Shojo Beat

Kaze Hikaru

30

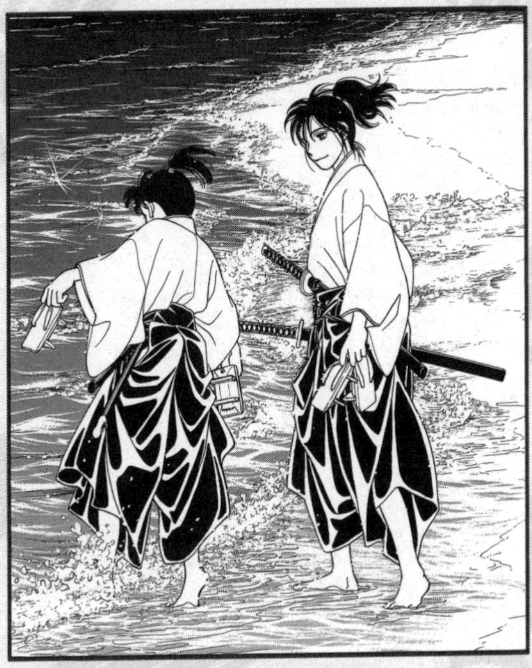

Story & Art by

Taeko Watanabe

Contents

Story Thus Far

It is the end of the Bakufu era, the third year of Bunkyu (1863) in Kyoto. The Shinsengumi is a band of warriors formed to protect the shogun.

Tominaga Sei, the daughter of a former Bakufu *bushi*, joined the Shinsengumi disguised as a boy by the name of Kamiya Seizaburo to avenge her father and brother. She has continued her training under the only person in the Shinsengumi who knows her true identity, Okita Soji, and she aspires to become a true *bushi*.

Ito and Hijikata formulate a plan to install Tokugawa Yoshikatsu of Owari as the next shogun. But because Ito is unable to recognize how the times have changed, his plan fails. Meanwhile, as the two continue to scheme in private, the anti-Bakufu faction in Kyoto is vandalizing official noticeboards. The Shinsengumi is ordered to tamp down this act of rebellion, but Harada and the others are unable to focus on their duties. Witnessing this, Nakamura grows even more distrustful of the Shinsengumi and decides to single Kamiya out in hopes of distancing her from the other members...!!

Characters

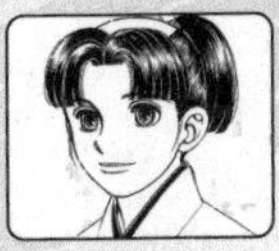

Tominaga Sei
She disguises herself as a boy to enter the Mibu-Roshi. She trains under Soji, aspiring to become a true *bushi*. But secretly, she is in love with Soji.

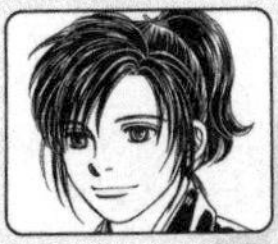

Okita Soji
Assistant vice captain of the Shinsengumi and licensed master of the Ten'nen Rishin-ryu. He supports the troop alongside Kondo and Hijikata and guides Seizaburo with a kind yet firm hand.

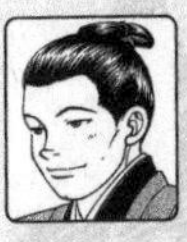

Kondo Isami
Captain of the Shinsengumi and fourth grandmaster of the Ten'nen Rishin-ryu. A passionate, warm, and well-respected leader.

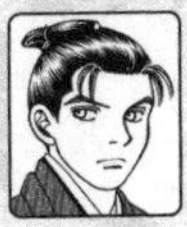

Hijikata Toshizo
Vice captain of the Shinsengumi. He commands both the group and himself with a rigid strictness. He is also known as "the Oni vice captain."

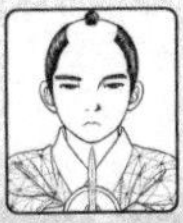

Saito Hajime
Assistant vice captain. He was a friend of Sei's older brother. Sei is attached to him in place of her lost brother.

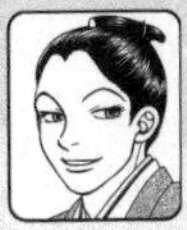

Ito Kashitaro
Councilor of the Shinsengumi. A skilled swordsman and an academic with anti-Bakufu sentiments, he plots to sway the direction of the troop.

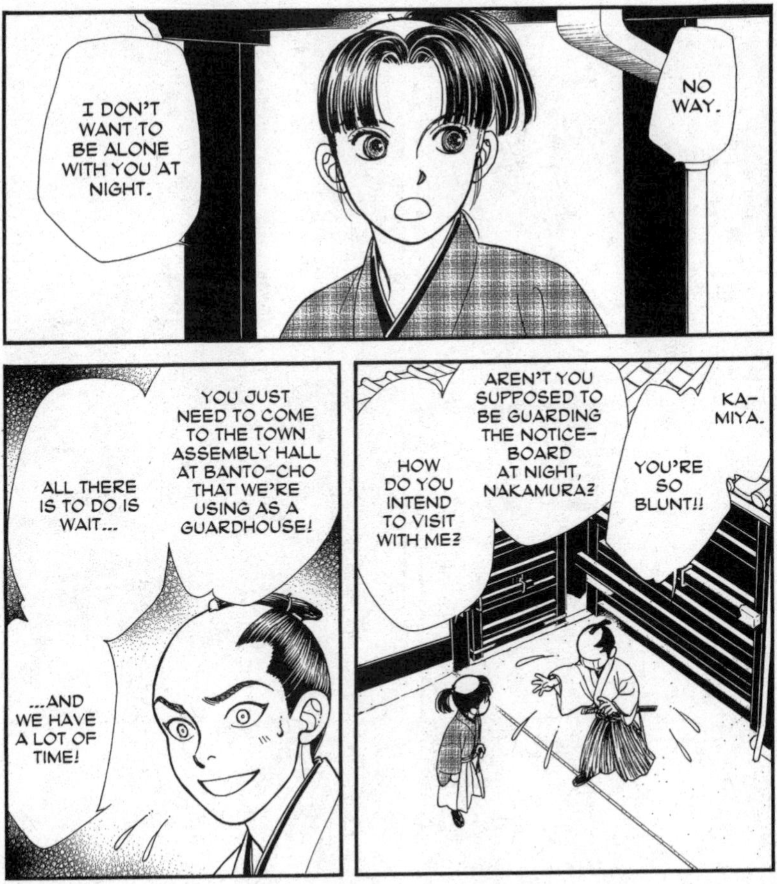
NO WAY.
I DON'T WANT TO BE ALONE WITH YOU AT NIGHT.
KA-MIYA.
YOU'RE SO BLUNT!!
AREN'T YOU SUPPOSED TO BE GUARDING THE NOTICE-BOARD AT NIGHT, NAKAMURA?
HOW DO YOU INTEND TO VISIT WITH ME?
YOU JUST NEED TO COME TO THE TOWN ASSEMBLY HALL AT BANTO-CHO THAT WE'RE USING AS A GUARDHOUSE!
ALL THERE IS TO DO IS WAIT...
...AND WE HAVE A LOT OF TIME!

KAZE HIKARU SENRYU

HE'S MADE A NEW NAME FOR HIMSELF BUT IF THERE IS JOY IN IT HE'S OKAY

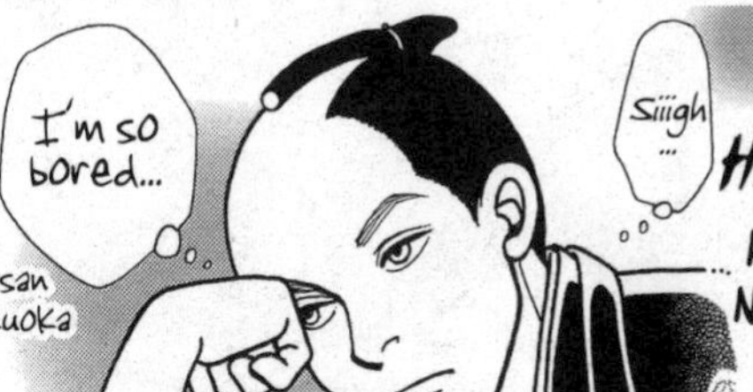
Siiigh...
I'm so bored...

By Miha-san from Fukuoka

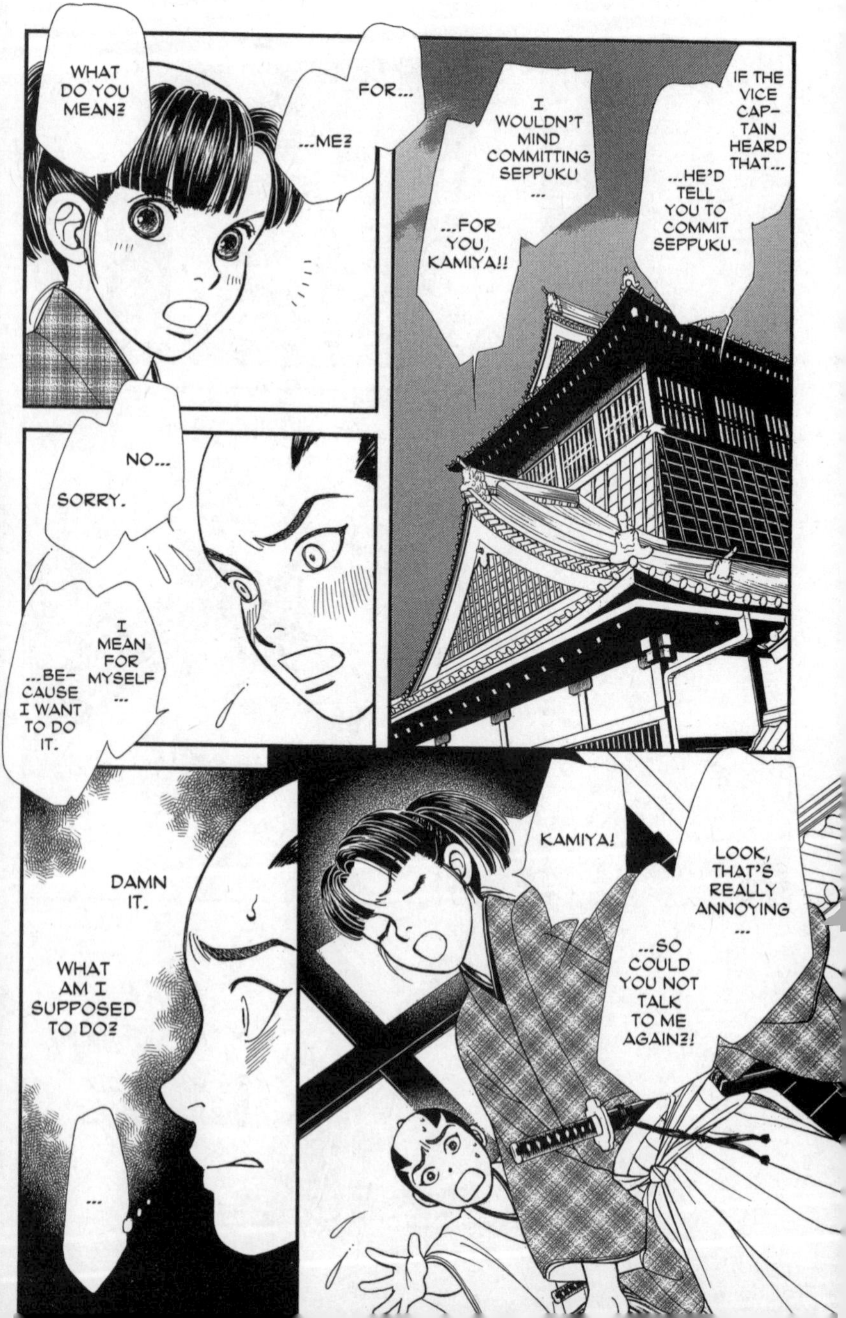
IF THE VICE CAP-TAIN HEARD THAT...
...HE'D TELL YOU TO COMMIT SEPPUKU.
I WOULDN'T MIND COMMITTING SEPPUKU ...
...FOR YOU, KAMIYA!!
FOR...
...ME?
WHAT DO YOU MEAN?
NO...
SORRY.
I MEAN FOR MYSELF ...
...BE-CAUSE I WANT TO DO IT.
LOOK, THAT'S REALLY ANNOYING ...
...SO COULD YOU NOT TALK TO ME AGAIN?!
KAMIYA!
DAMN IT.
WHAT AM I SUPPOSED TO DO?
...

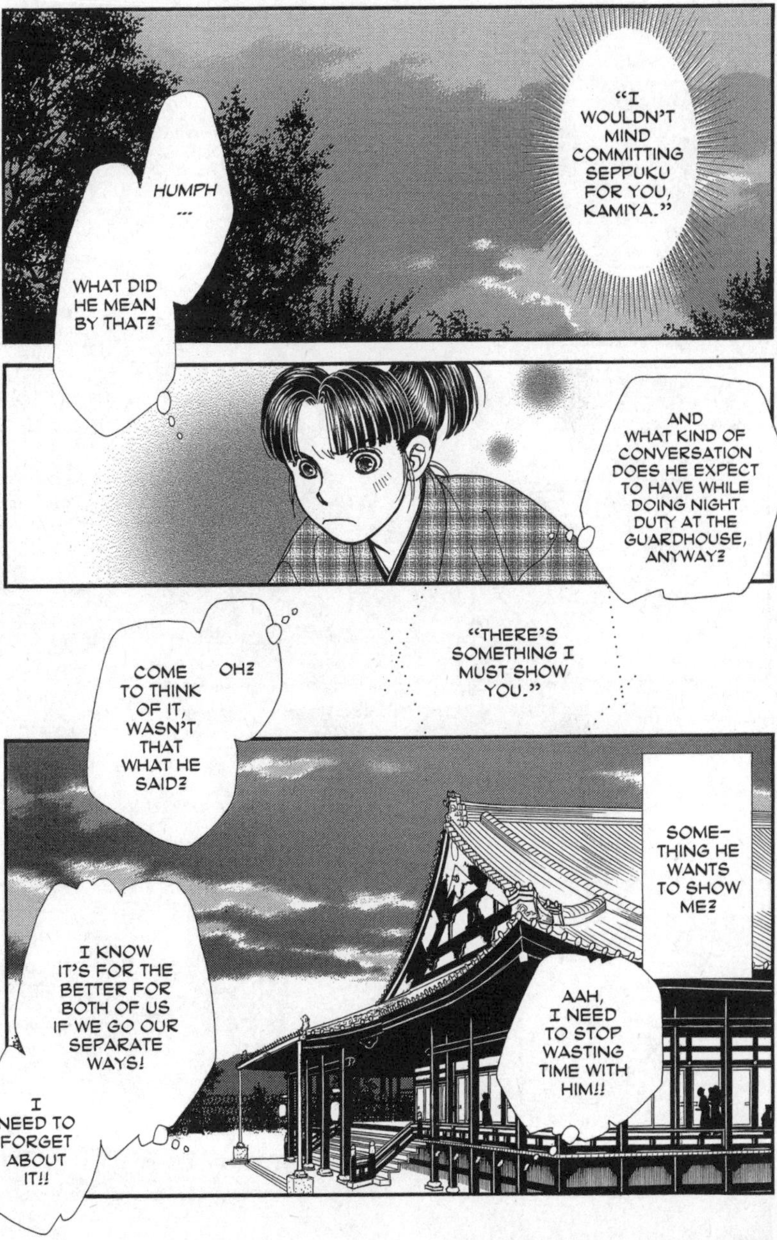
"I WOULDN'T MIND COMMITTING SEPPUKU FOR YOU, KAMIYA."
HUMPH...
WHAT DID HE MEAN BY THAT?
AND WHAT KIND OF CONVERSATION DOES HE EXPECT TO HAVE WHILE DOING NIGHT DUTY AT THE GUARDHOUSE, ANYWAY?
"THERE'S SOMETHING I MUST SHOW YOU."
OH?
COME TO THINK OF IT, WASN'T THAT WHAT HE SAID?
SOME-THING HE WANTS TO SHOW ME?
AAH, I NEED TO STOP WASTING TIME WITH HIM!!
I KNOW IT'S FOR THE BETTER FOR BOTH OF US IF WE GO OUR SEPARATE WAYS!
I NEED TO FORGET ABOUT IT!!

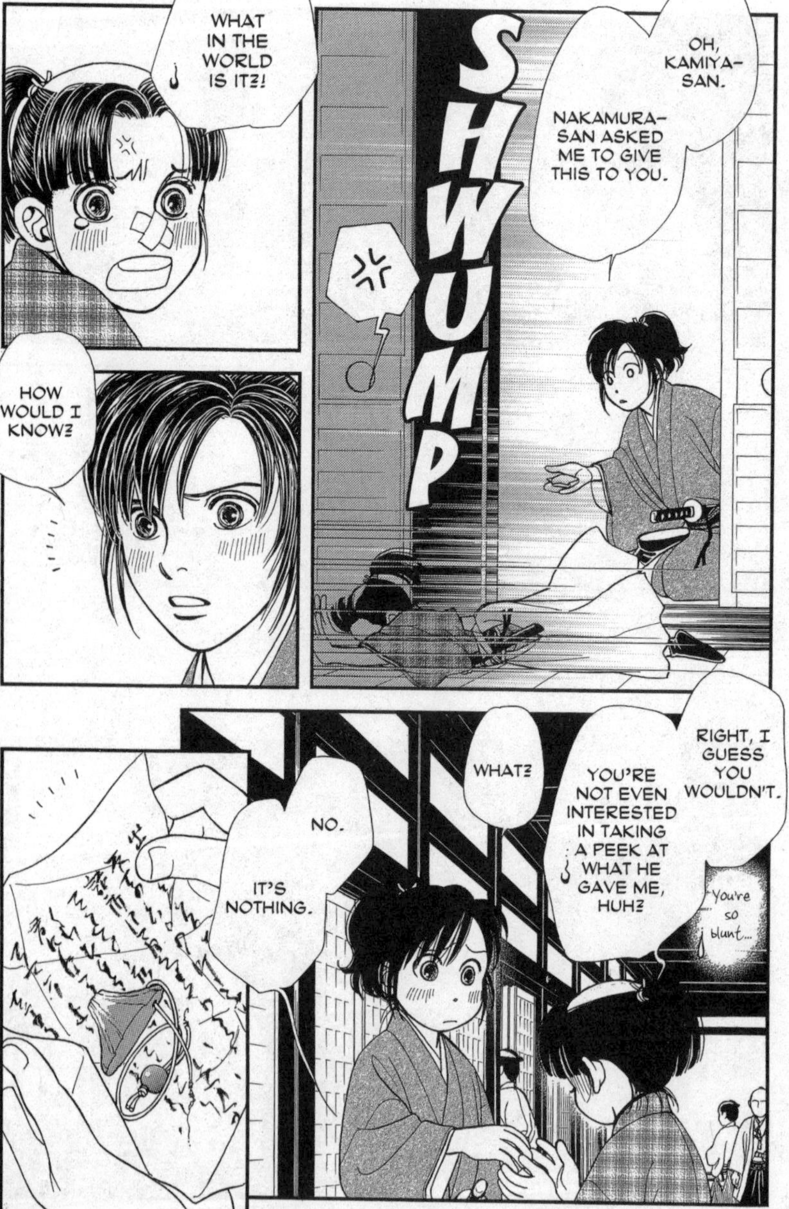
SHWUMP
OH, KAMIYA-SAN.
NAKAMURA-SAN ASKED ME TO GIVE THIS TO YOU.
WHAT IN THE WORLD IS IT?!
HOW WOULD I KNOW?
RIGHT, I GUESS YOU WOULDN'T.
YOU'RE NOT EVEN INTERESTED IN TAKING A PEEK AT WHAT HE GAVE ME, HUH?
You're so blunt...
WHAT?
NO.
IT'S NOTHING.

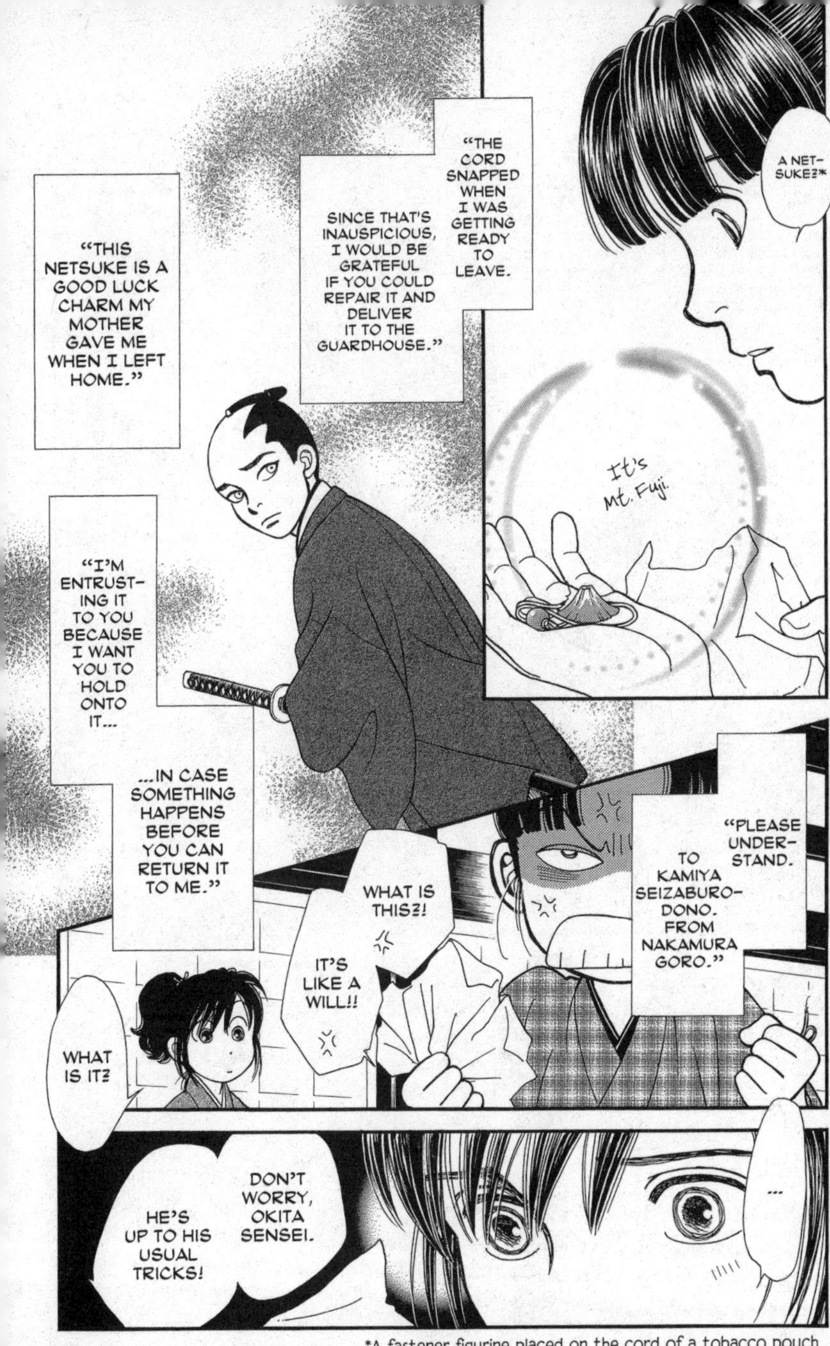
A NET-SUKE?*
It's Mt. Fuji.
"THE CORD SNAPPED WHEN I WAS GETTING READY TO LEAVE.
SINCE THAT'S INAUSPICIOUS, I WOULD BE GRATEFUL IF YOU COULD REPAIR IT AND DELIVER IT TO THE GUARDHOUSE."
"THIS NETSUKE IS A GOOD LUCK CHARM MY MOTHER GAVE ME WHEN I LEFT HOME."
"I'M ENTRUST-ING IT TO YOU BECAUSE I WANT YOU TO HOLD ONTO IT...
...IN CASE SOMETHING HAPPENS BEFORE YOU CAN RETURN IT TO ME."
"PLEASE UNDER-STAND.
TO KAMIYA SEIZABURO-DONO. FROM NAKAMURA GORO."
WHAT IS THIS?!
IT'S LIKE A WILL!!
WHAT IS IT?
...
DON'T WORRY, OKITA SENSEI.
HE'S UP TO HIS USUAL TRICKS!

*A fastener figurine placed on the cord of a tobacco pouch or other drawstring bag, allowing it to hang from an obi.

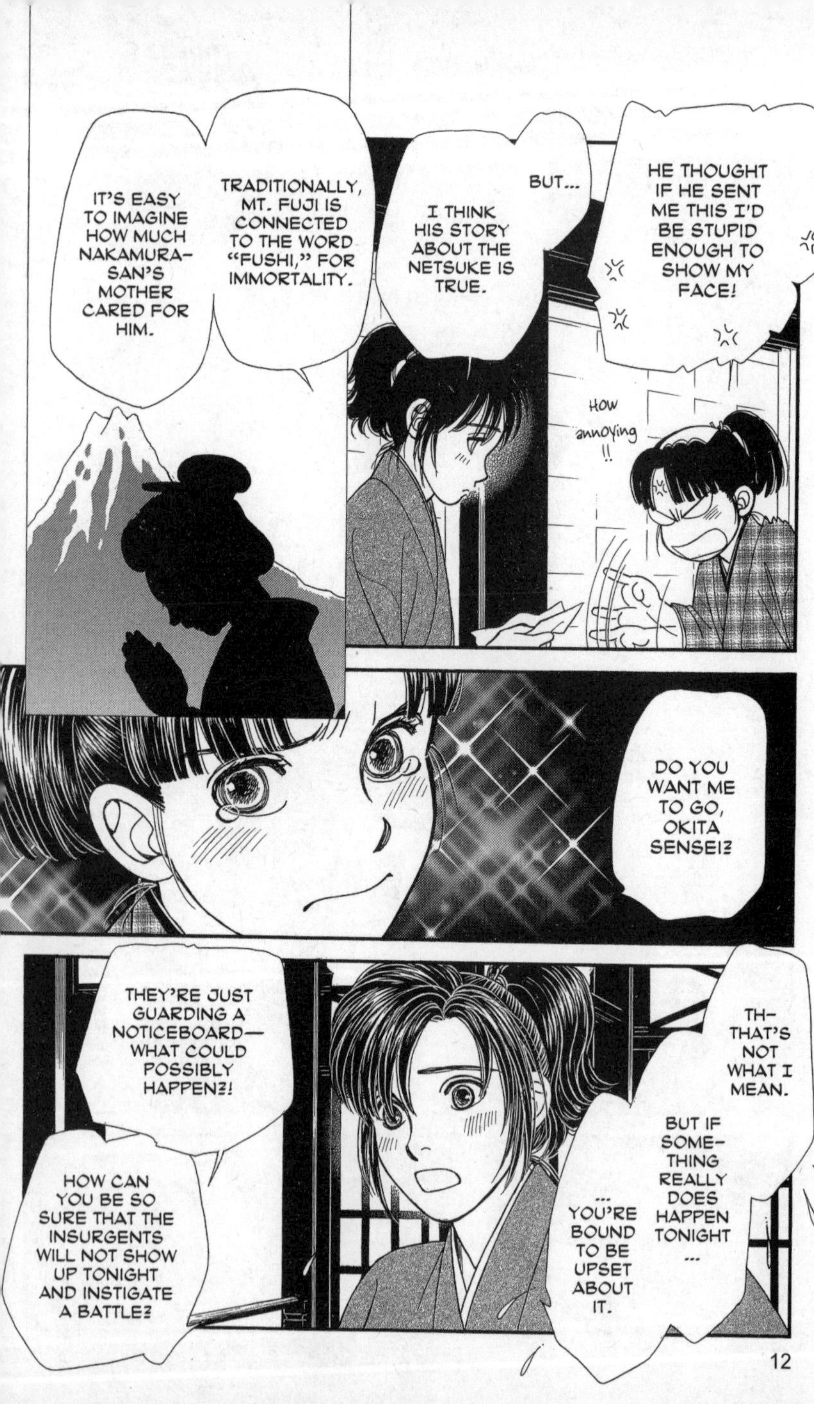
HE THOUGHT IF HE SENT ME THIS I'D BE STUPID ENOUGH TO SHOW MY FACE!
HOW annoying!!
BUT...
I THINK HIS STORY ABOUT THE NETSUKE IS TRUE.
TRADITIONALLY, MT. FUJI IS CONNECTED TO THE WORD "FUSHI," FOR IMMORTALITY.
IT'S EASY TO IMAGINE HOW MUCH NAKAMURA-SAN'S MOTHER CARED FOR HIM.
DO YOU WANT ME TO GO, OKITA SENSEI!?
TH-THAT'S NOT WHAT I MEAN.
BUT IF SOMETHING REALLY DOES HAPPEN TONIGHT...
...YOU'RE BOUND TO BE UPSET ABOUT IT.
THEY'RE JUST GUARDING A NOTICEBOARD—WHAT COULD POSSIBLY HAPPEN!?!
HOW CAN YOU BE SO SURE THAT THE INSURGENTS WILL NOT SHOW UP TONIGHT AND INSTIGATE A BATTLE!?

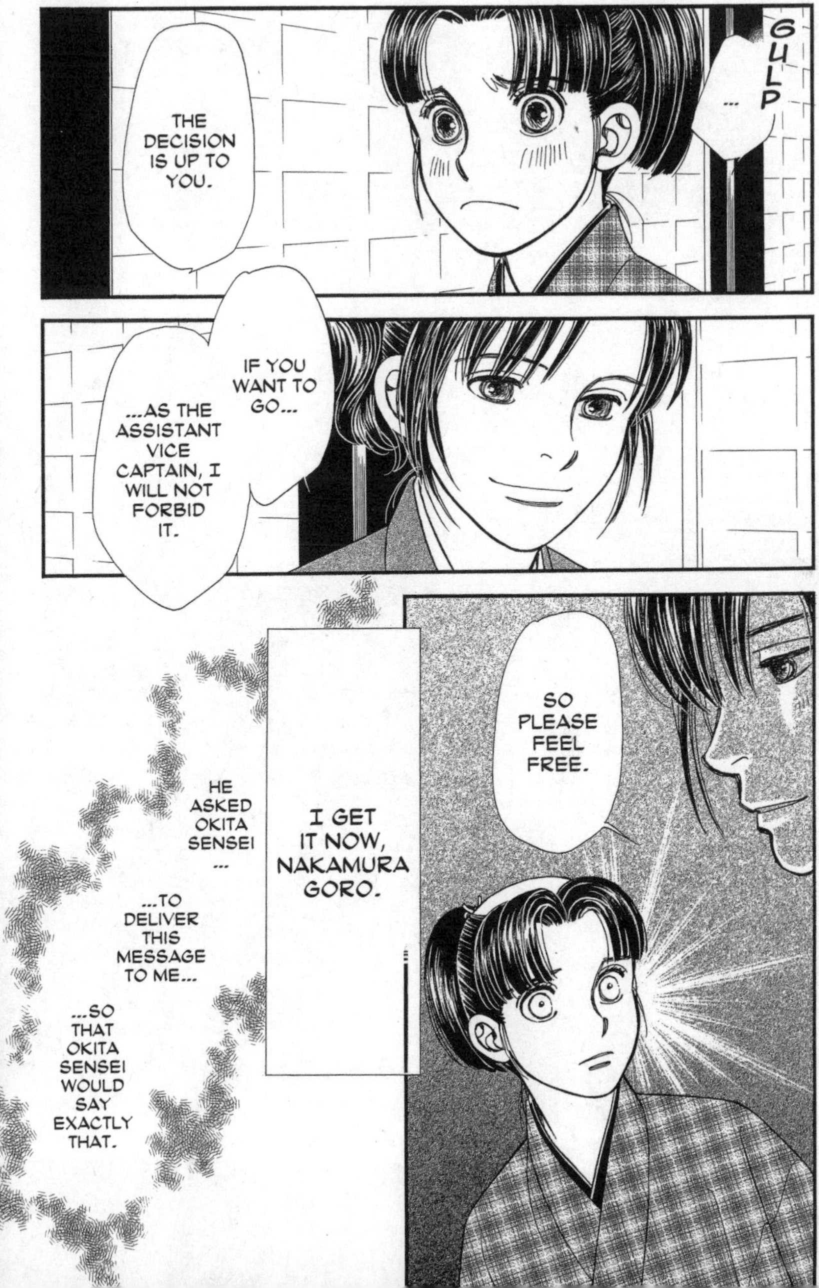
GULP
...
THE DECISION IS UP TO YOU.
IF YOU WANT TO GO...
...AS THE ASSISTANT VICE CAPTAIN, I WILL NOT FORBID IT.
SO PLEASE FEEL FREE.
I GET IT NOW, NAKAMURA GORO.
HE ASKED OKITA SENSEI ...
...TO DELIVER THIS MESSAGE TO ME...
...SO THAT OKITA SENSEI WOULD SAY EXACTLY THAT.

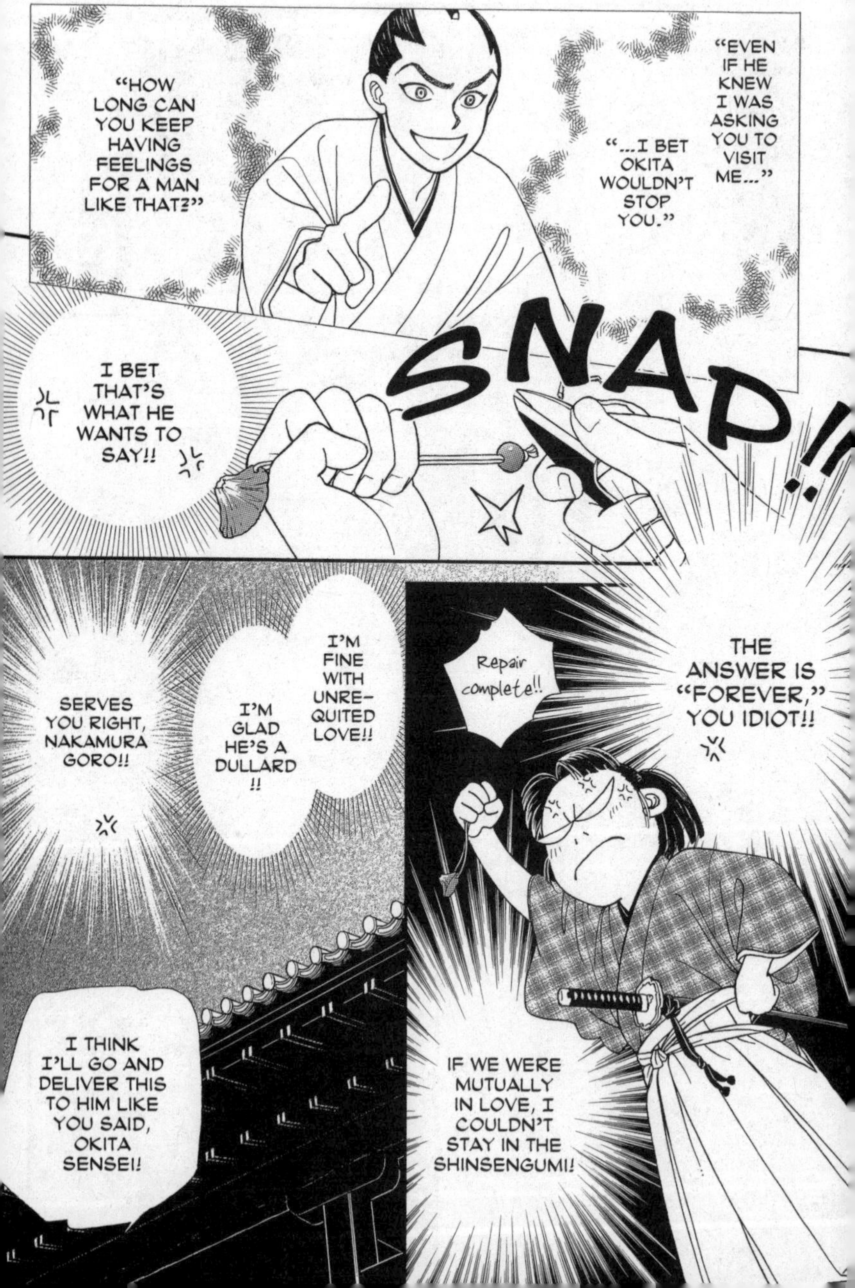
"EVEN IF HE KNEW I WAS ASKING YOU TO VISIT ME..."
"...I BET OKITA WOULDN'T STOP YOU."
"HOW LONG CAN YOU KEEP HAVING FEELINGS FOR A MAN LIKE THAT?"
SNAP!!
I BET THAT'S WHAT HE WANTS TO SAY!!
THE ANSWER IS "FOREVER," YOU IDIOT!!
Repair complete!!
IF WE WERE MUTUALLY IN LOVE, I COULDN'T STAY IN THE SHINSENGUMI!
I'M FINE WITH UNRE-QUITED LOVE!!
I'M GLAD HE'S A DULLARD!!
SERVES YOU RIGHT, NAKAMURA GORO!!
I THINK I'LL GO AND DELIVER THIS TO HIM LIKE YOU SAID, OKITA SENSEI!

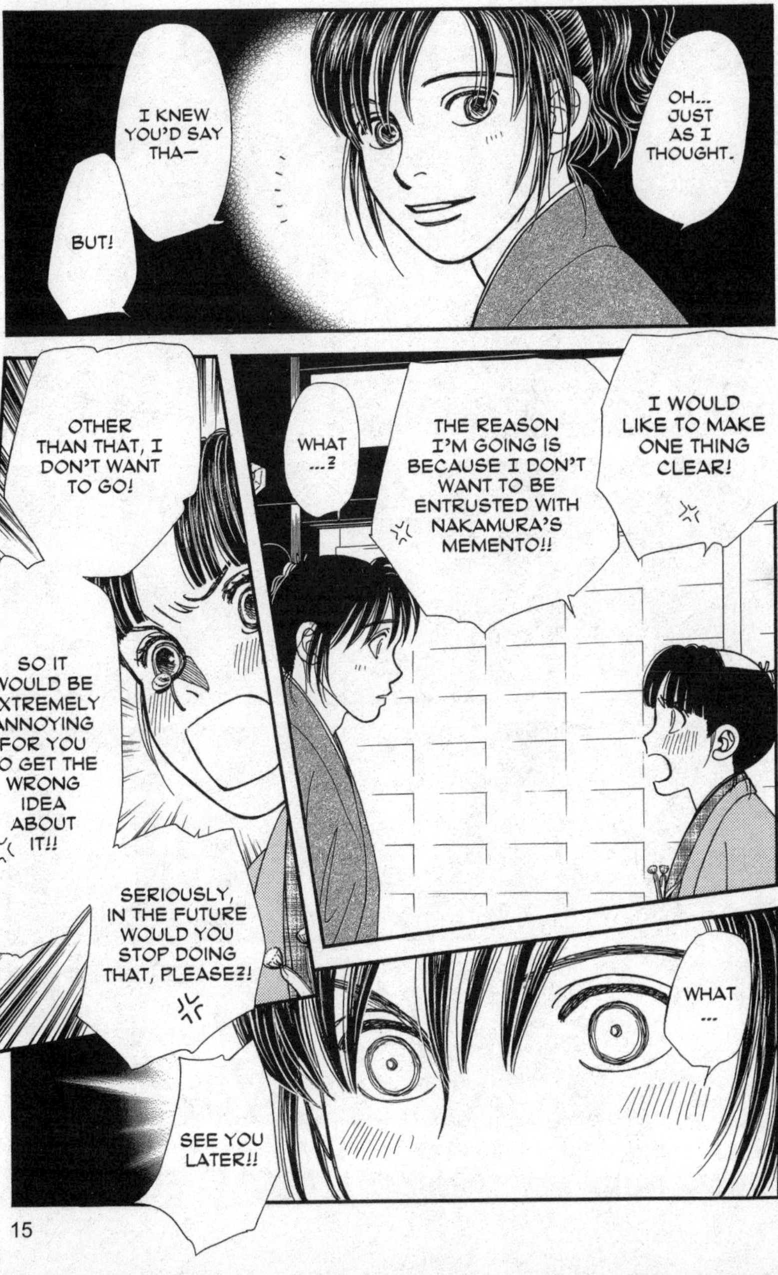
OH... JUST AS I THOUGHT.
I KNEW YOU'D SAY THA—
BUT!
I WOULD LIKE TO MAKE ONE THING CLEAR!
THE REASON I'M GOING IS BECAUSE I DON'T WANT TO BE ENTRUSTED WITH NAKAMURA'S MEMENTO!!
WHAT ...?
OTHER THAN THAT, I DON'T WANT TO GO!
SO IT WOULD BE EXTREMELY ANNOYING FOR YOU TO GET THE WRONG IDEA ABOUT IT!!
SERIOUSLY, IN THE FUTURE WOULD YOU STOP DOING THAT, PLEASE?!
WHAT ...
SEE YOU LATER!!

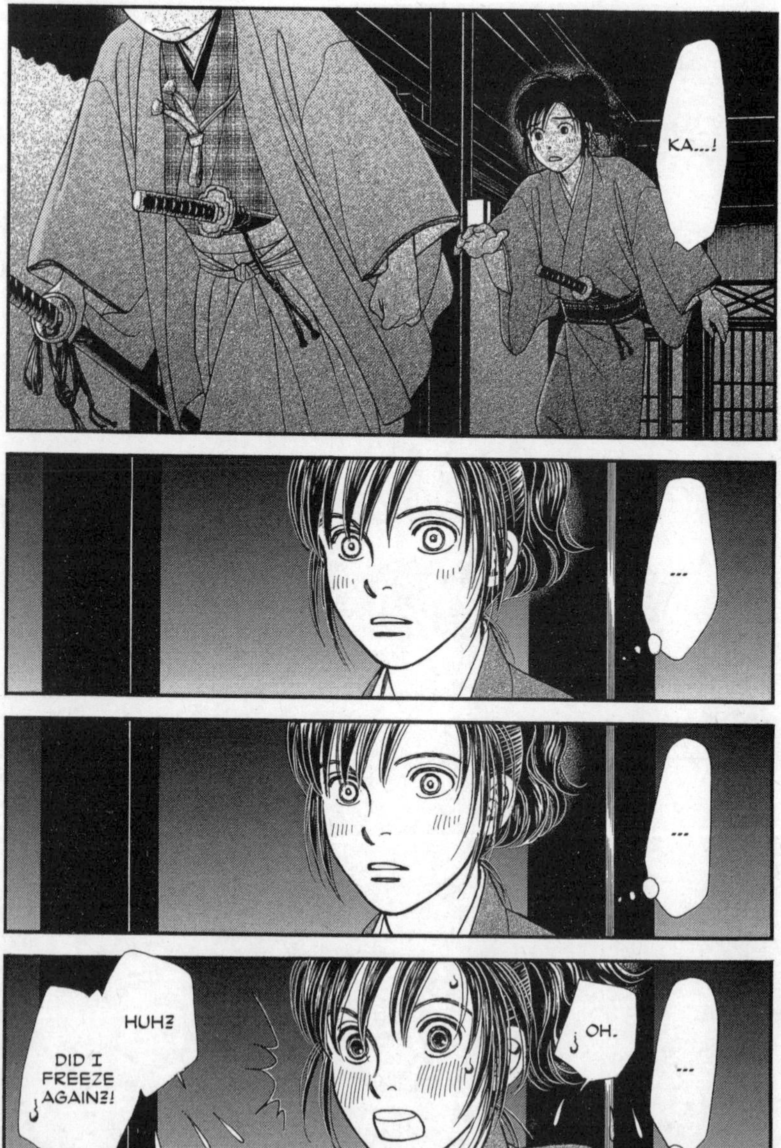
KA...!
...
...
...
OH.
HUH?
DID I FREEZE AGAIN?!

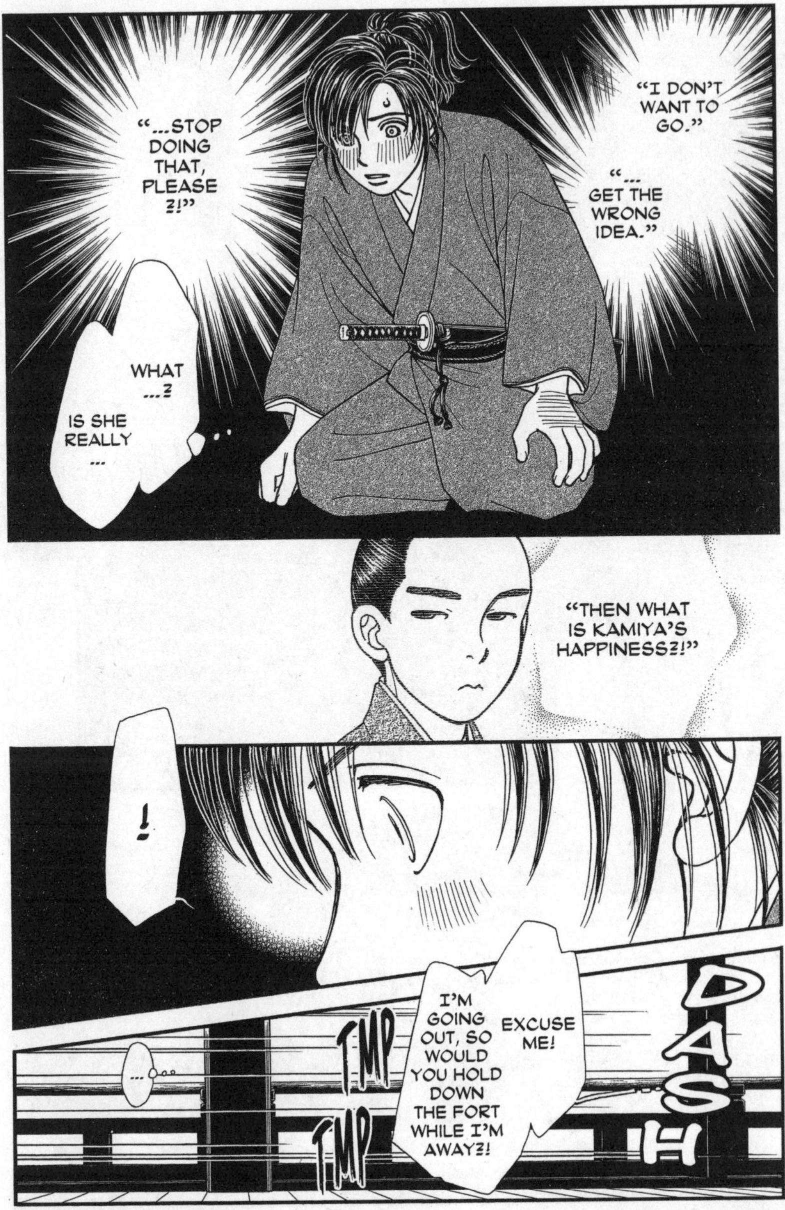
"I DON'T WANT TO GO."
"... GET THE WRONG IDEA."
"...STOP DOING THAT, PLEASE?!"
WHAT ...?
IS SHE REALLY ...
"THEN WHAT IS KAMIYA'S HAPPINESS?!"
!
DASH
EXCUSE ME!
I'M GOING OUT, SO WOULD YOU HOLD DOWN THE FORT WHILE I'M AWAY?!
TMP
TMP
...

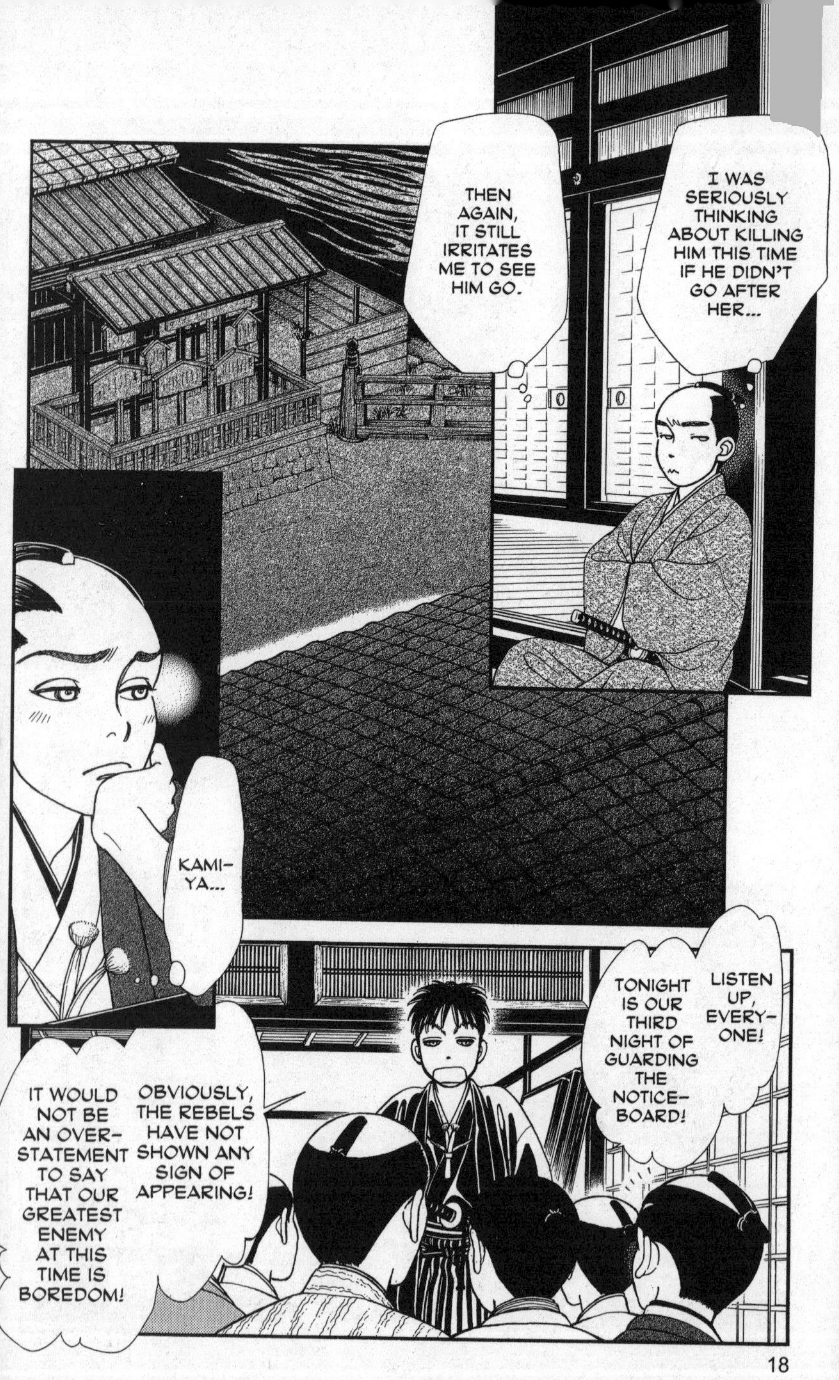

I WAS SERIOUSLY THINKING ABOUT KILLING HIM THIS TIME IF HE DIDN'T GO AFTER HER...
THEN AGAIN, IT STILL IRRITATES ME TO SEE HIM GO.
KAMI-YA...
LISTEN UP, EVERY-ONE!
TONIGHT IS OUR THIRD NIGHT OF GUARDING THE NOTICE-BOARD!
OBVIOUSLY, THE REBELS HAVE NOT SHOWN ANY SIGN OF APPEARING!
IT WOULD NOT BE AN OVER-STATEMENT TO SAY THAT OUR GREATEST ENEMY AT THIS TIME IS BOREDOM!

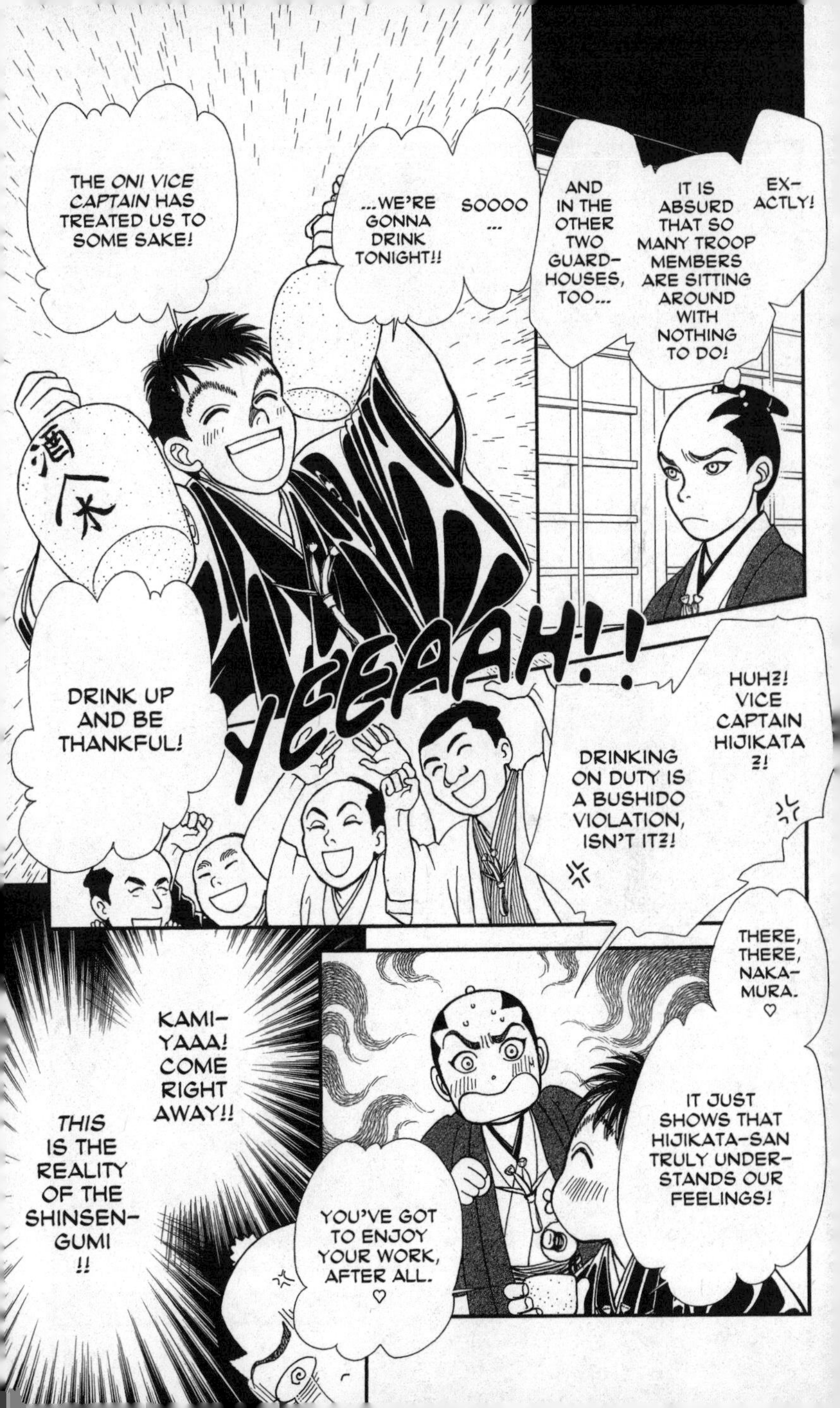
EX-ACTLY!
IT IS ABSURD THAT SO MANY TROOP MEMBERS ARE SITTING AROUND WITH NOTHING TO DO!
AND IN THE OTHER TWO GUARD-HOUSES, TOO...
SOOOO...
...WE'RE GONNA DRINK TONIGHT!!
THE *ONI VICE CAPTAIN* HAS TREATED US TO SOME SAKE!
DRINK UP AND BE THANKFUL!
YEEAAAH!!
HUH?! VICE CAPTAIN HIJIKATA?!
DRINKING ON DUTY IS A BUSHIDO VIOLATION, ISN'T IT?!
THERE, THERE, NAKA-MURA. ♡
IT JUST SHOWS THAT HIJIKATA-SAN TRULY UNDER-STANDS OUR FEELINGS!
YOU'VE GOT TO ENJOY YOUR WORK, AFTER ALL. ♡
KAMI-YAAA! COME RIGHT AWAY!!
THIS IS THE REALITY OF THE SHINSEN-GUMI !!

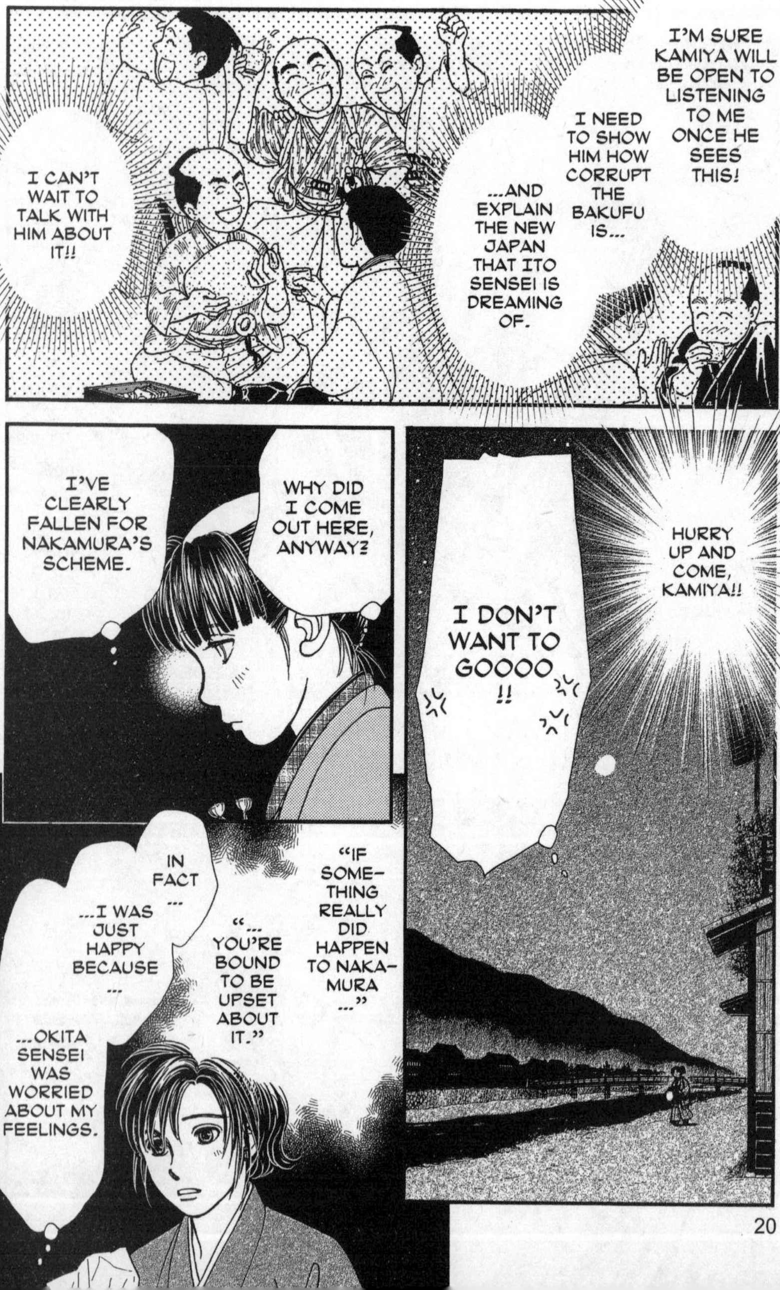
I'M SURE KAMIYA WILL BE OPEN TO LISTENING TO ME ONCE HE SEES THIS!
I NEED TO SHOW HIM HOW CORRUPT THE BAKUFU IS...
...AND EXPLAIN THE NEW JAPAN THAT ITO SENSEI IS DREAMING OF.
I CAN'T WAIT TO TALK WITH HIM ABOUT IT!!
HURRY UP AND COME, KAMIYA!!
I DON'T WANT TO GOOOO!!
WHY DID I COME OUT HERE, ANYWAY?
I'VE CLEARLY FALLEN FOR NAKAMURA'S SCHEME.
"IF SOMETHING REALLY DID HAPPEN TO NAKAMURA..."
"...YOU'RE BOUND TO BE UPSET ABOUT IT."
IN FACT...
...I WAS JUST HAPPY BECAUSE...
...OKITA SENSEI WAS WORRIED ABOUT MY FEELINGS.

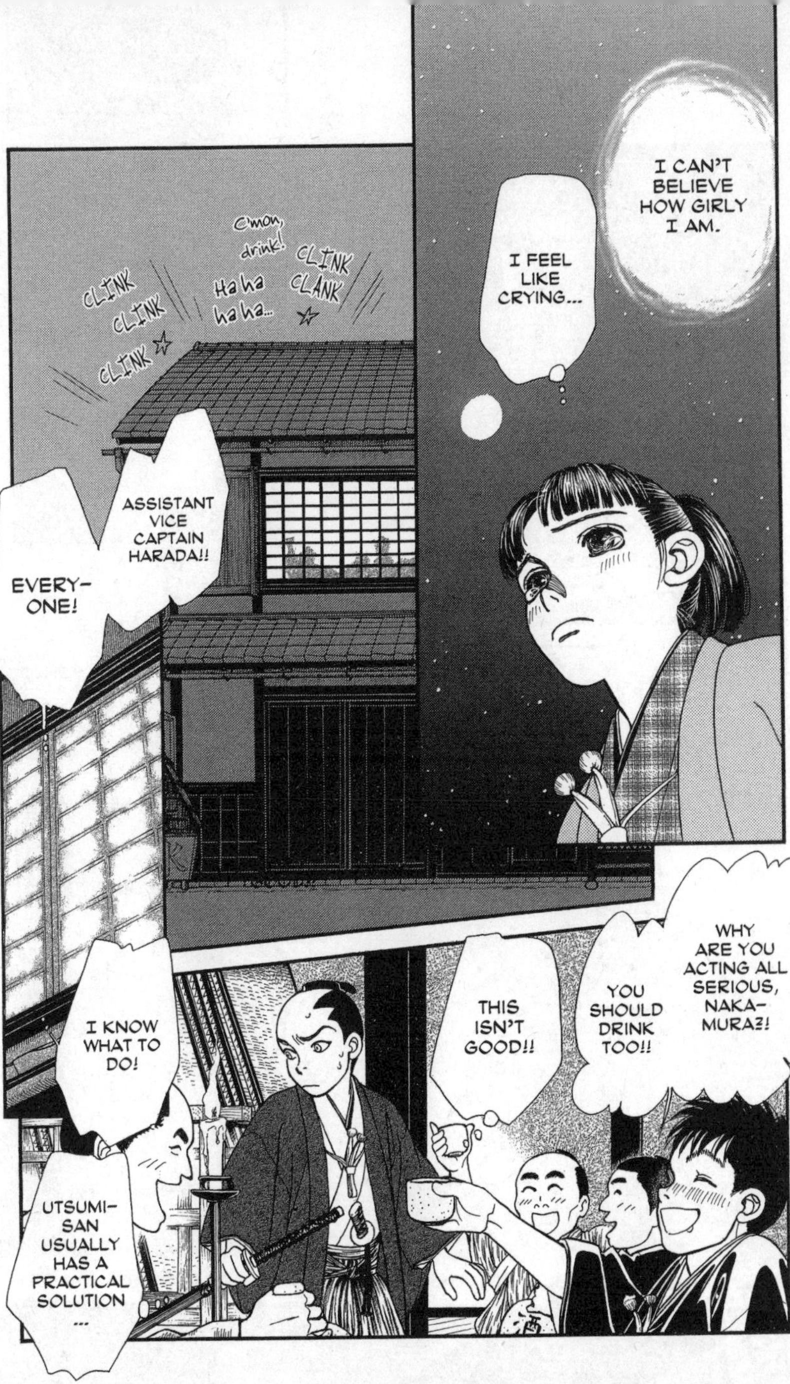
I CAN'T BELIEVE HOW GIRLY I AM.
I FEEL LIKE CRYING...
C'mon, drink!
CLINK CLANK
Ha ha ha ha...
CLINK CLINK CLINK
ASSISTANT VICE CAPTAIN HARADA!!
EVERYONE!
WHY ARE YOU ACTING ALL SERIOUS, NAKAMURA?!
YOU SHOULD DRINK TOO!!
THIS ISN'T GOOD!!
I KNOW WHAT TO DO!
UTSUMI-SAN USUALLY HAS A PRACTICAL SOLUTION ...

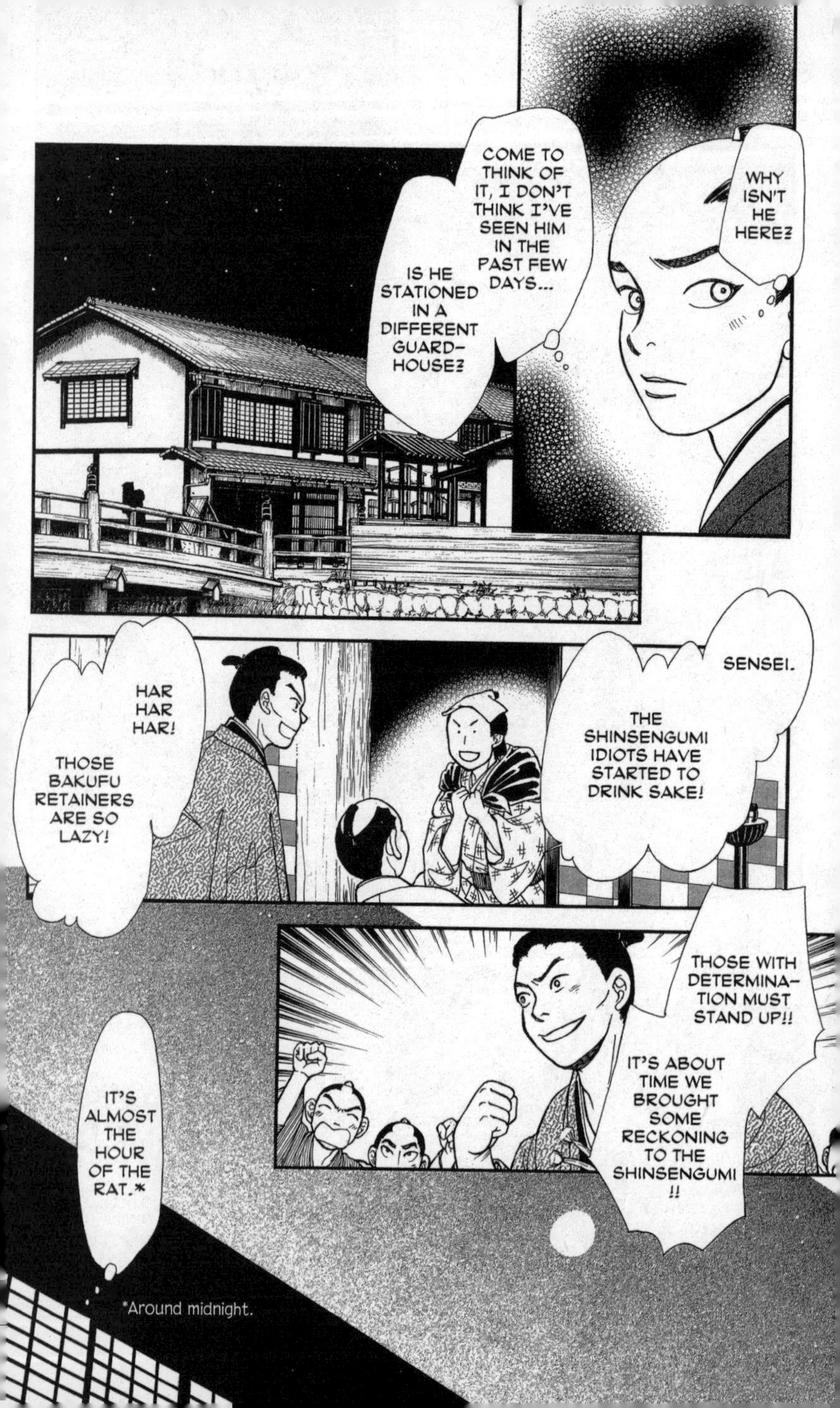
WHY ISN'T HE HERE?
COME TO THINK OF IT, I DON'T THINK I'VE SEEN HIM IN THE PAST FEW DAYS...
IS HE STATIONED IN A DIFFERENT GUARD-HOUSE?
SENSEI.
THE SHINSENGUMI IDIOTS HAVE STARTED TO DRINK SAKE!
HAR HAR HAR!
THOSE BAKUFU RETAINERS ARE SO LAZY!
THOSE WITH DETERMINATION MUST STAND UP!!
IT'S ABOUT TIME WE BROUGHT SOME RECKONING TO THE SHINSENGUMI!!
IT'S ALMOST THE HOUR OF THE RAT.*

*Around midnight.

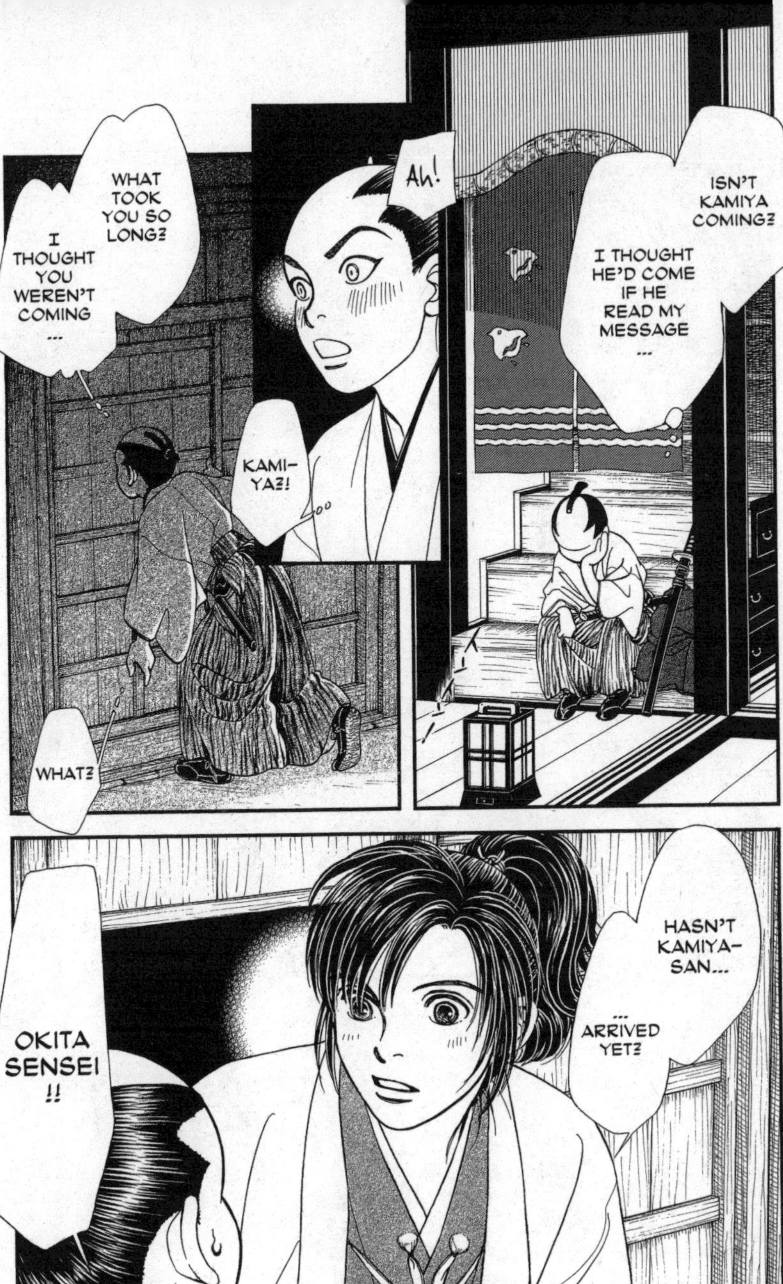
ISN'T KAMIYA COMING?
I THOUGHT HE'D COME IF HE READ MY MESSAGE ...
Ah!
KAMI-YA?!
WHAT TOOK YOU SO LONG?
I THOUGHT YOU WEREN'T COMING ...
WHAT?
HASN'T KAMIYA-SAN...
... ARRIVED YET?
OKITA SENSEI !!

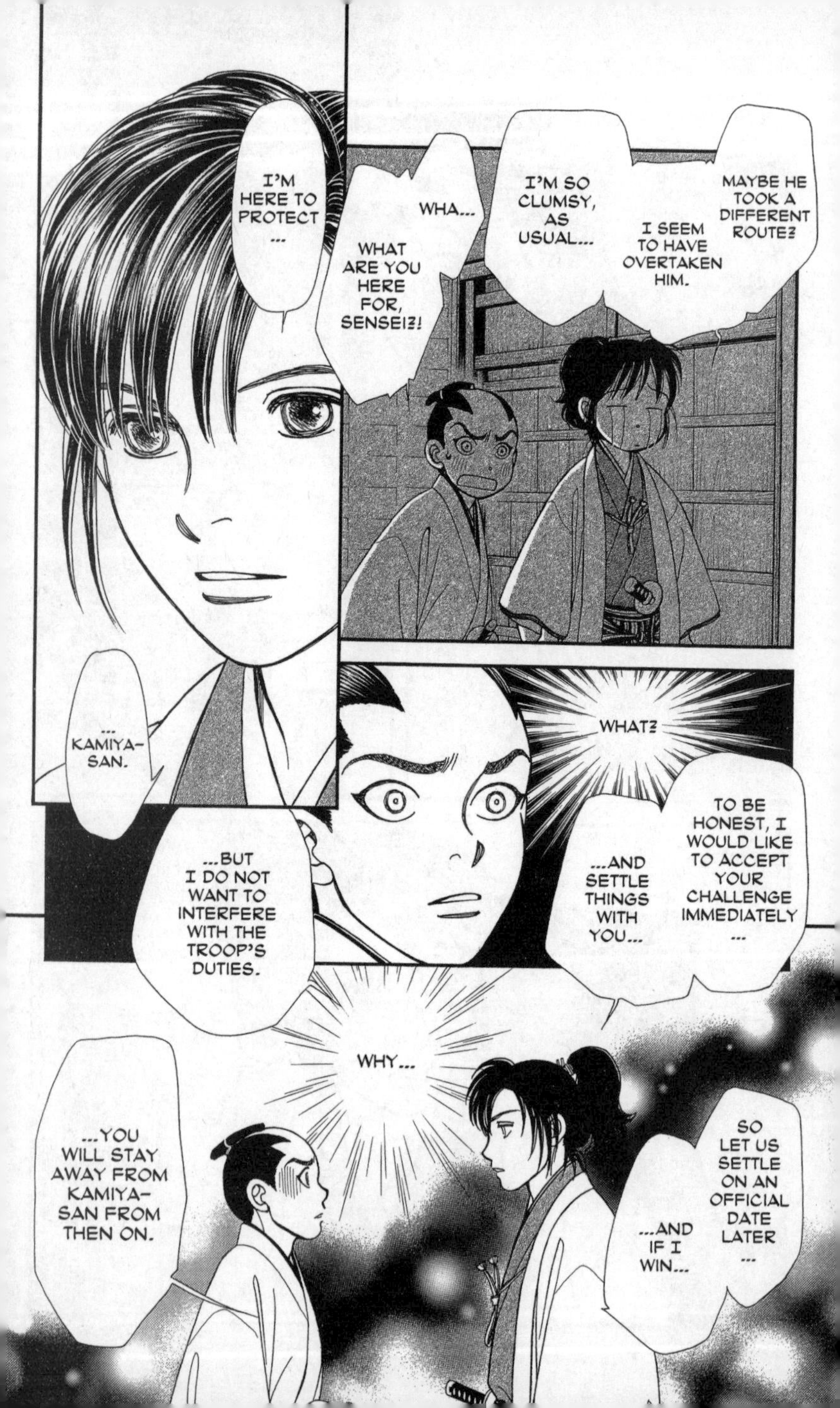
MAYBE HE TOOK A DIFFERENT ROUTE?
I'M SO CLUMSY, AS USUAL...
I SEEM TO HAVE OVERTAKEN HIM.
WHA...
WHAT ARE YOU HERE FOR, SENSEI?!
I'M HERE TO PROTECT...
...KAMIYA-SAN.
WHAT?
TO BE HONEST, I WOULD LIKE TO ACCEPT YOUR CHALLENGE IMMEDIATELY...
...AND SETTLE THINGS WITH YOU...
...BUT I DO NOT WANT TO INTERFERE WITH THE TROOP'S DUTIES.
SO LET US SETTLE ON AN OFFICIAL DATE LATER...
...AND IF I WIN...
WHY...
...YOU WILL STAY AWAY FROM KAMIYA-SAN FROM THEN ON.

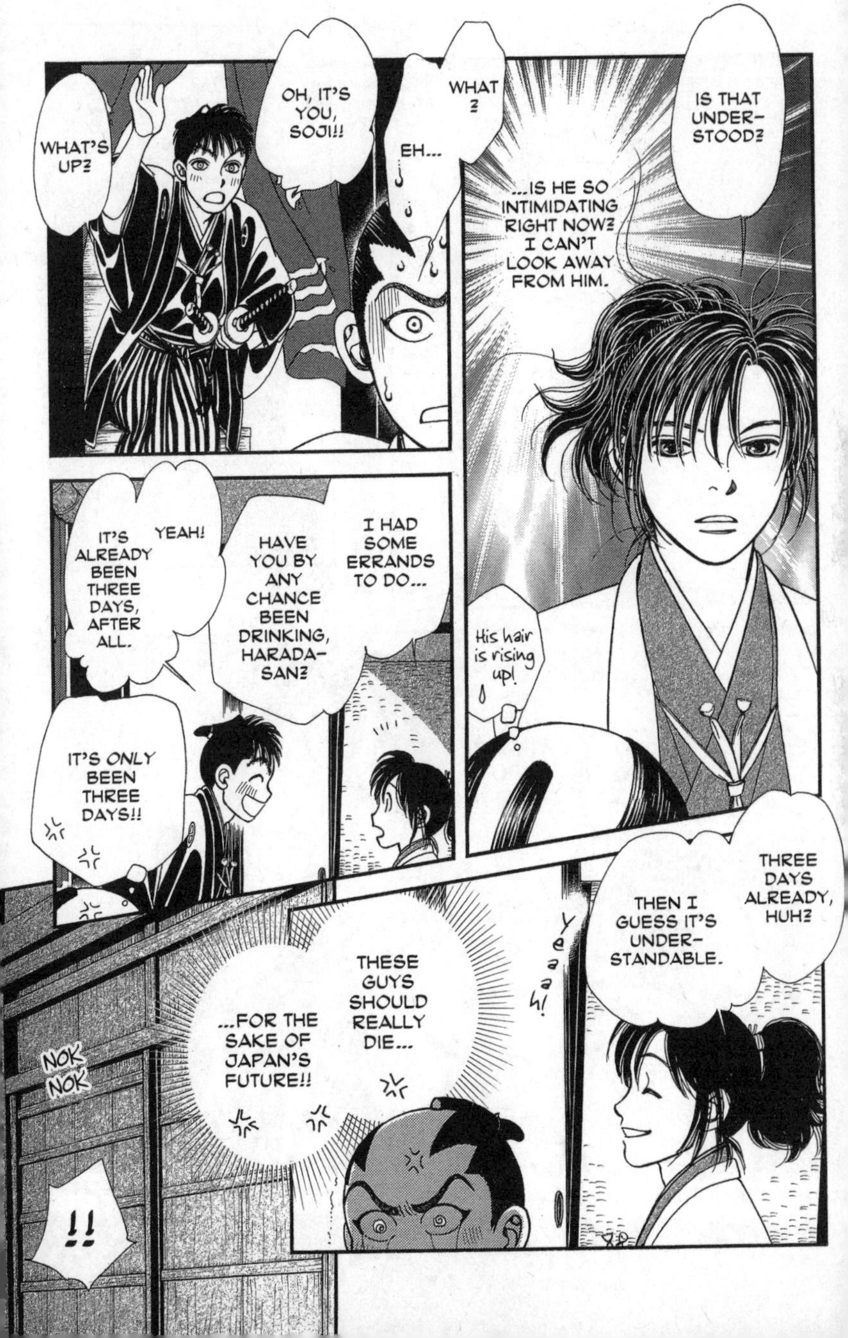
IS THAT UNDER-STOOD?
...IS HE SO INTIMIDATING RIGHT NOW? I CAN'T LOOK AWAY FROM HIM.
His hair is rising up!
WHAT?
EH...
OH, IT'S YOU, SOJI!!
WHAT'S UP?
I HAD SOME ERRANDS TO DO...
HAVE YOU BY ANY CHANCE BEEN DRINKING, HARADA-SAN?
YEAH!
IT'S ALREADY BEEN THREE DAYS, AFTER ALL.
IT'S ONLY BEEN THREE DAYS!!
THREE DAYS ALREADY, HUH?
THEN I GUESS IT'S UNDER-STANDABLE.
yeaah!
THESE GUYS SHOULD REALLY DIE...
...FOR THE SAKE OF JAPAN'S FUTURE!!
NOK NOK
!!

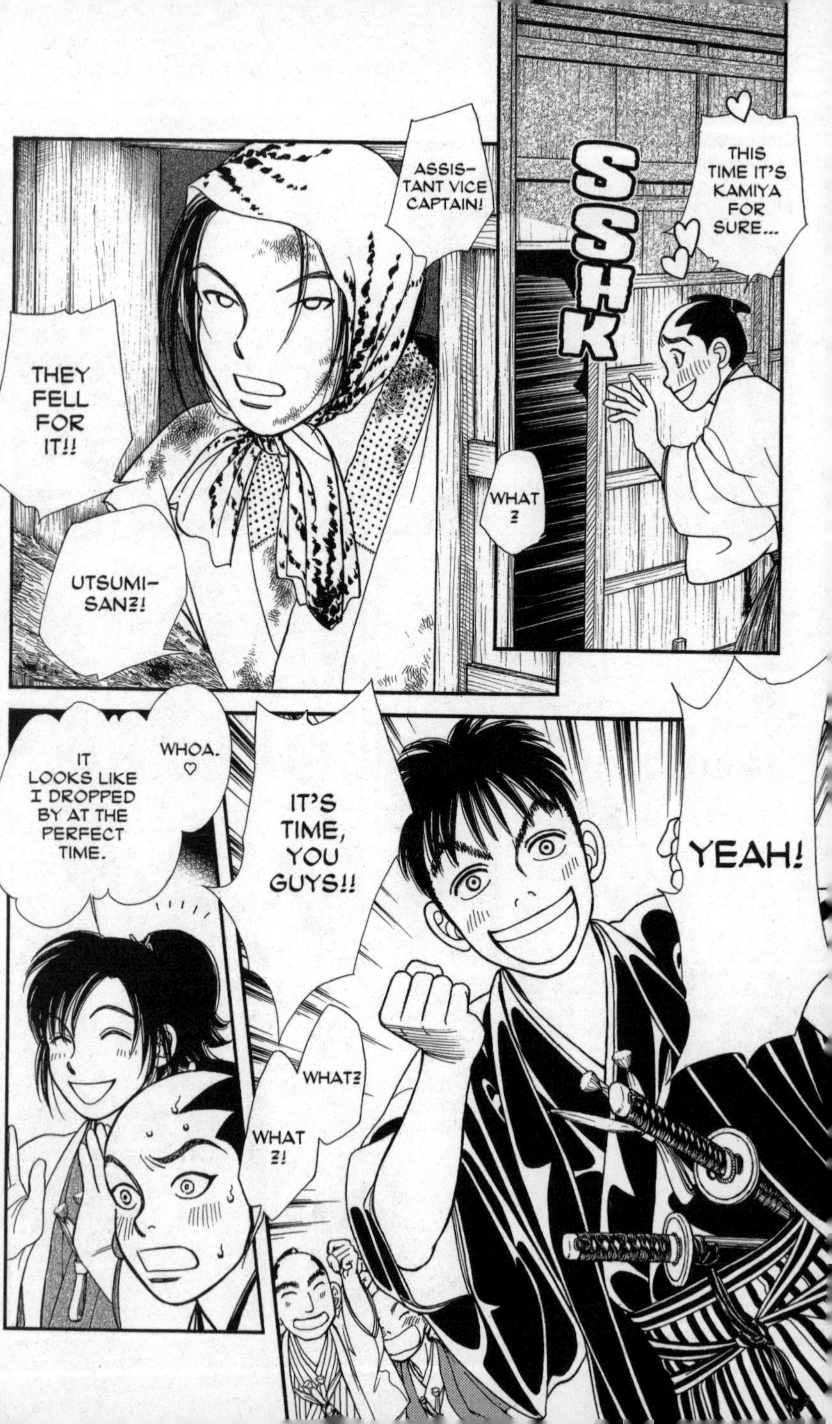
THIS TIME IT'S KAMIYA FOR SURE...
SSHK
WHAT?
ASSISTANT VICE CAPTAIN!
THEY FELL FOR IT!!
UTSUMI-SAN?!
YEAH!
IT'S TIME, YOU GUYS!!
WHOA. ♡
IT LOOKS LIKE I DROPPED BY AT THE PERFECT TIME.
WHAT?
WHAT?!

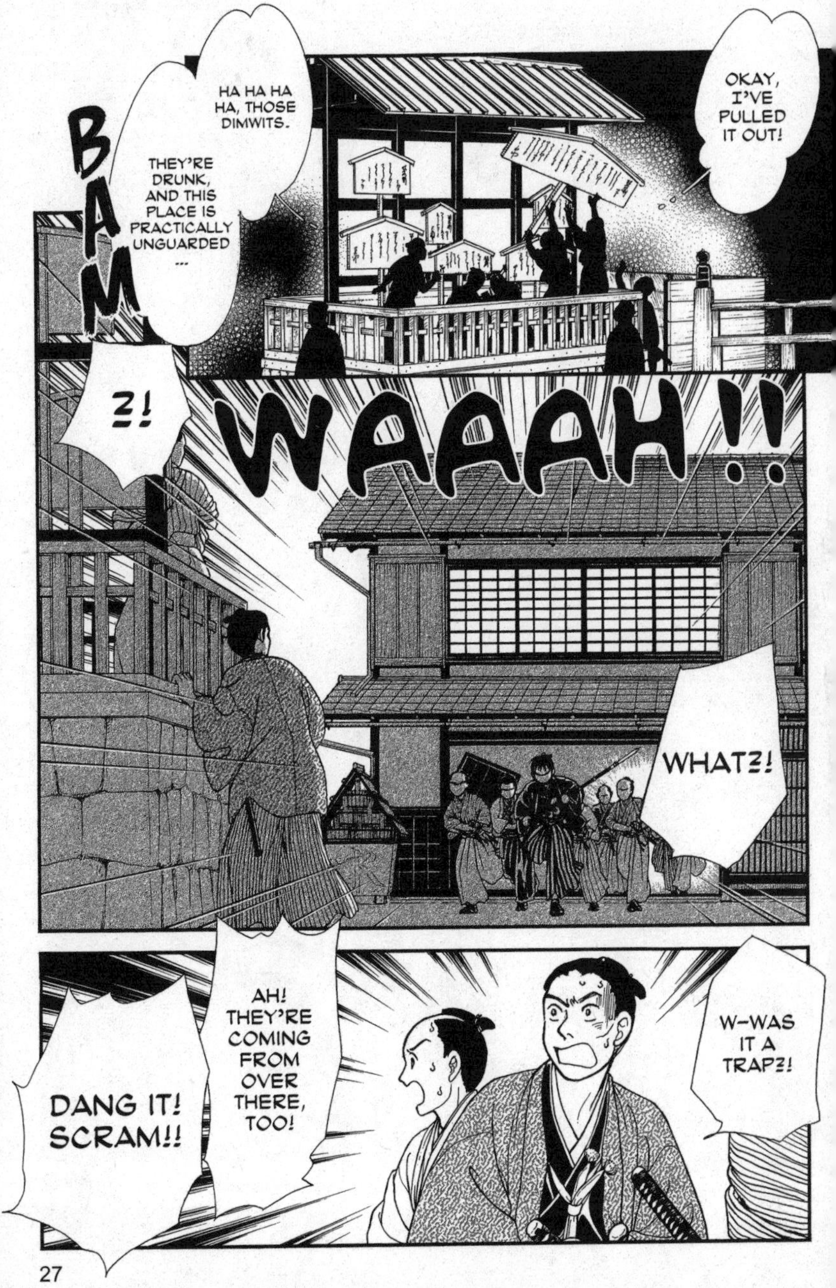
OKAY, I'VE PULLED IT OUT!
HA HA HA HA, THOSE DIMWITS.
THEY'RE DRUNK, AND THIS PLACE IS PRACTICALLY UNGUARDED ...
BAM
WAAAH!!
?!
WHAT?!
W-WAS IT A TRAP?!
AH! THEY'RE COMING FROM OVER THERE, TOO!
DANG IT! SCRAM!!

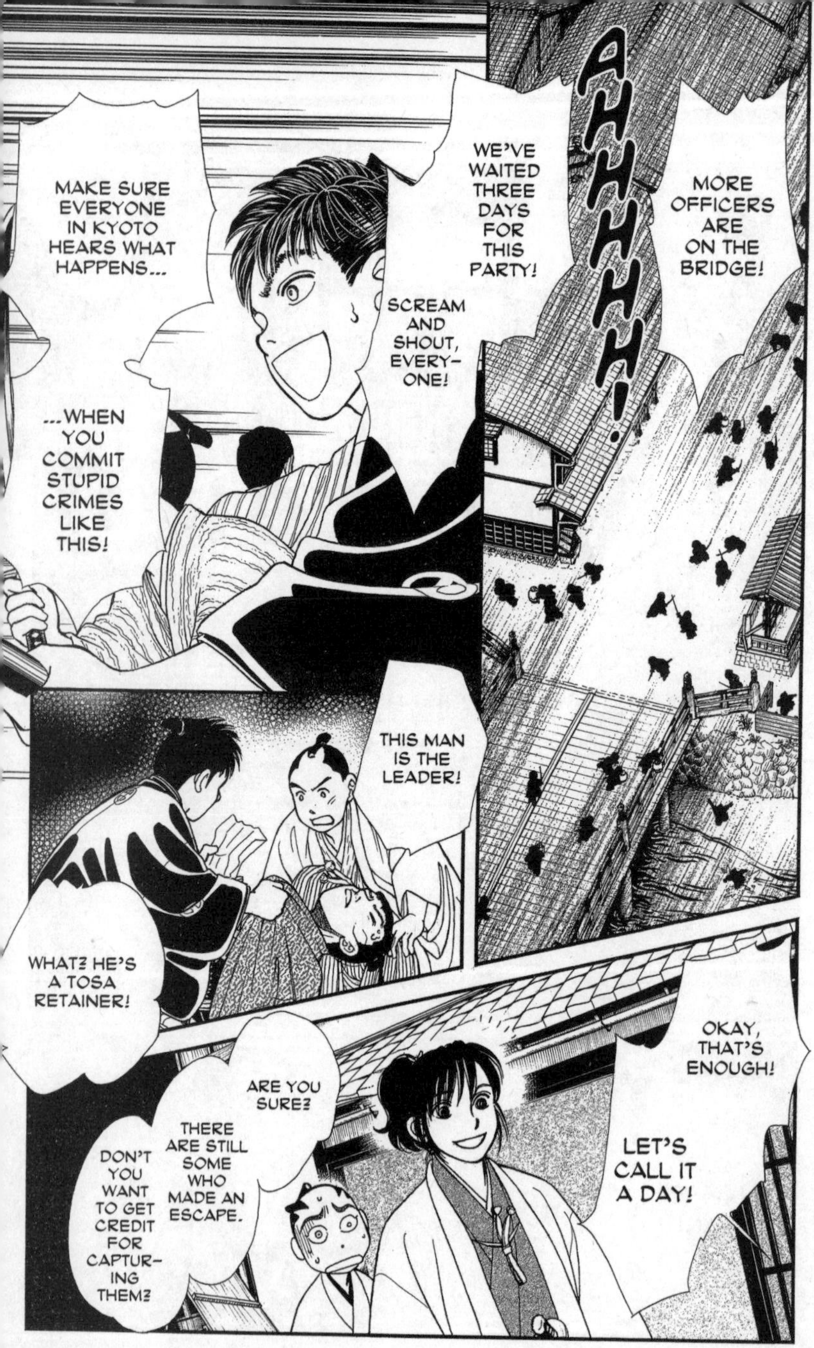
AHHHHH!
MORE OFFICERS ARE ON THE BRIDGE!
WE'VE WAITED THREE DAYS FOR THIS PARTY!
SCREAM AND SHOUT, EVERYONE!
MAKE SURE EVERYONE IN KYOTO HEARS WHAT HAPPENS...
...WHEN YOU COMMIT STUPID CRIMES LIKE THIS!
THIS MAN IS THE LEADER!
WHAT? HE'S A TOSA RETAINER!
OKAY, THAT'S ENOUGH!
LET'S CALL IT A DAY!
ARE YOU SURE?
THERE ARE STILL SOME WHO MADE AN ESCAPE.
DON'T YOU WANT TO GET CREDIT FOR CAPTURING THEM?

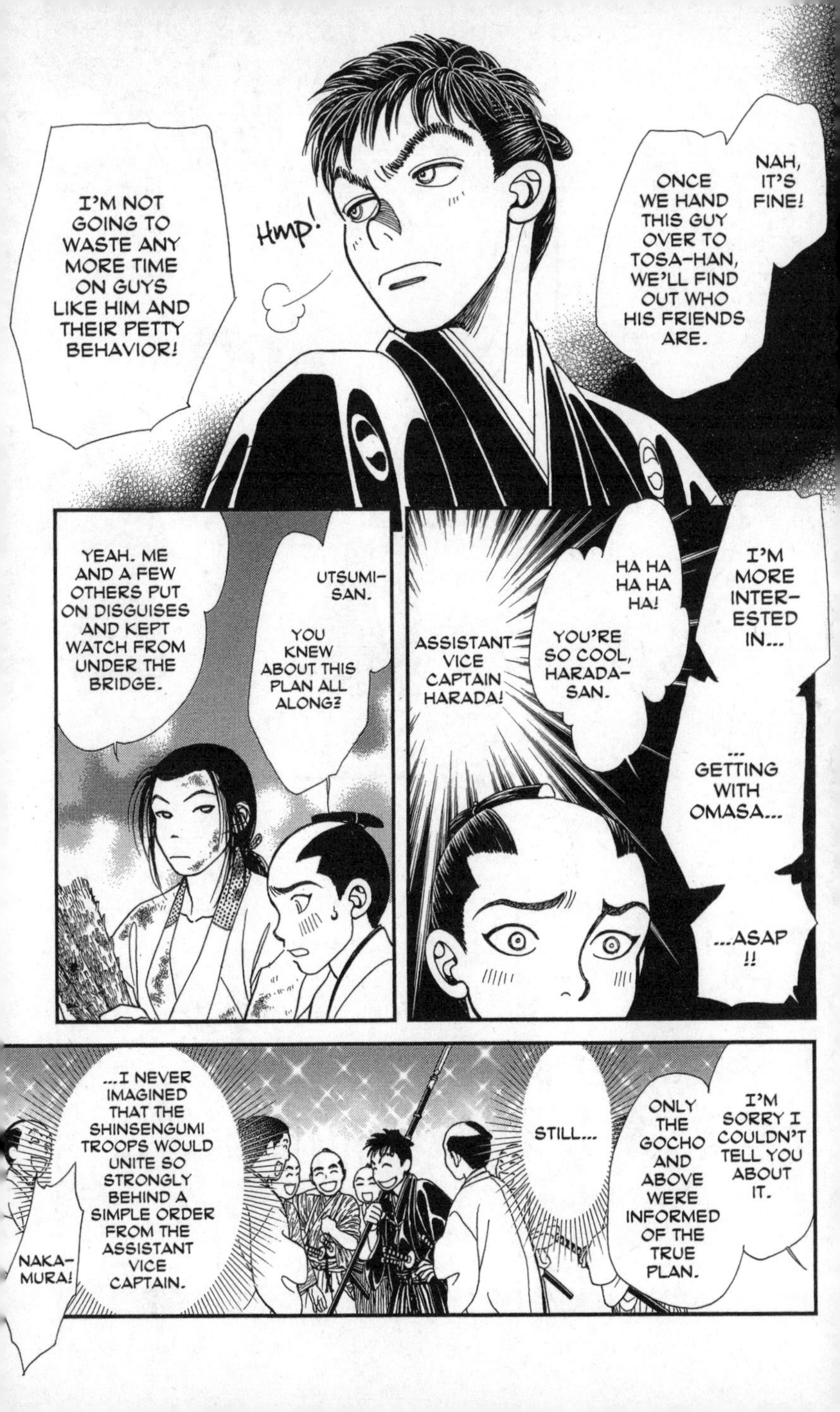
NAH, IT'S FINE!
ONCE WE HAND THIS GUY OVER TO TOSA-HAN, WE'LL FIND OUT WHO HIS FRIENDS ARE.
Hmp!
I'M NOT GOING TO WASTE ANY MORE TIME ON GUYS LIKE HIM AND THEIR PETTY BEHAVIOR!
I'M MORE INTER-ESTED IN...
...GETTING WITH OMASA...
...ASAP !!
HA HA HA HA HA!
YOU'RE SO COOL, HARADA-SAN.
ASSISTANT VICE CAPTAIN HARADA!
UTSUMI-SAN.
YOU KNEW ABOUT THIS PLAN ALL ALONG?
YEAH. ME AND A FEW OTHERS PUT ON DISGUISES AND KEPT WATCH FROM UNDER THE BRIDGE.
I'M SORRY I COULDN'T TELL YOU ABOUT IT.
ONLY THE GOCHO AND ABOVE WERE INFORMED OF THE TRUE PLAN.
STILL...
...I NEVER IMAGINED THAT THE SHINSENGUMI TROOPS WOULD UNITE SO STRONGLY BEHIND A SIMPLE ORDER FROM THE ASSISTANT VICE CAPTAIN.
NAKA-MURA!

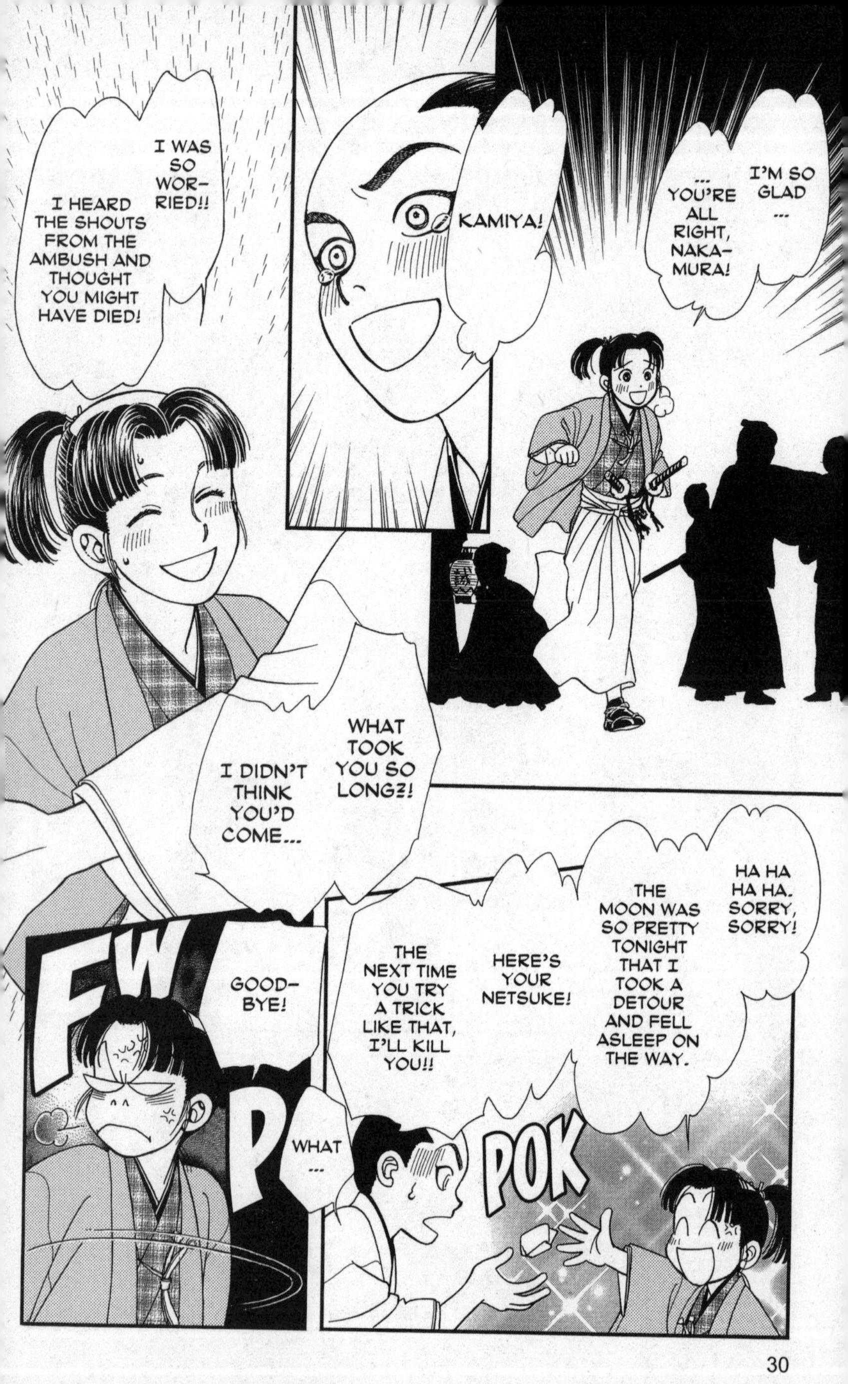
I'M SO GLAD ...
... YOU'RE ALL RIGHT, NAKAMURA!
KAMIYA!
I WAS SO WORRIED!!
I HEARD THE SHOUTS FROM THE AMBUSH AND THOUGHT YOU MIGHT HAVE DIED!
WHAT TOOK YOU SO LONG?!
I DIDN'T THINK YOU'D COME...
HA HA HA HA. SORRY, SORRY!
THE MOON WAS SO PRETTY TONIGHT THAT I TOOK A DETOUR AND FELL ASLEEP ON THE WAY.
HERE'S YOUR NETSUKE!
THE NEXT TIME YOU TRY A TRICK LIKE THAT, I'LL KILL YOU!!
POK
WHAT ...
FWP
GOOD-BYE!

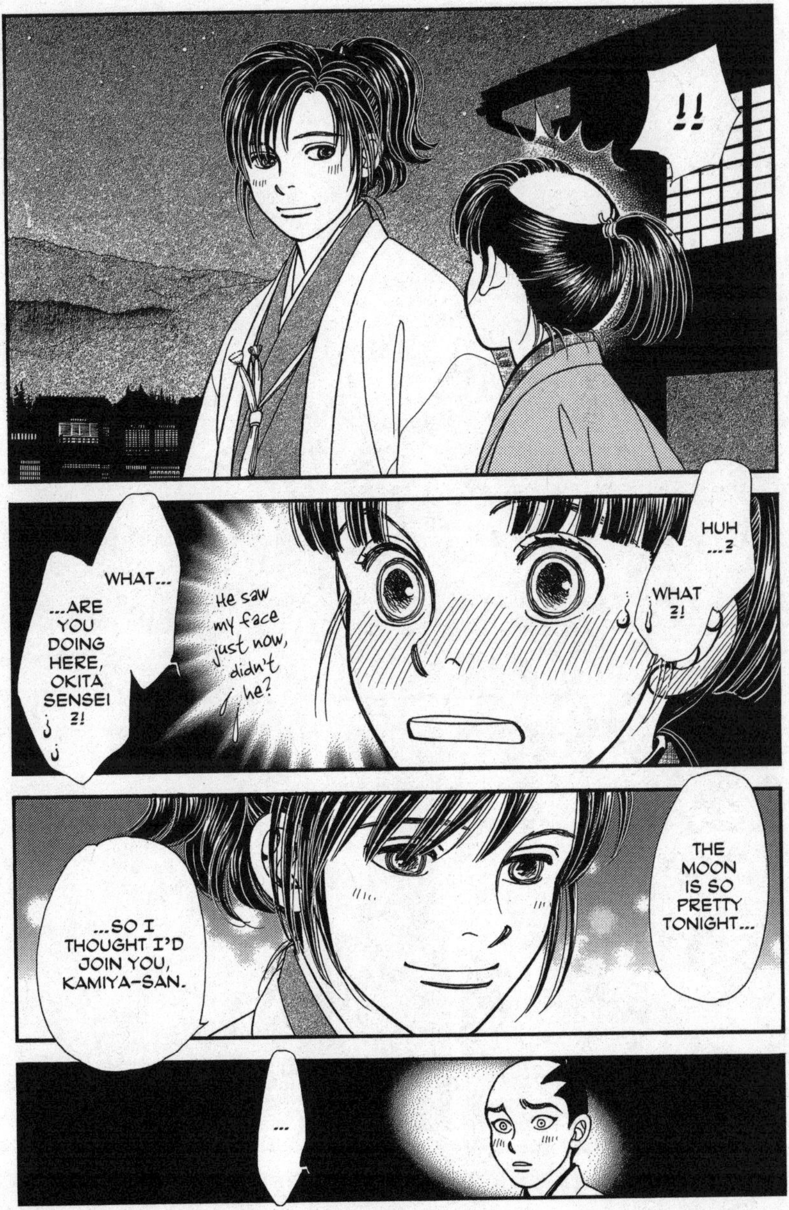
!!
HUH ...?
WHAT ?!
He saw my face just now, didn't he?
WHAT... ...ARE YOU DOING HERE, OKITA SENSEI ?!
THE MOON IS SO PRETTY TONIGHT...
...SO I THOUGHT I'D JOIN YOU, KAMIYA-SAN.
...

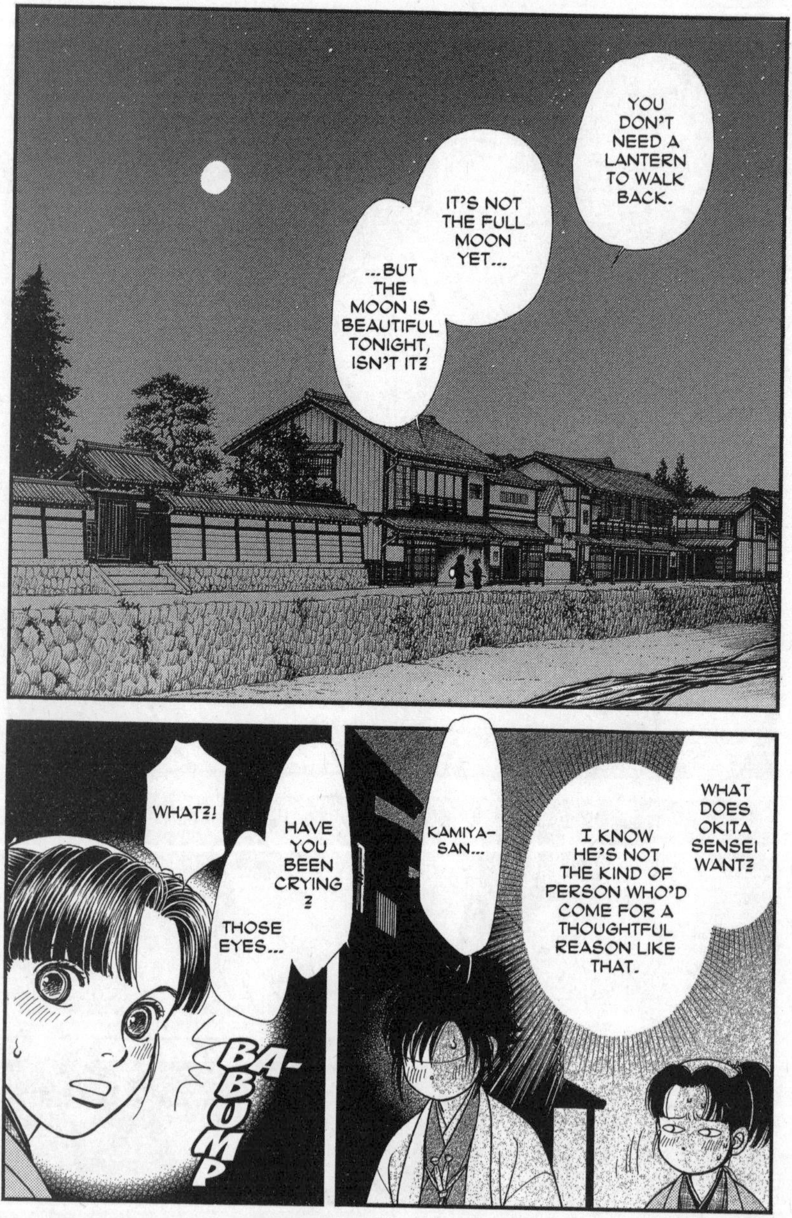
YOU DON'T NEED A LANTERN TO WALK BACK.
IT'S NOT THE FULL MOON YET...
...BUT THE MOON IS BEAUTIFUL TONIGHT, ISN'T IT?
WHAT DOES OKITA SENSEI WANT?
I KNOW HE'S NOT THE KIND OF PERSON WHO'D COME FOR A THOUGHTFUL REASON LIKE THAT.
KAMIYA-SAN...
HAVE YOU BEEN CRYING?
THOSE EYES...
WHAT?!
BA-BUMP

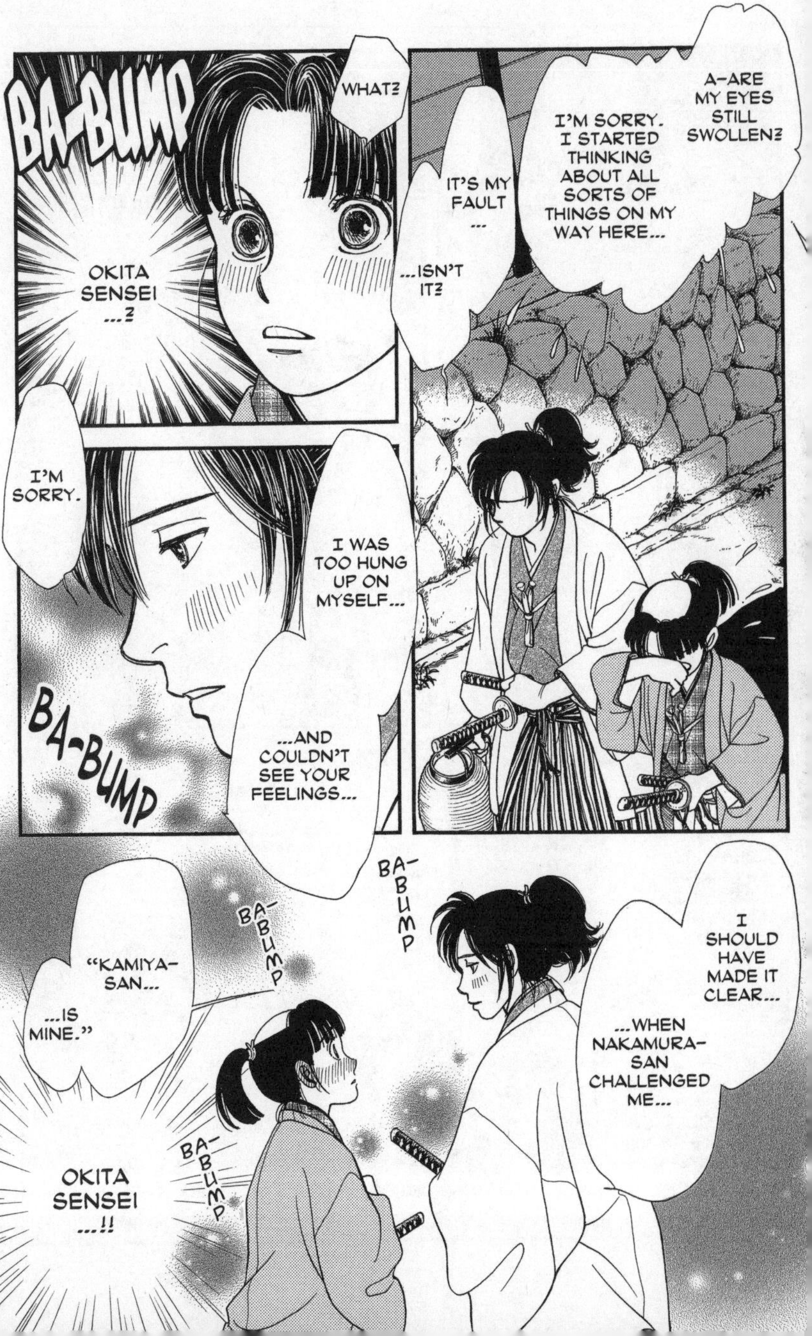
A-ARE MY EYES STILL SWOLLEN?
I'M SORRY. I STARTED THINKING ABOUT ALL SORTS OF THINGS ON MY WAY HERE...
IT'S MY FAULT ...
...ISN'T IT?
WHAT?
BA-BUMP
OKITA SENSEI ...?
I'M SORRY.
I WAS TOO HUNG UP ON MYSELF...
...AND COULDN'T SEE YOUR FEELINGS...
BA-BUMP
I SHOULD HAVE MADE IT CLEAR...
...WHEN NAKAMURA-SAN CHALLENGED ME...
BA-BUMP
BA-BUMP
"KAMIYA-SAN...
...IS MINE."
BA-BUMP
OKITA SENSEI ...!!

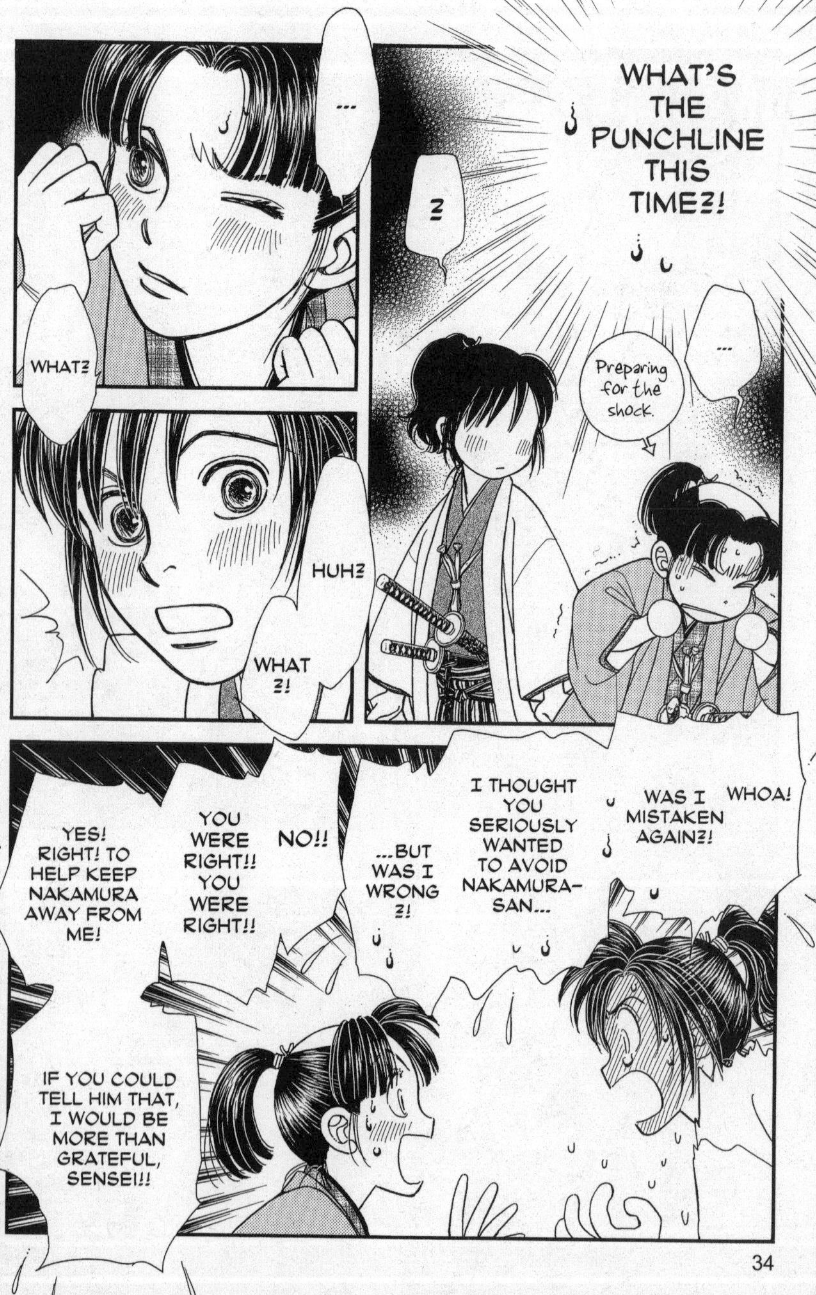
WHAT'S THE PUNCHLINE THIS TIME?!
...
Preparing for the shock.
?
...
WHAT?
HUH?
WHAT?!
WHOA!
WAS I MISTAKEN AGAIN?!
I THOUGHT YOU SERIOUSLY WANTED TO AVOID NAKAMURA-SAN...
...BUT WAS I WRONG?!
NO!!
YOU WERE RIGHT!! YOU WERE RIGHT!!
YES! RIGHT! TO HELP KEEP NAKAMURA AWAY FROM ME!
IF YOU COULD TELL HIM THAT, I WOULD BE MORE THAN GRATEFUL, SENSEI!!

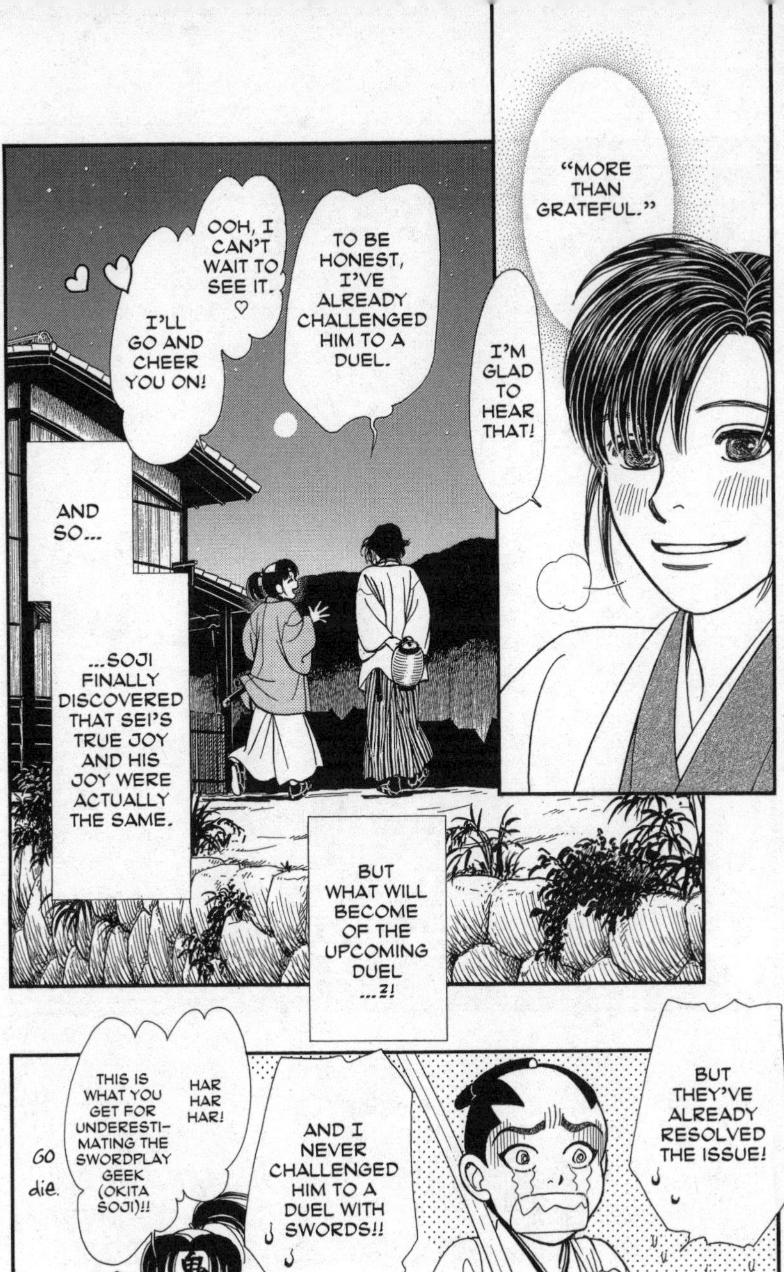
"MORE THAN GRATEFUL."
I'M GLAD TO HEAR THAT!
TO BE HONEST, I'VE ALREADY CHALLENGED HIM TO A DUEL.
OOH, I CAN'T WAIT TO SEE IT. ♡
I'LL GO AND CHEER YOU ON!
AND SO...
...SOJI FINALLY DISCOVERED THAT SEI'S TRUE JOY AND HIS JOY WERE ACTUALLY THE SAME.
BUT WHAT WILL BECOME OF THE UPCOMING DUEL ...?!
BUT THEY'VE ALREADY RESOLVED THE ISSUE!
AND I NEVER CHALLENGED HIM TO A DUEL WITH SWORDS!!
HAR HAR HAR!
THIS IS WHAT YOU GET FOR UNDERESTIMATING THE SWORDPLAY GEEK (OKITA SOJI)!!
GO die.
VICTORY
SOJI

Sei's headband: Oni

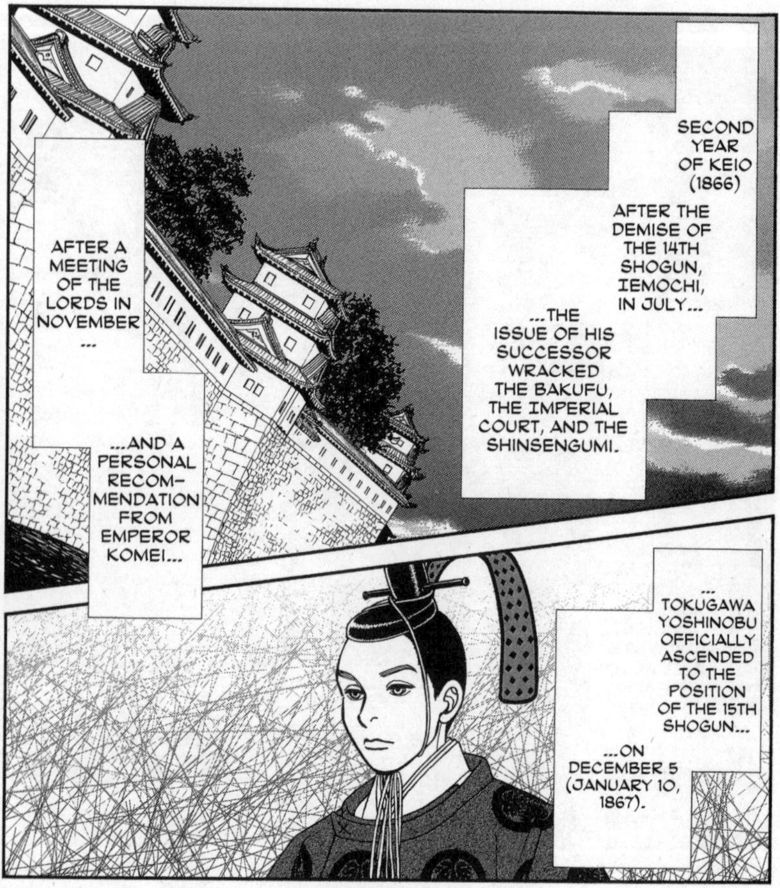
SECOND YEAR OF KEIO (1866)
AFTER THE DEMISE OF THE 14TH SHOGUN, IEMOCHI, IN JULY...
...THE ISSUE OF HIS SUCCESSOR WRACKED THE BAKUFU, THE IMPERIAL COURT, AND THE SHINSENGUMI.
AFTER A MEETING OF THE LORDS IN NOVEMBER ...
...AND A PERSONAL RECOM-MENDATION FROM EMPEROR KOMEI...
...TOKUGAWA YOSHINOBU OFFICIALLY ASCENDED TO THE POSITION OF THE 15TH SHOGUN...
...ON DECEMBER 5 (JANUARY 10, 1867).

KAZE HIKARU SENRYU
OUT OF THE QUESTION BUT ACCEPTABLE AS A FRIEND

By Misako Toshimitsu from Oita

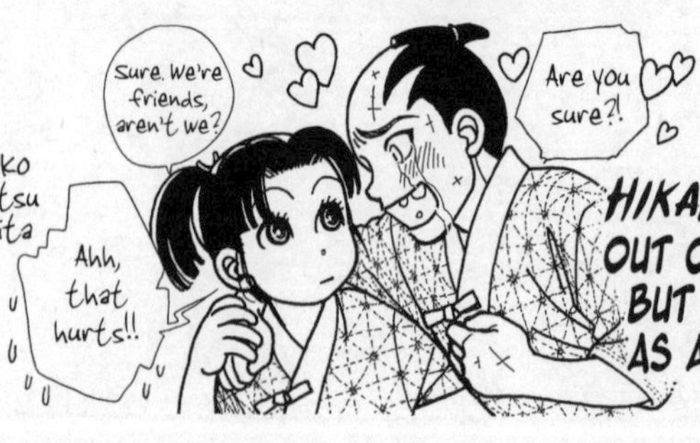
Are you sure?!
Sure. We're friends, aren't we?
Ahh, that hurts!!

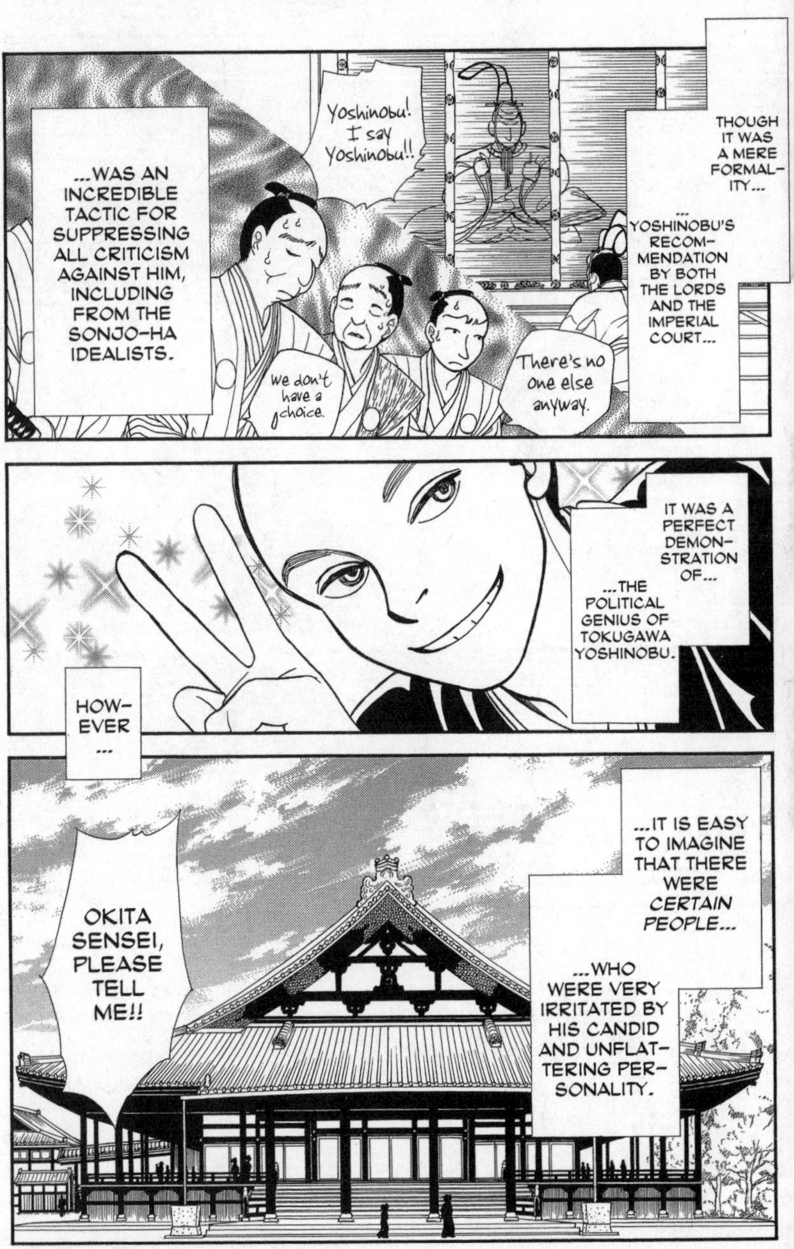
THOUGH IT WAS A MERE FORMALITY...
...YOSHINOBU'S RECOMMENDATION BY BOTH THE LORDS AND THE IMPERIAL COURT...
Yoshinobu! I say Yoshinobu!!
There's no one else anyway.
We don't have a choice.
...WAS AN INCREDIBLE TACTIC FOR SUPPRESSING ALL CRITICISM AGAINST HIM, INCLUDING FROM THE SONJO-HA IDEALISTS.
IT WAS A PERFECT DEMONSTRATION OF...
...THE POLITICAL GENIUS OF TOKUGAWA YOSHINOBU.
HOWEVER...
...IT IS EASY TO IMAGINE THAT THERE WERE *CERTAIN PEOPLE*...
...WHO WERE VERY IRRITATED BY HIS CANDID AND UNFLATTERING PERSONALITY.
OKITA SENSEI, PLEASE TELL ME!!

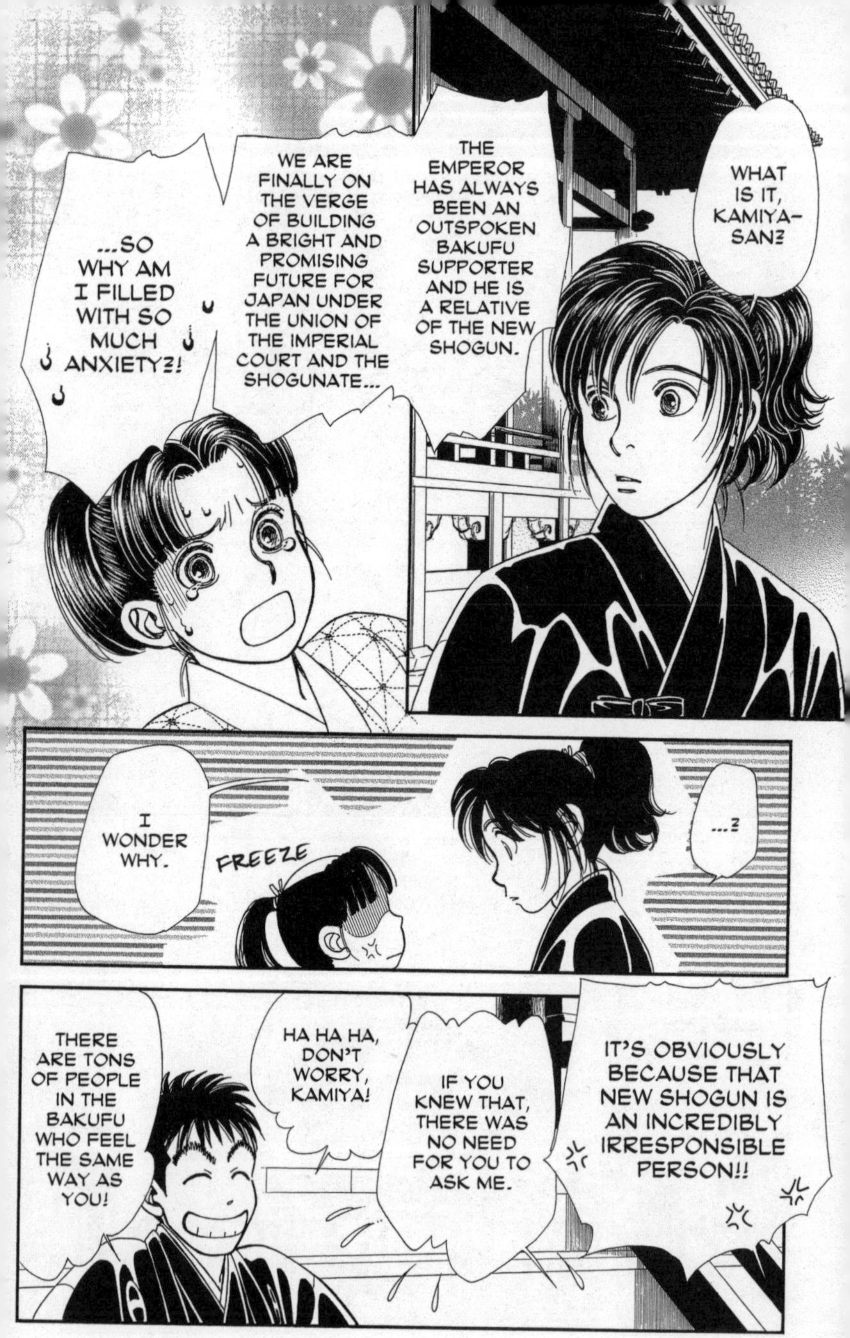
WHAT IS IT, KAMIYA-SAN?
THE EMPEROR HAS ALWAYS BEEN AN OUTSPOKEN BAKUFU SUPPORTER AND HE IS A RELATIVE OF THE NEW SHOGUN.
WE ARE FINALLY ON THE VERGE OF BUILDING A BRIGHT AND PROMISING FUTURE FOR JAPAN UNDER THE UNION OF THE IMPERIAL COURT AND THE SHOGUNATE...
...SO WHY AM I FILLED WITH SO MUCH ANXIETY?!
...?
I WONDER WHY.
FREEZE
IT'S OBVIOUSLY BECAUSE THAT NEW SHOGUN IS AN INCREDIBLY IRRESPONSIBLE PERSON!!
IF YOU KNEW THAT, THERE WAS NO NEED FOR YOU TO ASK ME.
HA HA HA, DON'T WORRY, KAMIYA!
THERE ARE TONS OF PEOPLE IN THE BAKUFU WHO FEEL THE SAME WAY AS YOU!

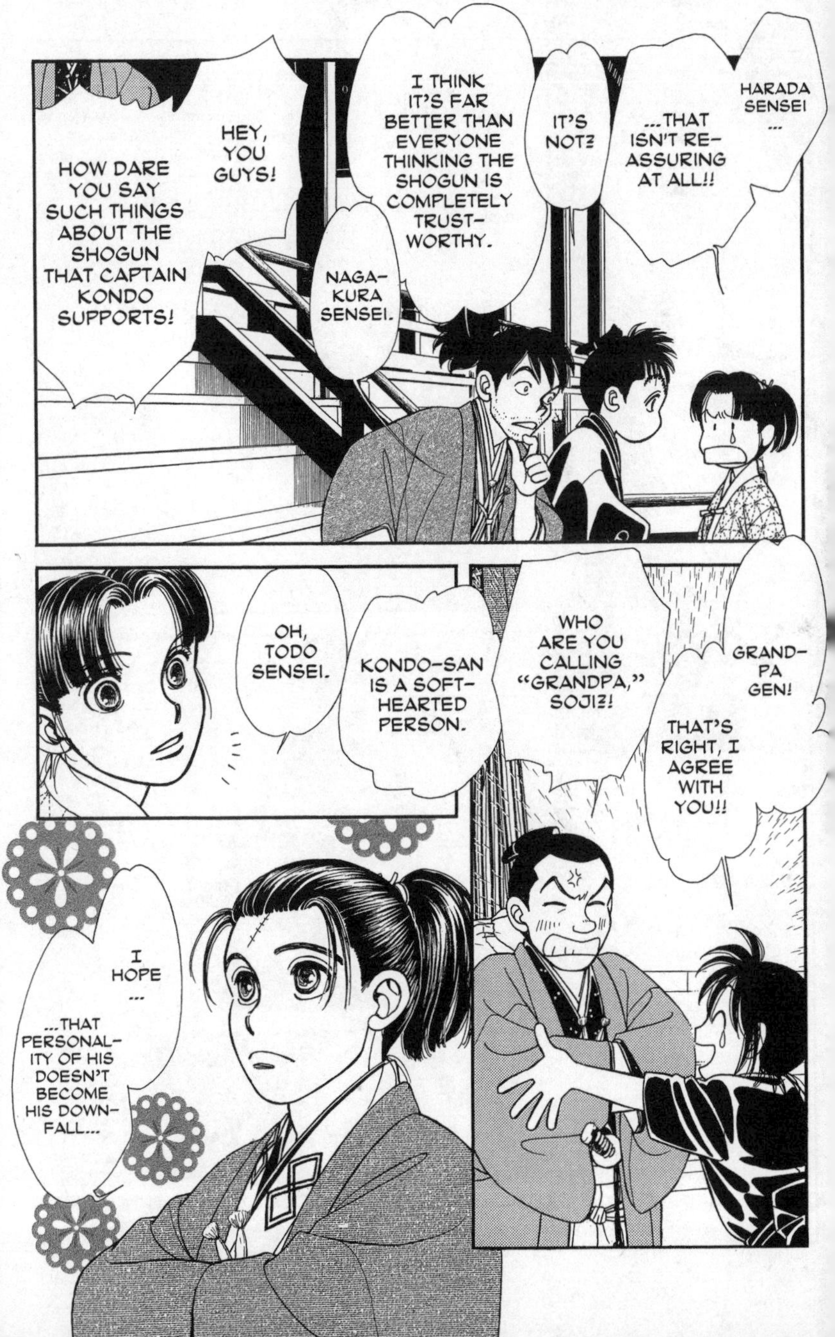
HARADA SENSEI ...
...THAT ISN'T RE-ASSURING AT ALL!!
IT'S NOT?
I THINK IT'S FAR BETTER THAN EVERYONE THINKING THE SHOGUN IS COMPLETELY TRUST-WORTHY.
NAGA-KURA SENSEI.
HEY, YOU GUYS!
HOW DARE YOU SAY SUCH THINGS ABOUT THE SHOGUN THAT CAPTAIN KONDO SUPPORTS!
GRAND-PA GEN!
THAT'S RIGHT, I AGREE WITH YOU!!
WHO ARE YOU CALLING "GRANDPA," SOJI?!
KONDO-SAN IS A SOFT-HEARTED PERSON.
OH, TODO SENSEI.
I HOPE ...
...THAT PERSONAL-ITY OF HIS DOESN'T BECOME HIS DOWN-FALL...

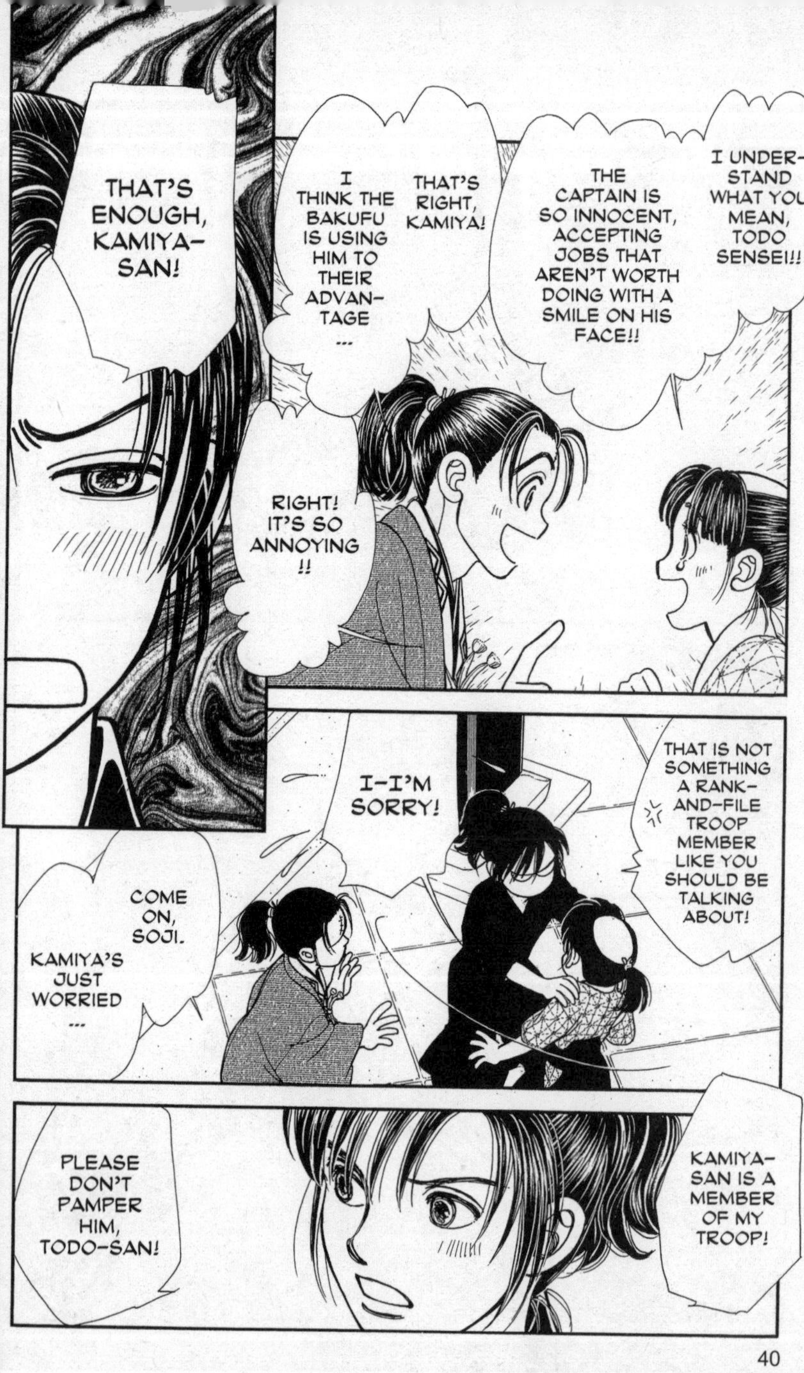
I UNDER-STAND WHAT YOU MEAN, TODO SENSEI!!
THE CAPTAIN IS SO INNOCENT, ACCEPTING JOBS THAT AREN'T WORTH DOING WITH A SMILE ON HIS FACE!!
THAT'S RIGHT, KAMIYA!
I THINK THE BAKUFU IS USING HIM TO THEIR ADVAN-TAGE ...
RIGHT! IT'S SO ANNOYING !!
THAT'S ENOUGH, KAMIYA-SAN!
THAT IS NOT SOMETHING A RANK-AND-FILE TROOP MEMBER LIKE YOU SHOULD BE TALKING ABOUT!
I-I'M SORRY!
COME ON, SOJI.
KAMIYA'S JUST WORRIED ...
KAMIYA-SAN IS A MEMBER OF MY TROOP!
PLEASE DON'T PAMPER HIM, TODO-SAN!

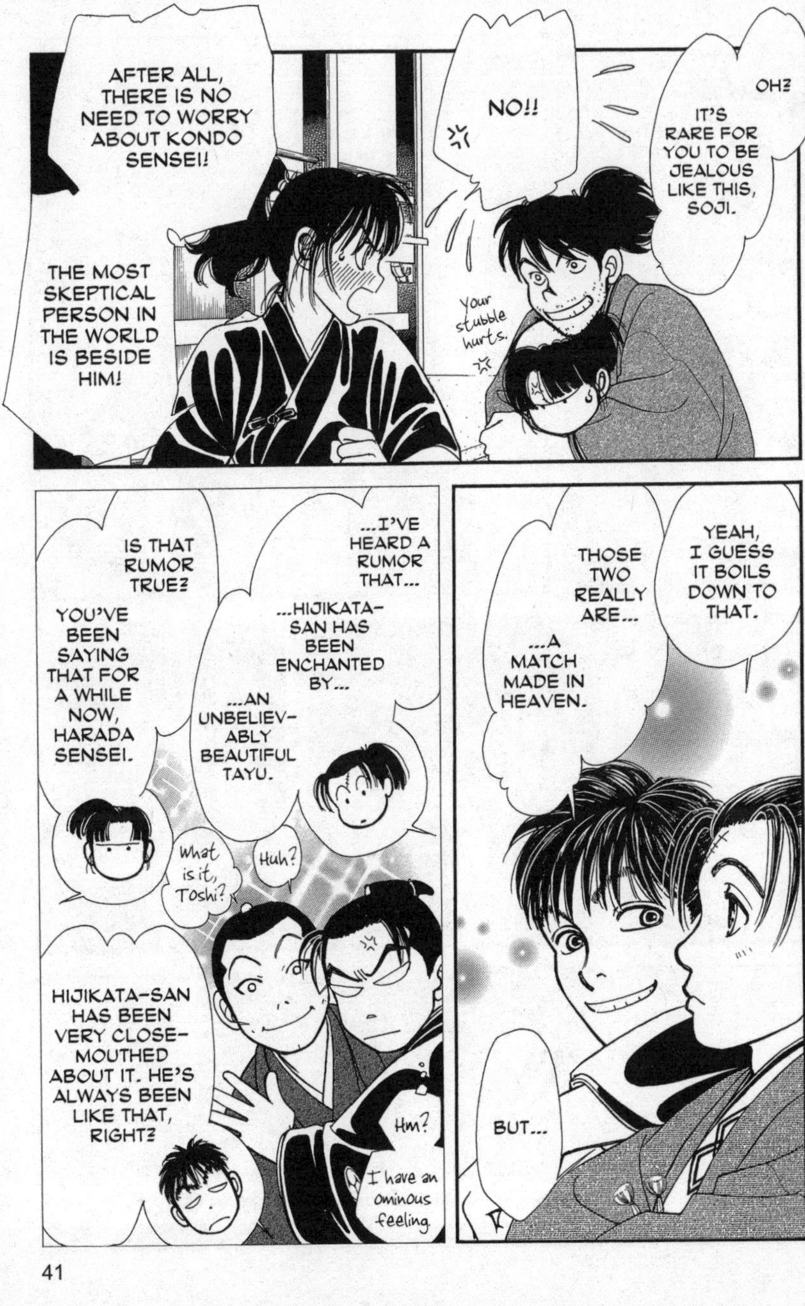
OH? IT'S RARE FOR YOU TO BE JEALOUS LIKE THIS, SOJI.
NO!!
AFTER ALL, THERE IS NO NEED TO WORRY ABOUT KONDO SENSEI!
Your stubble hurts.
THE MOST SKEPTICAL PERSON IN THE WORLD IS BESIDE HIM!
YEAH, I GUESS IT BOILS DOWN TO THAT.
THOSE TWO REALLY ARE...
...A MATCH MADE IN HEAVEN.
BUT...
...I'VE HEARD A RUMOR THAT...
...HIJIKATA-SAN HAS BEEN ENCHANTED BY...
...AN UNBELIEV-ABLY BEAUTIFUL TAYU.
IS THAT RUMOR TRUE?
YOU'VE BEEN SAYING THAT FOR A WHILE NOW, HARADA SENSEI.
Huh?
What is it, Toshi?
HIJIKATA-SAN HAS BEEN VERY CLOSE-MOUTHED ABOUT IT. HE'S ALWAYS BEEN LIKE THAT, RIGHT?
Hm?
I have an ominous feeling.

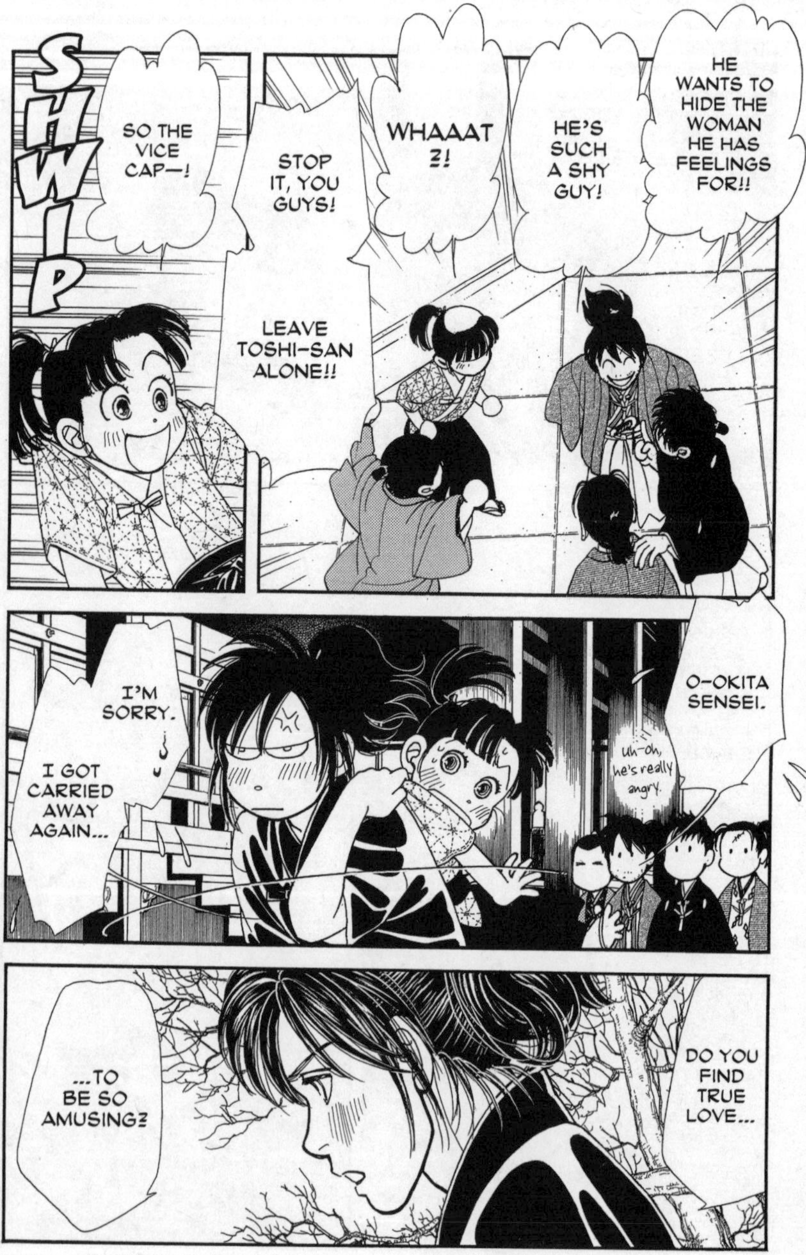

HE WANTS TO HIDE THE WOMAN HE HAS FEELINGS FOR!!
HE'S SUCH A SHY GUY!
WHAAAT?!
STOP IT, YOU GUYS!
LEAVE TOSHI-SAN ALONE!!
SHWIP
SO THE VICE CAP—!
O-OKITA SENSEI.
Uh-oh, he's really angry.
I'M SORRY.
I GOT CARRIED AWAY AGAIN...
DO YOU FIND TRUE LOVE...
...TO BE SO AMUSING?

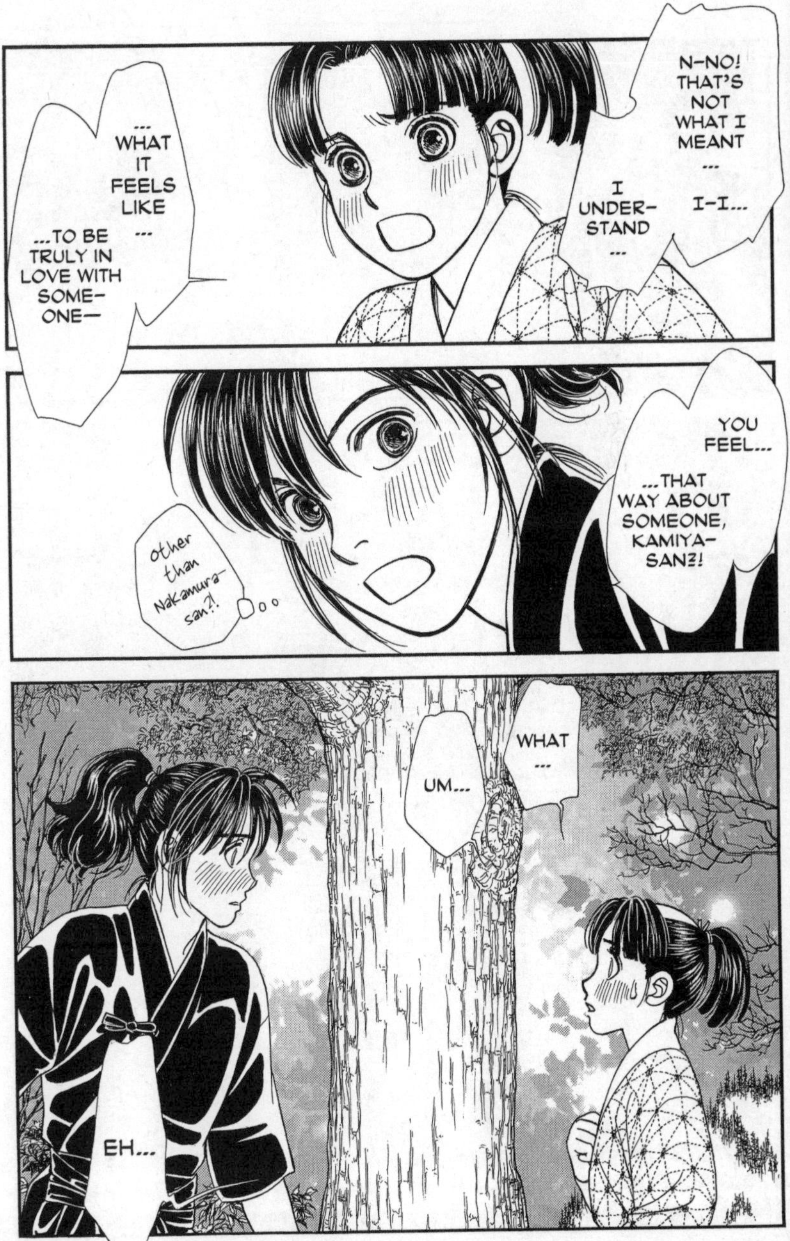
N-NO! THAT'S NOT WHAT I MEANT... I-I...
I UNDERSTAND...
...WHAT IT FEELS LIKE...
...TO BE TRULY IN LOVE WITH SOMEONE—
YOU FEEL...
...THAT WAY ABOUT SOMEONE, KAMIYA-SAN?!
other than Nakamura-san?!
WHAT...
UM...
EH...

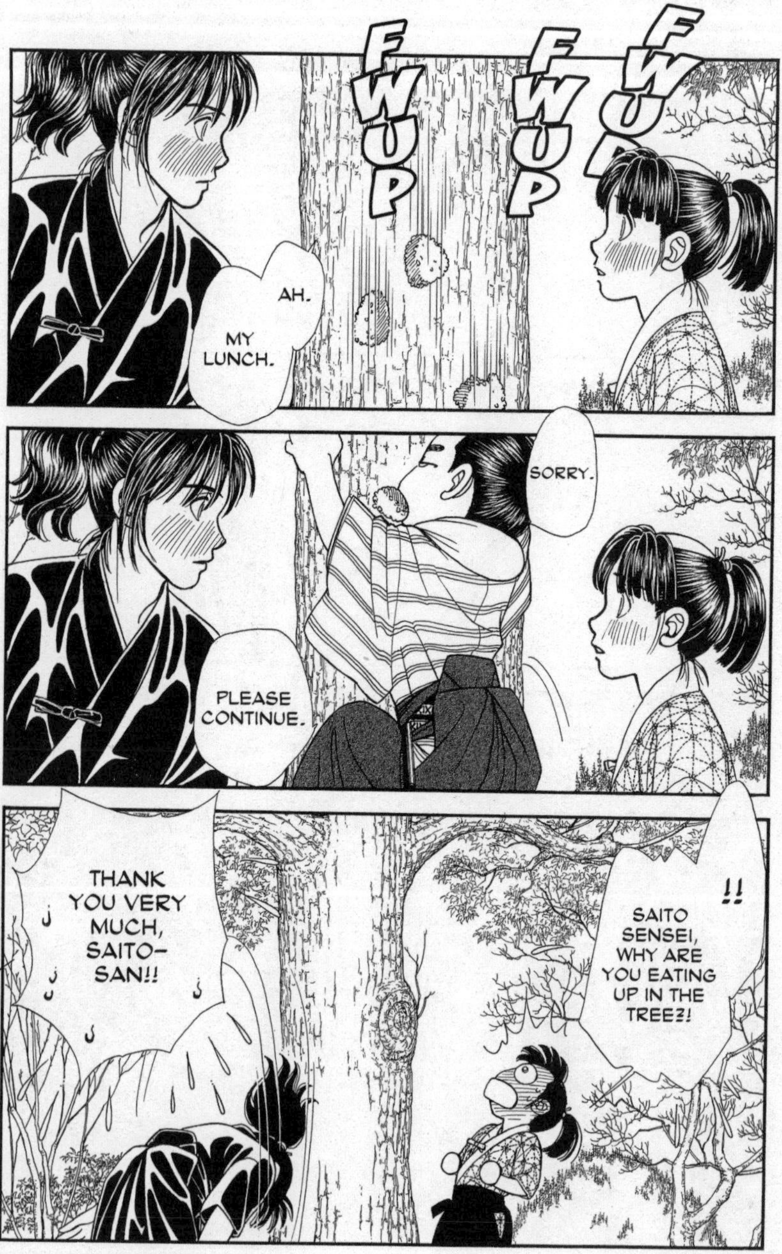
FWUP
FWUP
FWUP
AH.
MY LUNCH.
SORRY.
PLEASE CONTINUE.
!!
SAITO SENSEI, WHY ARE YOU EATING UP IN THE TREE?!
THANK YOU VERY MUCH, SAITO-SAN!!

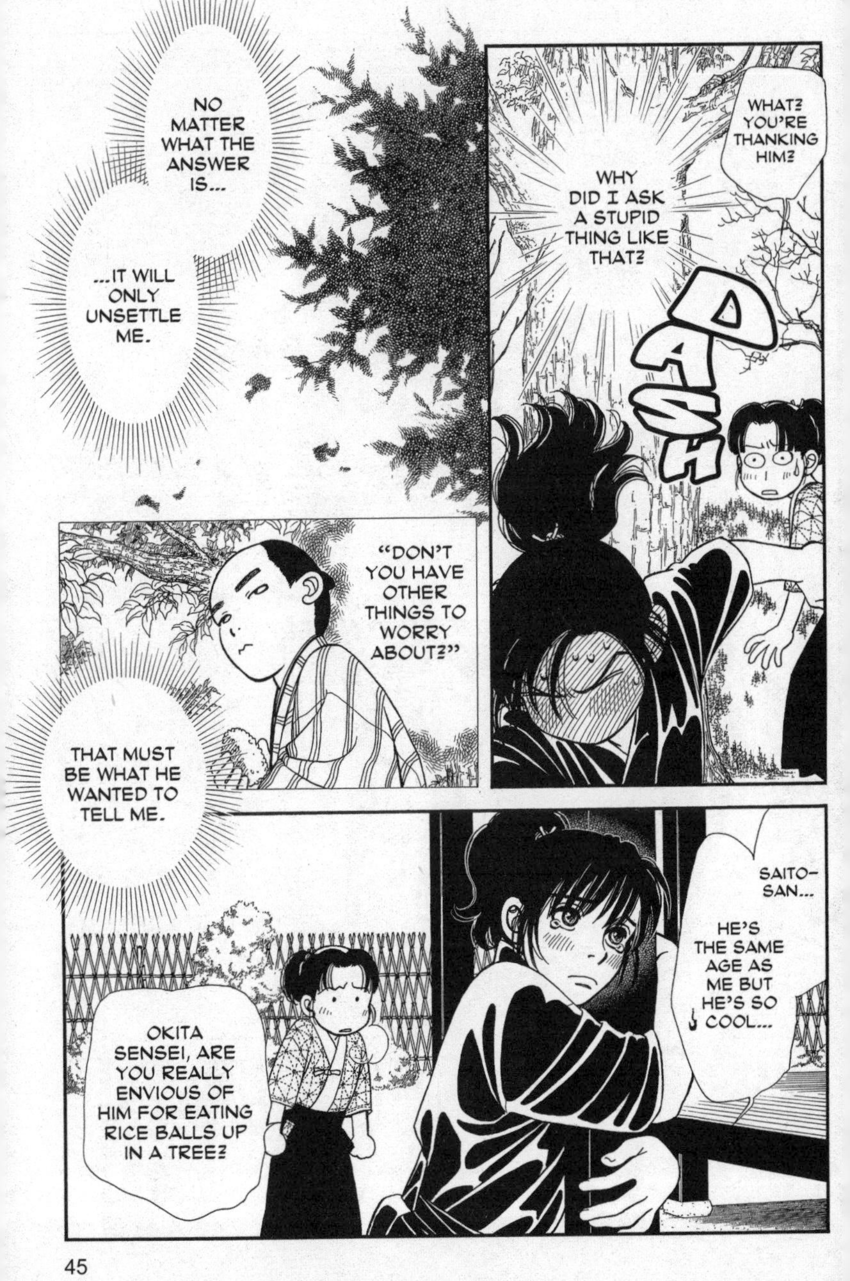
WHAT? YOU'RE THANKING HIM?
WHY DID I ASK A STUPID THING LIKE THAT?
DASH
NO MATTER WHAT THE ANSWER IS...
...IT WILL ONLY UNSETTLE ME.
"DON'T YOU HAVE OTHER THINGS TO WORRY ABOUT?"
THAT MUST BE WHAT HE WANTED TO TELL ME.
SAITO-SAN...
HE'S THE SAME AGE AS ME BUT HE'S SO COOL...
OKITA SENSEI, ARE YOU REALLY ENVIOUS OF HIM FOR EATING RICE BALLS UP IN A TREE?

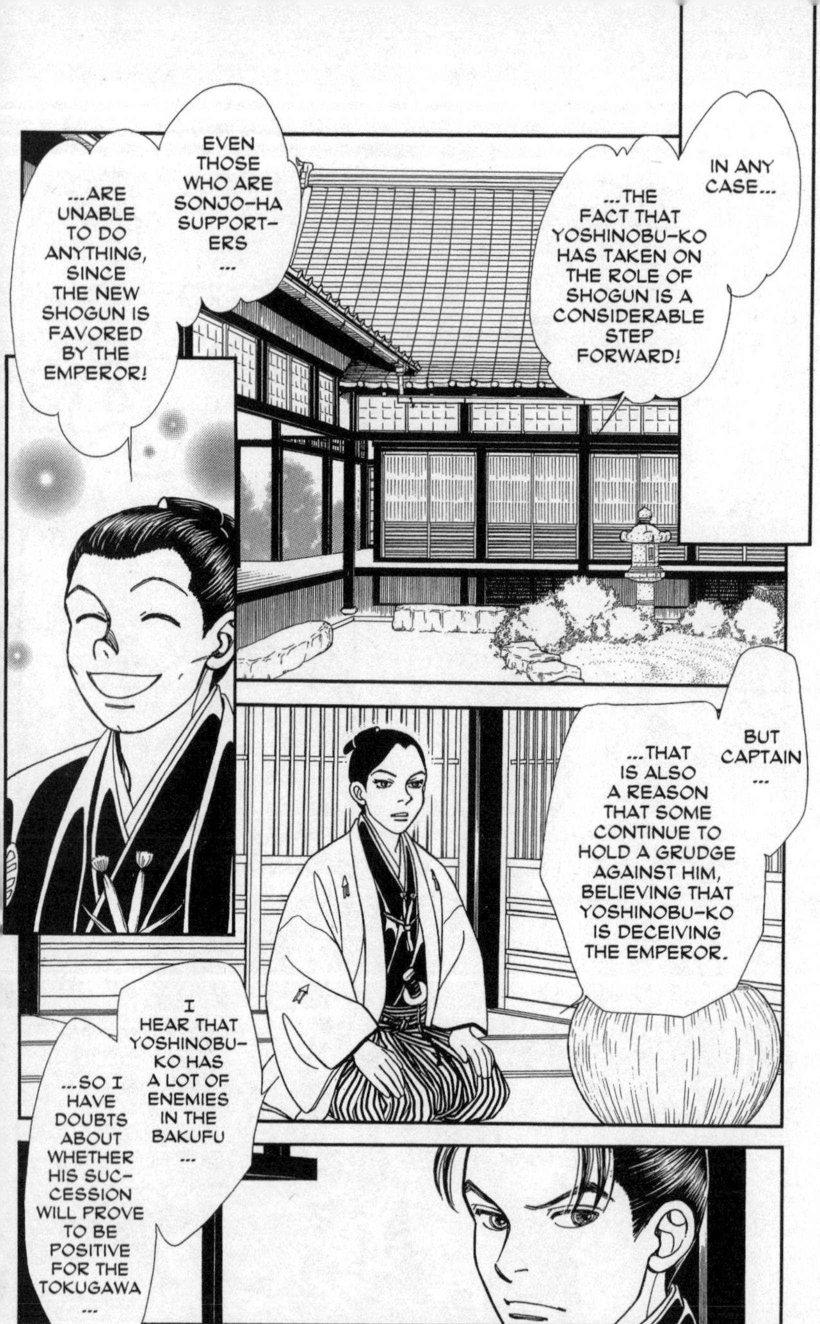
IN ANY CASE...
...THE FACT THAT YOSHINOBU-KO HAS TAKEN ON THE ROLE OF SHOGUN IS A CONSIDERABLE STEP FORWARD!
EVEN THOSE WHO ARE SONJO-HA SUPPORTERS...
...ARE UNABLE TO DO ANYTHING, SINCE THE NEW SHOGUN IS FAVORED BY THE EMPEROR!
BUT CAPTAIN...
...THAT IS ALSO A REASON THAT SOME CONTINUE TO HOLD A GRUDGE AGAINST HIM, BELIEVING THAT YOSHINOBU-KO IS DECEIVING THE EMPEROR.
I HEAR THAT YOSHINOBU-KO HAS A LOT OF ENEMIES IN THE BAKUFU...
...SO I HAVE DOUBTS ABOUT WHETHER HIS SUCCESSION WILL PROVE TO BE POSITIVE FOR THE TOKUGAWA...

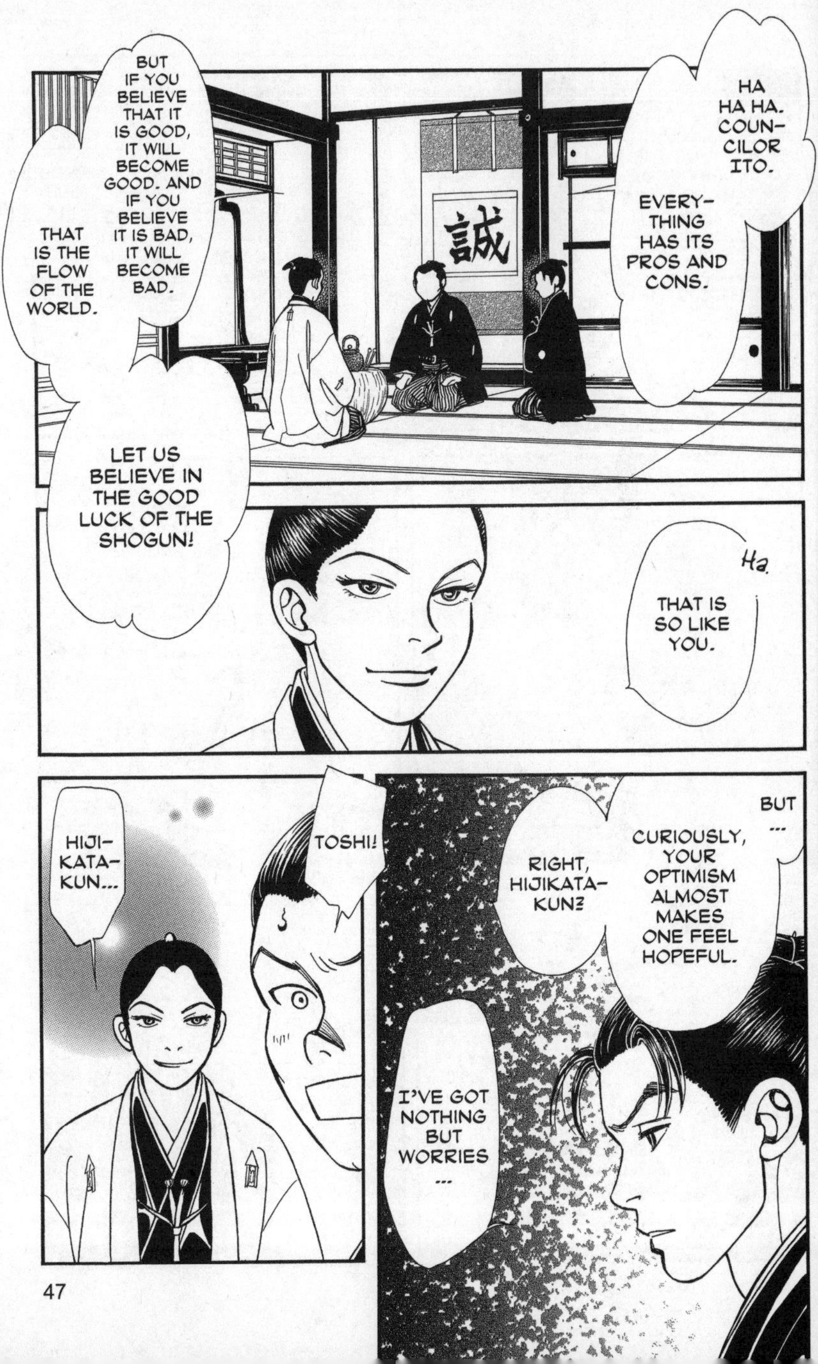
HA HA HA. COUNCILOR ITO.
EVERYTHING HAS ITS PROS AND CONS.
BUT IF YOU BELIEVE THAT IT IS GOOD, IT WILL BECOME GOOD. AND IF YOU BELIEVE IT IS BAD, IT WILL BECOME BAD.
THAT IS THE FLOW OF THE WORLD.
LET US BELIEVE IN THE GOOD LUCK OF THE SHOGUN!
Ha.
THAT IS SO LIKE YOU.
BUT ...
CURIOUSLY, YOUR OPTIMISM ALMOST MAKES ONE FEEL HOPEFUL.
RIGHT, HIJIKATA-KUN?
I'VE GOT NOTHING BUT WORRIES ...
TOSHI!
HIJIKATA-KUN...

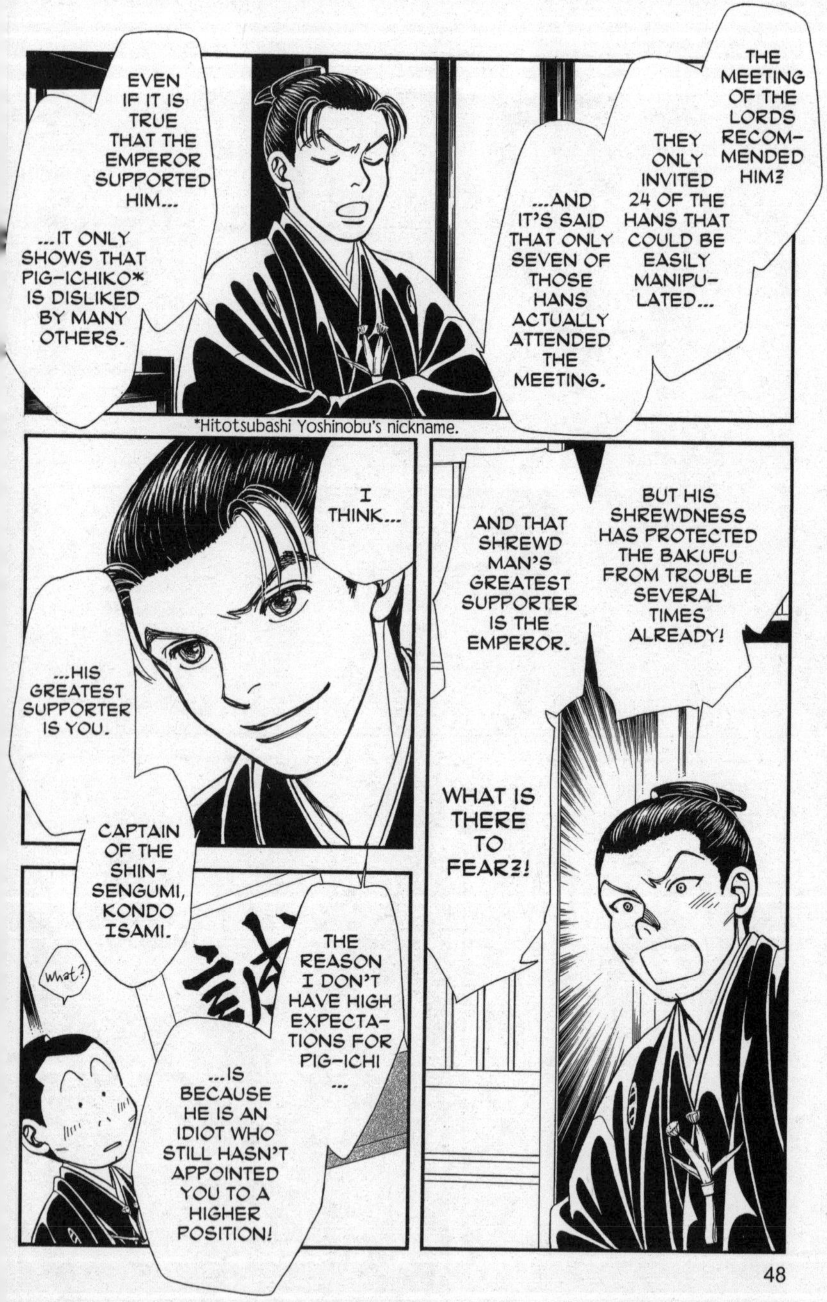
THE MEETING OF THE LORDS RECOMMENDED HIM?
THEY ONLY INVITED 24 OF THE HANS THAT COULD BE EASILY MANIPULATED...
...AND IT'S SAID THAT ONLY SEVEN OF THOSE HANS ACTUALLY ATTENDED THE MEETING.
EVEN IF IT IS TRUE THAT THE EMPEROR SUPPORTED HIM...
...IT ONLY SHOWS THAT PIG-ICHIKO* IS DISLIKED BY MANY OTHERS.
*Hitotsubashi Yoshinobu's nickname.
BUT HIS SHREWDNESS HAS PROTECTED THE BAKUFU FROM TROUBLE SEVERAL TIMES ALREADY!
AND THAT SHREWD MAN'S GREATEST SUPPORTER IS THE EMPEROR.
WHAT IS THERE TO FEAR?!
I THINK...
...HIS GREATEST SUPPORTER IS YOU.
CAPTAIN OF THE SHIN-SENGUMI, KONDO ISAMI.
THE REASON I DON'T HAVE HIGH EXPECTATIONS FOR PIG-ICHI...
...IS BECAUSE HE IS AN IDIOT WHO STILL HASN'T APPOINTED YOU TO A HIGHER POSITION!
what?

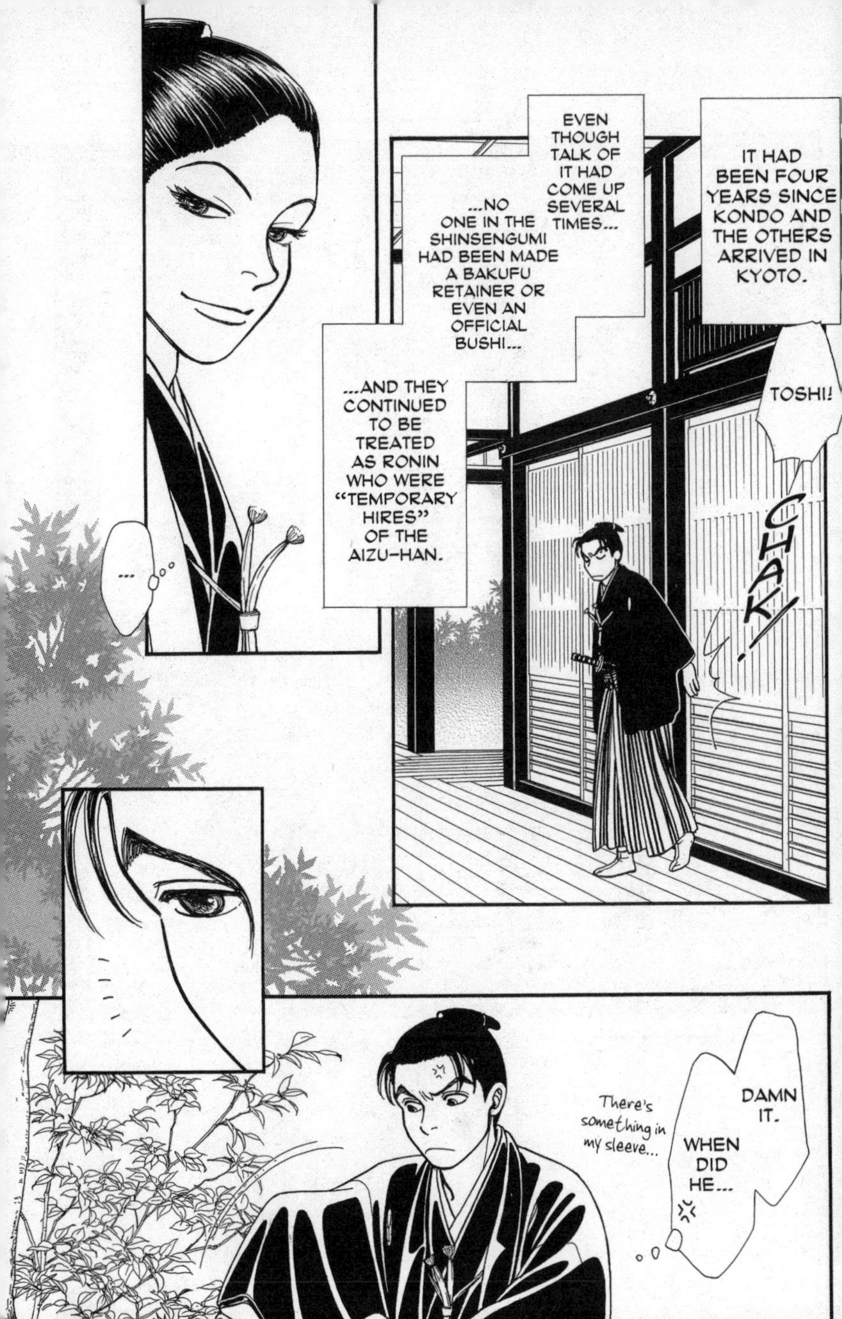
IT HAD BEEN FOUR YEARS SINCE KONDO AND THE OTHERS ARRIVED IN KYOTO.
EVEN THOUGH TALK OF IT HAD COME UP SEVERAL TIMES...
...NO ONE IN THE SHINSENGUMI HAD BEEN MADE A BAKUFU RETAINER OR EVEN AN OFFICIAL BUSHI...
...AND THEY CONTINUED TO BE TREATED AS RONIN WHO WERE "TEMPORARY HIRES" OF THE AIZU-HAN.
TOSHI!
CHAK!
...
DAMN IT.
WHEN DID HE...
There's something in my sleeve...

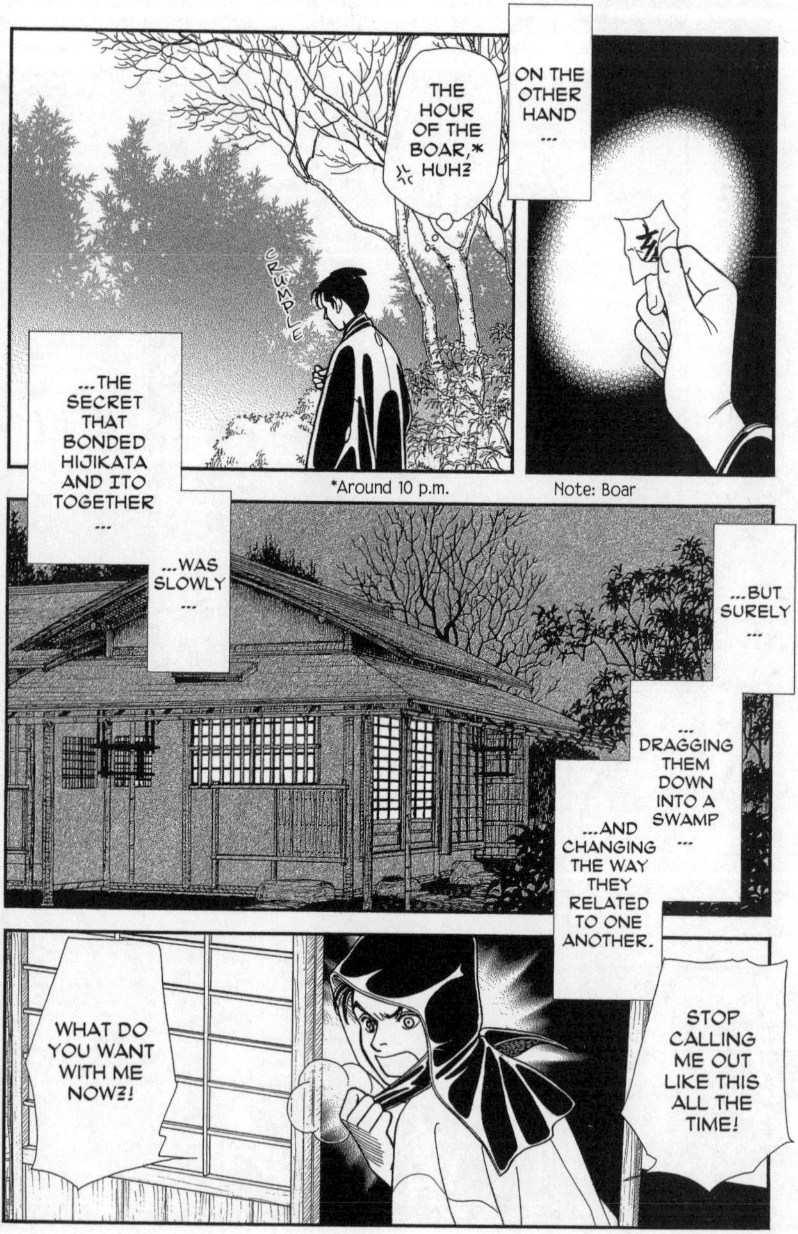
ON THE OTHER HAND ...
Note: Boar
THE HOUR OF THE BOAR,* HUH?
CRUMPLE
...THE SECRET THAT BONDED HIJIKATA AND ITO TOGETHER ...
*Around 10 p.m.
...WAS SLOWLY ...
...BUT SURELY ...
... DRAGGING THEM DOWN INTO A SWAMP ...
...AND CHANGING THE WAY THEY RELATED TO ONE ANOTHER.
STOP CALLING ME OUT LIKE THIS ALL THE TIME!
WHAT DO YOU WANT WITH ME NOW?!

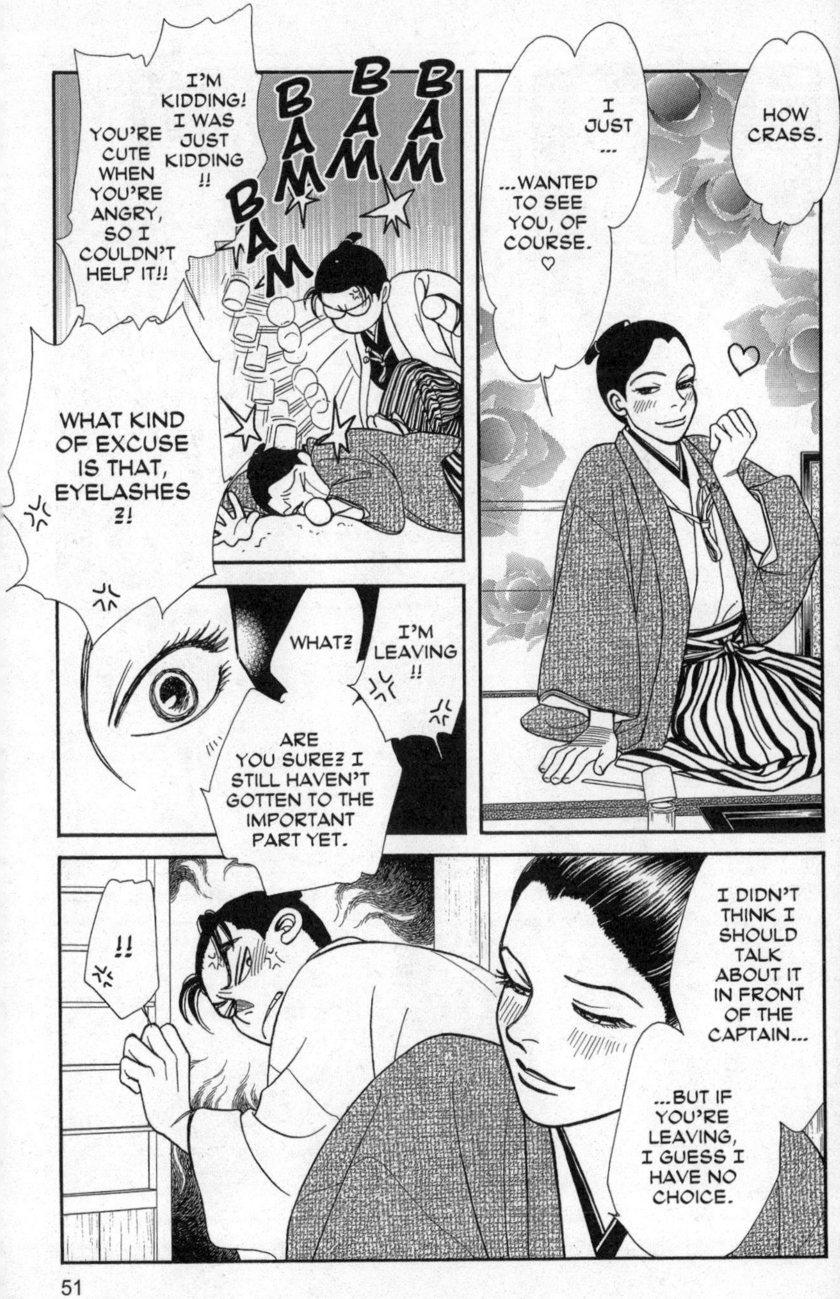
HOW CRASS.
I JUST...
...WANTED TO SEE YOU, OF COURSE. ♡
BAM BAMM BAMM BAM
I'M KIDDING! I WAS JUST KIDDING!!
YOU'RE CUTE WHEN YOU'RE ANGRY, SO I COULDN'T HELP IT!!
WHAT KIND OF EXCUSE IS THAT, EYELASHES?!
I'M LEAVING!!
WHAT?
ARE YOU SURE? I STILL HAVEN'T GOTTEN TO THE IMPORTANT PART YET.
I DIDN'T THINK I SHOULD TALK ABOUT IT IN FRONT OF THE CAPTAIN...
...BUT IF YOU'RE LEAVING, I GUESS I HAVE NO CHOICE.
!!

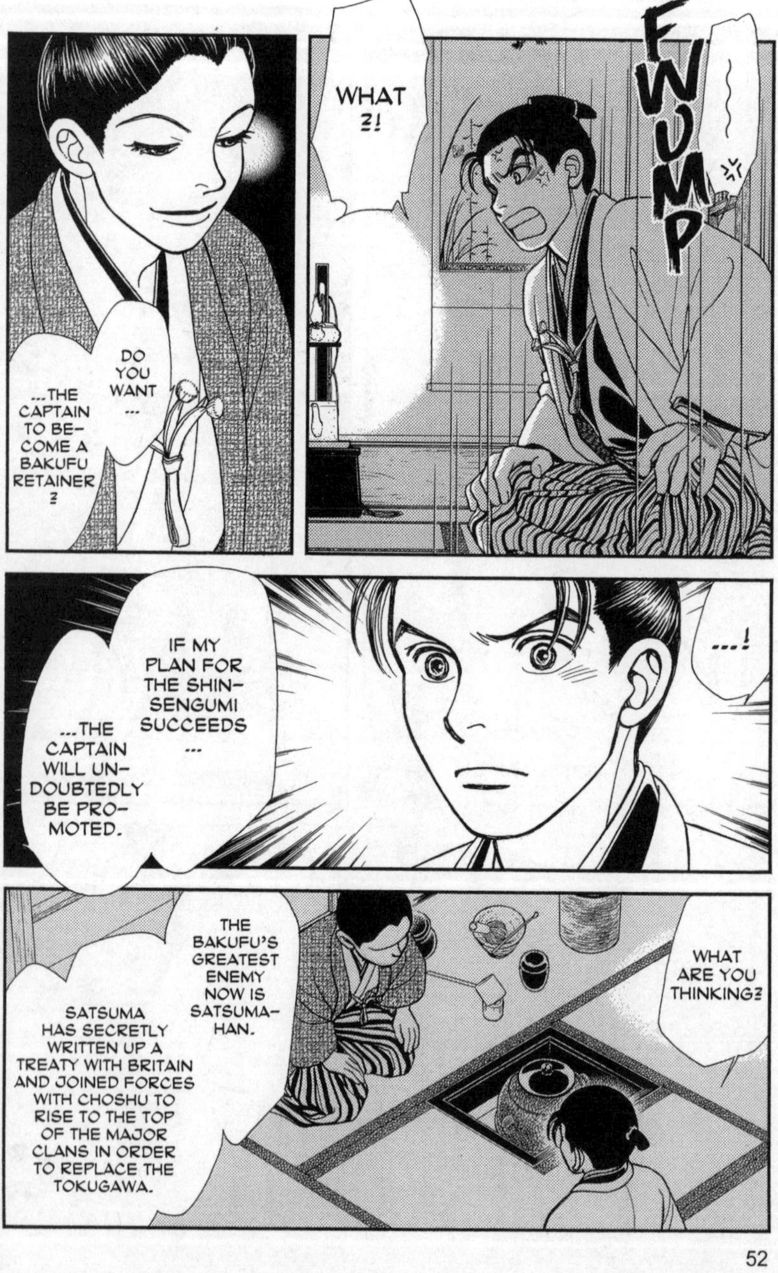
FWUMP
WHAT?!
DO YOU WANT...
...THE CAPTAIN TO BECOME A BAKUFU RETAINER?
...!
IF MY PLAN FOR THE SHINSENGUMI SUCCEEDS...
...THE CAPTAIN WILL UNDOUBTEDLY BE PROMOTED.
WHAT ARE YOU THINKING?
THE BAKUFU'S GREATEST ENEMY NOW IS SATSUMA-HAN.
SATSUMA HAS SECRETLY WRITTEN UP A TREATY WITH BRITAIN AND JOINED FORCES WITH CHOSHU TO RISE TO THE TOP OF THE MAJOR CLANS IN ORDER TO REPLACE THE TOKUGAWA.

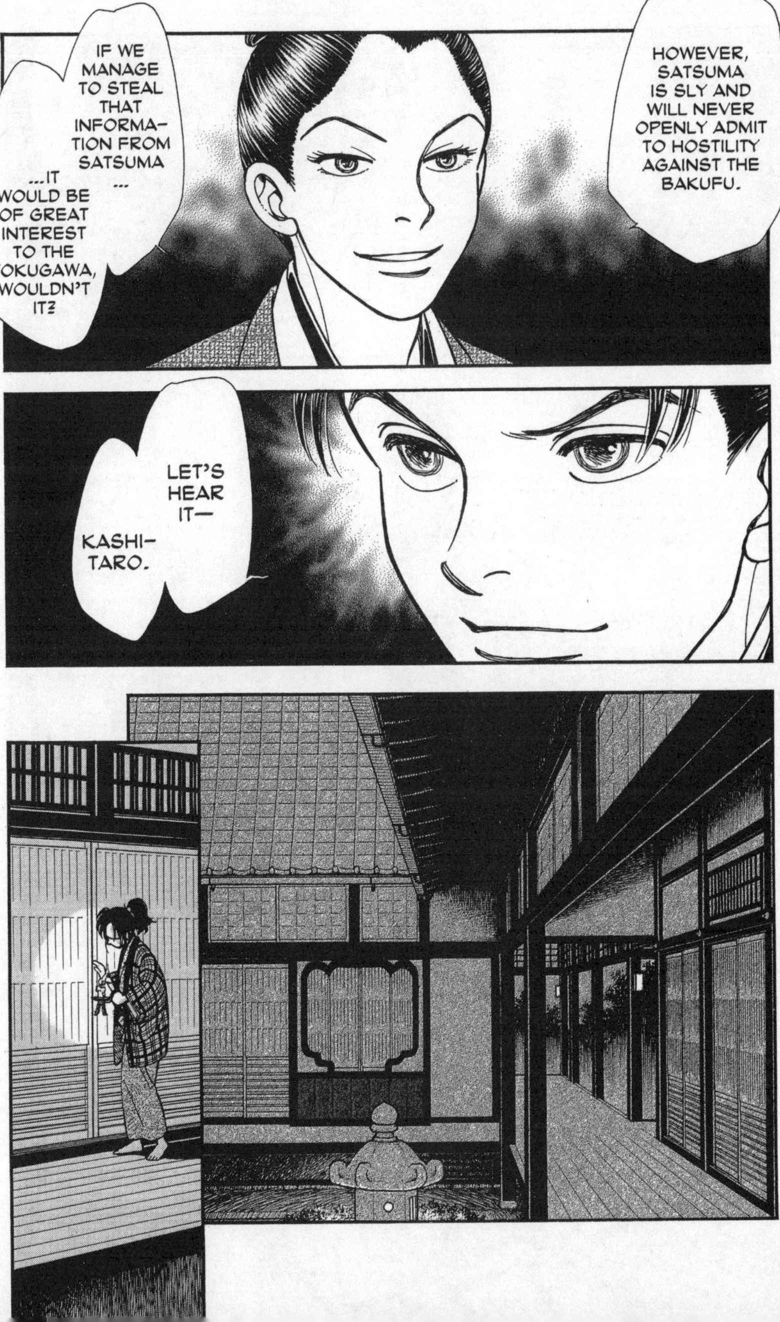
HOWEVER, SATSUMA IS SLY AND WILL NEVER OPENLY ADMIT TO HOSTILITY AGAINST THE BAKUFU.
IF WE MANAGE TO STEAL THAT INFORMATION FROM SATSUMA ...
...IT WOULD BE OF GREAT INTEREST TO THE TOKUGAWA, WOULDN'T IT?
LET'S HEAR IT—
KASHI-TARO.

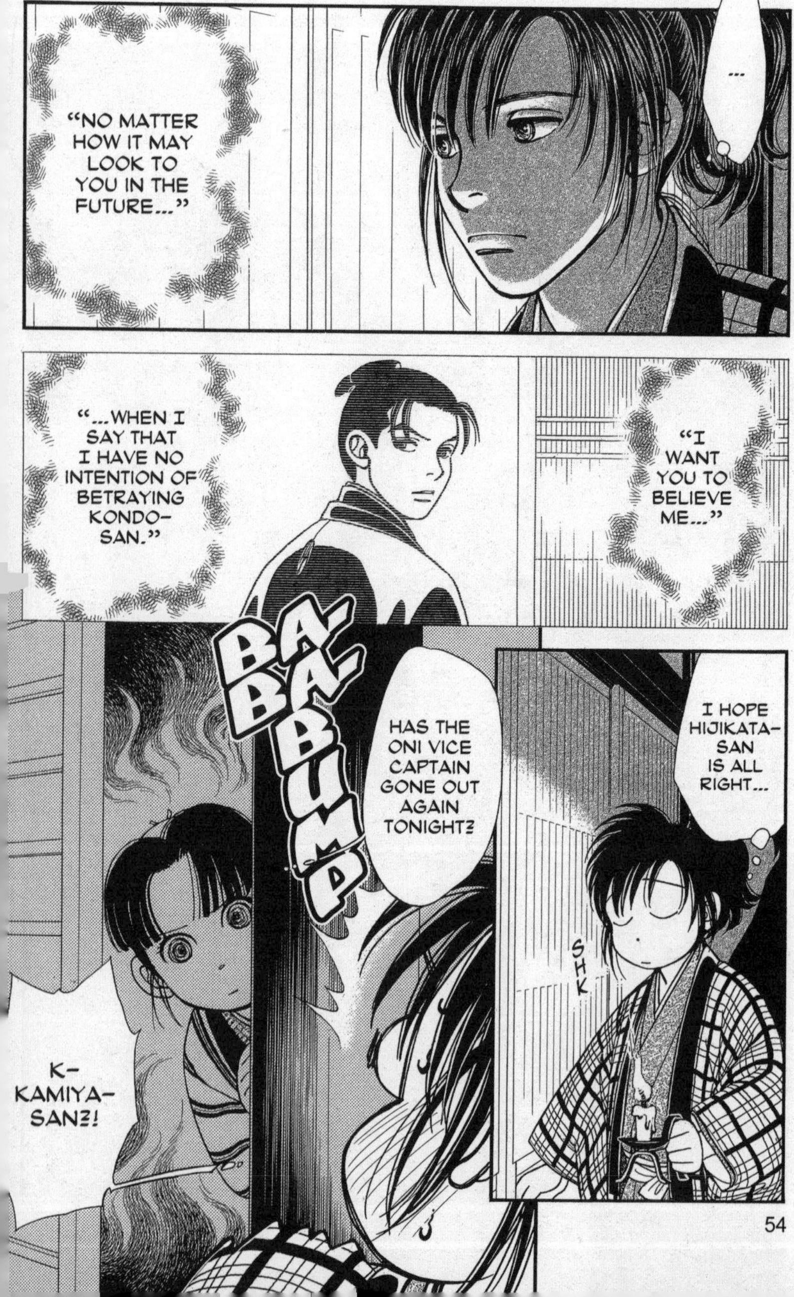
...
"NO MATTER HOW IT MAY LOOK TO YOU IN THE FUTURE..."
"I WANT YOU TO BELIEVE ME..."
"...WHEN I SAY THAT I HAVE NO INTENTION OF BETRAYING KONDO-SAN."
I HOPE HIJIKATA-SAN IS ALL RIGHT...
SHK
HAS THE ONI VICE CAPTAIN GONE OUT AGAIN TONIGHT?
BA-BA-BUMP
K-KAMIYA-SAN?!

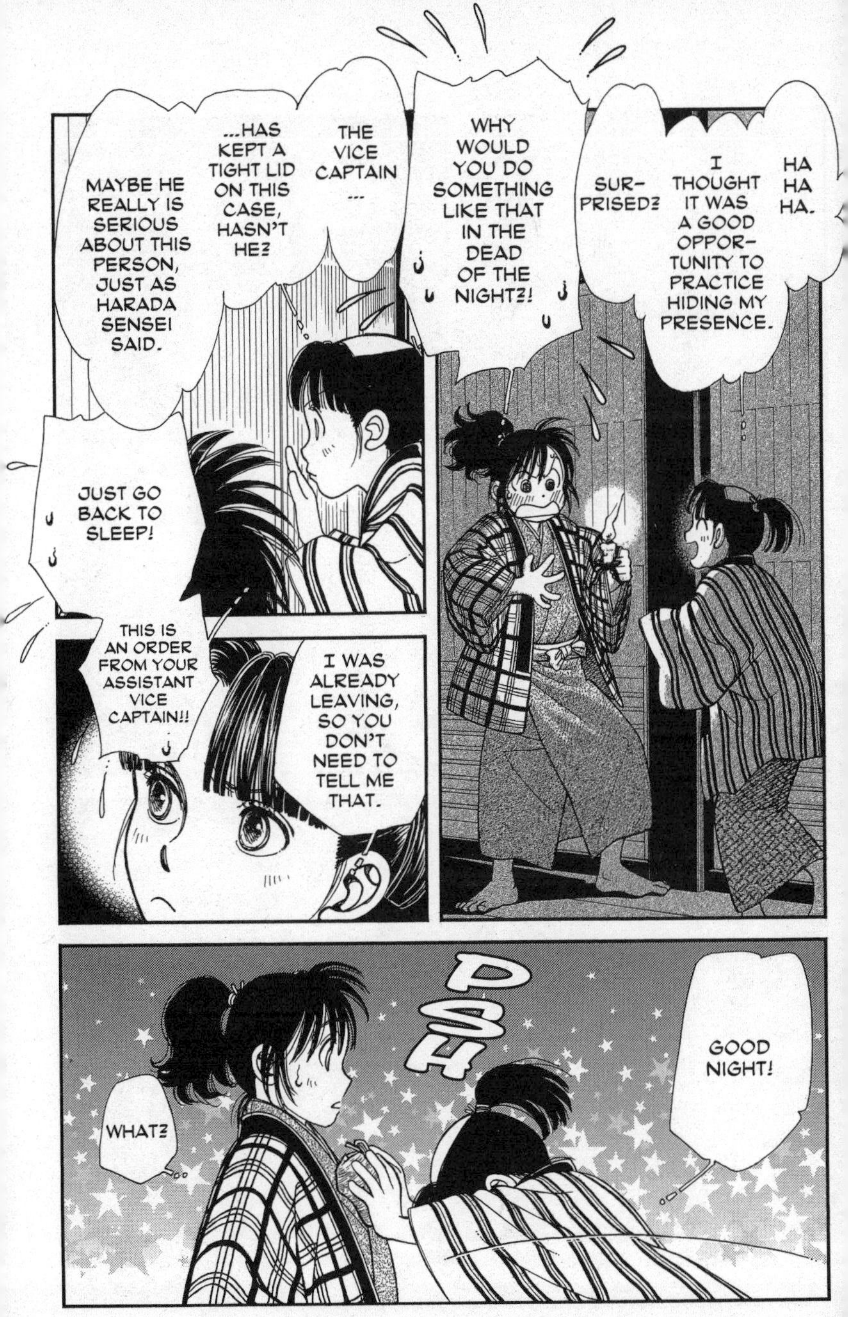
HA HA HA.
I THOUGHT IT WAS A GOOD OPPORTUNITY TO PRACTICE HIDING MY PRESENCE.
SURPRISED?
WHY WOULD YOU DO SOMETHING LIKE THAT IN THE DEAD OF THE NIGHT?!
THE VICE CAPTAIN...
...HAS KEPT A TIGHT LID ON THIS CASE, HASN'T HE?
MAYBE HE REALLY IS SERIOUS ABOUT THIS PERSON, JUST AS HARADA SENSEI SAID.
JUST GO BACK TO SLEEP!
THIS IS AN ORDER FROM YOUR ASSISTANT VICE CAPTAIN!!
I WAS ALREADY LEAVING, SO YOU DON'T NEED TO TELL ME THAT.
PSH
GOOD NIGHT!
WHAT?

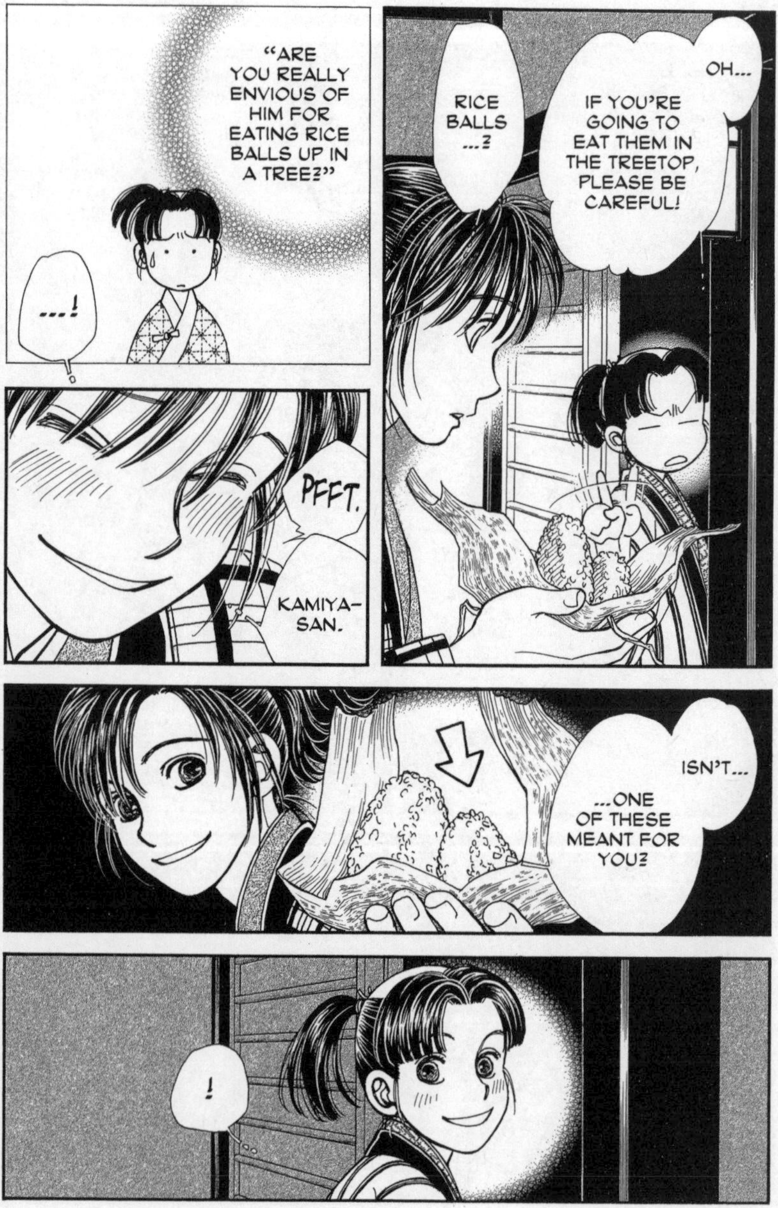

OH...
IF YOU'RE GOING TO EAT THEM IN THE TREETOP, PLEASE BE CAREFUL!
RICE BALLS ...?
"ARE YOU REALLY ENVIOUS OF HIM FOR EATING RICE BALLS UP IN A TREE?"
...!
PFFT.
KAMIYA-SAN.
ISN'T...
...ONE OF THESE MEANT FOR YOU?
!

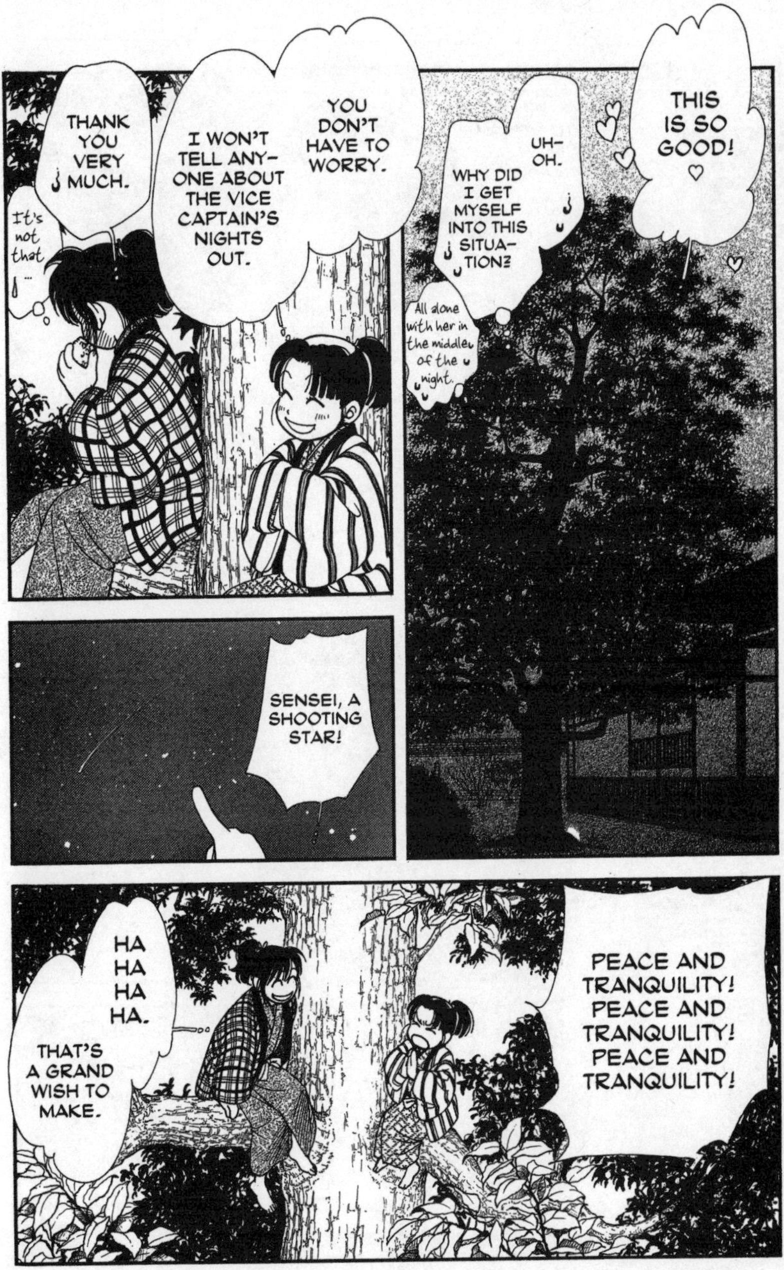
THIS IS SO GOOD!
UH-OH.
WHY DID I GET MYSELF INTO THIS SITUATION?
All alone with her in the middle of the night.
YOU DON'T HAVE TO WORRY.
I WON'T TELL ANYONE ABOUT THE VICE CAPTAIN'S NIGHTS OUT.
THANK YOU VERY MUCH.
It's not that ...
SENSEI, A SHOOTING STAR!
PEACE AND TRANQUILITY! PEACE AND TRANQUILITY! PEACE AND TRANQUILITY!
HA HA HA HA.
THAT'S A GRAND WISH TO MAKE.

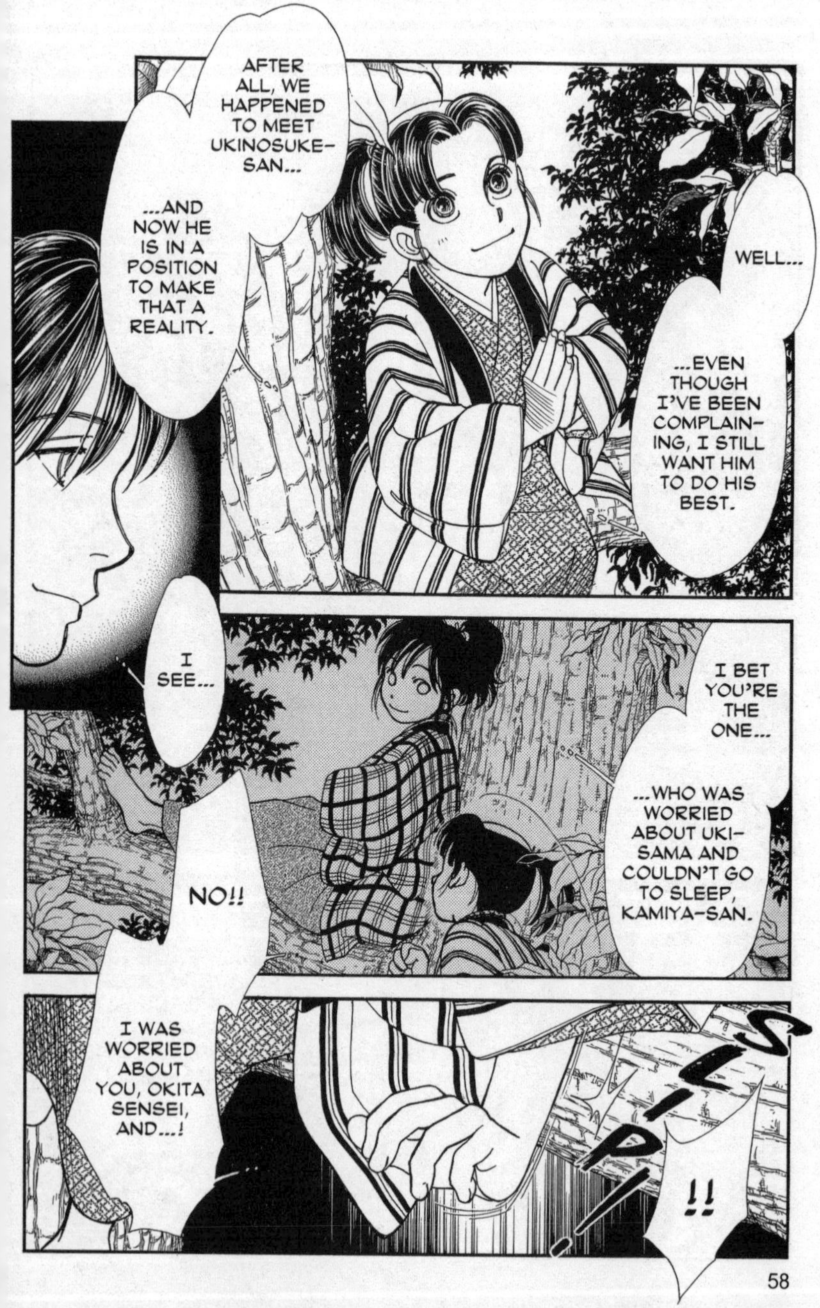
WELL...
...EVEN THOUGH I'VE BEEN COMPLAIN-ING, I STILL WANT HIM TO DO HIS BEST.
AFTER ALL, WE HAPPENED TO MEET UKINOSUKE-SAN...
...AND NOW HE IS IN A POSITION TO MAKE THAT A REALITY.
I SEE...
I BET YOU'RE THE ONE...
...WHO WAS WORRIED ABOUT UKI-SAMA AND COULDN'T GO TO SLEEP, KAMIYA-SAN.
NO!!
I WAS WORRIED ABOUT YOU, OKITA SENSEI, AND...!
SLIP!!

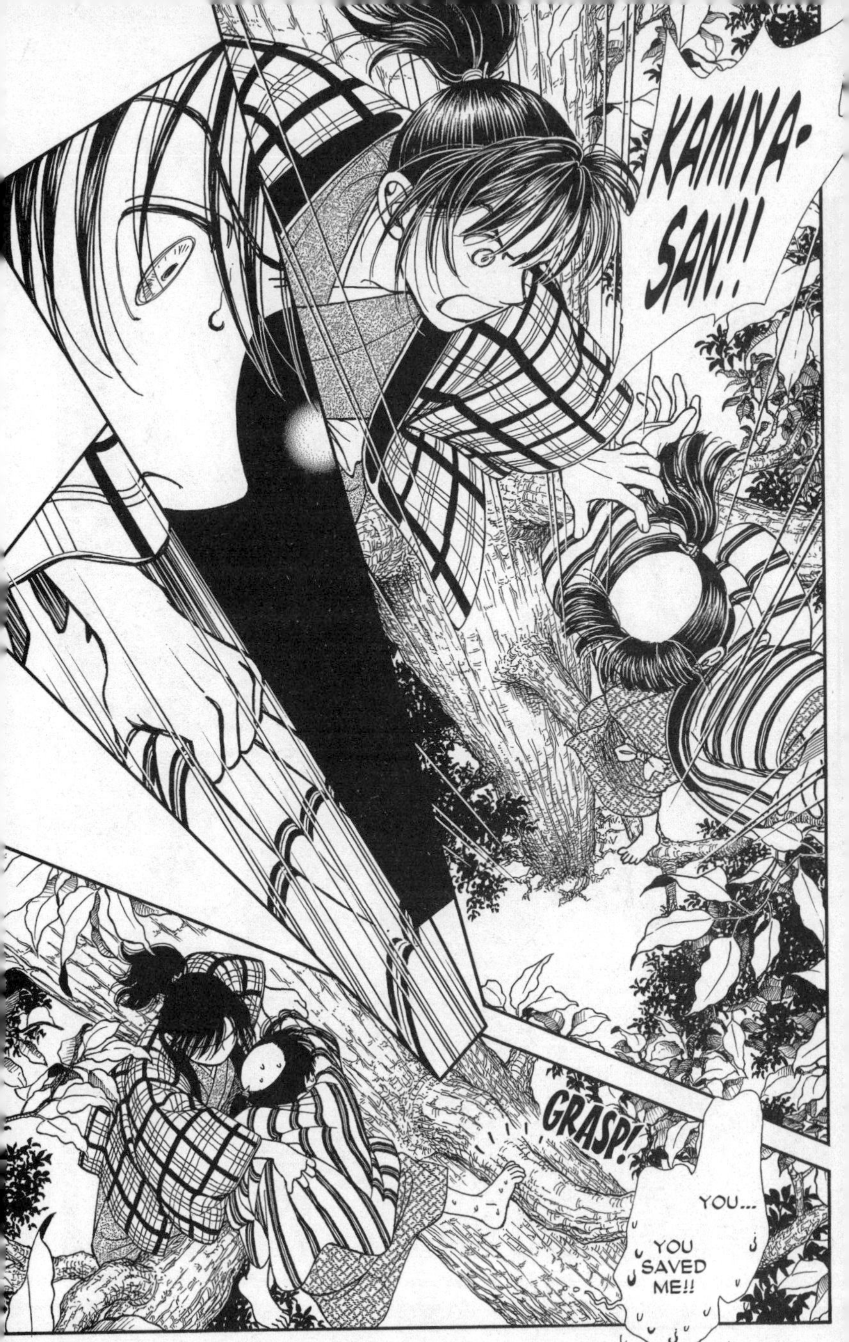
KAMIYA-SAN!!
GRASP!
YOU...
YOU SAVED ME!!

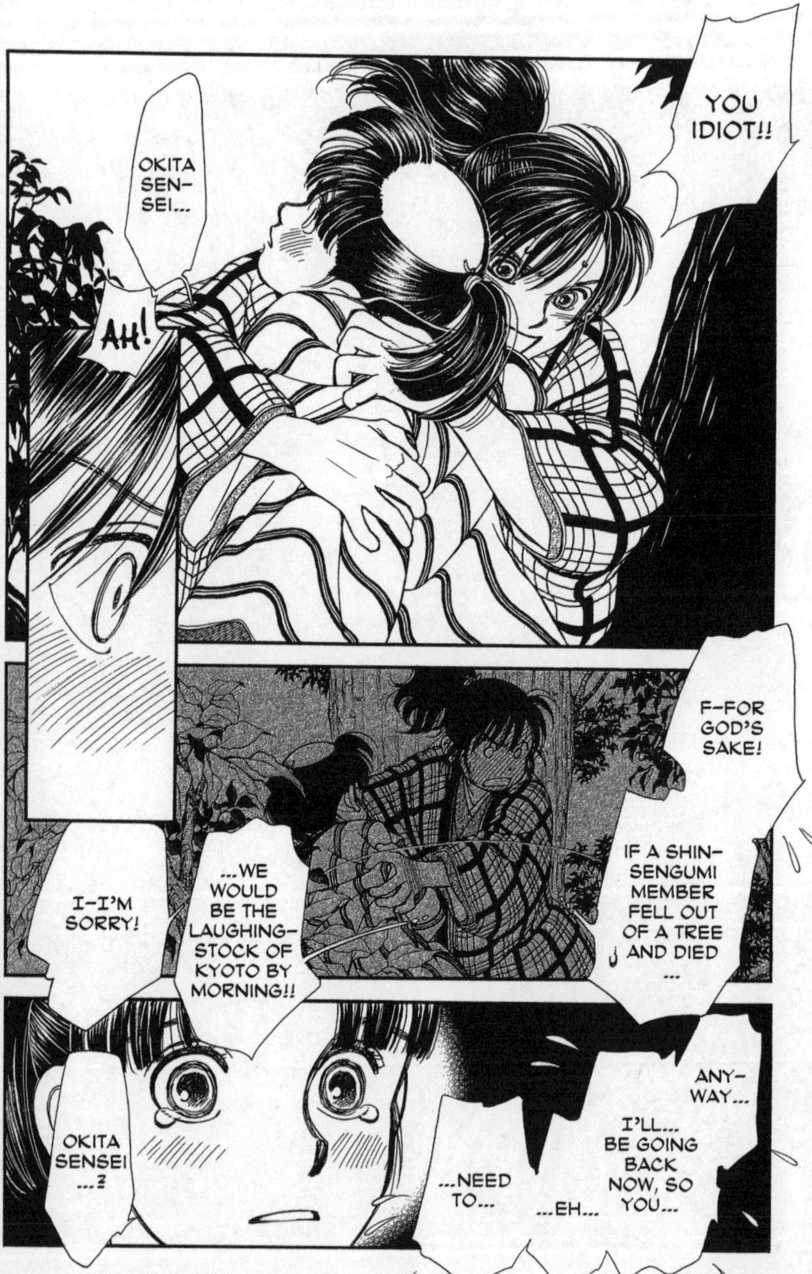
YOU IDIOT!!
OKITA SEN-SEI...
AH!
F-FOR GOD'S SAKE!
IF A SHIN-SENGUMI MEMBER FELL OUT OF A TREE AND DIED ...
...WE WOULD BE THE LAUGHING-STOCK OF KYOTO BY MORNING!!
I-I'M SORRY!
ANY-WAY...
I'LL... BE GOING BACK NOW, SO YOU...
...EH...
...NEED TO...
OKITA SENSEI ...?

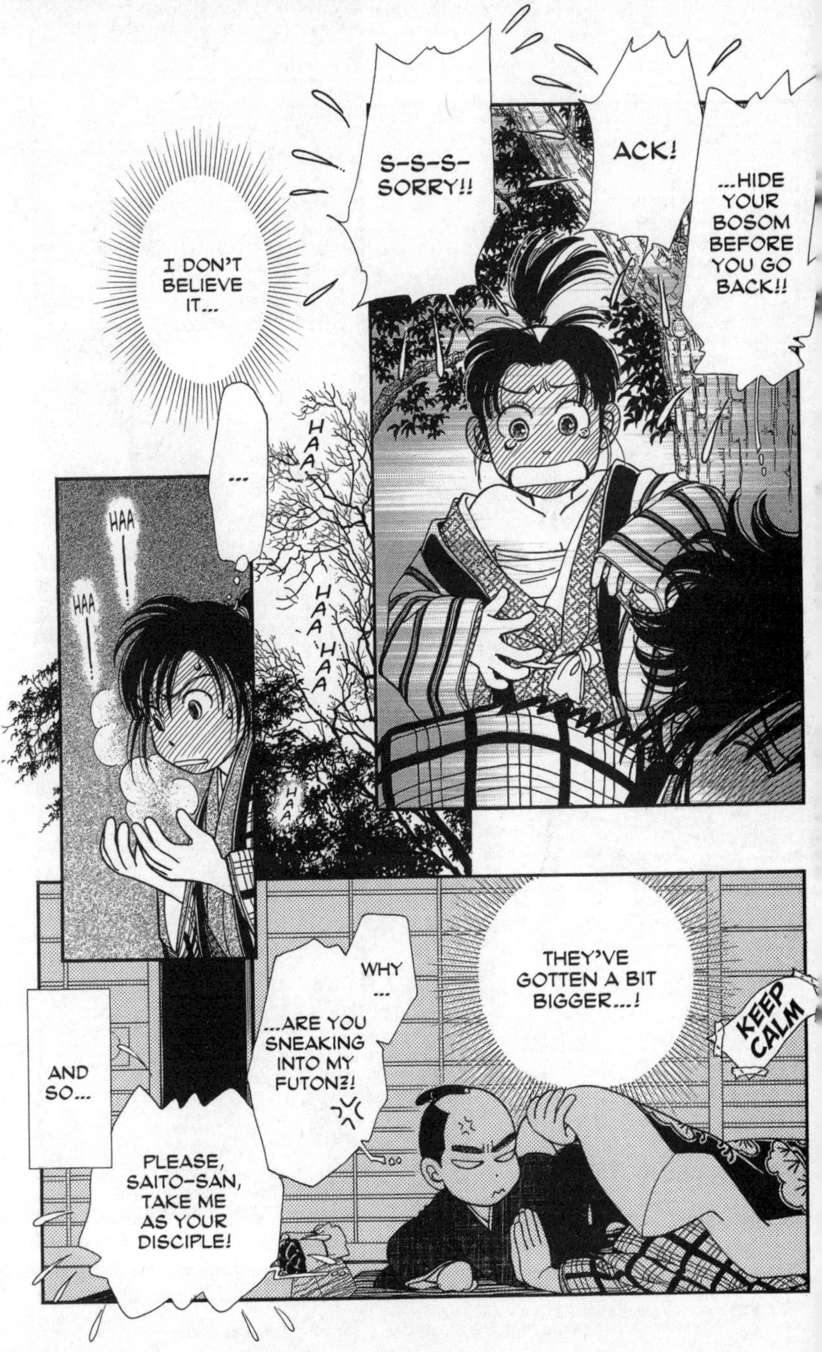
...HIDE YOUR BOSOM BEFORE YOU GO BACK!!
ACK!
S-S-S-SORRY!!
I DON'T BELIEVE IT...
HAA HAA
HAA HAA HAA
HAA
...
HAA
HAA
KEEP CALM
THEY'VE GOTTEN A BIT BIGGER...!
WHY ...
...ARE YOU SNEAKING INTO MY FUTON?!
AND SO...
PLEASE, SAITO-SAN, TAKE ME AS YOUR DISCIPLE!

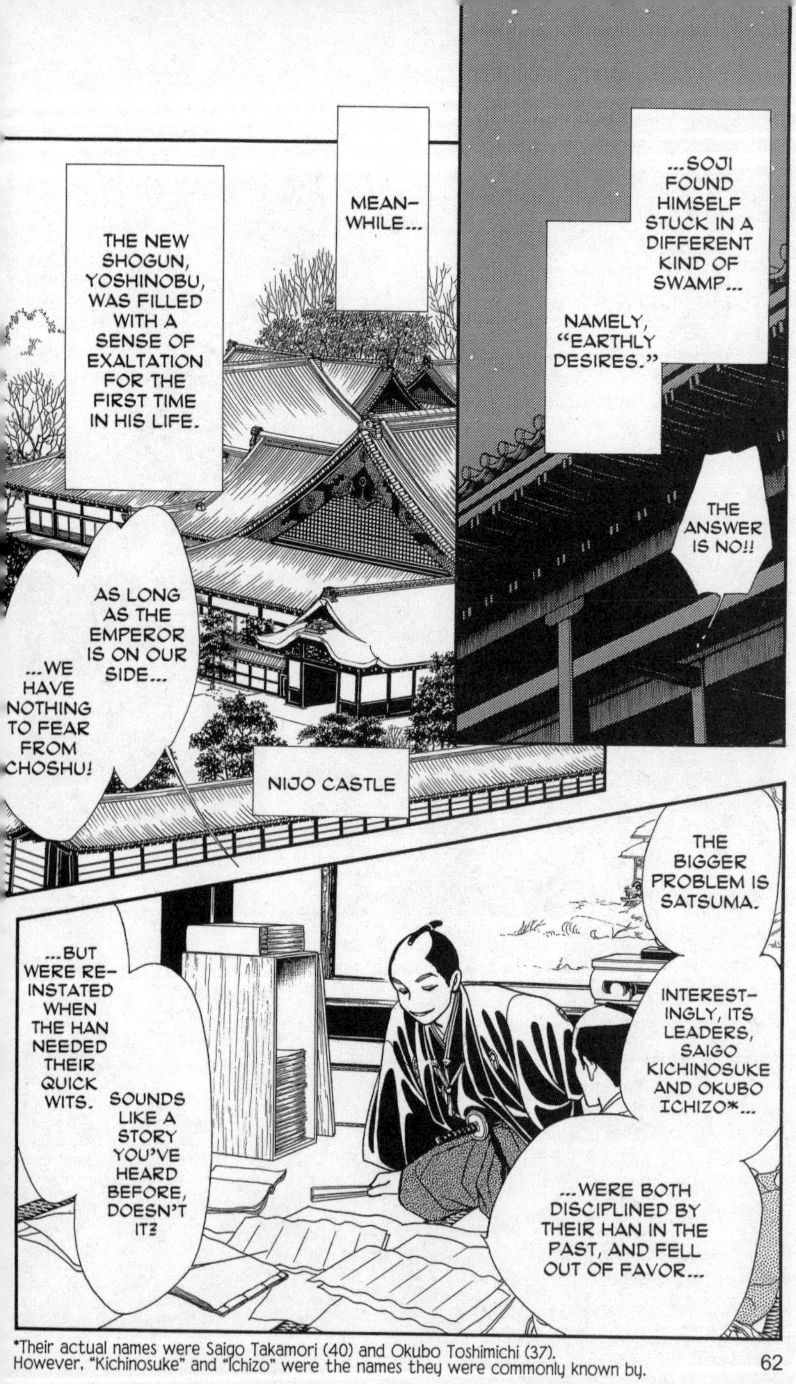
...SOJI FOUND HIMSELF STUCK IN A DIFFERENT KIND OF SWAMP...
NAMELY, "EARTHLY DESIRES."
THE ANSWER IS NO!!
MEAN-WHILE...
THE NEW SHOGUN, YOSHINOBU, WAS FILLED WITH A SENSE OF EXALTATION FOR THE FIRST TIME IN HIS LIFE.
AS LONG AS THE EMPEROR IS ON OUR SIDE...
...WE HAVE NOTHING TO FEAR FROM CHOSHU!
NIJO CASTLE
THE BIGGER PROBLEM IS SATSUMA.
INTEREST-INGLY, ITS LEADERS, SAIGO KICHINOSUKE AND OKUBO ICHIZO*...
...WERE BOTH DISCIPLINED BY THEIR HAN IN THE PAST, AND FELL OUT OF FAVOR...
...BUT WERE RE-INSTATED WHEN THE HAN NEEDED THEIR QUICK WITS.
SOUNDS LIKE A STORY YOU'VE HEARD BEFORE, DOESN'T IT?

*Their actual names were Saigo Takamori (40) and Okubo Toshimichi (37). However, "Kichinosuke" and "Ichizo" were the names they were commonly known by.

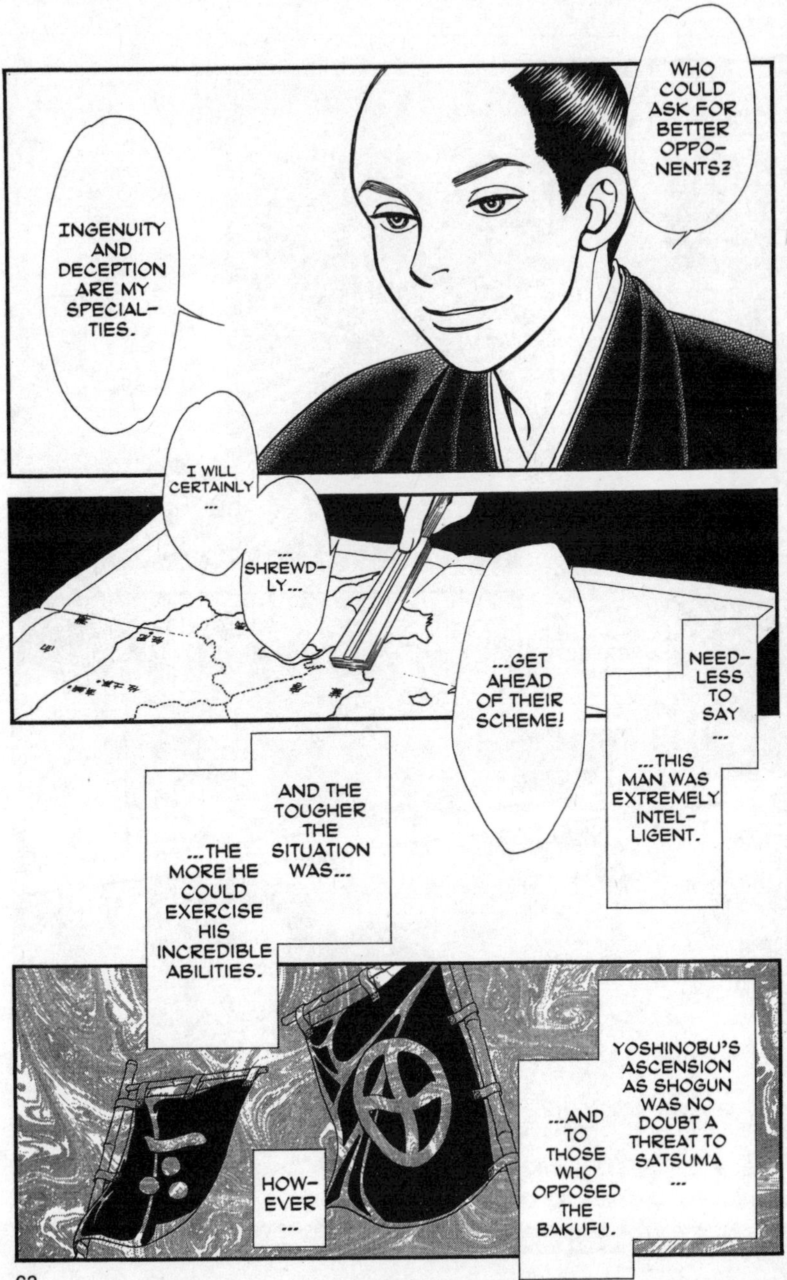
WHO COULD ASK FOR BETTER OPPONENTS?
INGENUITY AND DECEPTION ARE MY SPECIALTIES.
I WILL CERTAINLY...
...SHREWDLY...
...GET AHEAD OF THEIR SCHEME!
NEEDLESS TO SAY...
...THIS MAN WAS EXTREMELY INTELLIGENT.
AND THE TOUGHER THE SITUATION WAS...
...THE MORE HE COULD EXERCISE HIS INCREDIBLE ABILITIES.
YOSHINOBU'S ASCENSION AS SHOGUN WAS NO DOUBT A THREAT TO SATSUMA...
...AND TO THOSE WHO OPPOSED THE BAKUFU.
HOWEVER...

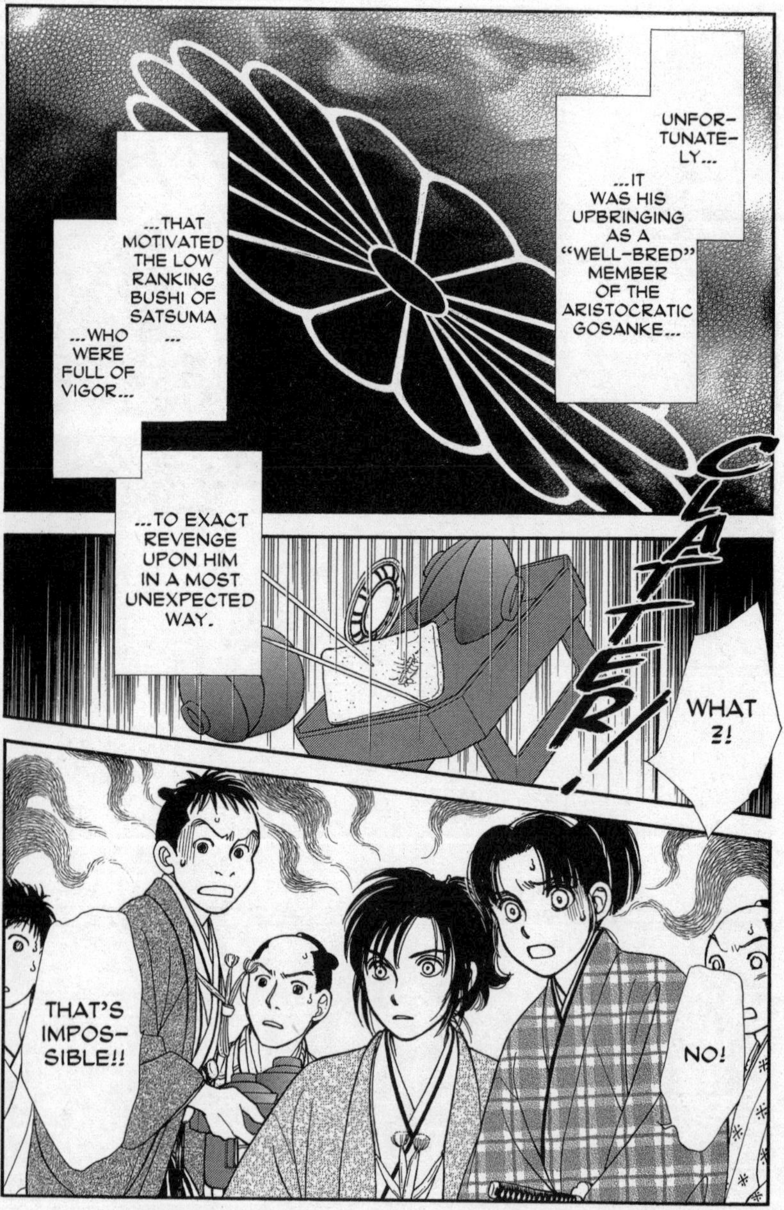
UNFOR-TUNATE-LY...
...IT WAS HIS UPBRINGING AS A "WELL-BRED" MEMBER OF THE ARISTOCRATIC GOSANKE...
...THAT MOTIVATED THE LOW RANKING BUSHI OF SATSUMA ...
...WHO WERE FULL OF VIGOR...
...TO EXACT REVENGE UPON HIM IN A MOST UNEXPECTED WAY.
CLATTER!
WHAT?!
NO!
THAT'S IMPOS-SIBLE!!

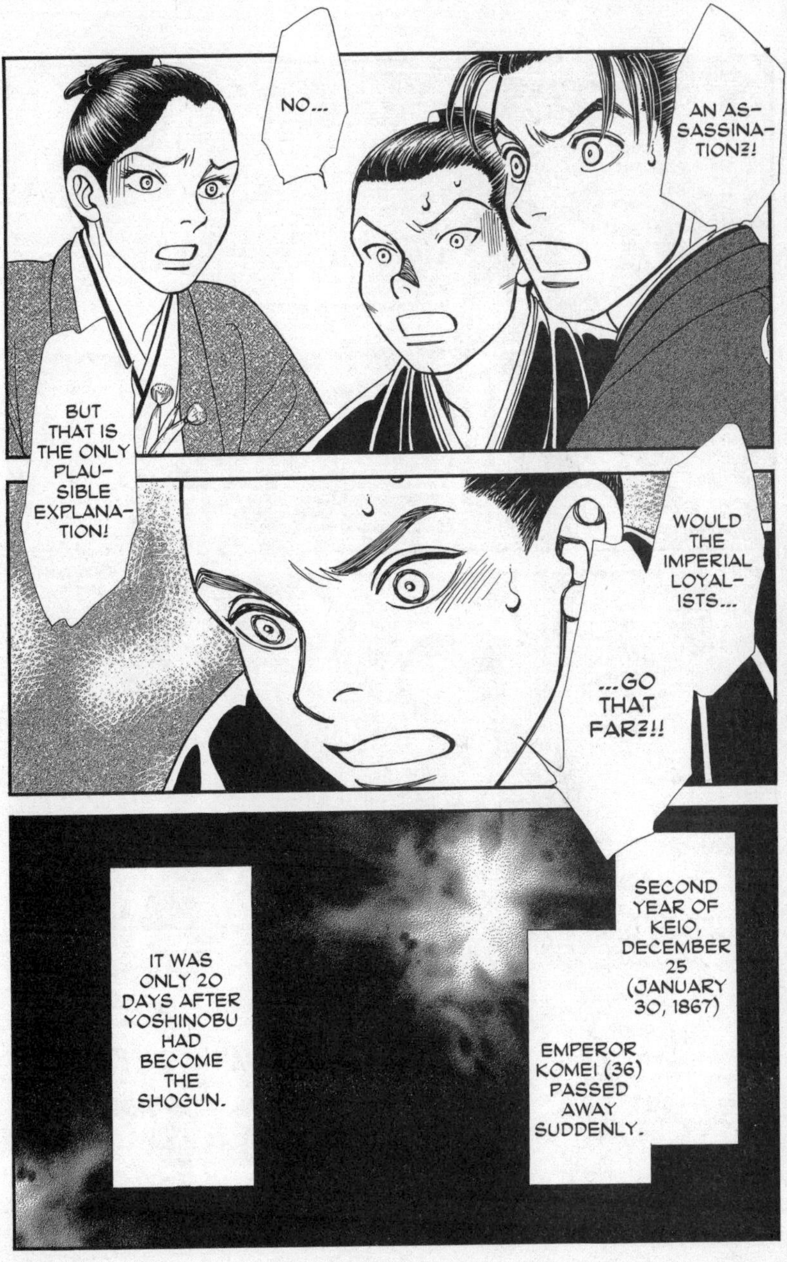
AN ASSASSINATION?!
NO...
BUT THAT IS THE ONLY PLAUSIBLE EXPLANATION!
WOULD THE IMPERIAL LOYALISTS...
...GO THAT FAR?!!
SECOND YEAR OF KEIO, DECEMBER 25 (JANUARY 30, 1867)
EMPEROR KOMEI (36) PASSED AWAY SUDDENLY.
IT WAS ONLY 20 DAYS AFTER YOSHINOBU HAD BECOME THE SHOGUN.

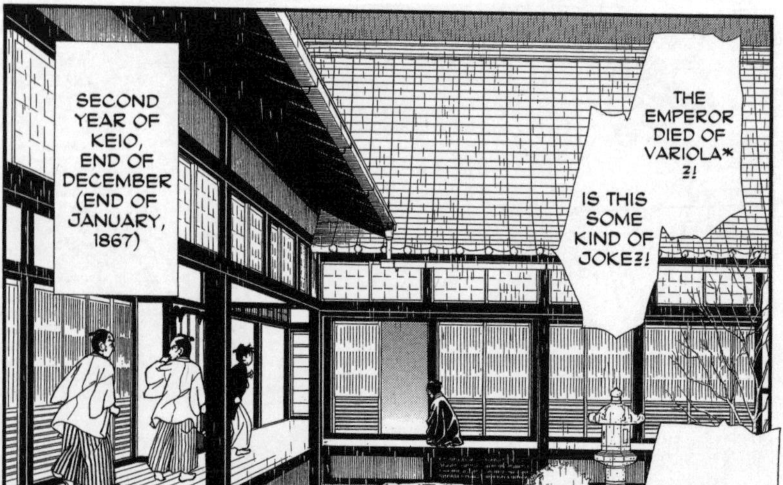
THE EMPEROR DIED OF VARIOLA* ?!
IS THIS SOME KIND OF JOKE?!
SECOND YEAR OF KEIO, END OF DECEMBER (END OF JANUARY, 1867)
VARIOLA DOESN'T SPREAD IN THIS SEASON...
...SO HOW COULD THE EMPEROR HAVE CAUGHT IT?!
THE EMPEROR HAD AN EXTREME ANTIPATHY TO FOR-EIGNERS...
...SO I WOULD NOT BE SURPRISED IF HE HADN'T RECEIVED A WESTERN-STYLE VACCINA-TION, BUT...

*Smallpox. A highly infectious disease that is controlled by law in contemporary times. Smallpox epidemics were frequent in the Edo period because the virus easily infects the respiratory tract. However, the frequency of epidemics decreased rapidly during the Bakumatsu period due to the use of the smallpox vaccine.

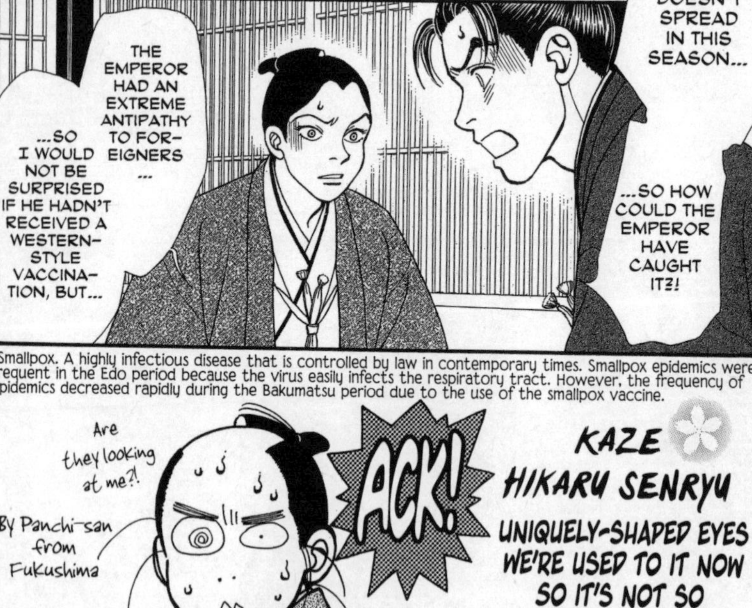
KAZE HIKARU SENRYU
UNIQUELY-SHAPED EYES
WE'RE USED TO IT NOW
SO IT'S NOT SO
UNIQUE ANYMORE
ACK!
Are they looking at me?!
By Panchi-san from Fukushima

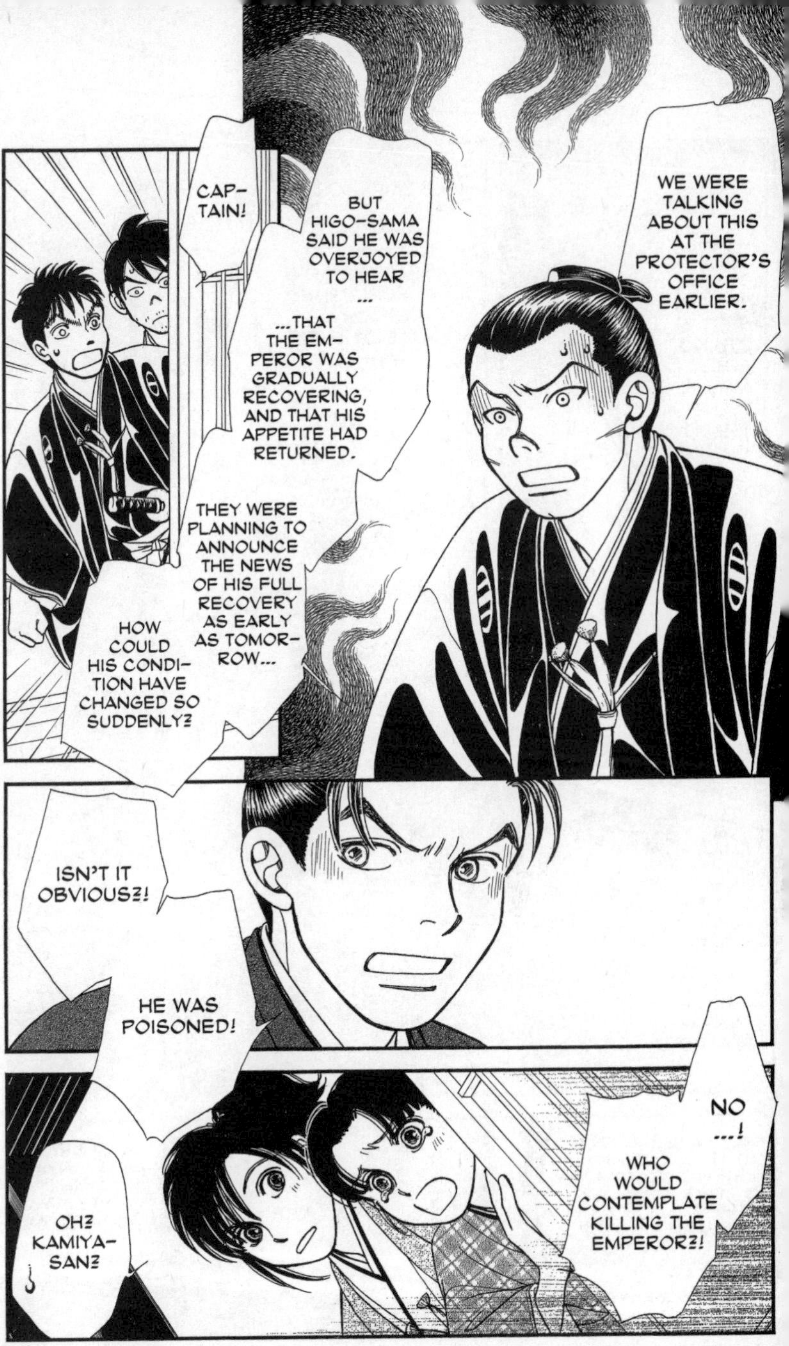
WE WERE TALKING ABOUT THIS AT THE PROTECTOR'S OFFICE EARLIER.
BUT HIGO-SAMA SAID HE WAS OVERJOYED TO HEAR ...
...THAT THE EM-PEROR WAS GRADUALLY RECOVERING, AND THAT HIS APPETITE HAD RETURNED.
THEY WERE PLANNING TO ANNOUNCE THE NEWS OF HIS FULL RECOVERY AS EARLY AS TOMOR-ROW...
CAP-TAIN!
HOW COULD HIS CONDI-TION HAVE CHANGED SO SUDDENLY?
ISN'T IT OBVIOUS?!
HE WAS POISONED!
NO ...!
WHO WOULD CONTEMPLATE KILLING THE EMPEROR?!
OH? KAMIYA-SAN?

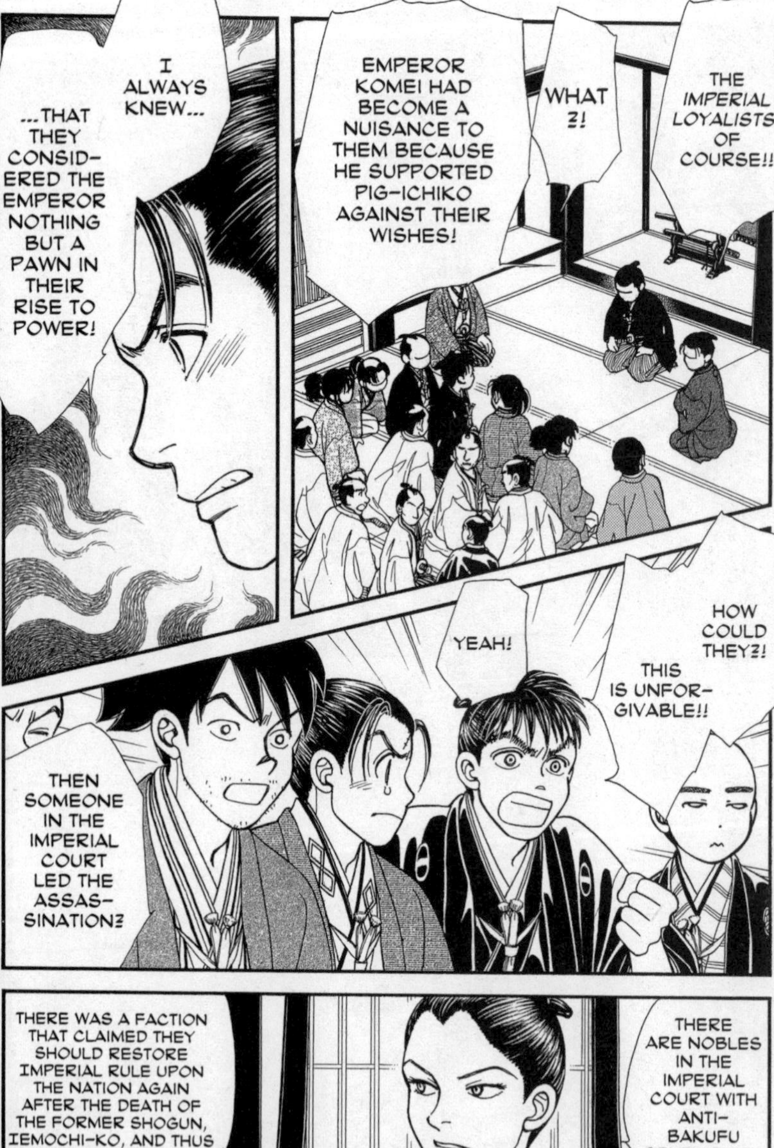
THE IMPERIAL LOYALISTS, OF COURSE!!
WHAT?!
EMPEROR KOMEI HAD BECOME A NUISANCE TO THEM BECAUSE HE SUPPORTED PIG-ICHIKO AGAINST THEIR WISHES!
I ALWAYS KNEW...
...THAT THEY CONSID-ERED THE EMPEROR NOTHING BUT A PAWN IN THEIR RISE TO POWER!
HOW COULD THEY?!
THIS IS UNFORGIVABLE!!
YEAH!
THEN SOMEONE IN THE IMPERIAL COURT LED THE ASSAS-SINATION?
THERE ARE NOBLES IN THE IMPERIAL COURT WITH ANTI-BAKUFU SENTIMENTS.
THERE WAS A FACTION THAT CLAIMED THEY SHOULD RESTORE IMPERIAL RULE UPON THE NATION AGAIN AFTER THE DEATH OF THE FORMER SHOGUN, IEMOCHI-KO, AND THUS INVITED THE ANGER OF EMPEROR KOMEI.

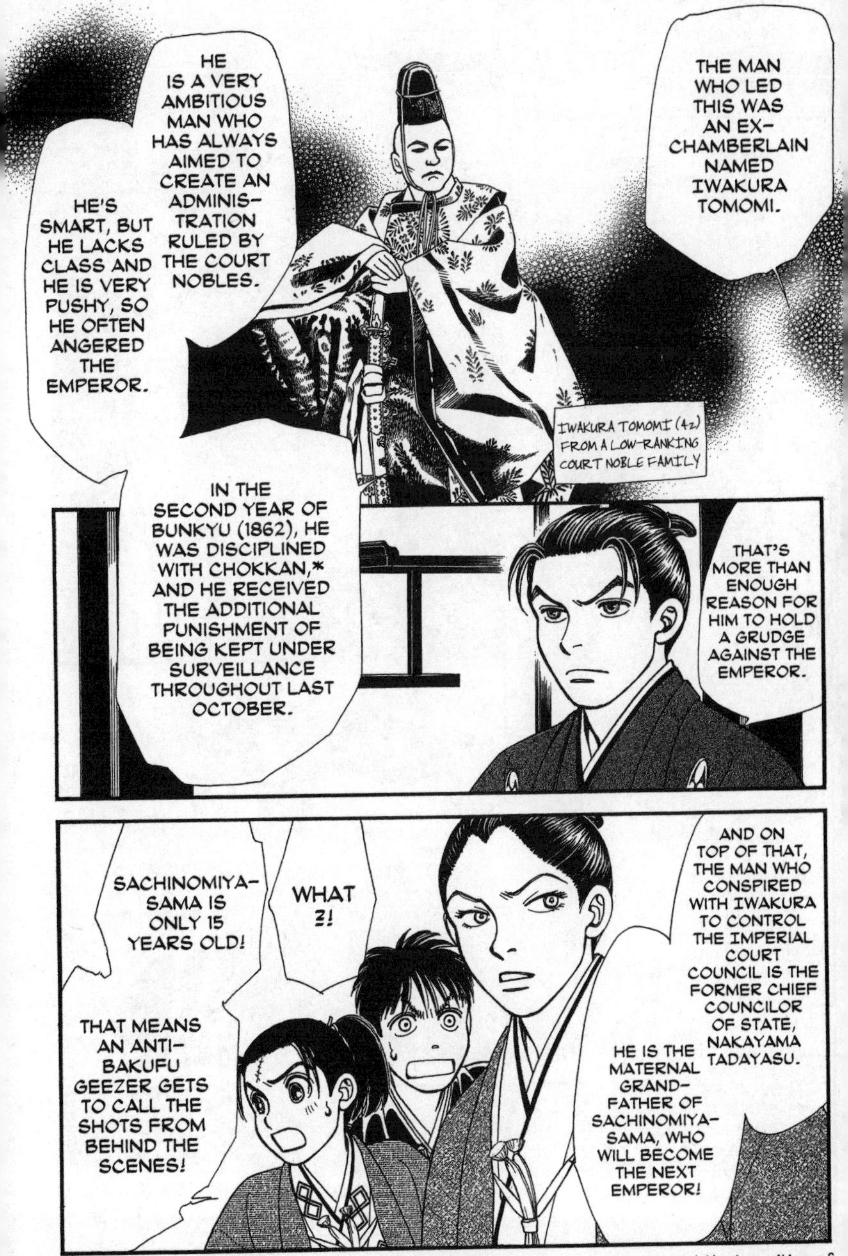

THE MAN WHO LED THIS WAS AN EX-CHAMBERLAIN NAMED IWAKURA TOMOMI.
HE IS A VERY AMBITIOUS MAN WHO HAS ALWAYS AIMED TO CREATE AN ADMINISTRATION RULED BY THE COURT NOBLES.
HE'S SMART, BUT HE LACKS CLASS AND HE IS VERY PUSHY, SO HE OFTEN ANGERED THE EMPEROR.
IWAKURA TOMOMI (42) FROM A LOW-RANKING COURT NOBLE FAMILY
IN THE SECOND YEAR OF BUNKYU (1862), HE WAS DISCIPLINED WITH CHOKKAN,* AND HE RECEIVED THE ADDITIONAL PUNISHMENT OF BEING KEPT UNDER SURVEILLANCE THROUGHOUT LAST OCTOBER.
THAT'S MORE THAN ENOUGH REASON FOR HIM TO HOLD A GRUDGE AGAINST THE EMPEROR.
AND ON TOP OF THAT, THE MAN WHO CONSPIRED WITH IWAKURA TO CONTROL THE IMPERIAL COURT COUNCIL IS THE FORMER CHIEF COUNCILOR OF STATE, NAKAYAMA TADAYASU.
HE IS THE MATERNAL GRANDFATHER OF SACHINOMIYA-SAMA, WHO WILL BECOME THE NEXT EMPEROR!
WHAT?!
SACHINOMIYA-SAMA IS ONLY 15 YEARS OLD!
THAT MEANS AN ANTI-BAKUFU GEEZER GETS TO CALL THE SHOTS FROM BEHIND THE SCENES!

*Being disowned by the emperor, and the imposition of Chikyo punishment until forgiveness is granted.

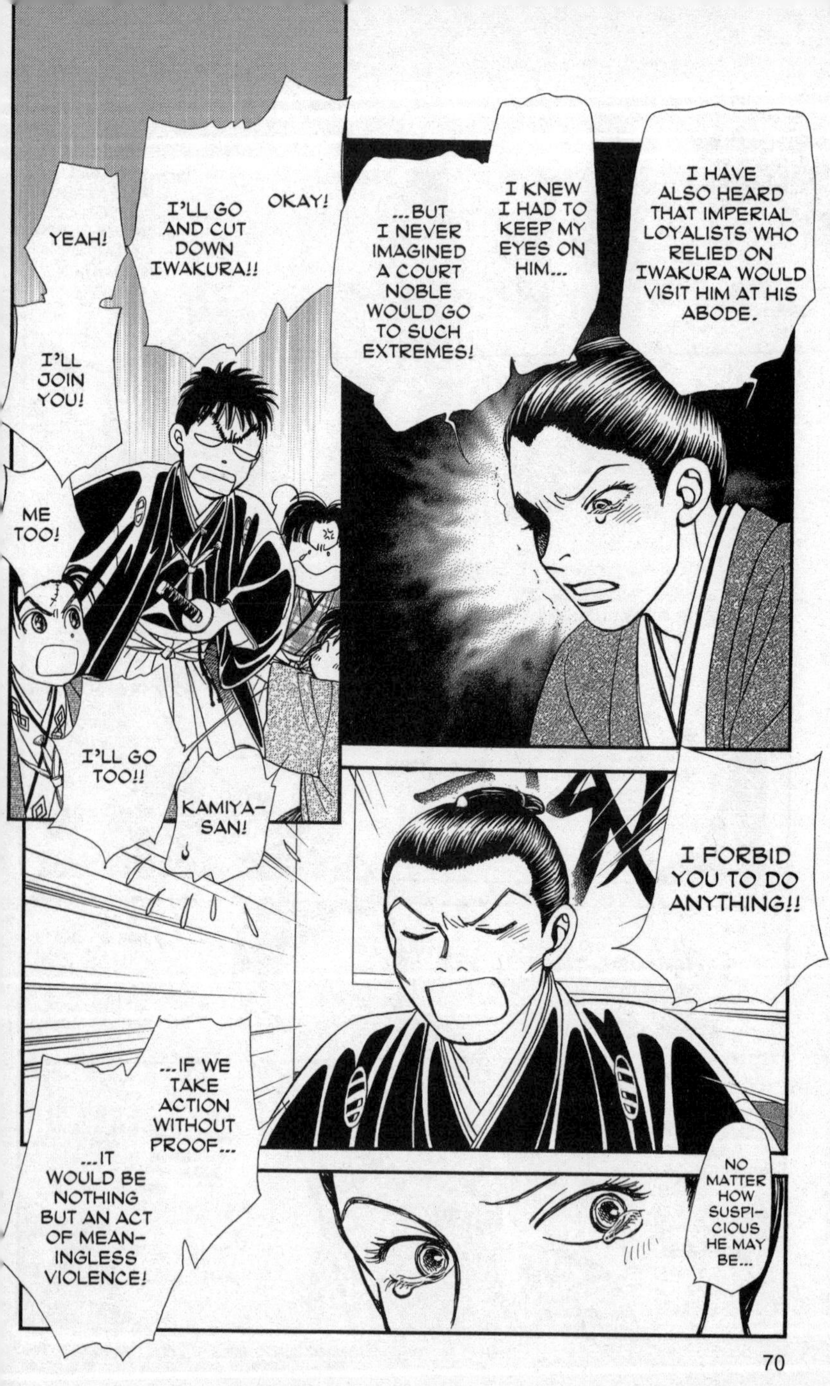
I HAVE ALSO HEARD THAT IMPERIAL LOYALISTS WHO RELIED ON IWAKURA WOULD VISIT HIM AT HIS ABODE.
I KNEW I HAD TO KEEP MY EYES ON HIM...
...BUT I NEVER IMAGINED A COURT NOBLE WOULD GO TO SUCH EXTREMES!
OKAY!
I'LL GO AND CUT DOWN IWAKURA!!
YEAH!
I'LL JOIN YOU!
ME TOO!
I'LL GO TOO!!
KAMIYA-SAN!
I FORBID YOU TO DO ANYTHING!!
NO MATTER HOW SUSPICIOUS HE MAY BE...
...IF WE TAKE ACTION WITHOUT PROOF...
...IT WOULD BE NOTHING BUT AN ACT OF MEANINGLESS VIOLENCE!

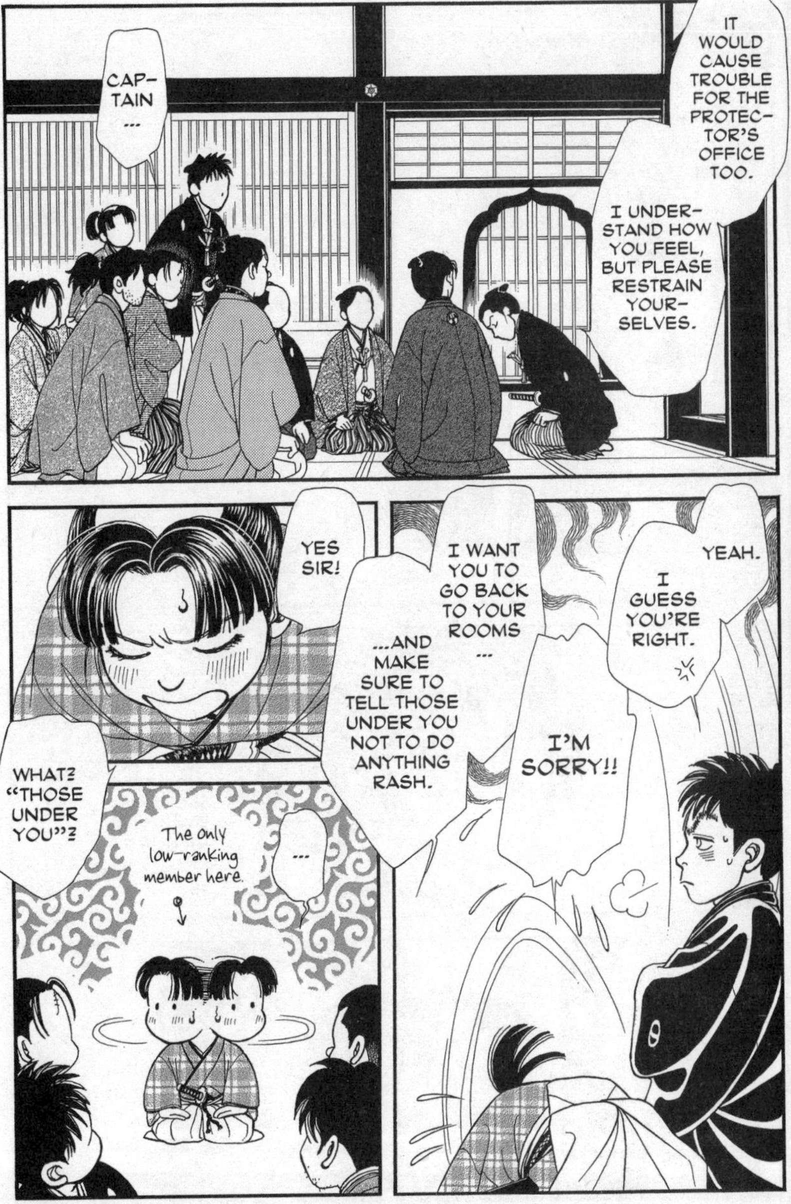
IT WOULD CAUSE TROUBLE FOR THE PROTECTOR'S OFFICE TOO.
I UNDERSTAND HOW YOU FEEL, BUT PLEASE RESTRAIN YOURSELVES.
CAPTAIN...
YEAH.
I GUESS YOU'RE RIGHT.
I WANT YOU TO GO BACK TO YOUR ROOMS...
...AND MAKE SURE TO TELL THOSE UNDER YOU NOT TO DO ANYTHING RASH.
I'M SORRY!!
YES SIR!
WHAT? "THOSE UNDER YOU"?
...
The only low-ranking member here.

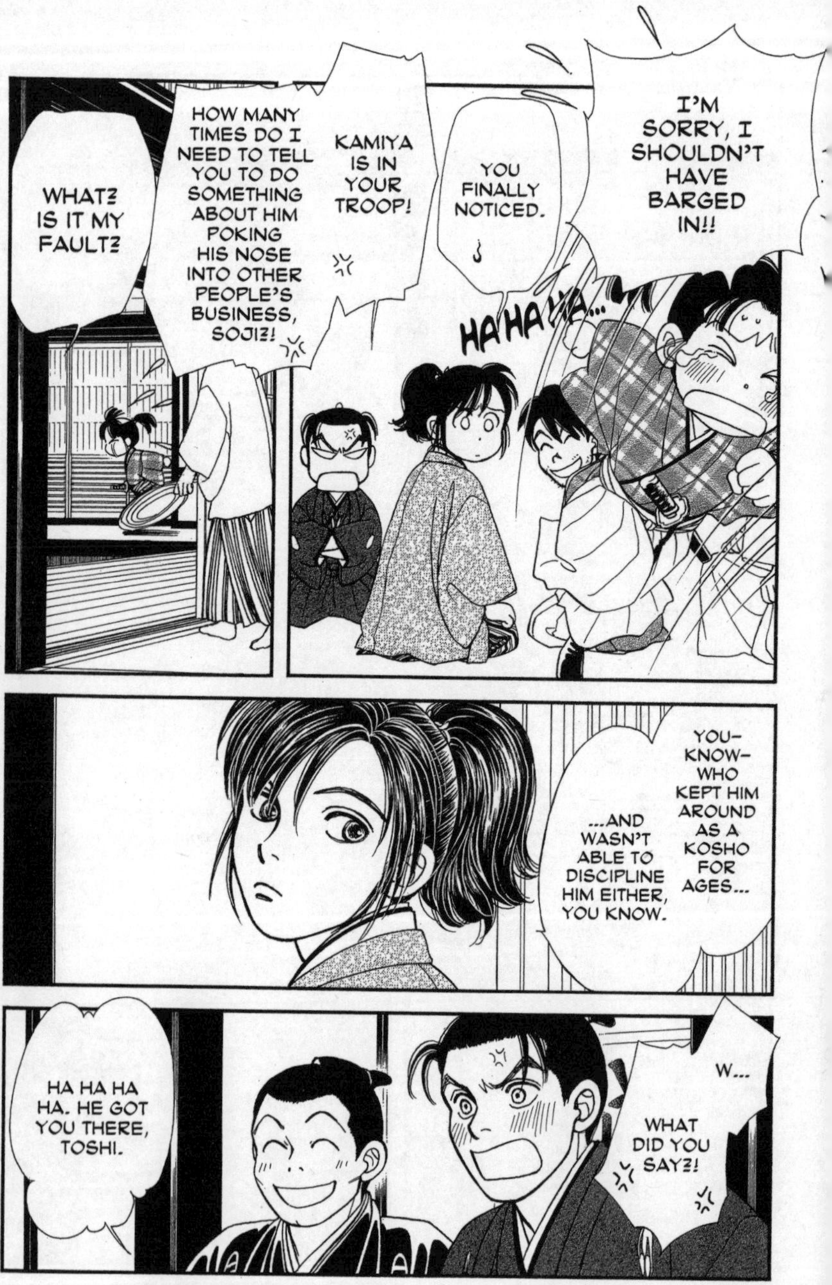
I'M SORRY, I SHOULDN'T HAVE BARGED IN!!
HA HA HA...
YOU FINALLY NOTICED.
KAMIYA IS IN YOUR TROOP!
HOW MANY TIMES DO I NEED TO TELL YOU TO DO SOMETHING ABOUT HIM POKING HIS NOSE INTO OTHER PEOPLE'S BUSINESS, SOJI?!
WHAT? IS IT MY FAULT?
YOU-KNOW-WHO KEPT HIM AROUND AS A KOSHO FOR AGES...
...AND WASN'T ABLE TO DISCIPLINE HIM EITHER, YOU KNOW.
W...
WHAT DID YOU SAY?!
HA HA HA HA. HE GOT YOU THERE, TOSHI.

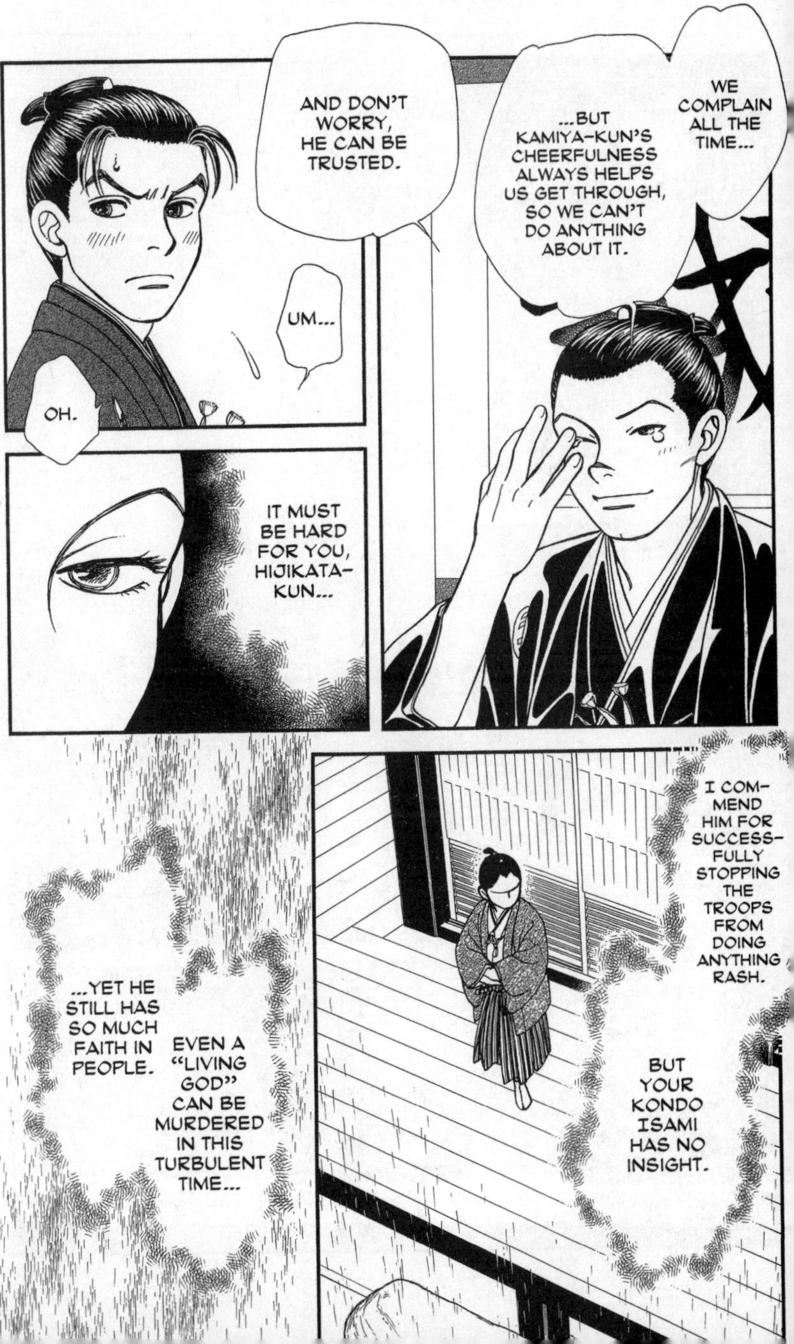
WE COMPLAIN ALL THE TIME...
...BUT KAMIYA-KUN'S CHEERFULNESS ALWAYS HELPS US GET THROUGH, SO WE CAN'T DO ANYTHING ABOUT IT.
AND DON'T WORRY, HE CAN BE TRUSTED.
UM...
OH.
IT MUST BE HARD FOR YOU, HIJIKATA-KUN...
I COMMEND HIM FOR SUCCESSFULLY STOPPING THE TROOPS FROM DOING ANYTHING RASH.
BUT YOUR KONDO ISAMI HAS NO INSIGHT.
EVEN A "LIVING GOD" CAN BE MURDERED IN THIS TURBULENT TIME...
...YET HE STILL HAS SO MUCH FAITH IN PEOPLE.

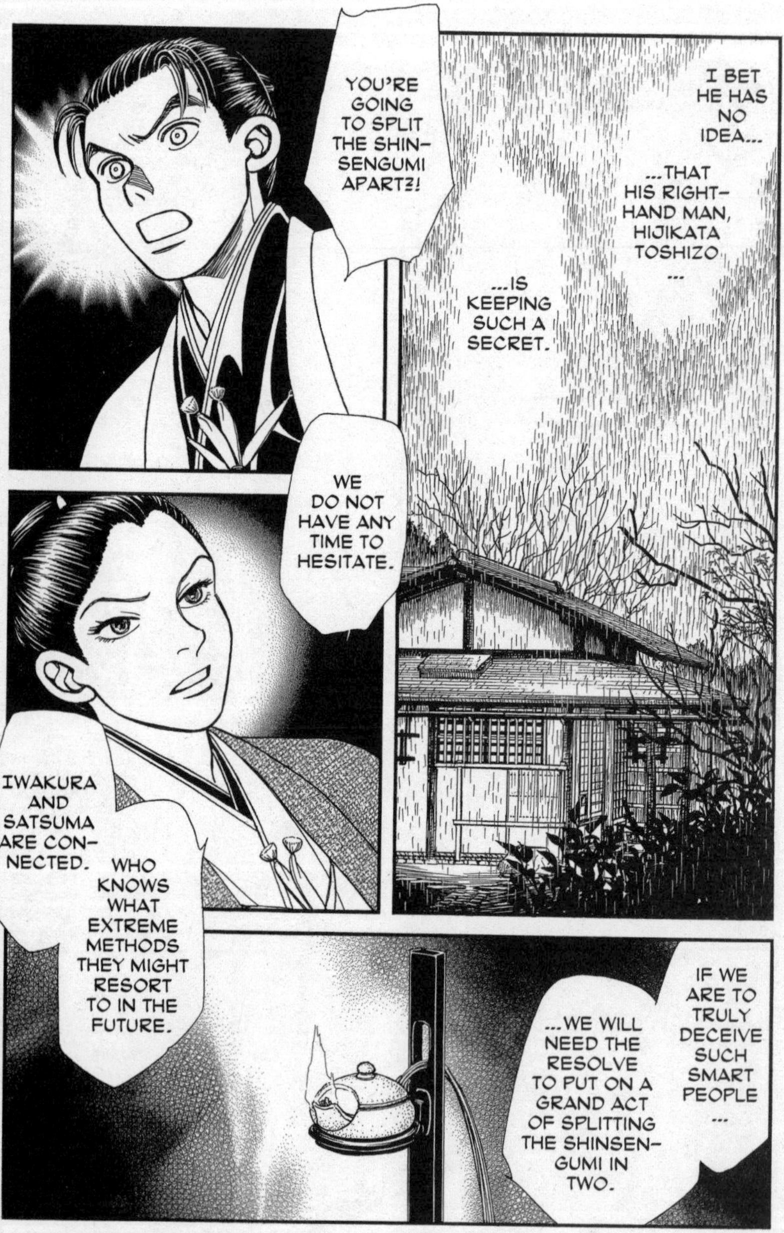
I BET HE HAS NO IDEA...
...THAT HIS RIGHT-HAND MAN, HIJIKATA TOSHIZO ...
...IS KEEPING SUCH A SECRET.
YOU'RE GOING TO SPLIT THE SHIN-SENGUMI APART?!
WE DO NOT HAVE ANY TIME TO HESITATE.
IWAKURA AND SATSUMA ARE CON-NECTED.
WHO KNOWS WHAT EXTREME METHODS THEY MIGHT RESORT TO IN THE FUTURE.
IF WE ARE TO TRULY DECEIVE SUCH SMART PEOPLE ...
...WE WILL NEED THE RESOLVE TO PUT ON A GRAND ACT OF SPLITTING THE SHINSEN-GUMI IN TWO.

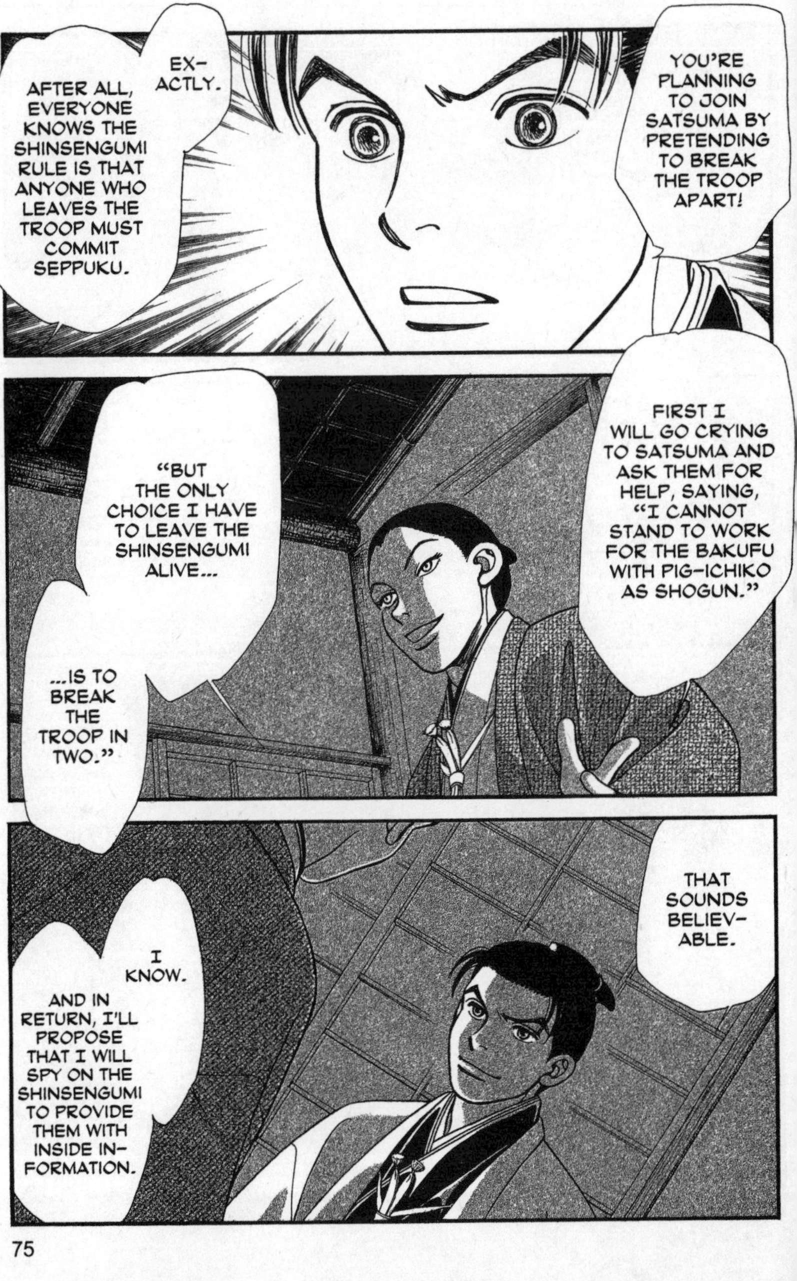
YOU'RE PLANNING TO JOIN SATSUMA BY PRETENDING TO BREAK THE TROOP APART!
EX-ACTLY.
AFTER ALL, EVERYONE KNOWS THE SHINSENGUMI RULE IS THAT ANYONE WHO LEAVES THE TROOP MUST COMMIT SEPPUKU.
FIRST I WILL GO CRYING TO SATSUMA AND ASK THEM FOR HELP, SAYING, "I CANNOT STAND TO WORK FOR THE BAKUFU WITH PIG-ICHIKO AS SHOGUN."
"BUT THE ONLY CHOICE I HAVE TO LEAVE THE SHINSENGUMI ALIVE...
...IS TO BREAK THE TROOP IN TWO."
THAT SOUNDS BELIEV-ABLE.
I KNOW.
AND IN RETURN, I'LL PROPOSE THAT I WILL SPY ON THE SHINSENGUMI TO PROVIDE THEM WITH INSIDE IN-FORMATION.

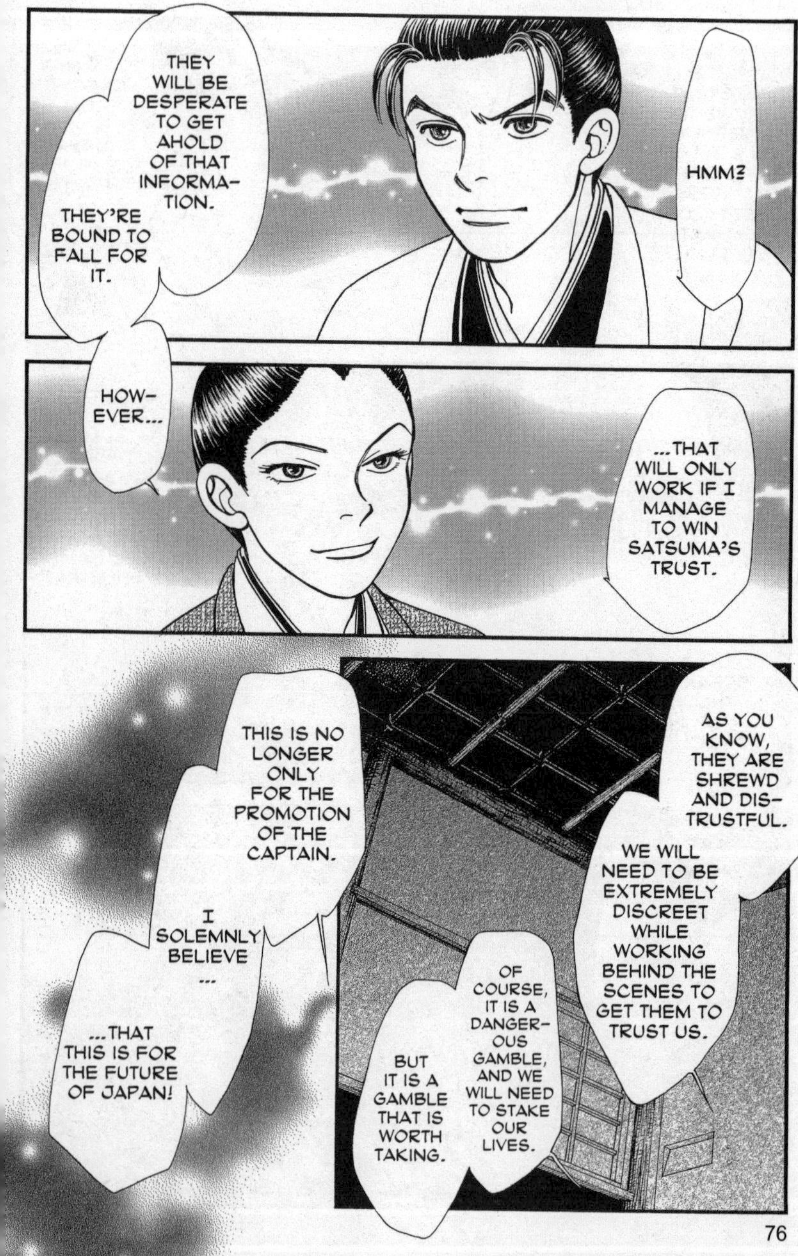
HMM?
THEY WILL BE DESPERATE TO GET AHOLD OF THAT INFORMATION.
THEY'RE BOUND TO FALL FOR IT.
HOW-EVER...
...THAT WILL ONLY WORK IF I MANAGE TO WIN SATSUMA'S TRUST.
AS YOU KNOW, THEY ARE SHREWD AND DISTRUSTFUL.
WE WILL NEED TO BE EXTREMELY DISCREET WHILE WORKING BEHIND THE SCENES TO GET THEM TO TRUST US.
OF COURSE, IT IS A DANGEROUS GAMBLE, AND WE WILL NEED TO STAKE OUR LIVES.
BUT IT IS A GAMBLE THAT IS WORTH TAKING.
THIS IS NO LONGER ONLY FOR THE PROMOTION OF THE CAPTAIN.
I SOLEMNLY BELIEVE...
...THAT THIS IS FOR THE FUTURE OF JAPAN!

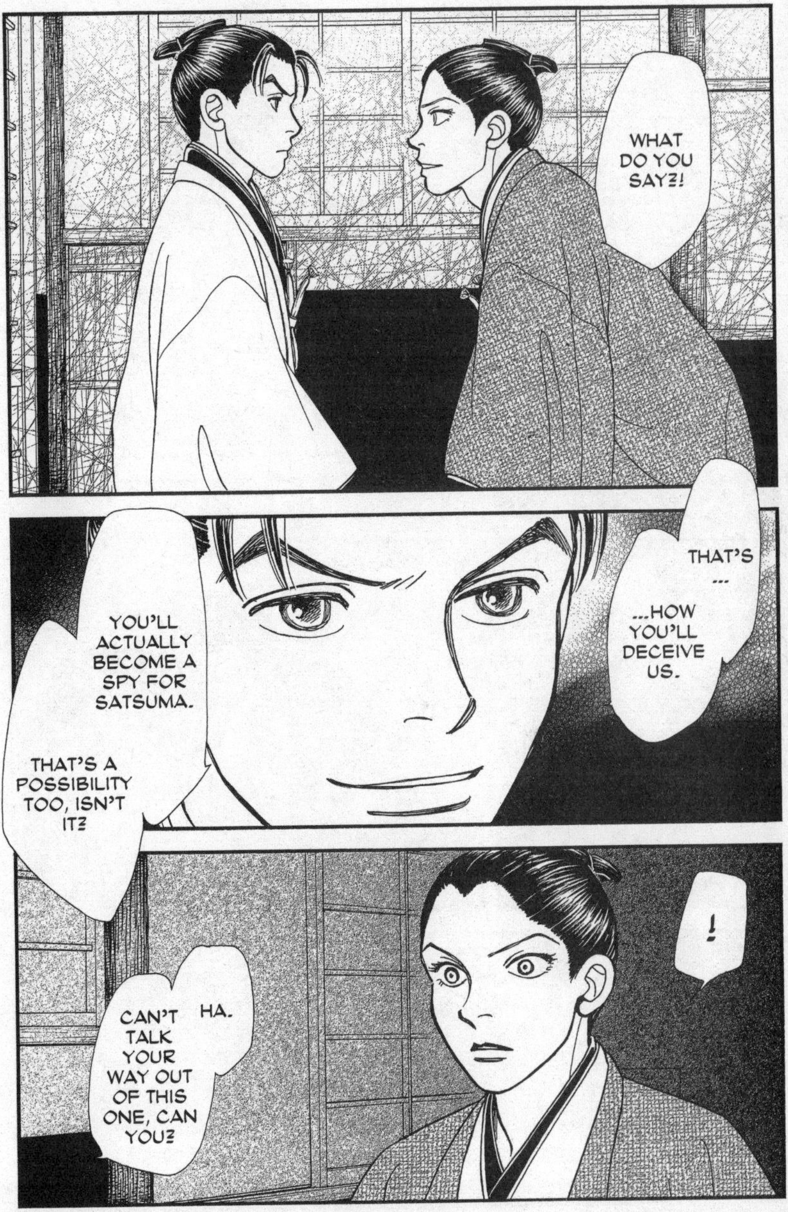
WHAT DO YOU SAY?!
THAT'S ...
...HOW YOU'LL DECEIVE US.
YOU'LL ACTUALLY BECOME A SPY FOR SATSUMA.
THAT'S A POSSIBILITY TOO, ISN'T IT?
!
HA.
CAN'T TALK YOUR WAY OUT OF THIS ONE, CAN YOU?

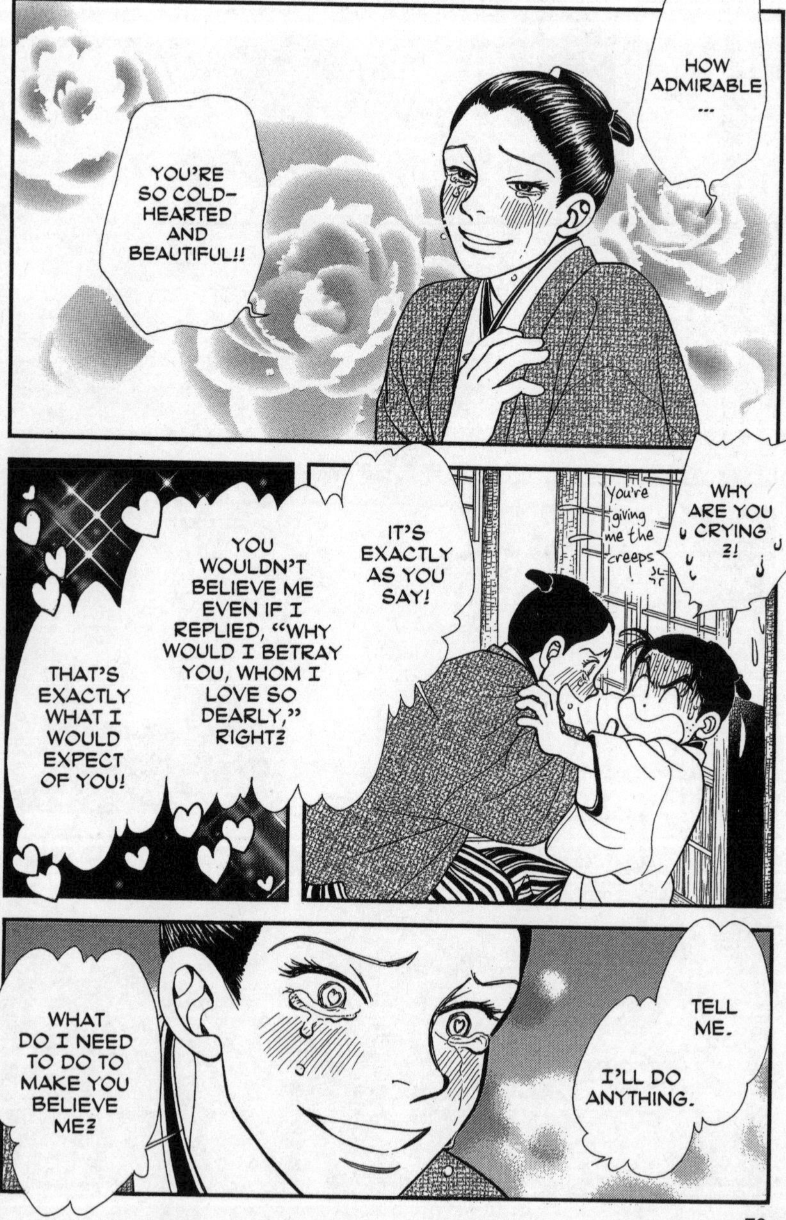
HOW ADMIRABLE ...
YOU'RE SO COLD-HEARTED AND BEAUTIFUL!!
WHY ARE YOU CRYING?!
You're giving me the creeps!
IT'S EXACTLY AS YOU SAY!
YOU WOULDN'T BELIEVE ME EVEN IF I REPLIED, "WHY WOULD I BETRAY YOU, WHOM I LOVE SO DEARLY," RIGHT?
THAT'S EXACTLY WHAT I WOULD EXPECT OF YOU!
TELL ME.
I'LL DO ANYTHING.
WHAT DO I NEED TO DO TO MAKE YOU BELIEVE ME?

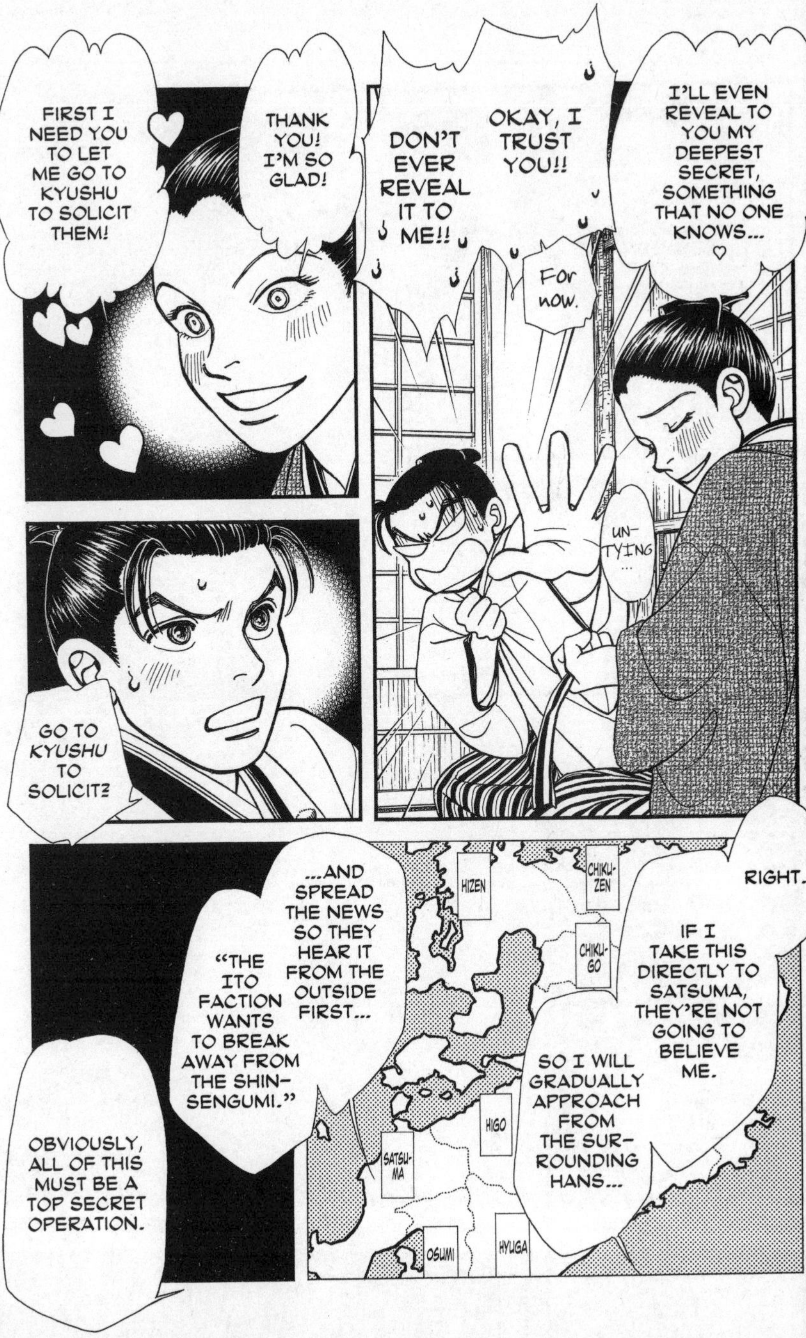
I'LL EVEN REVEAL TO YOU MY DEEPEST SECRET, SOMETHING THAT NO ONE KNOWS... ♡
OKAY, I TRUST YOU!!
DON'T EVER REVEAL IT TO ME!!
For now.
UN-TYING ...
THANK YOU! I'M SO GLAD!
FIRST I NEED YOU TO LET ME GO TO KYUSHU TO SOLICIT THEM!
GO TO KYUSHU TO SOLICIT?
RIGHT.
IF I TAKE THIS DIRECTLY TO SATSUMA, THEY'RE NOT GOING TO BELIEVE ME.
SO I WILL GRADUALLY APPROACH FROM THE SUR-ROUNDING HANS...
...AND SPREAD THE NEWS SO THEY HEAR IT FROM THE OUTSIDE FIRST...
"THE ITO FACTION WANTS TO BREAK AWAY FROM THE SHIN-SENGUMI."
OBVIOUSLY, ALL OF THIS MUST BE A TOP SECRET OPERATION.
CHIKU-ZEN
HIZEN
CHIKU-GO
HIGO
SATSU-MA
HYUGA
OSUMI

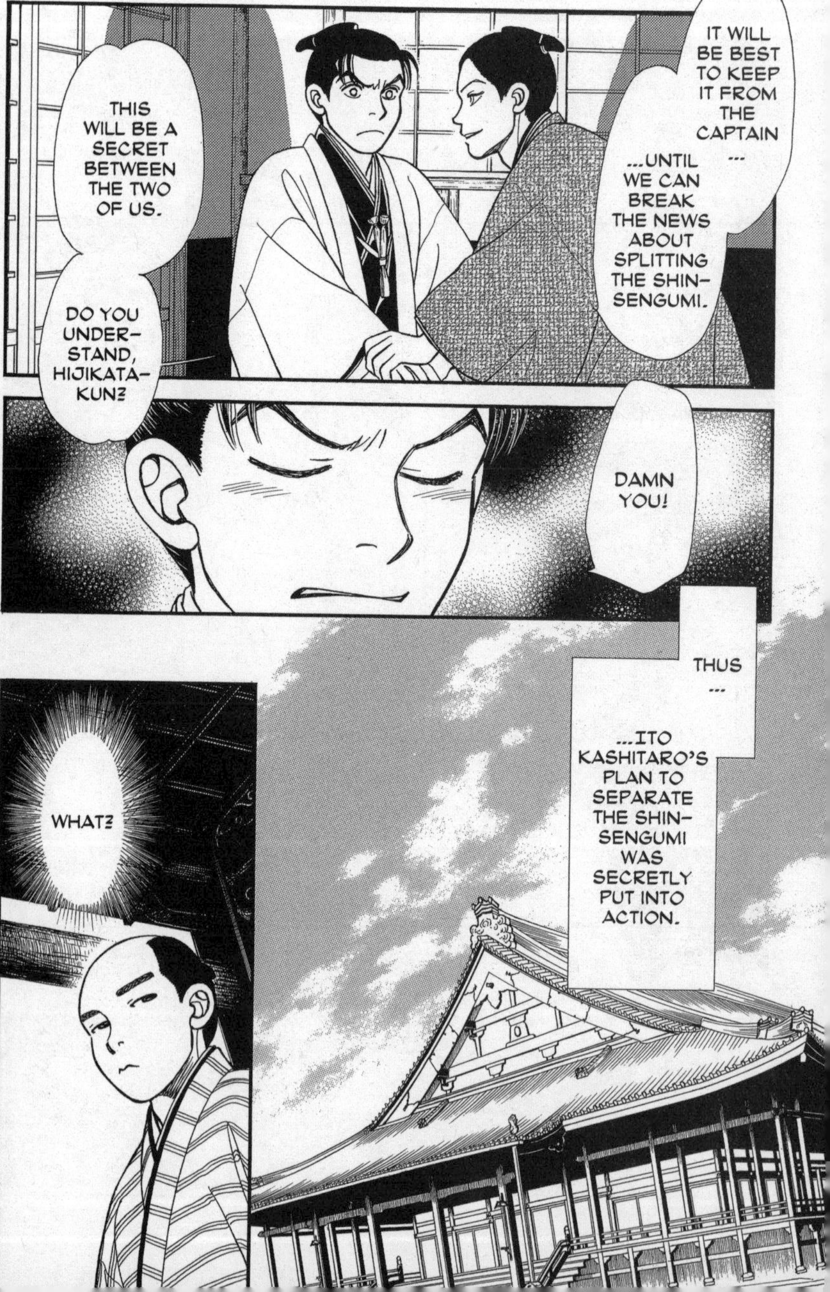
IT WILL BE BEST TO KEEP IT FROM THE CAPTAIN ---
...UNTIL WE CAN BREAK THE NEWS ABOUT SPLITTING THE SHIN-SENGUMI.
THIS WILL BE A SECRET BETWEEN THE TWO OF US.
DO YOU UNDERSTAND, HIJIKATA-KUN?
DAMN YOU!
THUS ---
...ITO KASHITARO'S PLAN TO SEPARATE THE SHIN-SENGUMI WAS SECRETLY PUT INTO ACTION.
WHAT?

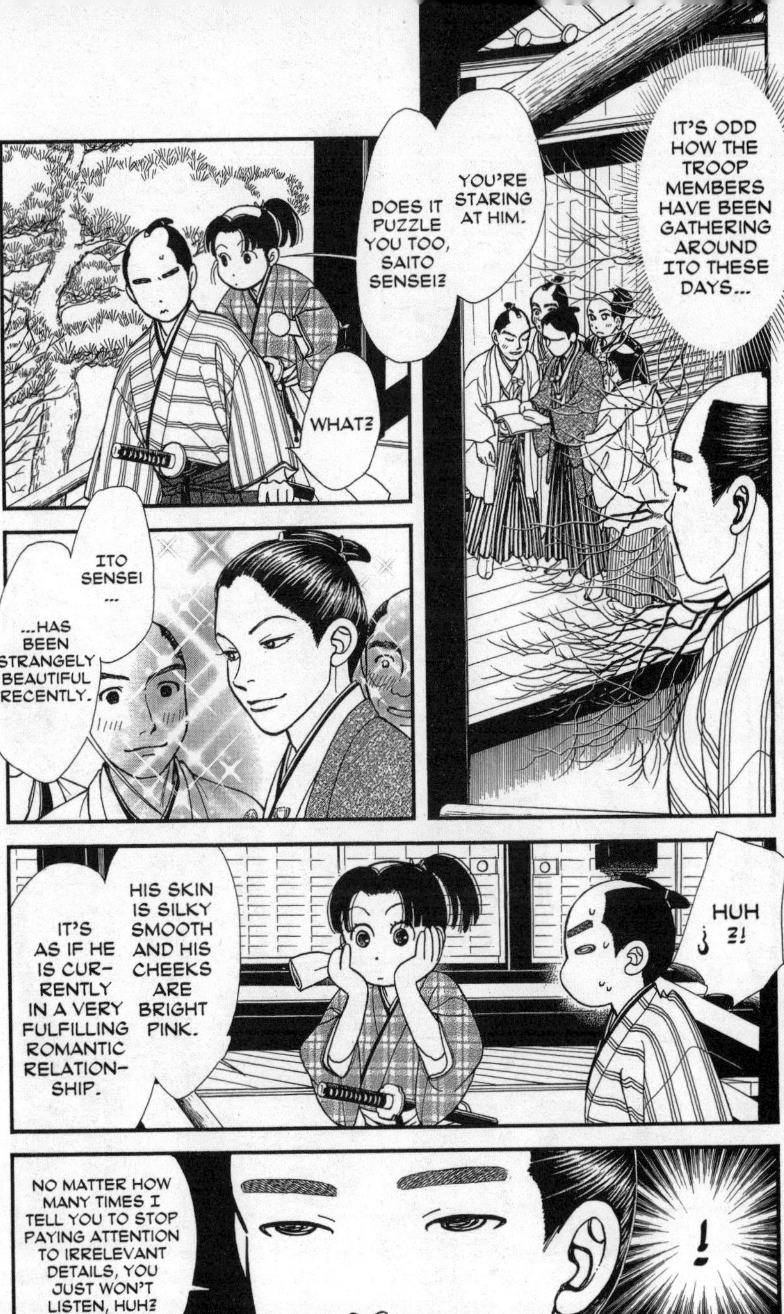
IT'S ODD HOW THE TROOP MEMBERS HAVE BEEN GATHERING AROUND ITO THESE DAYS...
YOU'RE STARING AT HIM.
DOES IT PUZZLE YOU TOO, SAITO SENSEI?
WHAT?
ITO SENSEI...
...HAS BEEN STRANGELY BEAUTIFUL RECENTLY.
HUH?!
HIS SKIN IS SILKY SMOOTH AND HIS CHEEKS ARE BRIGHT PINK.
IT'S AS IF HE IS CURRENTLY IN A VERY FULFILLING ROMANTIC RELATIONSHIP.
!
NO MATTER HOW MANY TIMES I TELL YOU TO STOP PAYING ATTENTION TO IRRELEVANT DETAILS, YOU JUST WON'T LISTEN, HUH?

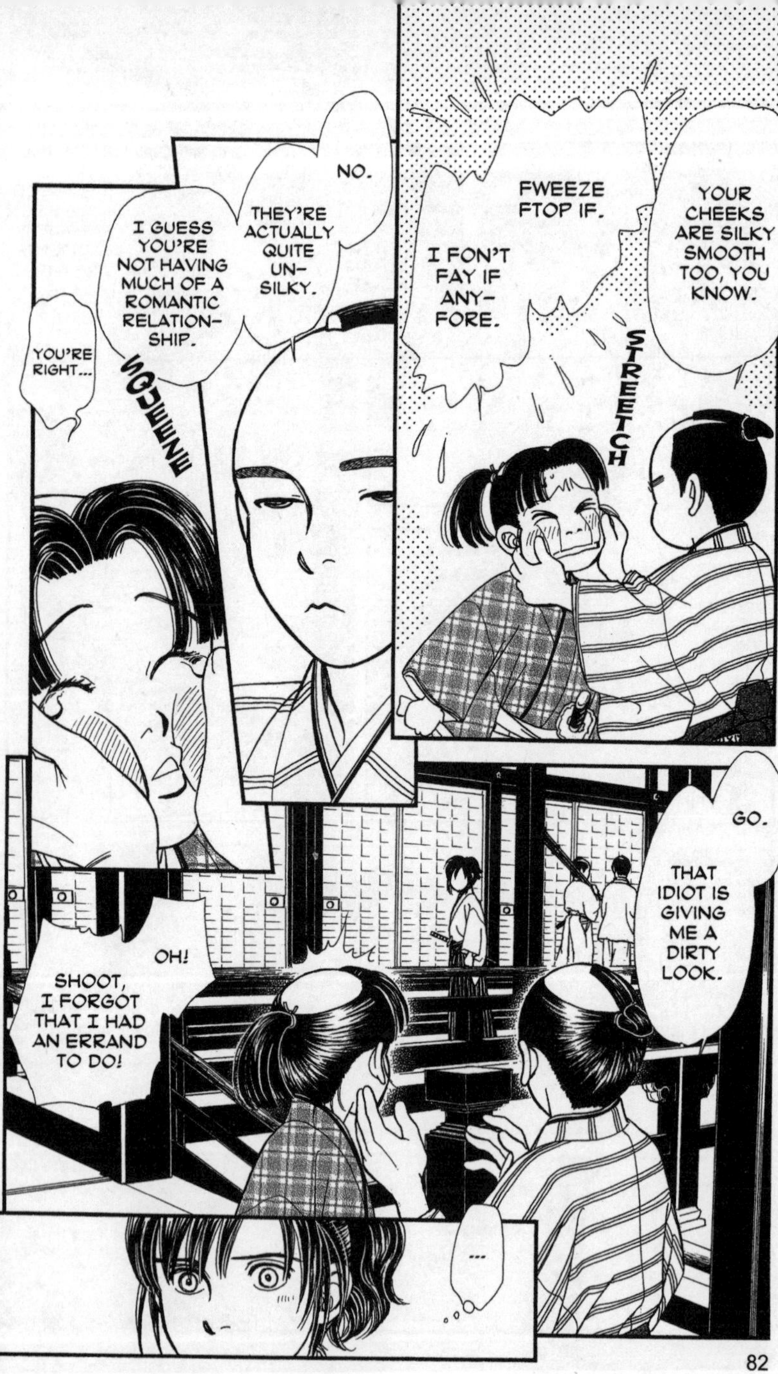
YOUR CHEEKS ARE SILKY SMOOTH TOO, YOU KNOW.
FWEEZE FTOP IF.
I FON'T FAY IF ANY-FORE.
STREETCH
NO.
THEY'RE ACTUALLY QUITE UN-SILKY.
I GUESS YOU'RE NOT HAVING MUCH OF A ROMANTIC RELATION-SHIP.
YOU'RE RIGHT...
SQUEEZE
GO.
THAT IDIOT IS GIVING ME A DIRTY LOOK.
OH!
SHOOT, I FORGOT THAT I HAD AN ERRAND TO DO!
...

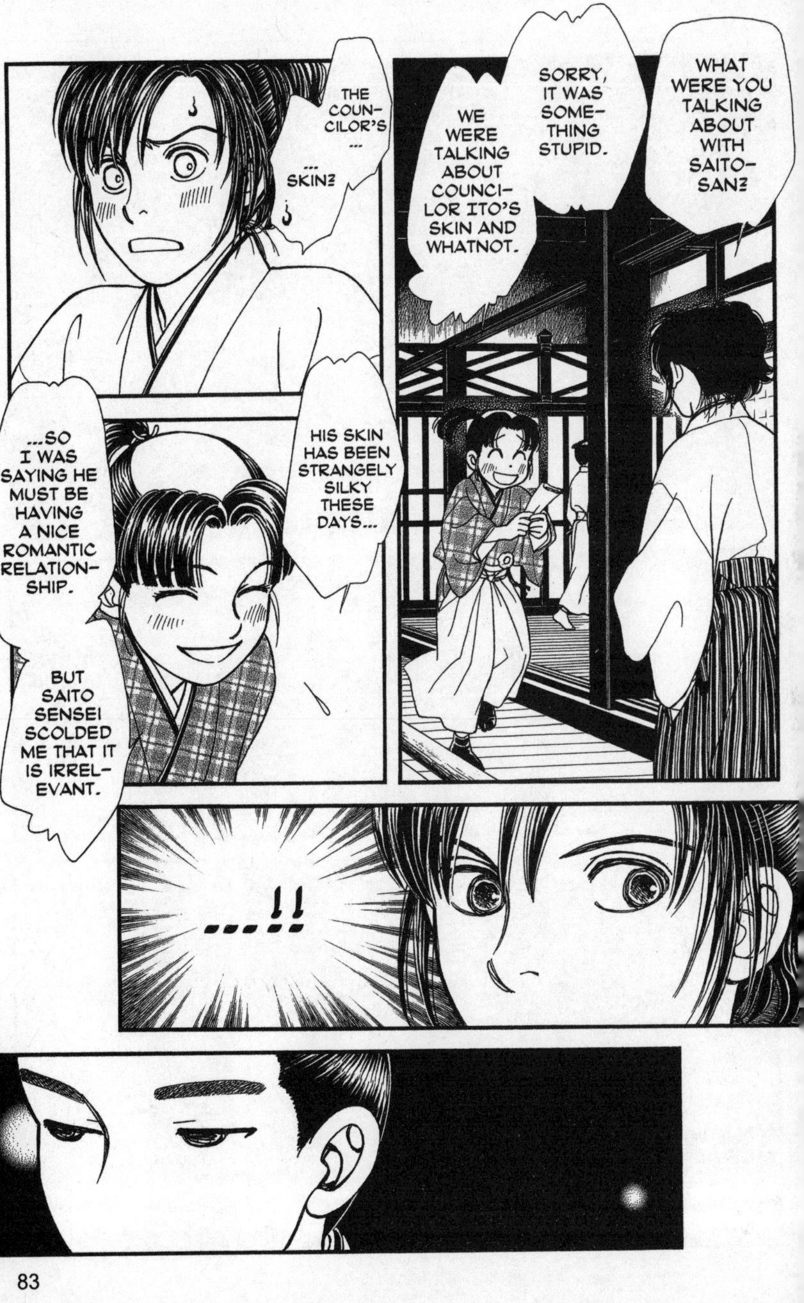
WHAT WERE YOU TALKING ABOUT WITH SAITO-SAN?
SORRY, IT WAS SOME-THING STUPID.
WE WERE TALKING ABOUT COUNCI-LOR ITO'S SKIN AND WHATNOT.
THE COUN-CILOR'S ...
... SKIN?
HIS SKIN HAS BEEN STRANGELY SILKY THESE DAYS...
...SO I WAS SAYING HE MUST BE HAVING A NICE ROMANTIC RELATION-SHIP.
BUT SAITO SENSEI SCOLDED ME THAT IT IS IRREL-EVANT.
...!!

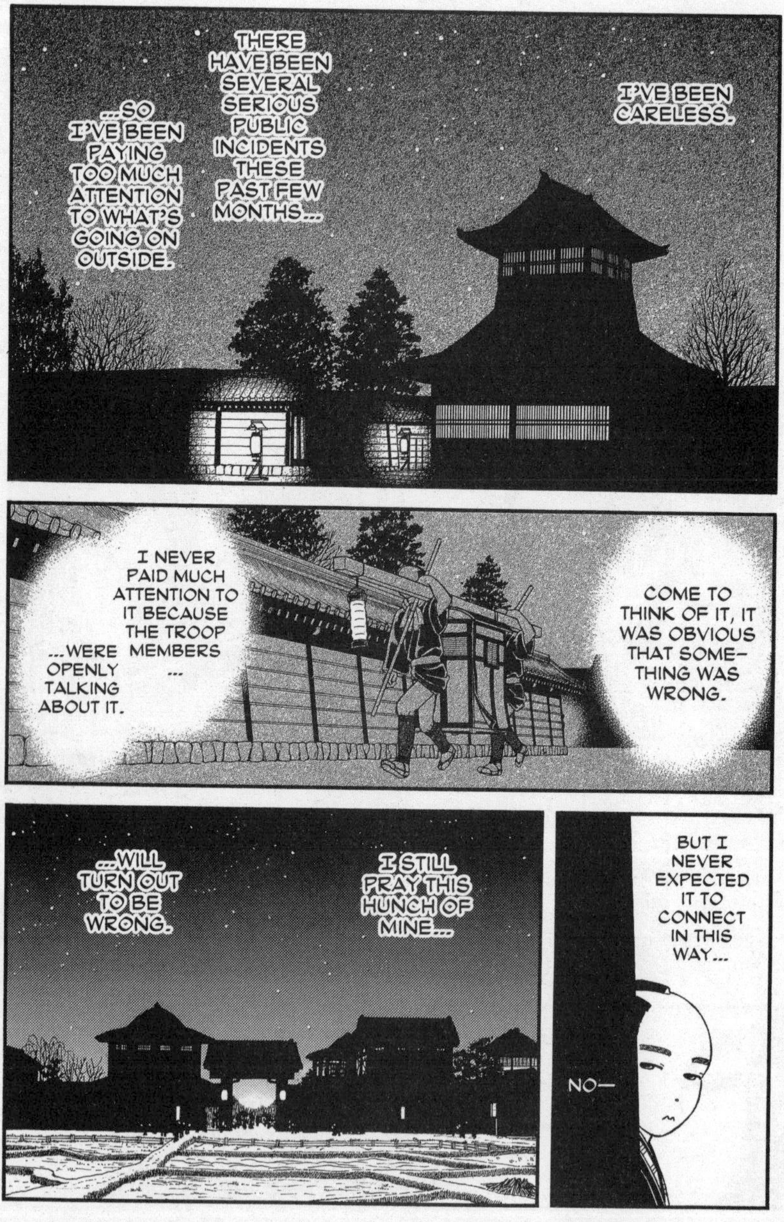
I'VE BEEN CARELESS.
THERE HAVE BEEN SEVERAL SERIOUS PUBLIC INCIDENTS THESE PAST FEW MONTHS...
...SO I'VE BEEN PAYING TOO MUCH ATTENTION TO WHAT'S GOING ON OUTSIDE.
COME TO THINK OF IT, IT WAS OBVIOUS THAT SOME-THING WAS WRONG.
I NEVER PAID MUCH ATTENTION TO IT BECAUSE THE TROOP MEMBERS ...
...WERE OPENLY TALKING ABOUT IT.
BUT I NEVER EXPECTED IT TO CONNECT IN THIS WAY...
NO—
I STILL PRAY THIS HUNCH OF MINE...
...WILL TURN OUT TO BE WRONG.

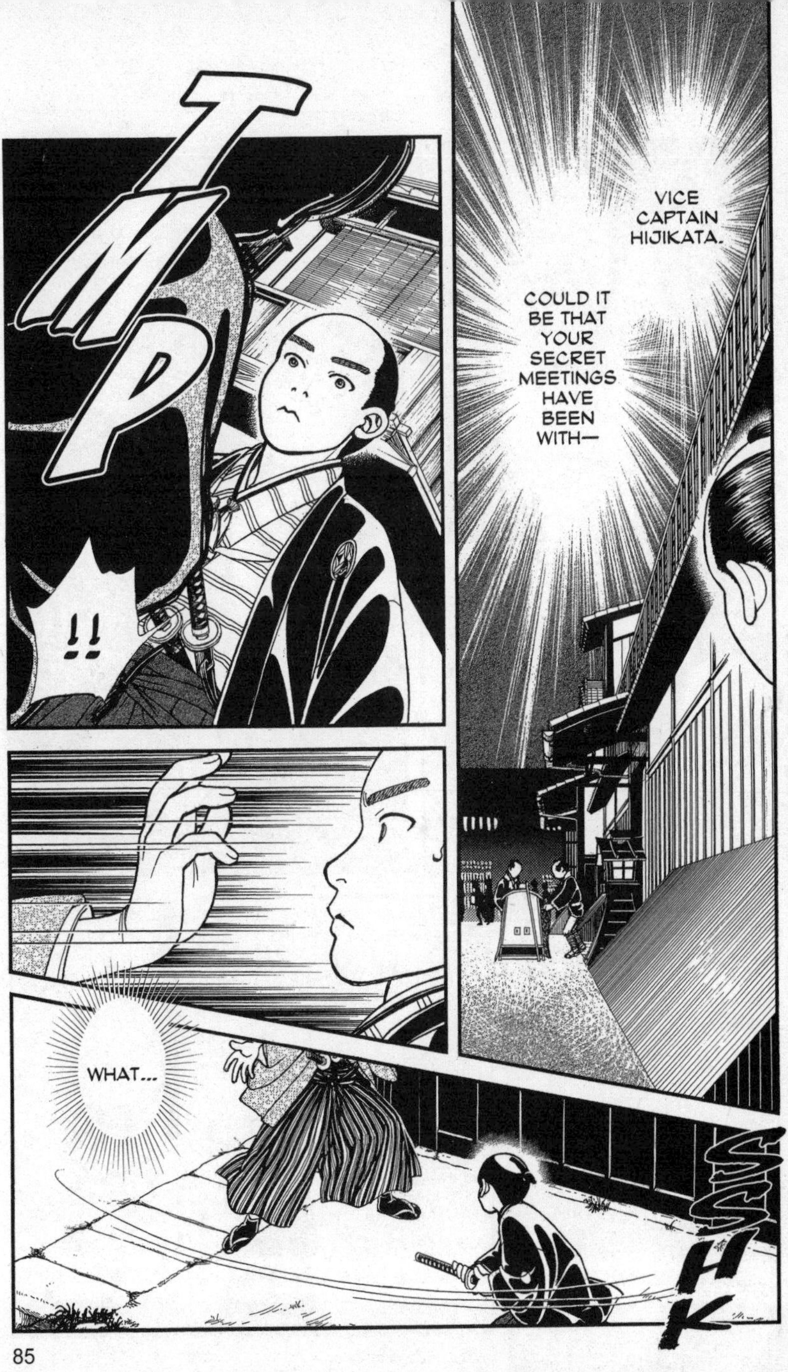
VICE CAPTAIN HIJIKATA.
COULD IT BE THAT YOUR SECRET MEETINGS HAVE BEEN WITH—
TMP
!!
WHAT...
SSHK

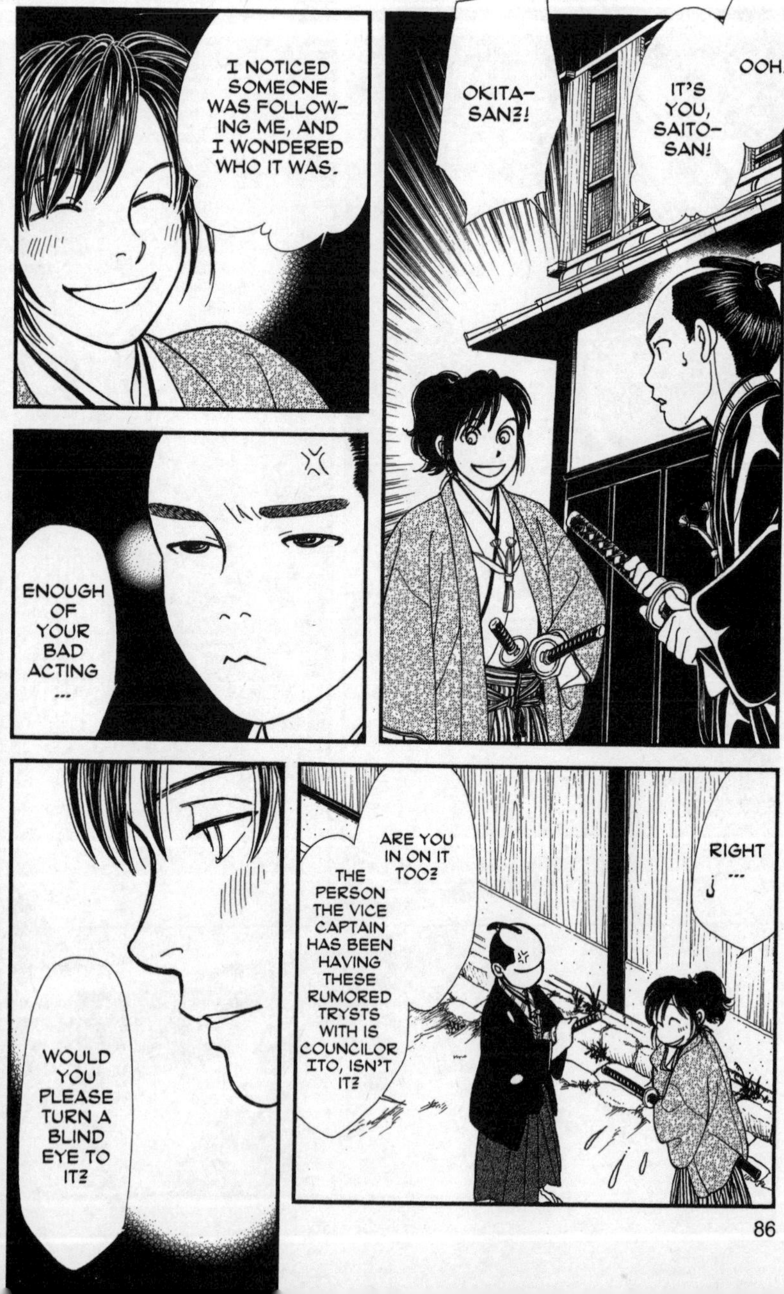
OOH. IT'S YOU, SAITO-SAN!
OKITA-SAN?!
I NOTICED SOMEONE WAS FOLLOWING ME, AND I WONDERED WHO IT WAS.
ENOUGH OF YOUR BAD ACTING...
RIGHT...
ARE YOU IN ON IT TOO?
THE PERSON THE VICE CAPTAIN HAS BEEN HAVING THESE RUMORED TRYSTS WITH IS COUNCILOR ITO, ISN'T IT?
WOULD YOU PLEASE TURN A BLIND EYE TO IT?

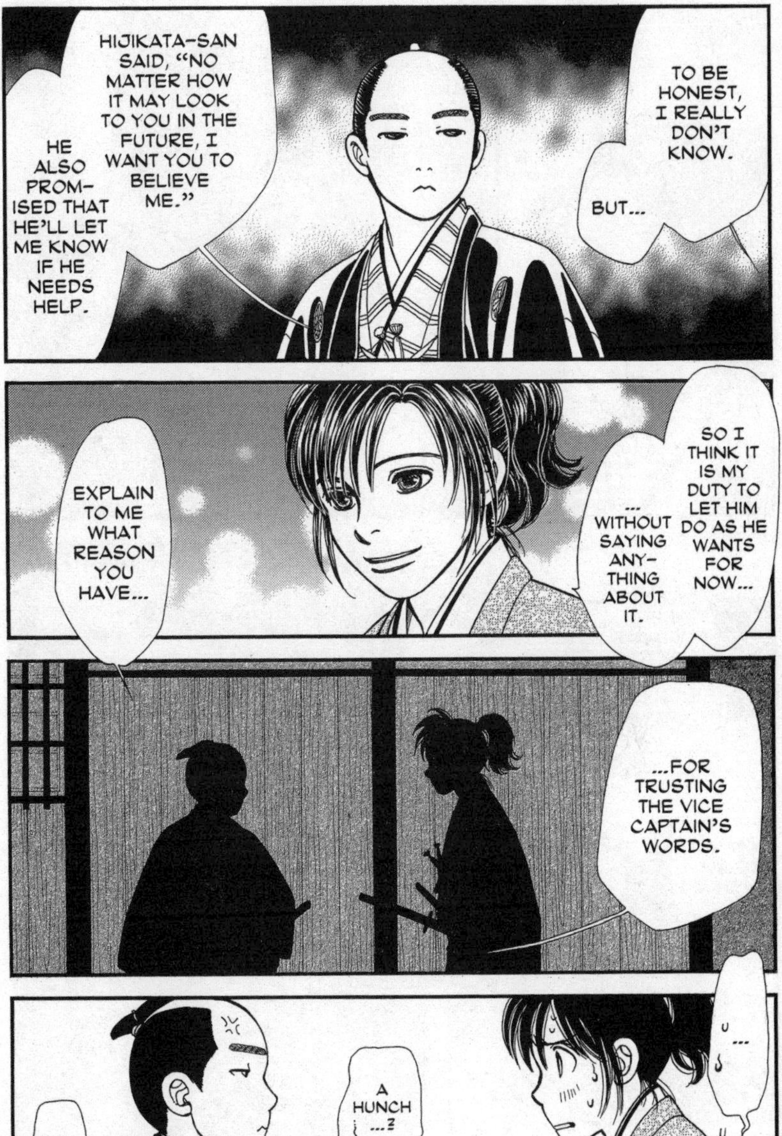
TO BE HONEST, I REALLY DON'T KNOW.
BUT...
HIJIKATA-SAN SAID, "NO MATTER HOW IT MAY LOOK TO YOU IN THE FUTURE, I WANT YOU TO BELIEVE ME."
HE ALSO PROMISED THAT HE'LL LET ME KNOW IF HE NEEDS HELP.
SO I THINK IT IS MY DUTY TO LET HIM DO AS HE WANTS FOR NOW...
...WITHOUT SAYING ANYTHING ABOUT IT.
EXPLAIN TO ME WHAT REASON YOU HAVE...
...FOR TRUSTING THE VICE CAPTAIN'S WORDS.
...
A HUNCH...?
...

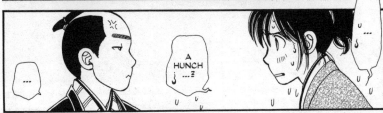

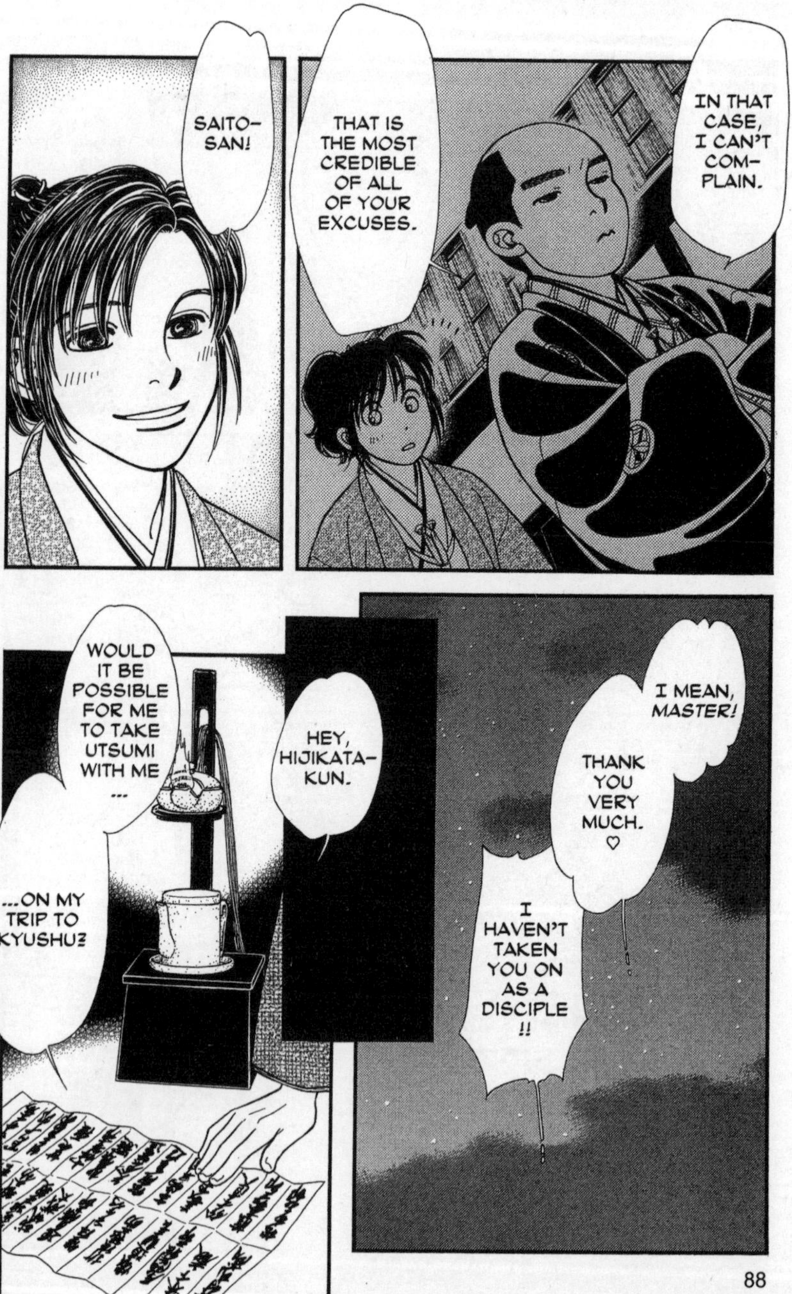
IN THAT CASE, I CAN'T COM-PLAIN.
THAT IS THE MOST CREDIBLE OF ALL OF YOUR EXCUSES.
SAITO-SAN!
I MEAN, MASTER!
THANK YOU VERY MUCH. ♡
I HAVEN'T TAKEN YOU ON AS A DISCIPLE !!
HEY, HIJIKATA-KUN.
WOULD IT BE POSSIBLE FOR ME TO TAKE UTSUMI WITH ME ...
...ON MY TRIP TO KYUSHU?

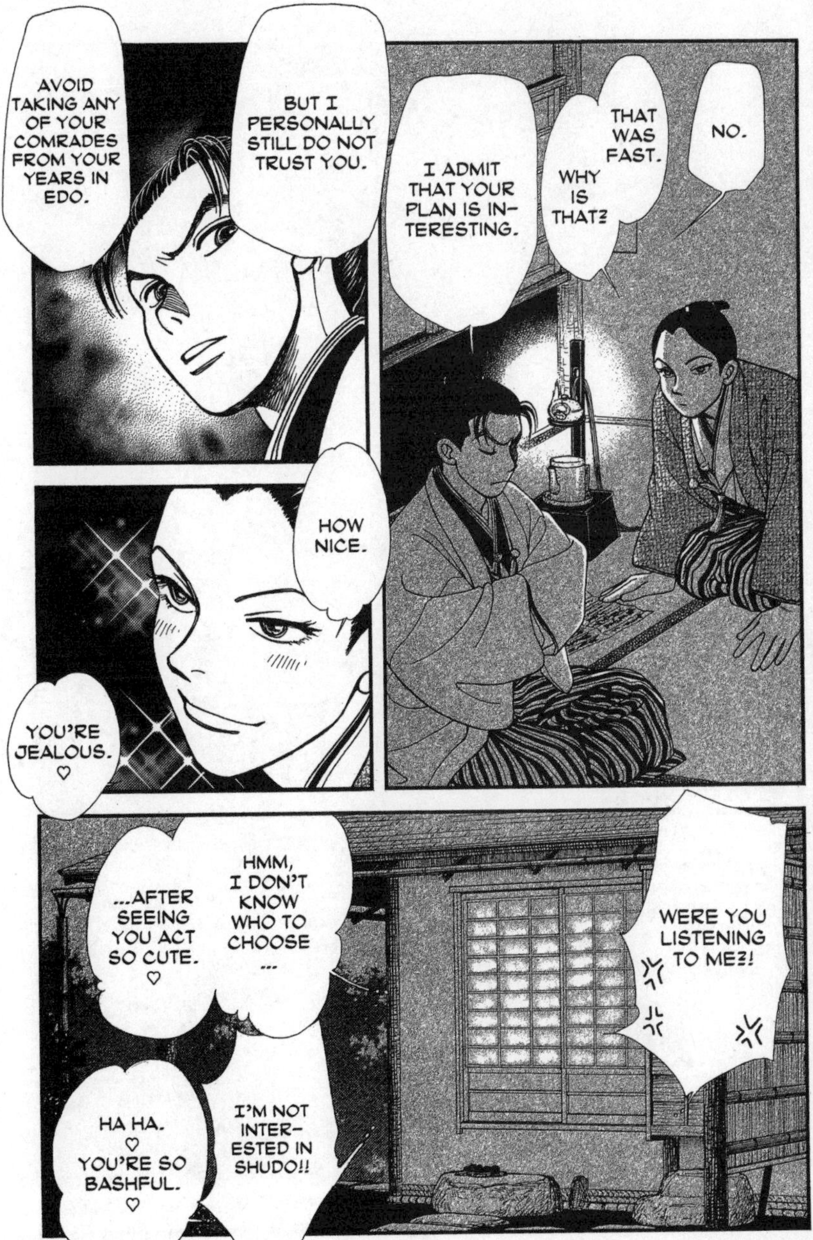
NO.
THAT WAS FAST.
WHY IS THAT?
I ADMIT THAT YOUR PLAN IS IN-TERESTING.
BUT I PERSONALLY STILL DO NOT TRUST YOU.
AVOID TAKING ANY OF YOUR COMRADES FROM YOUR YEARS IN EDO.
HOW NICE.
YOU'RE JEALOUS. ♡
WERE YOU LISTENING TO ME?!
HMM, I DON'T KNOW WHO TO CHOOSE...
...AFTER SEEING YOU ACT SO CUTE. ♡
I'M NOT INTER-ESTED IN SHUDO!!
HA HA. ♡ YOU'RE SO BASHFUL. ♡

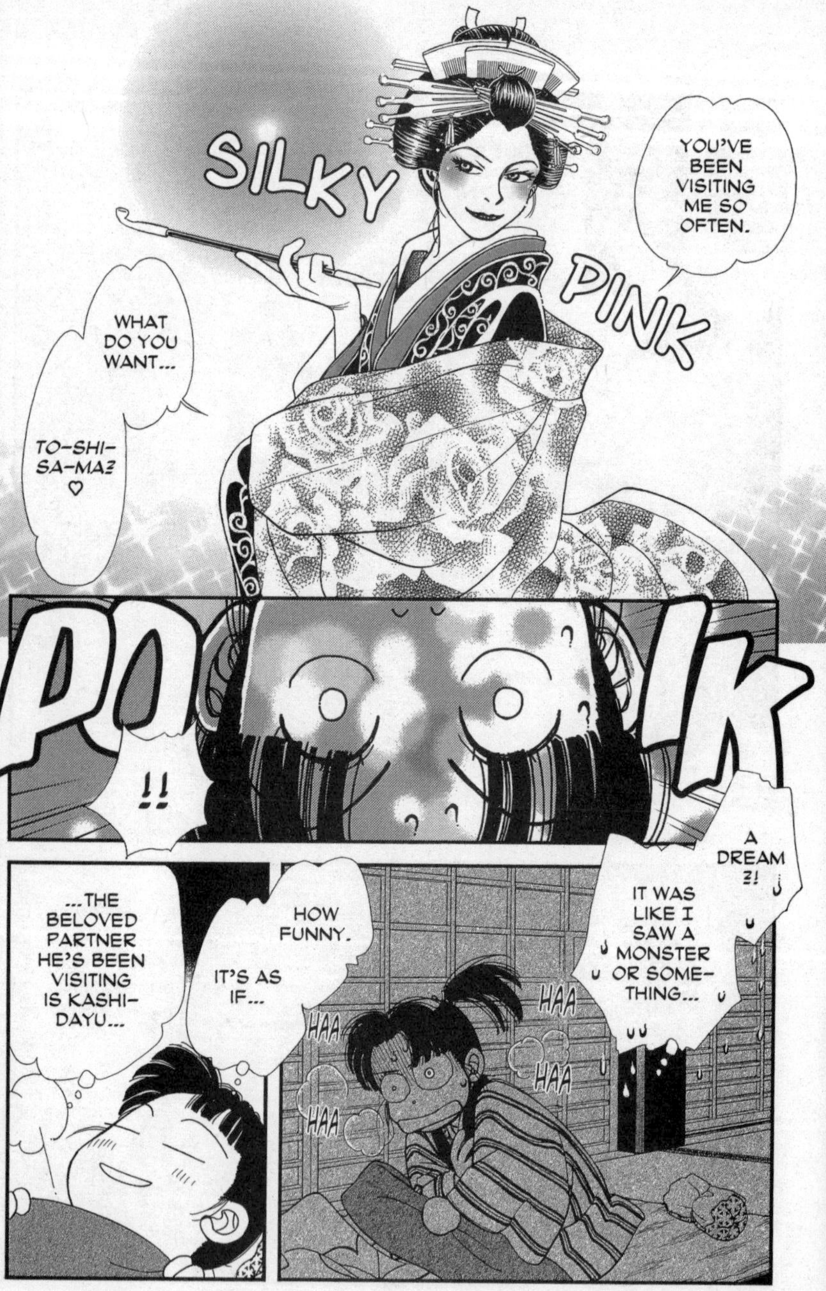
YOU'VE BEEN VISITING ME SO OFTEN.
SILKY
PINK
WHAT DO YOU WANT...
TO-SHI-SA-MA? ♡
PO
IK
!!
A DREAM?!
IT WAS LIKE I SAW A MONSTER OR SOME-THING...
HAA
HAA
HAA
HAA
HOW FUNNY.
IT'S AS IF...
...THE BELOVED PARTNER HE'S BEEN VISITING IS KASHI-DAYU...

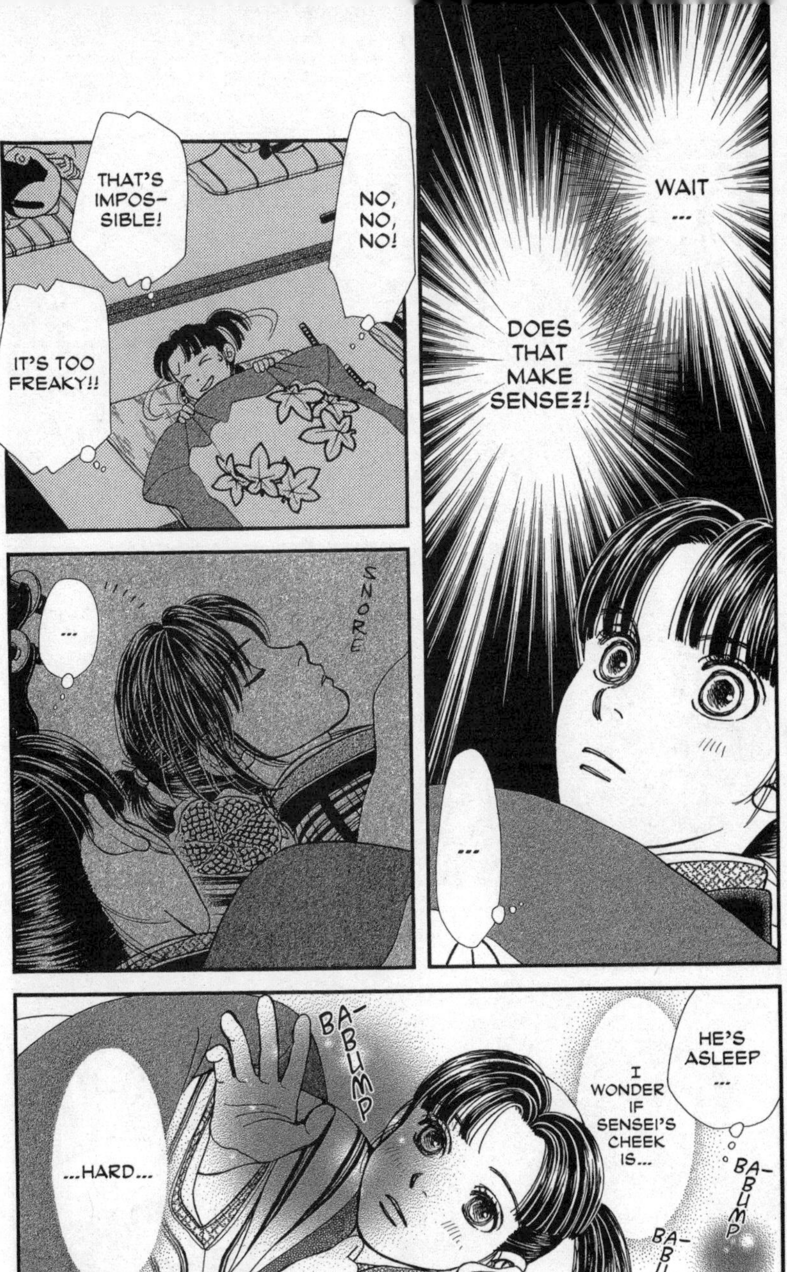
WAIT ...
DOES THAT MAKE SENSE?!
...
NO, NO, NO!
THAT'S IMPOSSIBLE!
IT'S TOO FREAKY!!
SNORE
...
HE'S ASLEEP ...
I WONDER IF SENSEI'S CHEEK IS...
BA-BUMP
BA-BUMP
BA-BUMP
...HARD...

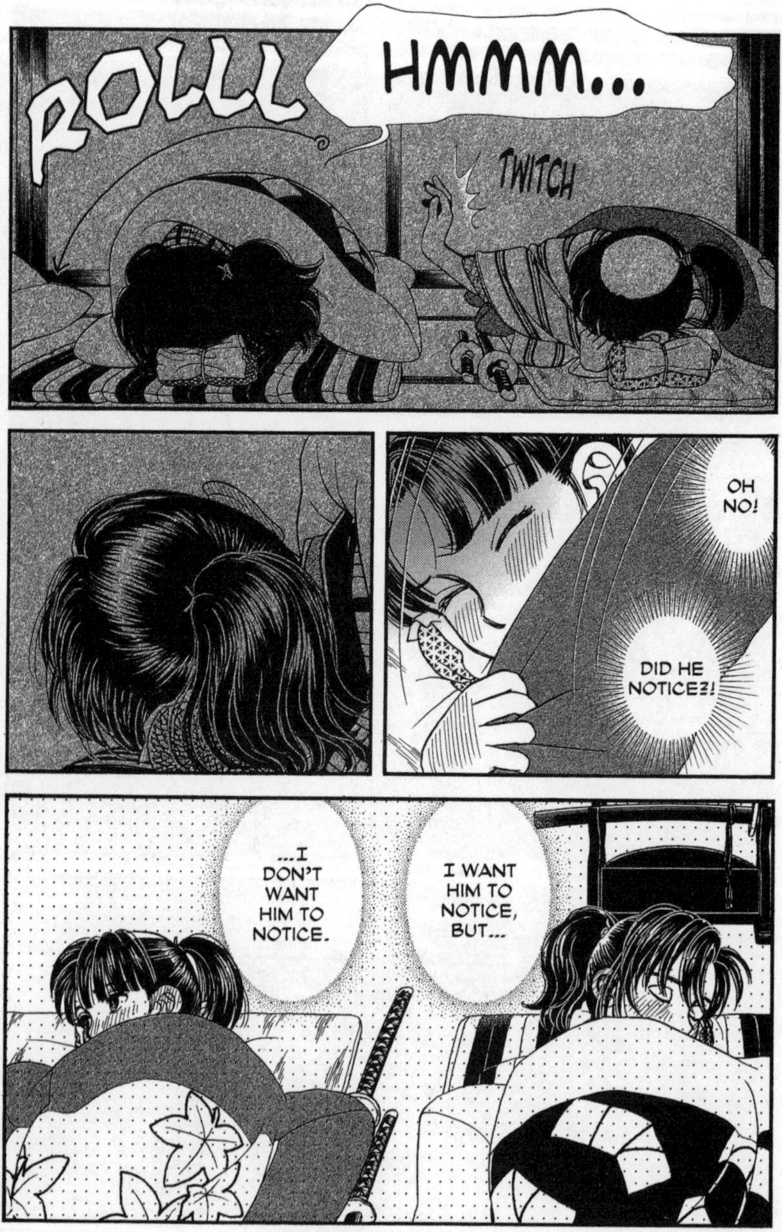
HMMM...
ROLL
TWITCH
OH NO!
DID HE NOTICE?!
I WANT HIM TO NOTICE, BUT...
...I DON'T WANT HIM TO NOTICE.

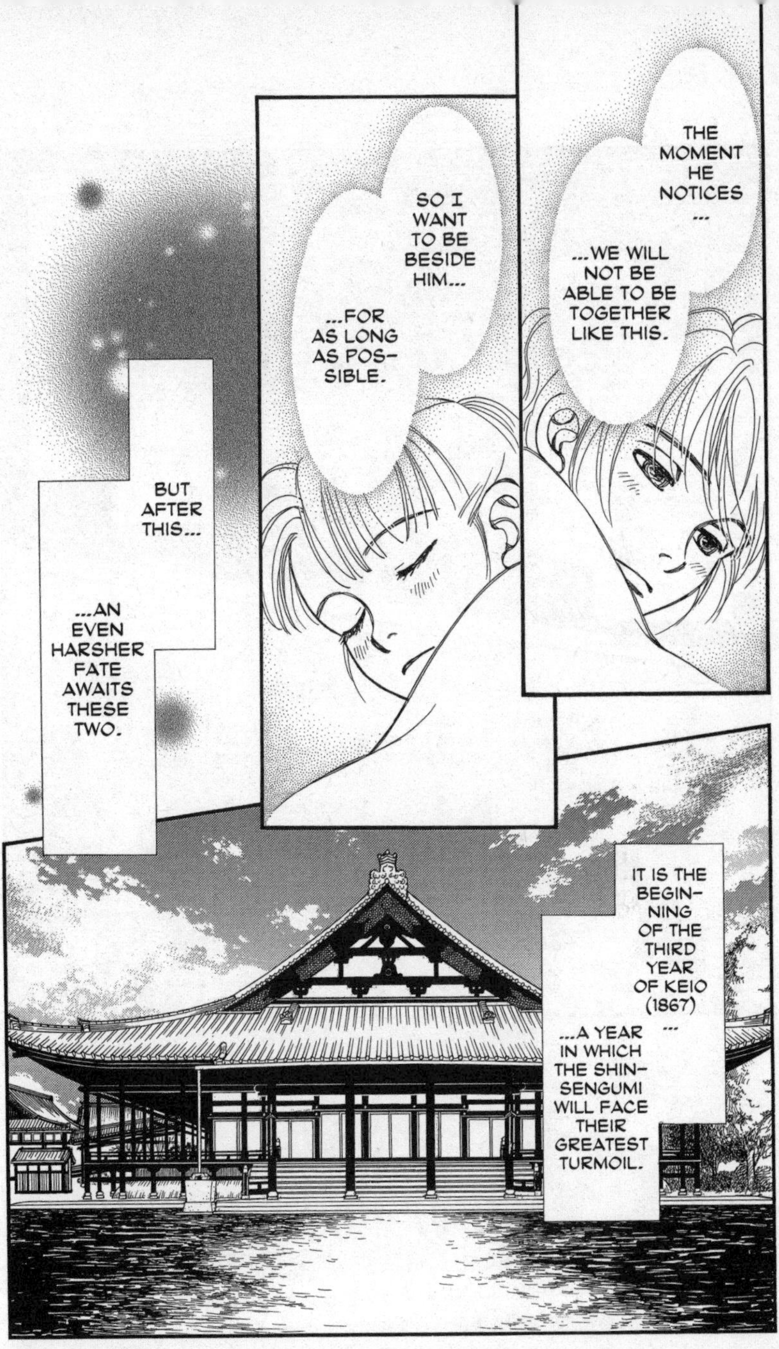
THE MOMENT HE NOTICES...
...WE WILL NOT BE ABLE TO BE TOGETHER LIKE THIS.
SO I WANT TO BE BESIDE HIM...
...FOR AS LONG AS POS-SIBLE.
BUT AFTER THIS...
...AN EVEN HARSHER FATE AWAITS THESE TWO.
IT IS THE BEGIN-NING OF THE THIRD YEAR OF KEIO (1867)...
...A YEAR IN WHICH THE SHIN-SENGUMI WILL FACE THEIR GREATEST TURMOIL.

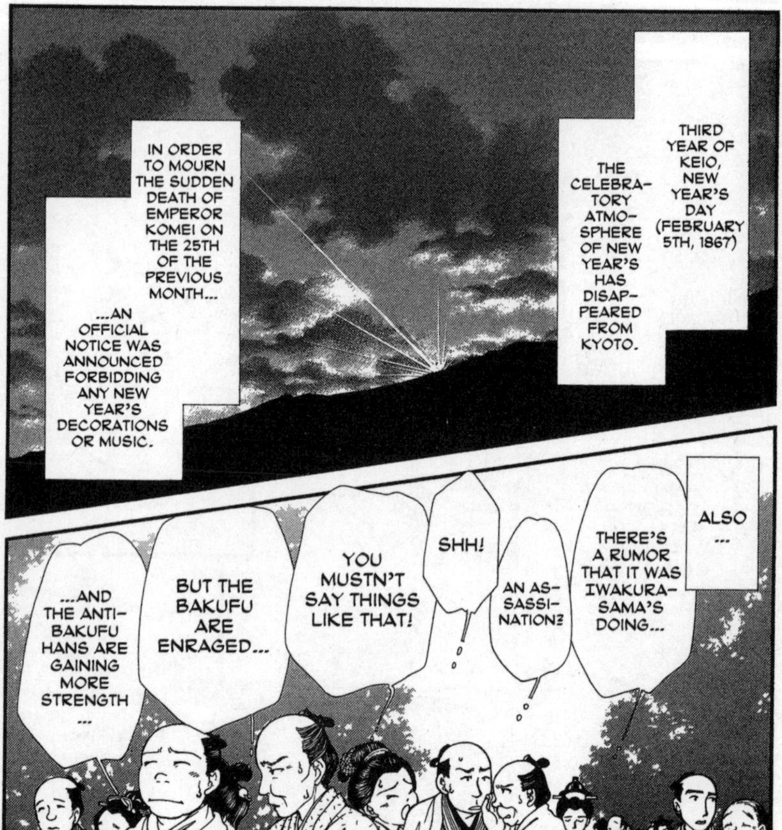
THIRD YEAR OF KEIO, NEW YEAR'S DAY (FEBRUARY 5TH, 1867)
THE CELEBRATORY ATMOSPHERE OF NEW YEAR'S HAS DISAPPEARED FROM KYOTO.
IN ORDER TO MOURN THE SUDDEN DEATH OF EMPEROR KOMEI ON THE 25TH OF THE PREVIOUS MONTH...
...AN OFFICIAL NOTICE WAS ANNOUNCED FORBIDDING ANY NEW YEAR'S DECORATIONS OR MUSIC.
ALSO...
THERE'S A RUMOR THAT IT WAS IWAKURA-SAMA'S DOING...
AN ASSASSINATION?
SHH!
YOU MUSTN'T SAY THINGS LIKE THAT!
BUT THE BAKUFU ARE ENRAGED...
...AND THE ANTI-BAKUFU HANS ARE GAINING MORE STRENGTH...

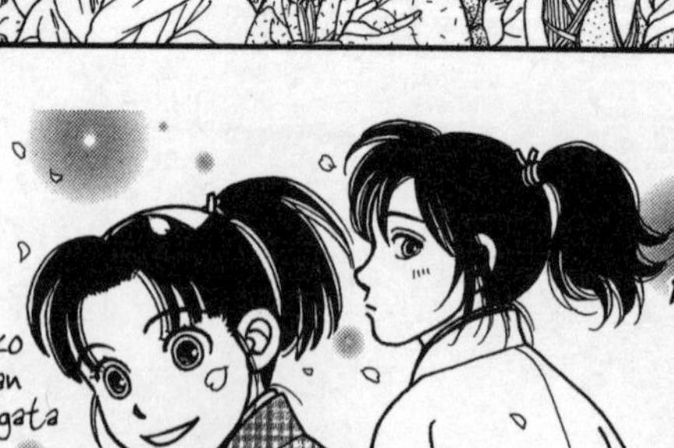

KAZE HIKARU SENRYU

SHINING SPRING
THE BEST TIME TO
SEE THE FLOWERS
DEPENDS ON THE WIND

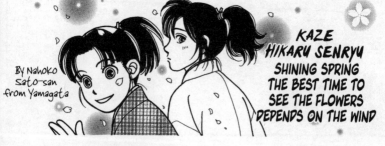

By Nahoko Sato-san from Yamagata

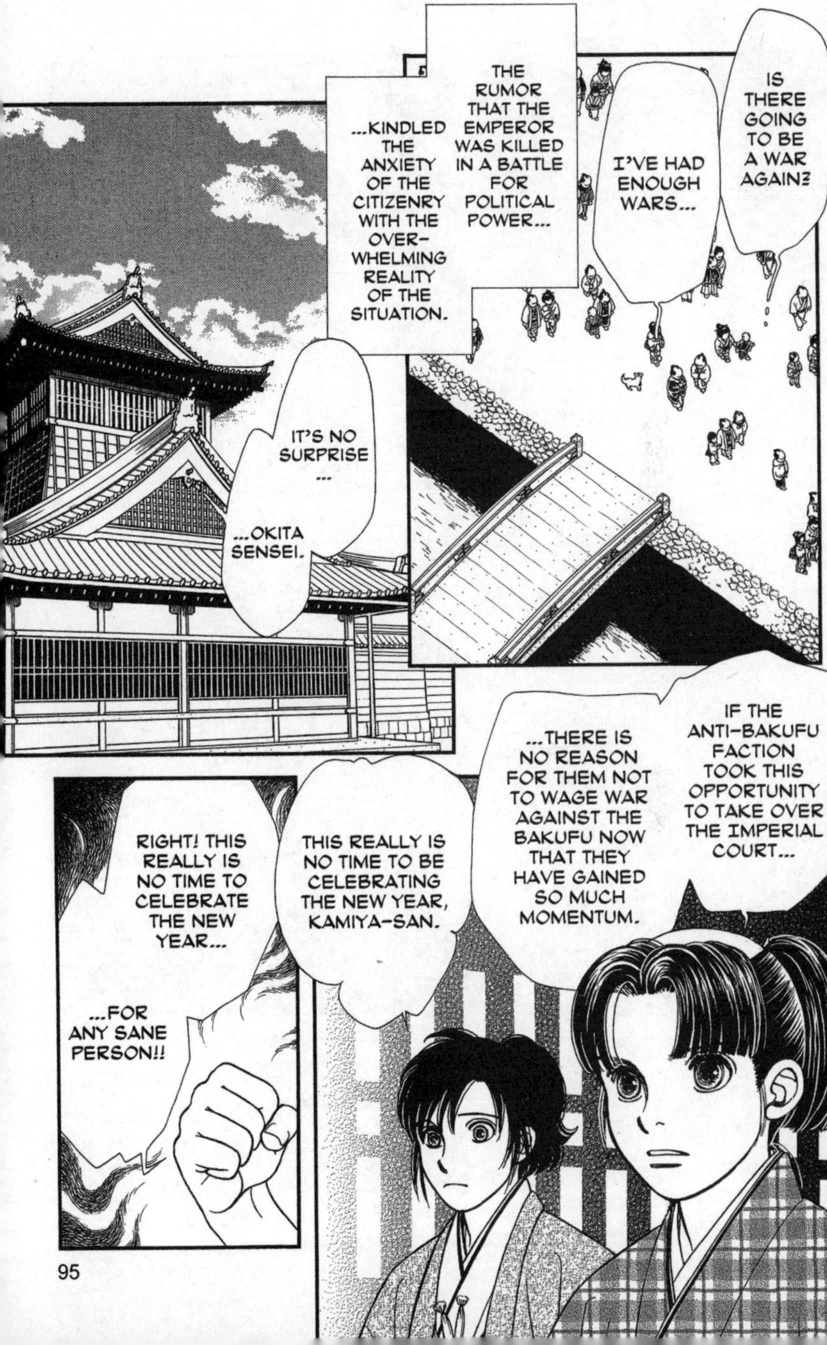
THE RUMOR THAT THE EMPEROR WAS KILLED IN A BATTLE FOR POLITICAL POWER...
...KINDLED THE ANXIETY OF THE CITIZENRY WITH THE OVER-WHELMING REALITY OF THE SITUATION.
IS THERE GOING TO BE A WAR AGAIN?
I'VE HAD ENOUGH WARS...
IT'S NO SURPRISE ...
...OKITA SENSEI.
IF THE ANTI-BAKUFU FACTION TOOK THIS OPPORTUNITY TO TAKE OVER THE IMPERIAL COURT...
...THERE IS NO REASON FOR THEM NOT TO WAGE WAR AGAINST THE BAKUFU NOW THAT THEY HAVE GAINED SO MUCH MOMENTUM.
THIS REALLY IS NO TIME TO BE CELEBRATING THE NEW YEAR, KAMIYA-SAN.
RIGHT! THIS REALLY IS NO TIME TO CELEBRATE THE NEW YEAR...
...FOR ANY SANE PERSON!!

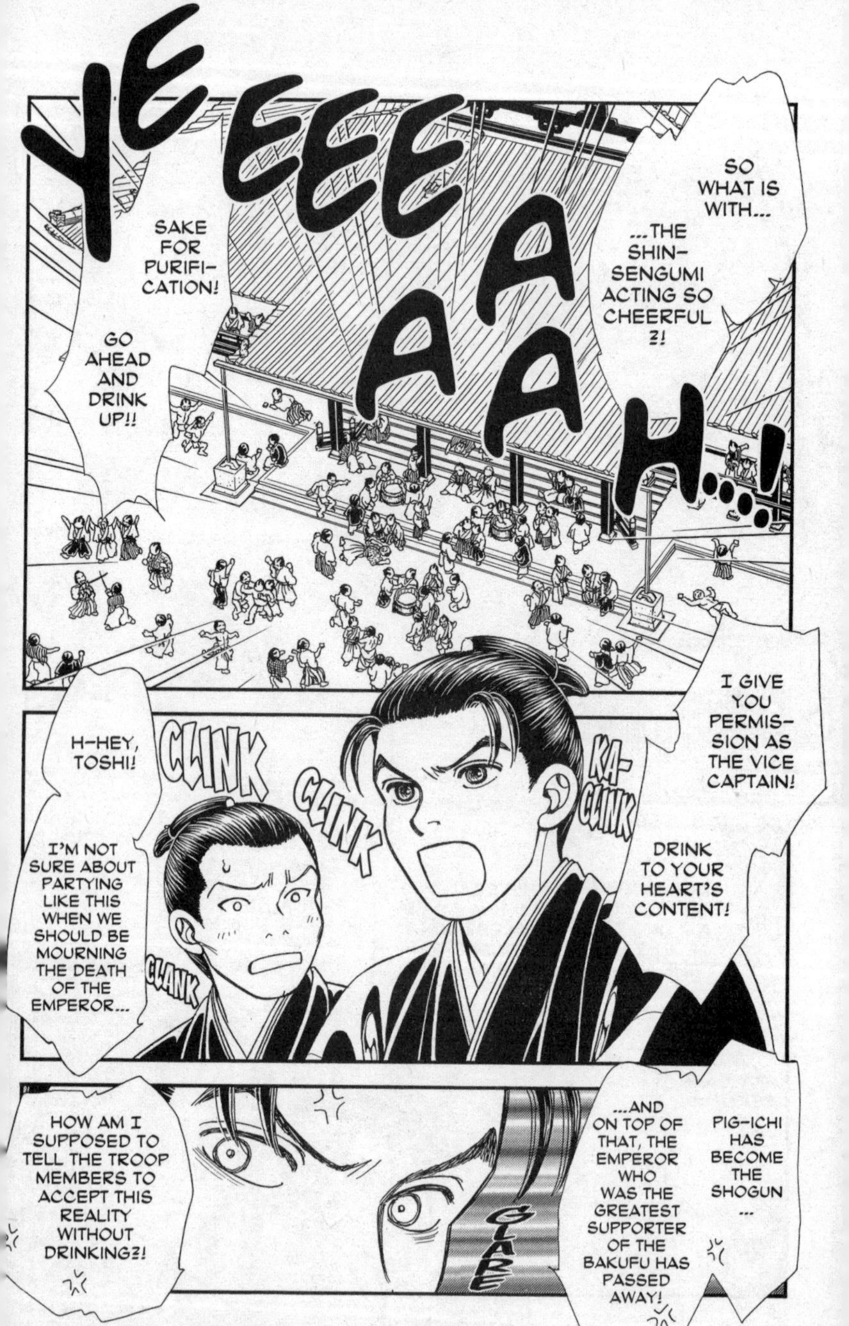
YEEEEAAAAH...!!
SO WHAT IS WITH...
...THE SHINSENGUMI ACTING SO CHEERFUL?!
SAKE FOR PURIFICATION!
GO AHEAD AND DRINK UP!!
I GIVE YOU PERMISSION AS THE VICE CAPTAIN!
DRINK TO YOUR HEART'S CONTENT!
KA-CLINK
CLINK
CLINK
H-HEY, TOSHI!
I'M NOT SURE ABOUT PARTYING LIKE THIS WHEN WE SHOULD BE MOURNING THE DEATH OF THE EMPEROR...
CLANK
PIG-ICHI HAS BECOME THE SHOGUN...
...AND ON TOP OF THAT, THE EMPEROR WHO WAS THE GREATEST SUPPORTER OF THE BAKUFU HAS PASSED AWAY!
GLARE
HOW AM I SUPPOSED TO TELL THE TROOP MEMBERS TO ACCEPT THIS REALITY WITHOUT DRINKING?!

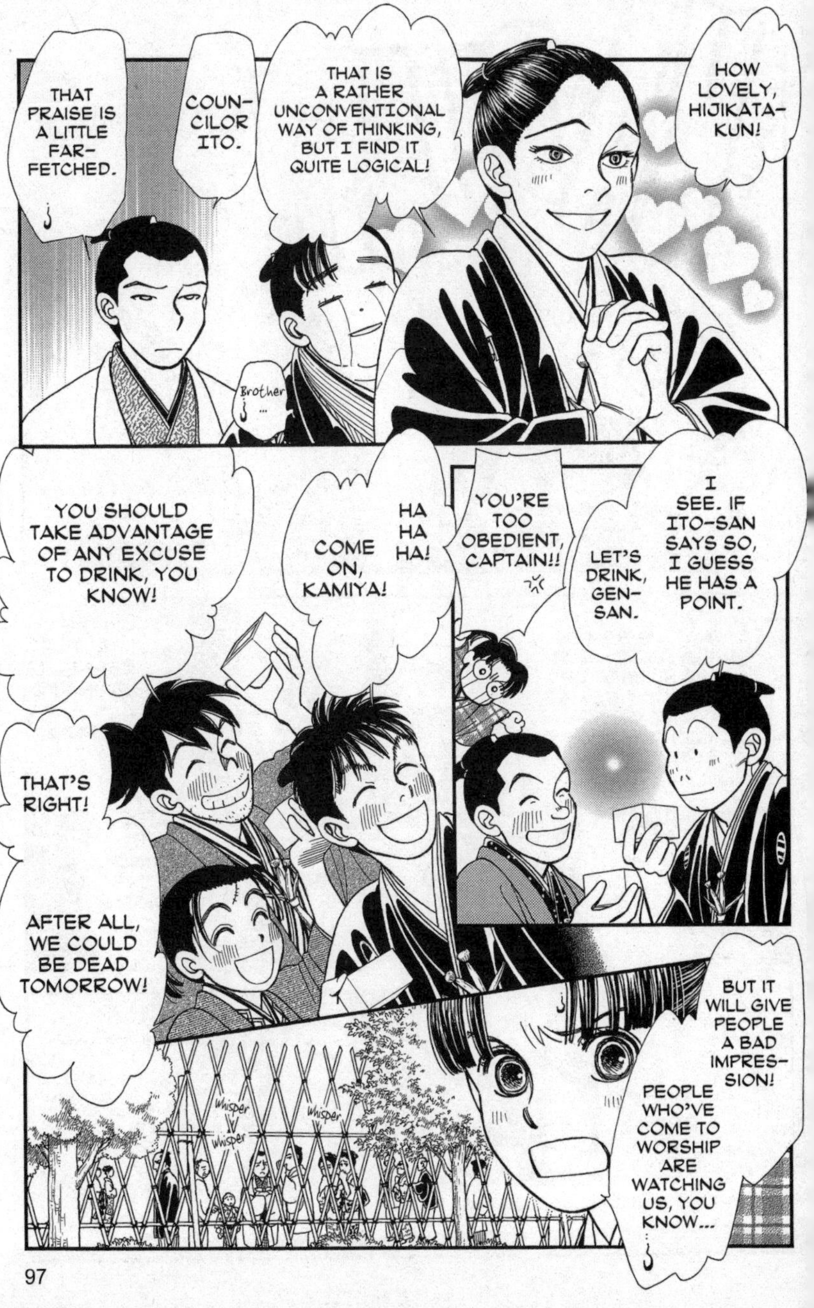
HOW LOVELY, HIJIKATA-KUN!
THAT IS A RATHER UNCONVENTIONAL WAY OF THINKING, BUT I FIND IT QUITE LOGICAL!
COUN-CILOR ITO.
THAT PRAISE IS A LITTLE FAR-FETCHED.
Brother...
I SEE. IF ITO-SAN SAYS SO, I GUESS HE HAS A POINT.
LET'S DRINK, GEN-SAN.
YOU'RE TOO OBEDIENT, CAPTAIN!!
HA HA HA!
COME ON, KAMIYA!
YOU SHOULD TAKE ADVANTAGE OF ANY EXCUSE TO DRINK, YOU KNOW!
THAT'S RIGHT!
AFTER ALL, WE COULD BE DEAD TOMORROW!
BUT IT WILL GIVE PEOPLE A BAD IMPRES-SION!
PEOPLE WHO'VE COME TO WORSHIP ARE WATCHING US, YOU KNOW...
Whisper
Whisper
Whisper

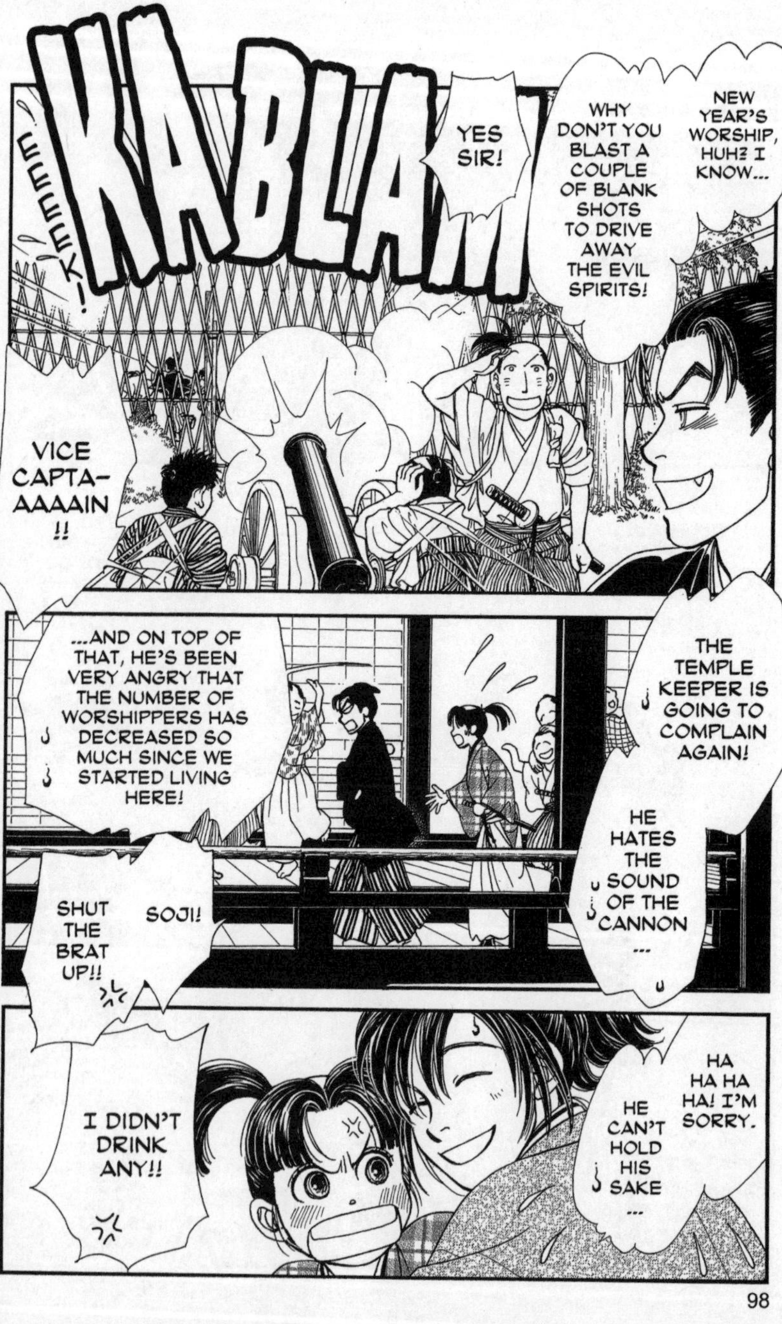
NEW YEAR'S WORSHIP, HUH? I KNOW...
WHY DON'T YOU BLAST A COUPLE OF BLANK SHOTS TO DRIVE AWAY THE EVIL SPIRITS!
YES SIR!
KABLAM
EEEEEK!
VICE CAPTA-AAAAIN!!
THE TEMPLE KEEPER IS GOING TO COMPLAIN AGAIN!
HE HATES THE SOUND OF THE CANNON ...
...AND ON TOP OF THAT, HE'S BEEN VERY ANGRY THAT THE NUMBER OF WORSHIPPERS HAS DECREASED SO MUCH SINCE WE STARTED LIVING HERE!
SOJI!
SHUT THE BRAT UP!!
HA HA HA HA! I'M SORRY.
HE CAN'T HOLD HIS SAKE ...
I DIDN'T DRINK ANY!!

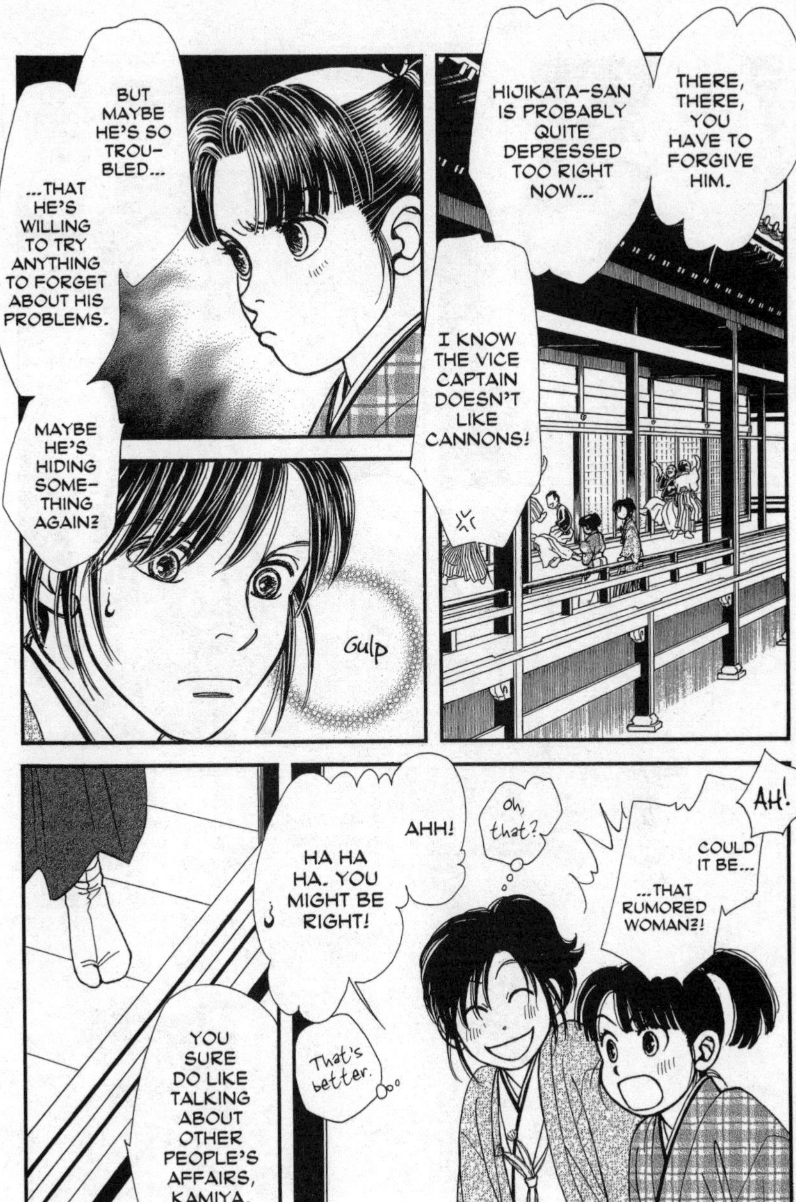
THERE, THERE, YOU HAVE TO FORGIVE HIM.
HIJIKATA-SAN IS PROBABLY QUITE DEPRESSED TOO RIGHT NOW...
I KNOW THE VICE CAPTAIN DOESN'T LIKE CANNONS!
BUT MAYBE HE'S SO TROUBLED...
...THAT HE'S WILLING TO TRY ANYTHING TO FORGET ABOUT HIS PROBLEMS.
MAYBE HE'S HIDING SOMETHING AGAIN?
Gulp
AH!
COULD IT BE...
...THAT RUMORED WOMAN?!
Oh, that?
AHH!
HA HA HA. YOU MIGHT BE RIGHT!
That's better.
YOU SURE DO LIKE TALKING ABOUT OTHER PEOPLE'S AFFAIRS, KAMIYA.

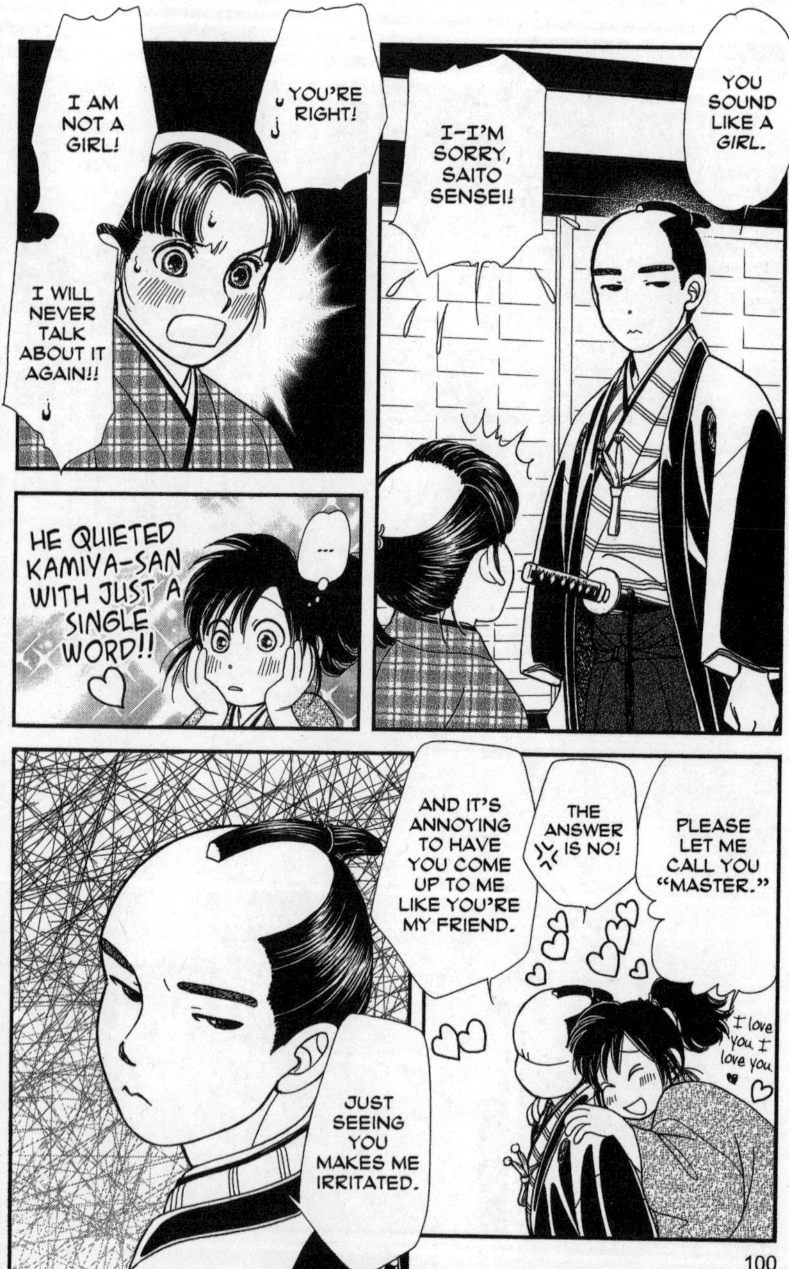
YOU SOUND LIKE A GIRL.
I-I'M SORRY, SAITO SENSEI!
YOU'RE RIGHT!
I AM NOT A GIRL!
I WILL NEVER TALK ABOUT IT AGAIN!!
...
HE QUIETED KAMIYA-SAN WITH JUST A SINGLE WORD!!
PLEASE LET ME CALL YOU "MASTER."
I love you. I love you.
THE ANSWER IS NO!
AND IT'S ANNOYING TO HAVE YOU COME UP TO ME LIKE YOU'RE MY FRIEND.
JUST SEEING YOU MAKES ME IRRITATED.

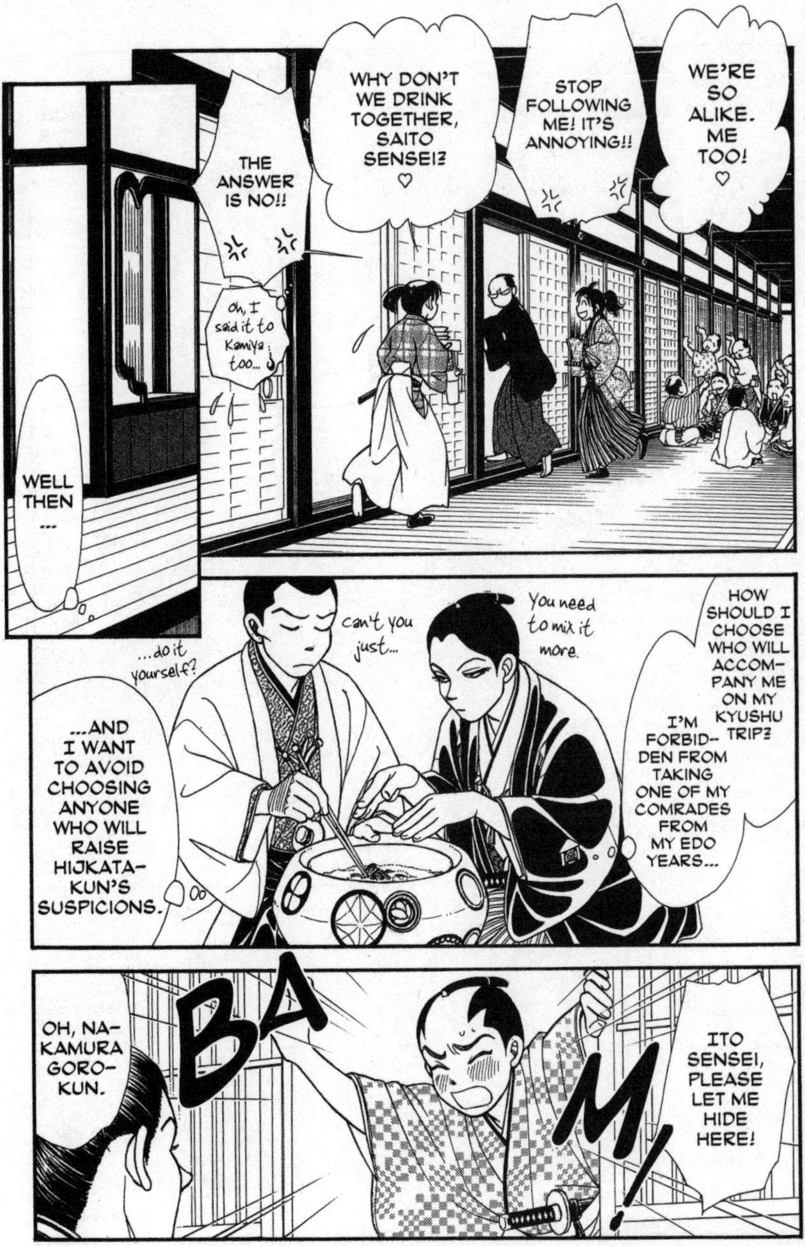
WE'RE SO ALIKE. ME TOO! ♡
STOP FOLLOWING ME! IT'S ANNOYING!!
WHY DON'T WE DRINK TOGETHER, SAITO SENSEI? ♡
THE ANSWER IS NO!!
Oh, I said it to Kamiya too...
WELL THEN ...
HOW SHOULD I CHOOSE WHO WILL ACCOMPANY ME ON MY KYUSHU TRIP?
I'M FORBID-DEN FROM TAKING ONE OF MY COMRADES FROM MY EDO YEARS...
You need to mix it more.
can't you just...
...do it yourself?
...AND I WANT TO AVOID CHOOSING ANYONE WHO WILL RAISE HIJKATA-KUN'S SUSPICIONS.
ITO SENSEI, PLEASE LET ME HIDE HERE!
BAM!
OH, NA-KAMURA GORO-KUN.

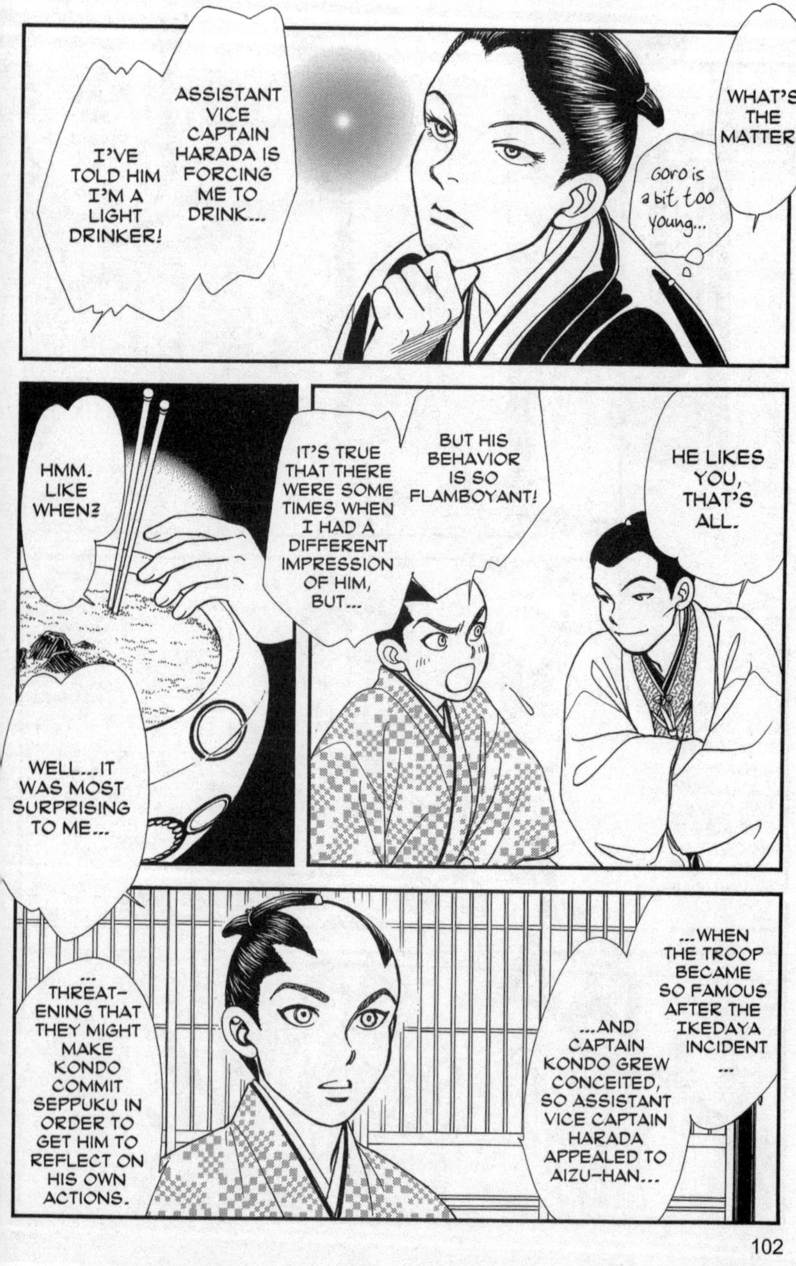
WHAT'S THE MATTER?
Goro is a bit too young...
ASSISTANT VICE CAPTAIN HARADA IS FORCING ME TO DRINK...
I'VE TOLD HIM I'M A LIGHT DRINKER!
HE LIKES YOU, THAT'S ALL.
BUT HIS BEHAVIOR IS SO FLAMBOYANT!
IT'S TRUE THAT THERE WERE SOME TIMES WHEN I HAD A DIFFERENT IMPRESSION OF HIM, BUT...
HMM. LIKE WHEN?
WELL...IT WAS MOST SURPRISING TO ME...
...WHEN THE TROOP BECAME SO FAMOUS AFTER THE IKEDAYA INCIDENT...
...AND CAPTAIN KONDO GREW CONCEITED, SO ASSISTANT VICE CAPTAIN HARADA APPEALED TO AIZU-HAN...
...THREAT-ENING THAT THEY MIGHT MAKE KONDO COMMIT SEPPUKU IN ORDER TO GET HIM TO REFLECT ON HIS OWN ACTIONS.

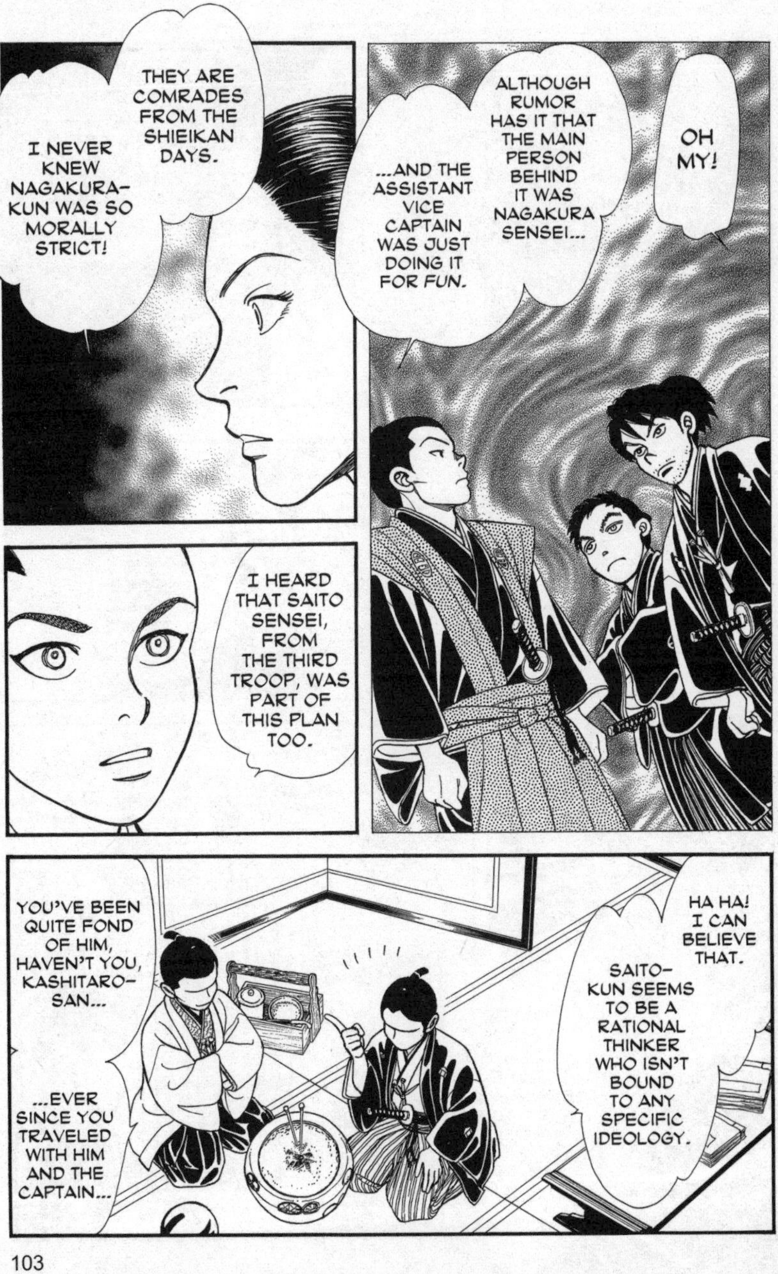
OH MY!
ALTHOUGH RUMOR HAS IT THAT THE MAIN PERSON BEHIND IT WAS NAGAKURA SENSEI...
...AND THE ASSISTANT VICE CAPTAIN WAS JUST DOING IT FOR *FUN*.
THEY ARE COMRADES FROM THE SHIEIKAN DAYS.
I NEVER KNEW NAGAKURA-KUN WAS SO MORALLY STRICT!
I HEARD THAT SAITO SENSEI, FROM THE THIRD TROOP, WAS PART OF THIS PLAN TOO.
HA HA! I CAN BELIEVE THAT.
SAITO-KUN SEEMS TO BE A RATIONAL THINKER WHO ISN'T BOUND TO ANY SPECIFIC IDEOLOGY.
YOU'VE BEEN QUITE FOND OF HIM, HAVEN'T YOU, KASHITARO-SAN...
...EVER SINCE YOU TRAVELED WITH HIM AND THE CAPTAIN...

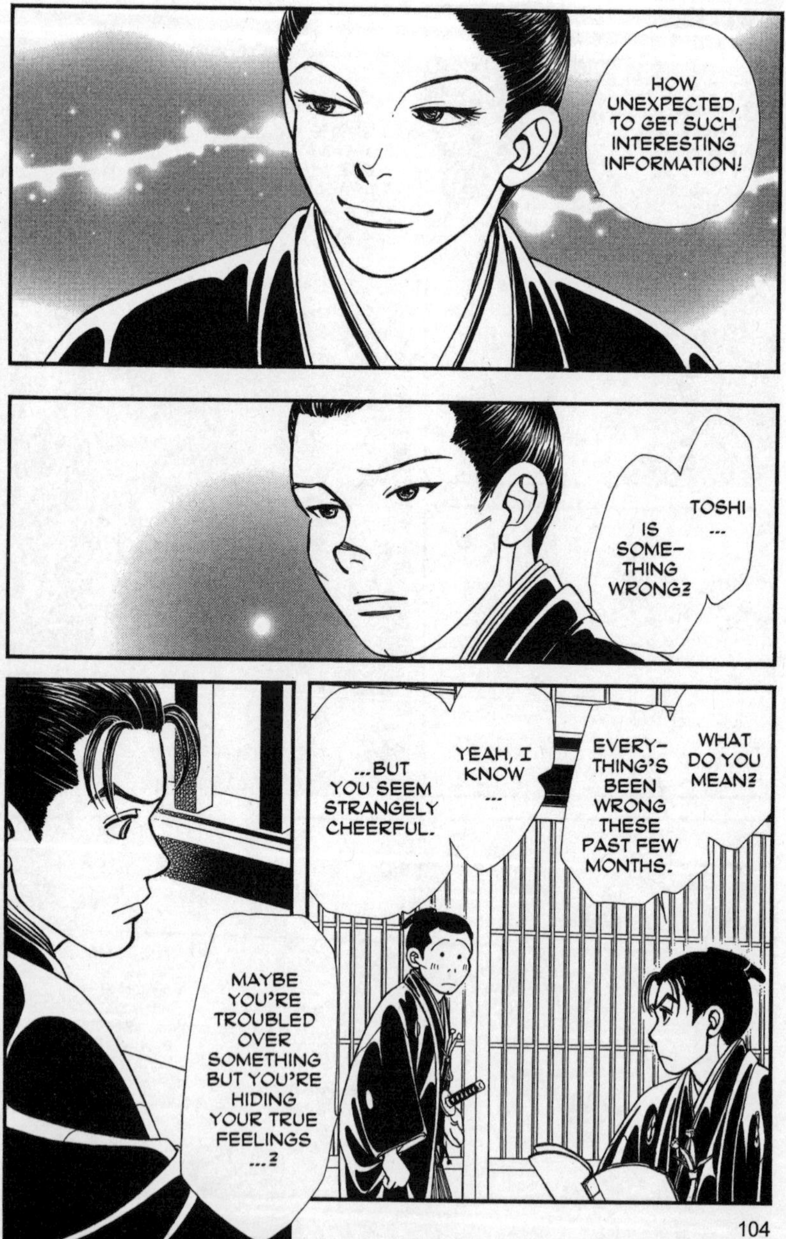
HOW UNEXPECTED, TO GET SUCH INTERESTING INFORMATION!
TOSHI ...
IS SOMETHING WRONG?
WHAT DO YOU MEAN?
EVERYTHING'S BEEN WRONG THESE PAST FEW MONTHS.
YEAH, I KNOW ...
...BUT YOU SEEM STRANGELY CHEERFUL.
MAYBE YOU'RE TROUBLED OVER SOMETHING BUT YOU'RE HIDING YOUR TRUE FEELINGS ...?

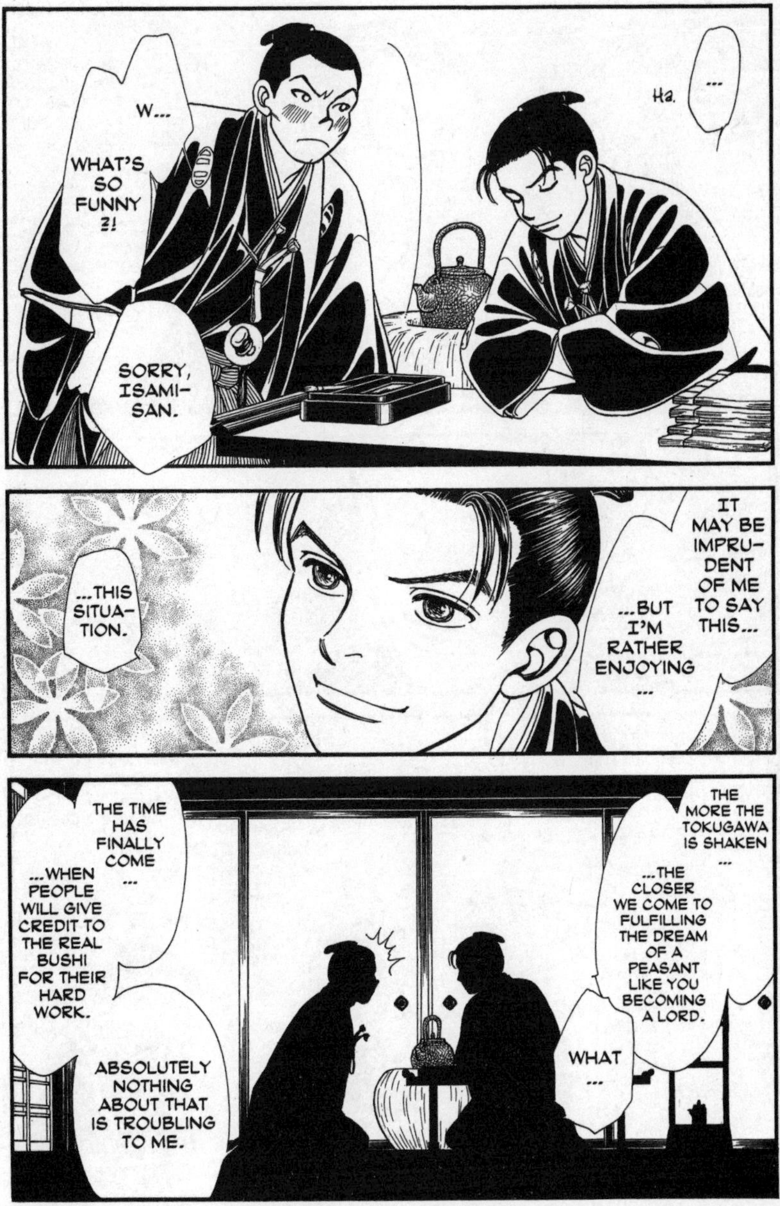
...
Ha.
W...
WHAT'S SO FUNNY?!
SORRY, ISAMI-SAN.
IT MAY BE IMPRU-DENT OF ME TO SAY THIS...
...BUT I'M RATHER ENJOYING...
...THIS SITUA-TION.
THE MORE THE TOKUGAWA IS SHAKEN...
...THE CLOSER WE COME TO FULFILLING THE DREAM OF A PEASANT LIKE YOU BECOMING A LORD.
WHAT...
THE TIME HAS FINALLY COME...
...WHEN PEOPLE WILL GIVE CREDIT TO THE REAL BUSHI FOR THEIR HARD WORK.
ABSOLUTELY NOTHING ABOUT THAT IS TROUBLING TO ME.

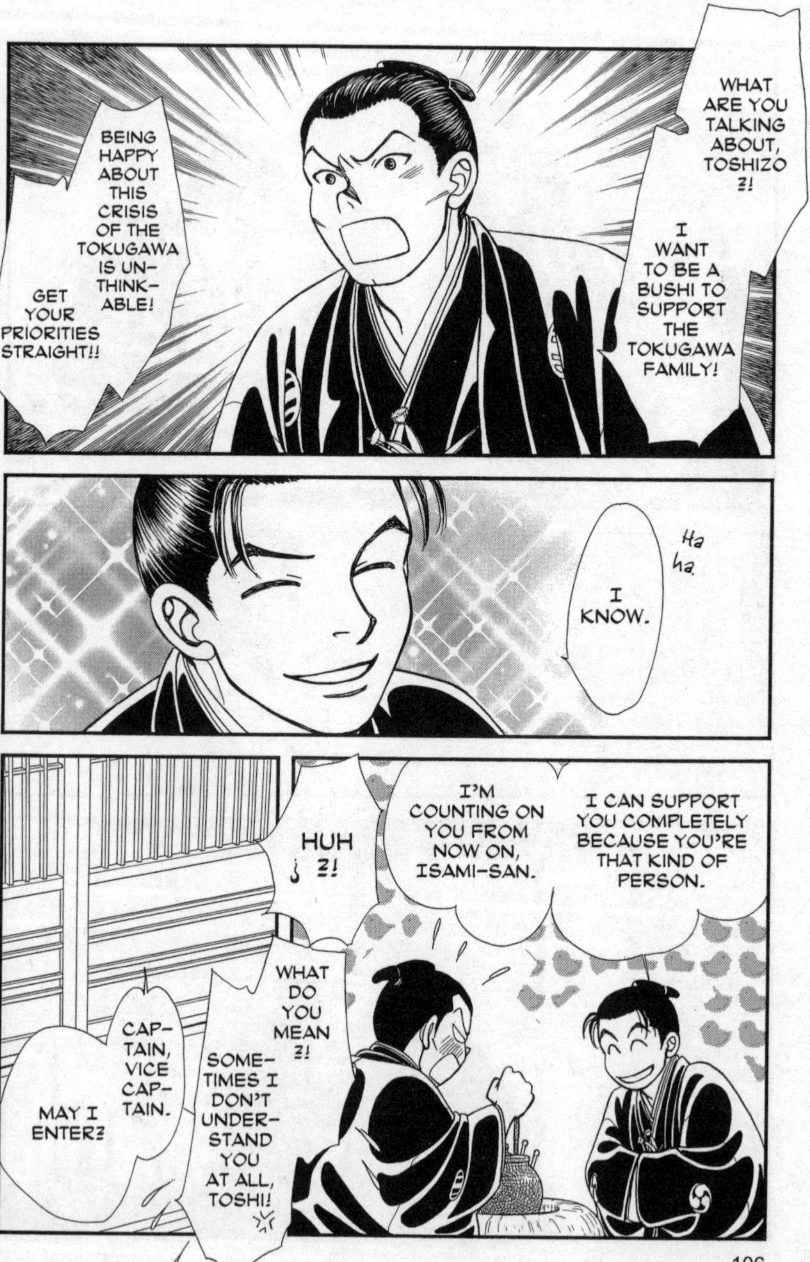
WHAT ARE YOU TALKING ABOUT, TOSHIZO?!
I WANT TO BE A BUSHI TO SUPPORT THE TOKUGAWA FAMILY!
BEING HAPPY ABOUT THIS CRISIS OF THE TOKUGAWA IS UNTHINKABLE!
GET YOUR PRIORITIES STRAIGHT!!
Ha ha.
I KNOW.
I CAN SUPPORT YOU COMPLETELY BECAUSE YOU'RE THAT KIND OF PERSON.
I'M COUNTING ON YOU FROM NOW ON, ISAMI-SAN.
HUH?!
WHAT DO YOU MEAN?!
SOMETIMES I DON'T UNDERSTAND YOU AT ALL, TOSHI!
CAPTAIN, VICE CAPTAIN.
MAY I ENTER?

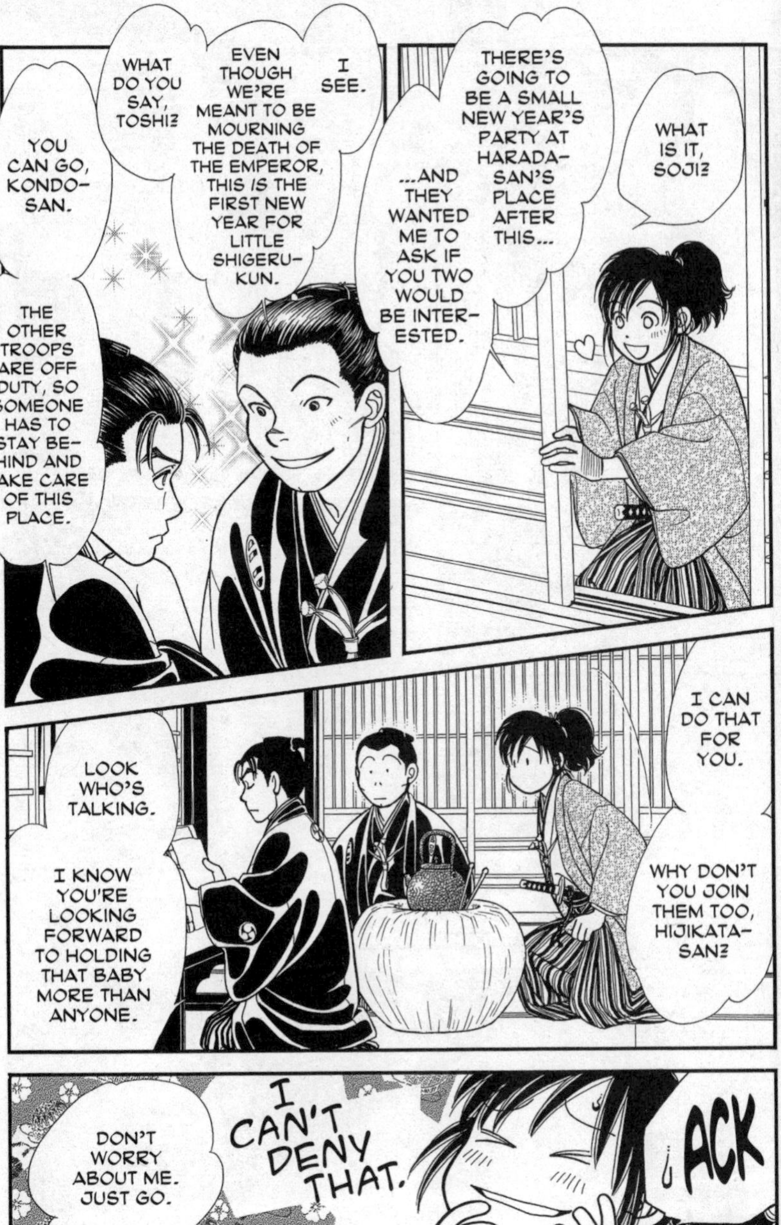
WHAT IS IT, SOJI?
THERE'S GOING TO BE A SMALL NEW YEAR'S PARTY AT HARADA-SAN'S PLACE AFTER THIS...
...AND THEY WANTED ME TO ASK IF YOU TWO WOULD BE INTER-ESTED.
I SEE.
EVEN THOUGH WE'RE MEANT TO BE MOURNING THE DEATH OF THE EMPEROR, THIS *IS* THE FIRST NEW YEAR FOR LITTLE SHIGERU-KUN.
WHAT DO YOU SAY, TOSHI?
YOU CAN GO, KONDO-SAN.
THE OTHER TROOPS ARE OFF DUTY, SO SOMEONE HAS TO STAY BE-HIND AND TAKE CARE OF THIS PLACE.
I CAN DO THAT FOR YOU.
WHY DON'T YOU JOIN THEM TOO, HIJIKATA-SAN?
LOOK WHO'S TALKING.
I KNOW YOU'RE LOOKING FORWARD TO HOLDING THAT BABY MORE THAN ANYONE.
ACK
I CAN'T DENY THAT.
DON'T WORRY ABOUT ME. JUST GO.

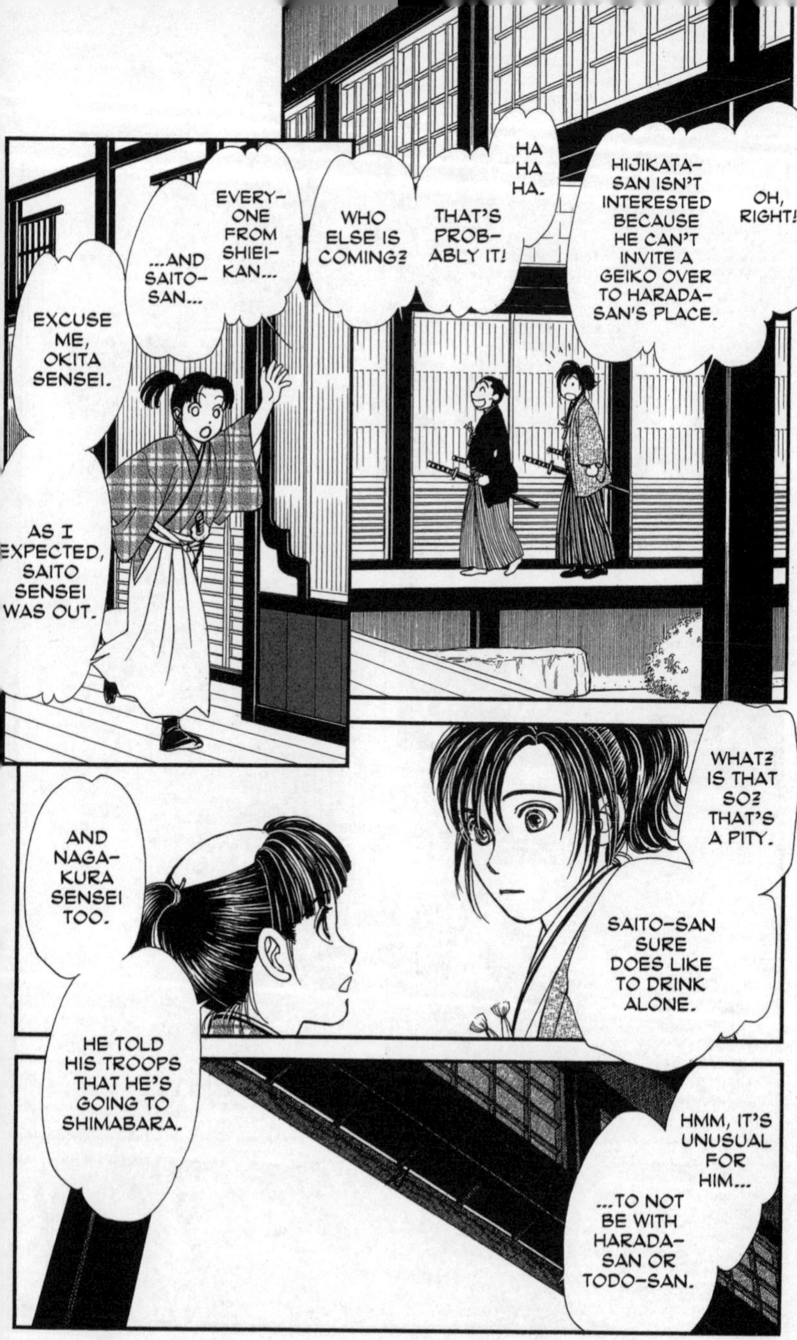
OH, RIGHT!
HIJIKATA-SAN ISN'T INTERESTED BECAUSE HE CAN'T INVITE A GEIKO OVER TO HARADA-SAN'S PLACE.
HA HA HA.
THAT'S PROB-ABLY IT!
WHO ELSE IS COMING?
EVERY-ONE FROM SHIEI-KAN...
...AND SAITO-SAN...
EXCUSE ME, OKITA SENSEI.
AS I EXPECTED, SAITO SENSEI WAS OUT.
WHAT? IS THAT SO? THAT'S A PITY.
SAITO-SAN SURE DOES LIKE TO DRINK ALONE.
AND NAGA-KURA SENSEI TOO.
HE TOLD HIS TROOPS THAT HE'S GOING TO SHIMABARA.
HMM, IT'S UNUSUAL FOR HIM...
...TO NOT BE WITH HARADA-SAN OR TODO-SAN.

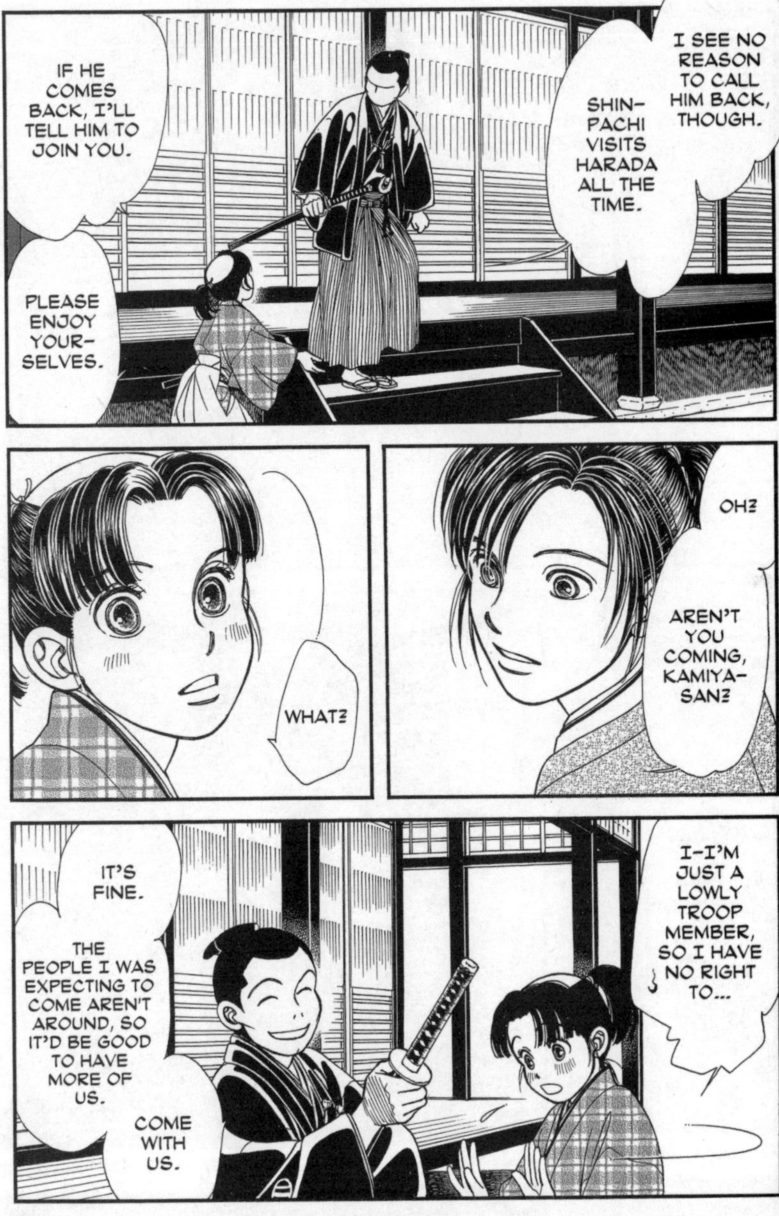
I SEE NO REASON TO CALL HIM BACK, THOUGH.
SHIN-PACHI VISITS HARADA ALL THE TIME.
IF HE COMES BACK, I'LL TELL HIM TO JOIN YOU.
PLEASE ENJOY YOUR-SELVES.
OH?
AREN'T YOU COMING, KAMIYA-SAN?
WHAT?
I-I'M JUST A LOWLY TROOP MEMBER, SO I HAVE NO RIGHT TO...
...
IT'S FINE.
THE PEOPLE I WAS EXPECTING TO COME AREN'T AROUND, SO IT'D BE GOOD TO HAVE MORE OF US.
COME WITH US.

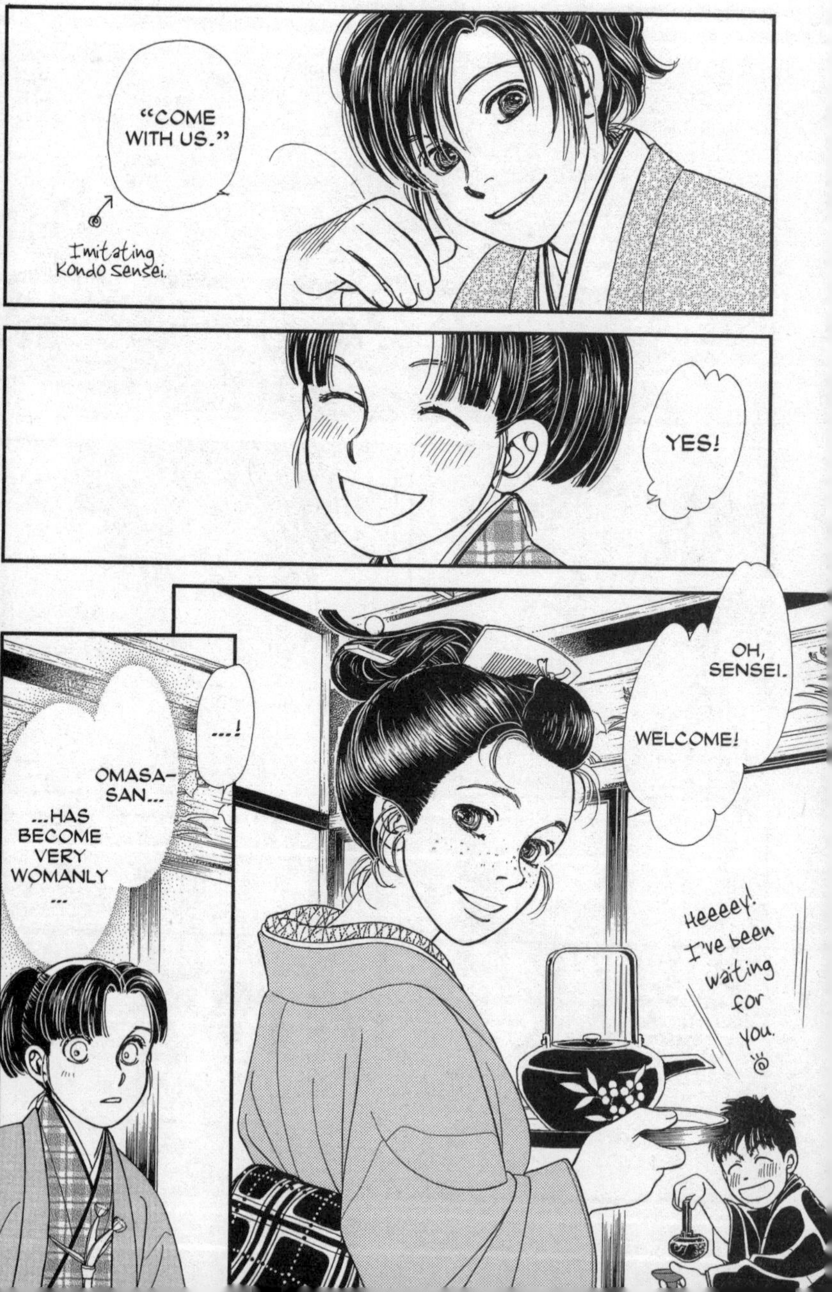
"COME WITH US."
Imitating Kondo Sensei.
YES!
OH, SENSEI.
WELCOME!
...!
Heeeey! I've been waiting for you.
OMASA-SAN...
...HAS BECOME VERY WOMANLY ...

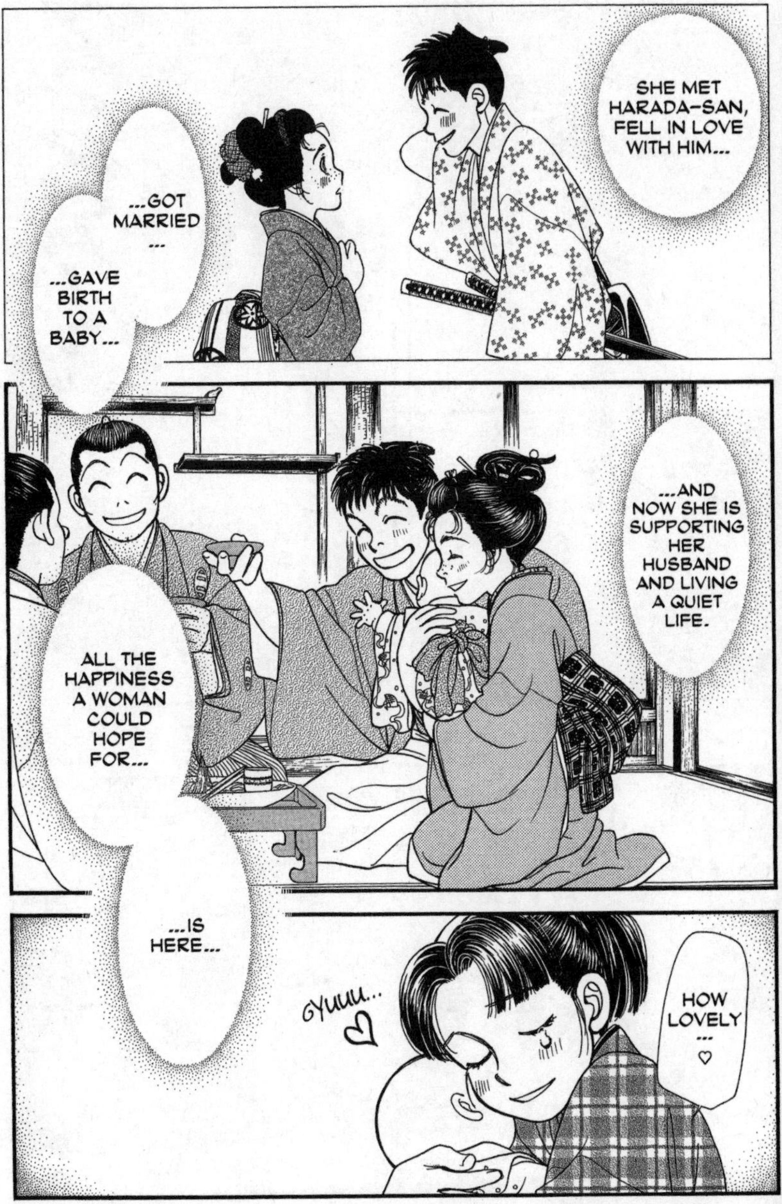
SHE MET HARADA-SAN, FELL IN LOVE WITH HIM...
...GOT MARRIED ...
...GAVE BIRTH TO A BABY...
...AND NOW SHE IS SUPPORTING HER HUSBAND AND LIVING A QUIET LIFE.
ALL THE HAPPINESS A WOMAN COULD HOPE FOR...
...IS HERE...
HOW LOVELY ... ♡
GYUUU... ♡

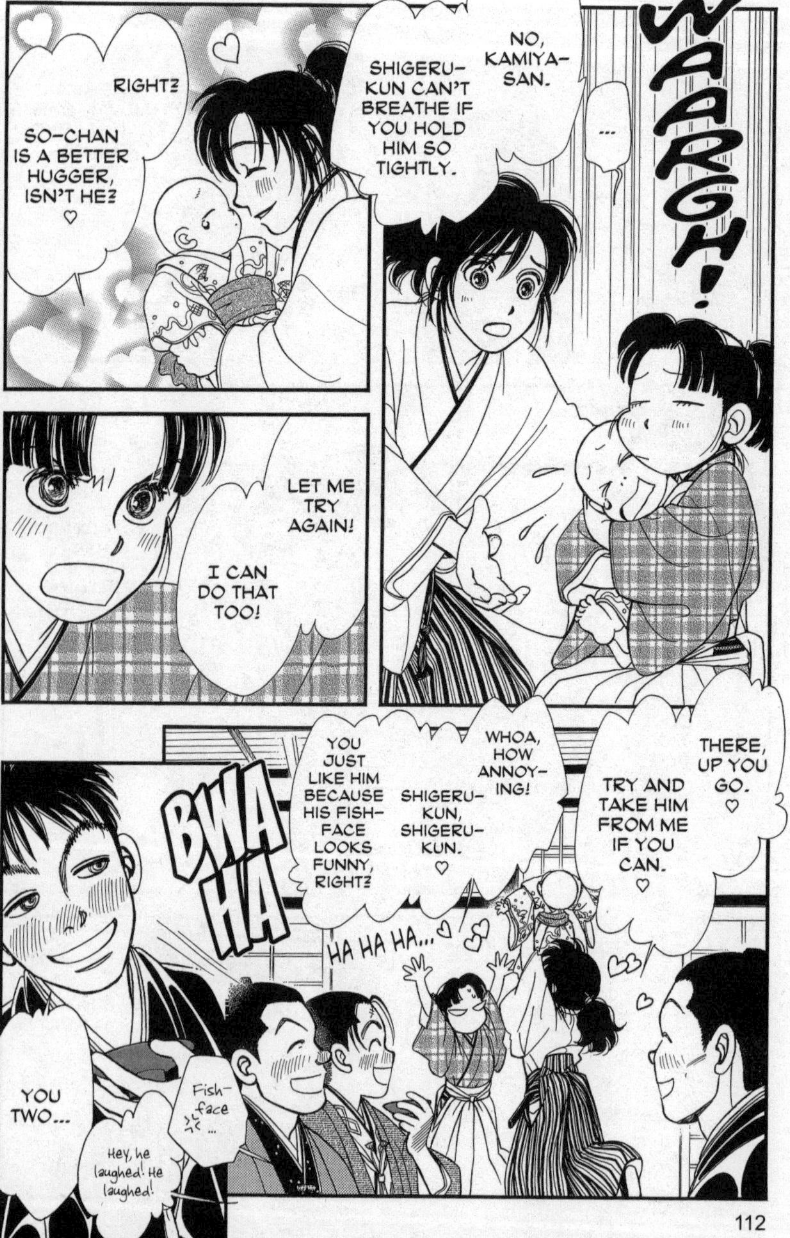
WAARGH!
...
NO, KAMIYA-SAN.
SHIGERU-KUN CAN'T BREATHE IF YOU HOLD HIM SO TIGHTLY.
RIGHT?
SO-CHAN IS A BETTER HUGGER, ISN'T HE? ♡
LET ME TRY AGAIN!
I CAN DO THAT TOO!
THERE, UP YOU GO. ♡
TRY AND TAKE HIM FROM ME IF YOU CAN. ♡
WHOA, HOW ANNOYING!
SHIGERU-KUN, SHIGERU-KUN. ♡
YOU JUST LIKE HIM BECAUSE HIS FISH-FACE LOOKS FUNNY, RIGHT?
BWA HA
HA HA HA...
YOU TWO...
Fish-face ...
Hey, he laughed! He laughed!

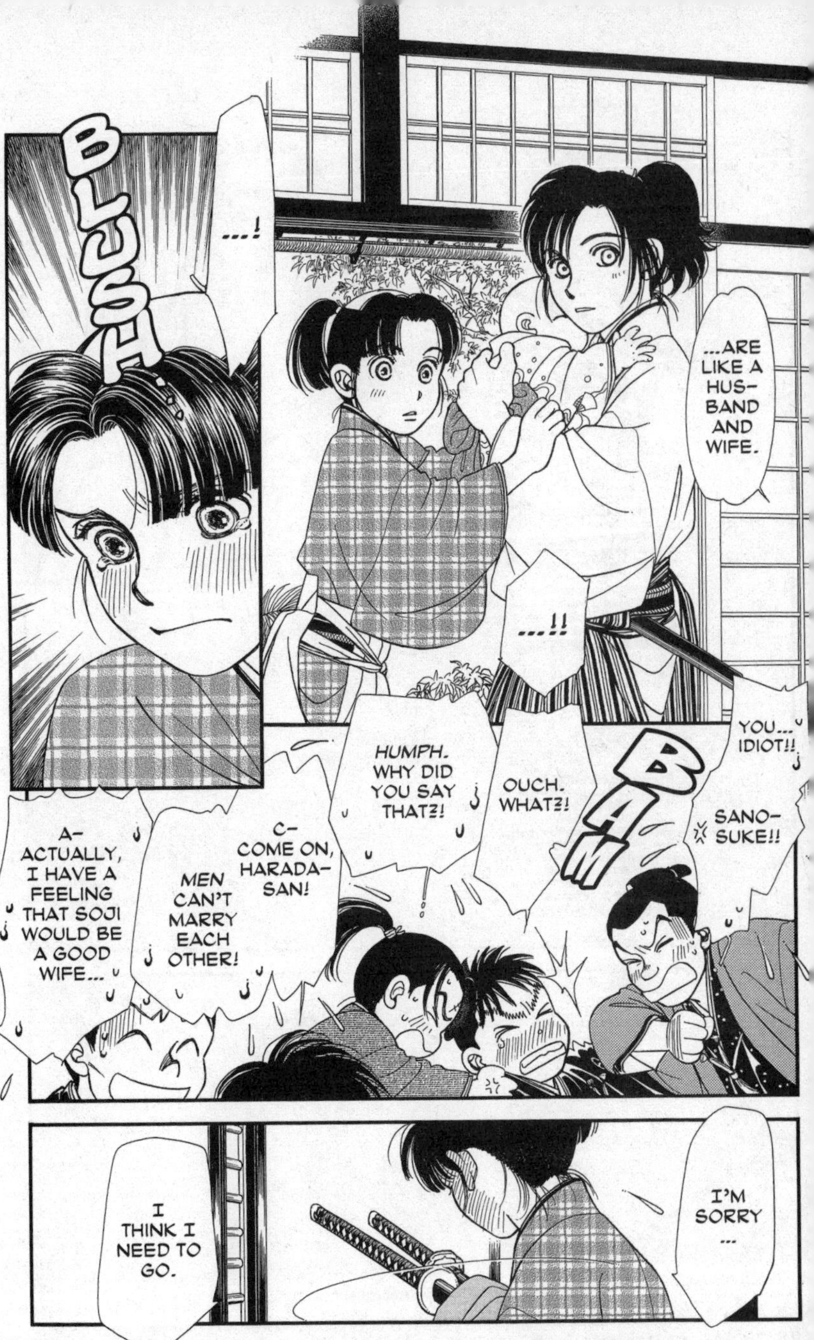
...ARE LIKE A HUS- BAND AND WIFE.
...!!
BLUSH
...!
YOU... IDIOT!!
SANO- SUKE!!
BAM
OUCH. WHAT?!
HUMPH. WHY DID YOU SAY THAT?!
C- COME ON, HARADA- SAN!
MEN CAN'T MARRY EACH OTHER!
A- ACTUALLY, I HAVE A FEELING THAT SOJI WOULD BE A GOOD WIFE...
I'M SORRY ...
I THINK I NEED TO GO.

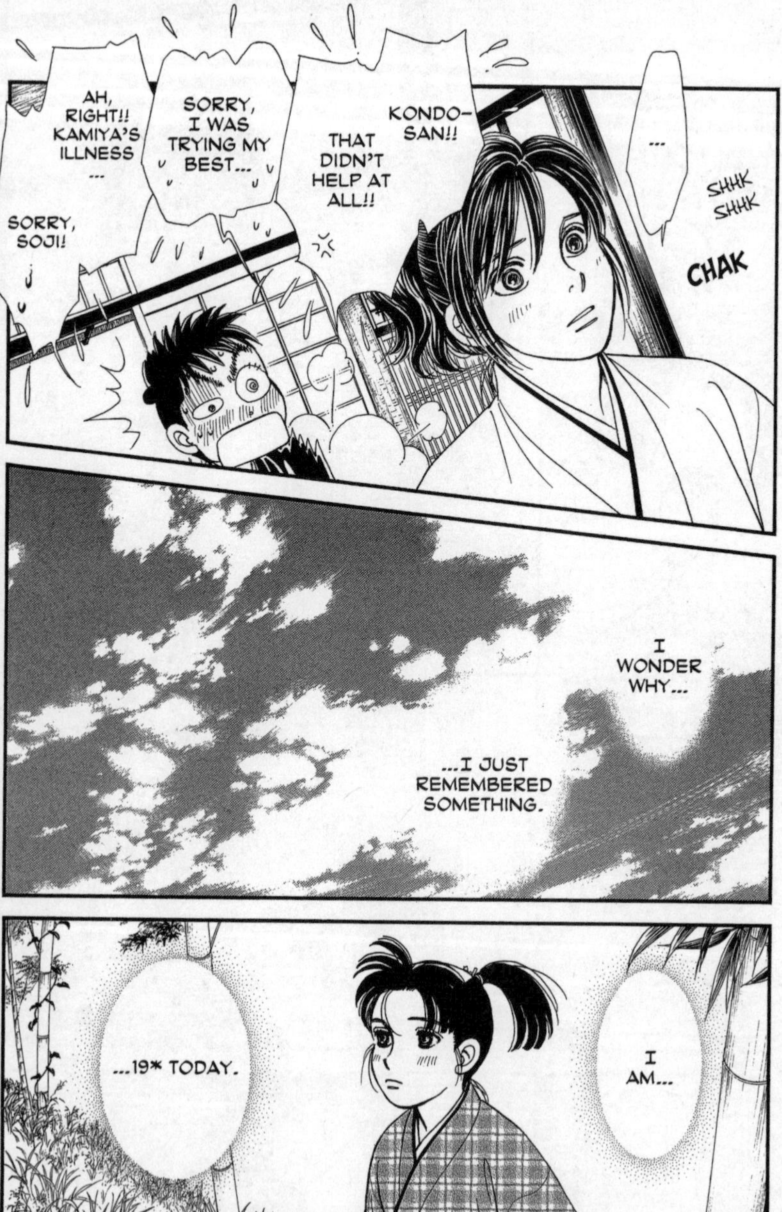
...
SHHK SHHK
CHAK
KONDO-SAN!!
THAT DIDN'T HELP AT ALL!!
SORRY, I WAS TRYING MY BEST...
AH, RIGHT!! KAMIYA'S ILLNESS ...
SORRY, SOJI!
I WONDER WHY...
...I JUST REMEMBERED SOMETHING.
I AM...
...19* TODAY.

*By East Asian age reckoning, you are one year old when you are born and then add one year to your age each New Year's day.

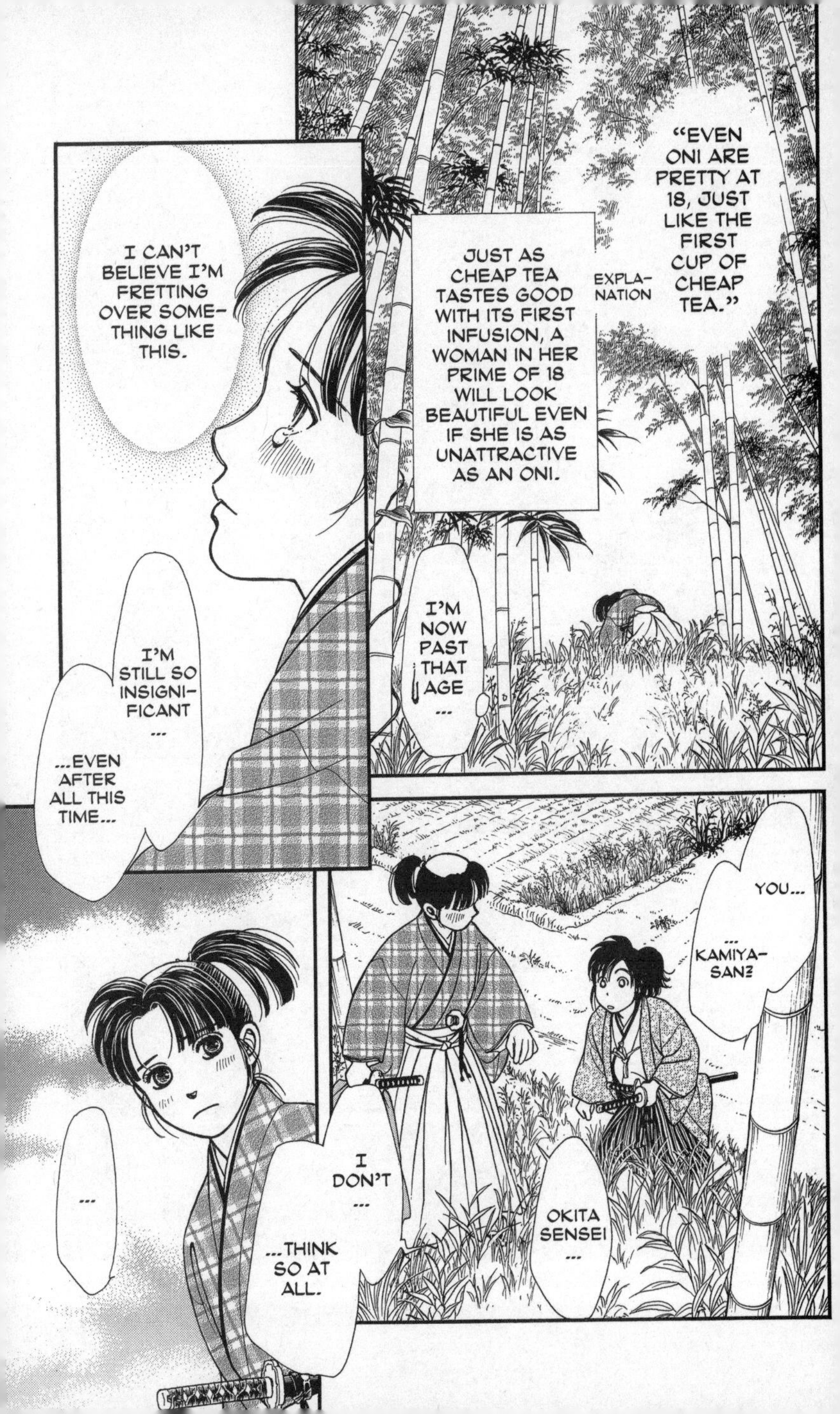
"EVEN ONI ARE PRETTY AT 18, JUST LIKE THE FIRST CUP OF CHEAP TEA."
EXPLANATION
JUST AS CHEAP TEA TASTES GOOD WITH ITS FIRST INFUSION, A WOMAN IN HER PRIME OF 18 WILL LOOK BEAUTIFUL EVEN IF SHE IS AS UNATTRACTIVE AS AN ONI.
I'M NOW PAST THAT AGE...
I CAN'T BELIEVE I'M FRETTING OVER SOMETHING LIKE THIS.
I'M STILL SO INSIGNIFICANT...
...EVEN AFTER ALL THIS TIME...
YOU...
...KAMIYA-SAN?
OKITA SENSEI...
...
I DON'T...
...THINK SO AT ALL.

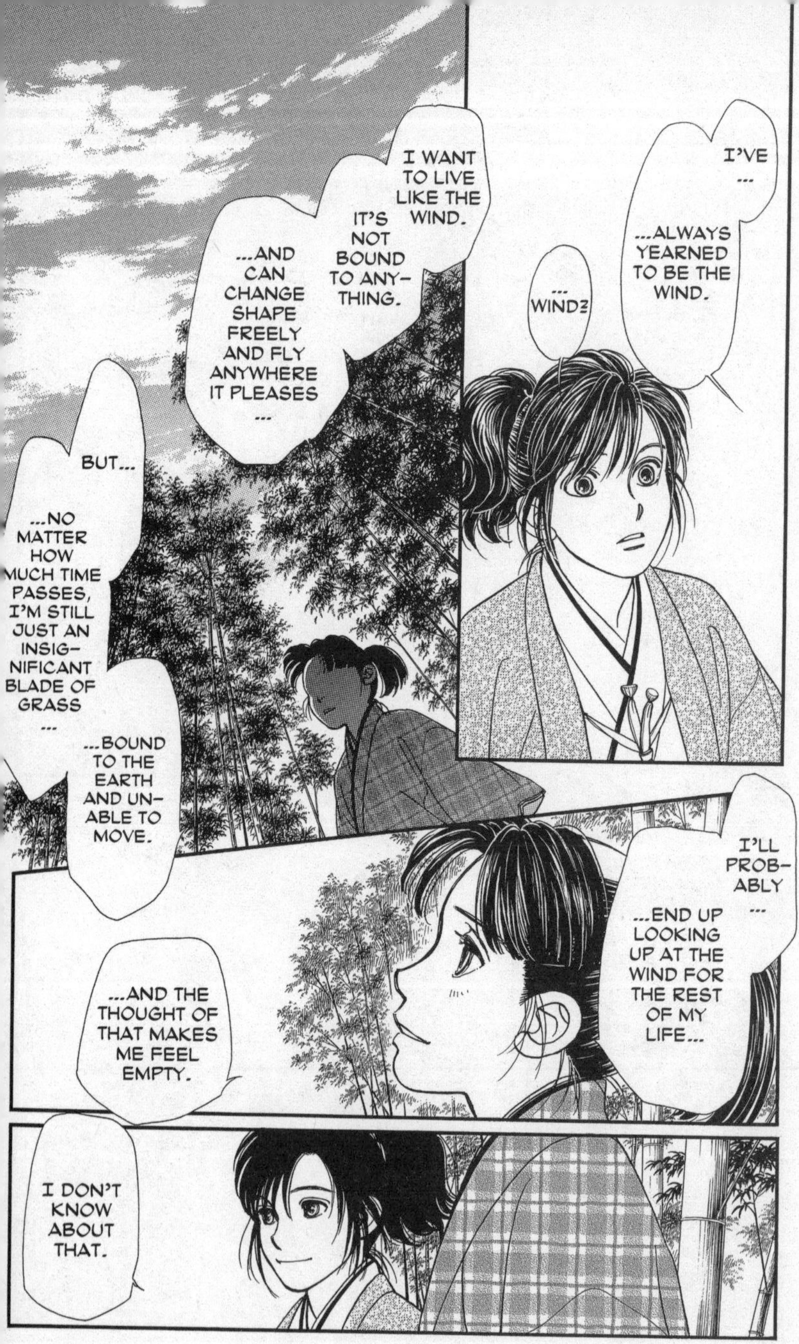
I'VE ...
...ALWAYS YEARNED TO BE THE WIND.
...WIND?
I WANT TO LIVE LIKE THE WIND.
IT'S NOT BOUND TO ANYTHING.
...AND CAN CHANGE SHAPE FREELY AND FLY ANYWHERE IT PLEASES ...
BUT...
...NO MATTER HOW MUCH TIME PASSES, I'M STILL JUST AN INSIGNIFICANT BLADE OF GRASS ...
...BOUND TO THE EARTH AND UNABLE TO MOVE.
I'LL PROBABLY ...
...END UP LOOKING UP AT THE WIND FOR THE REST OF MY LIFE...
...AND THE THOUGHT OF THAT MAKES ME FEEL EMPTY.
I DON'T KNOW ABOUT THAT.

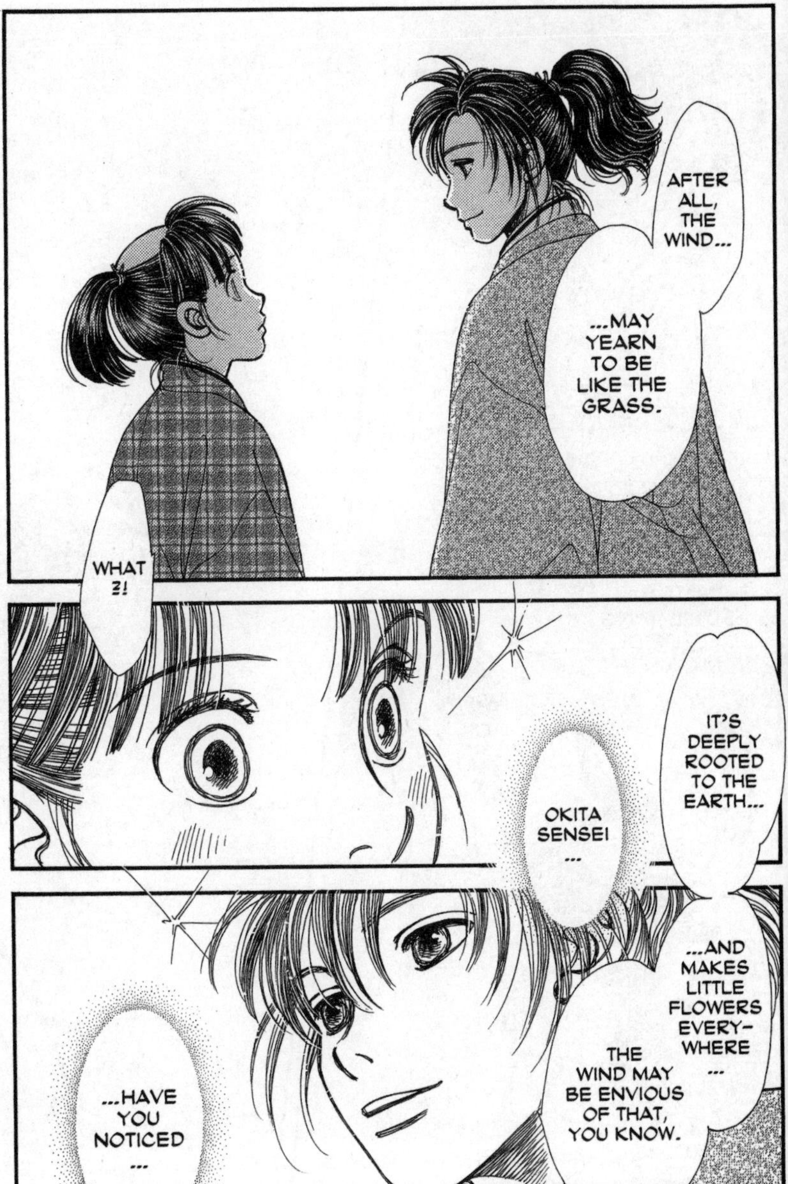
AFTER ALL, THE WIND...
...MAY YEARN TO BE LIKE THE GRASS.
WHAT?!
IT'S DEEPLY ROOTED TO THE EARTH...
OKITA SENSEI...
...AND MAKES LITTLE FLOWERS EVERYWHERE...
THE WIND MAY BE ENVIOUS OF THAT, YOU KNOW.
...HAVE YOU NOTICED...

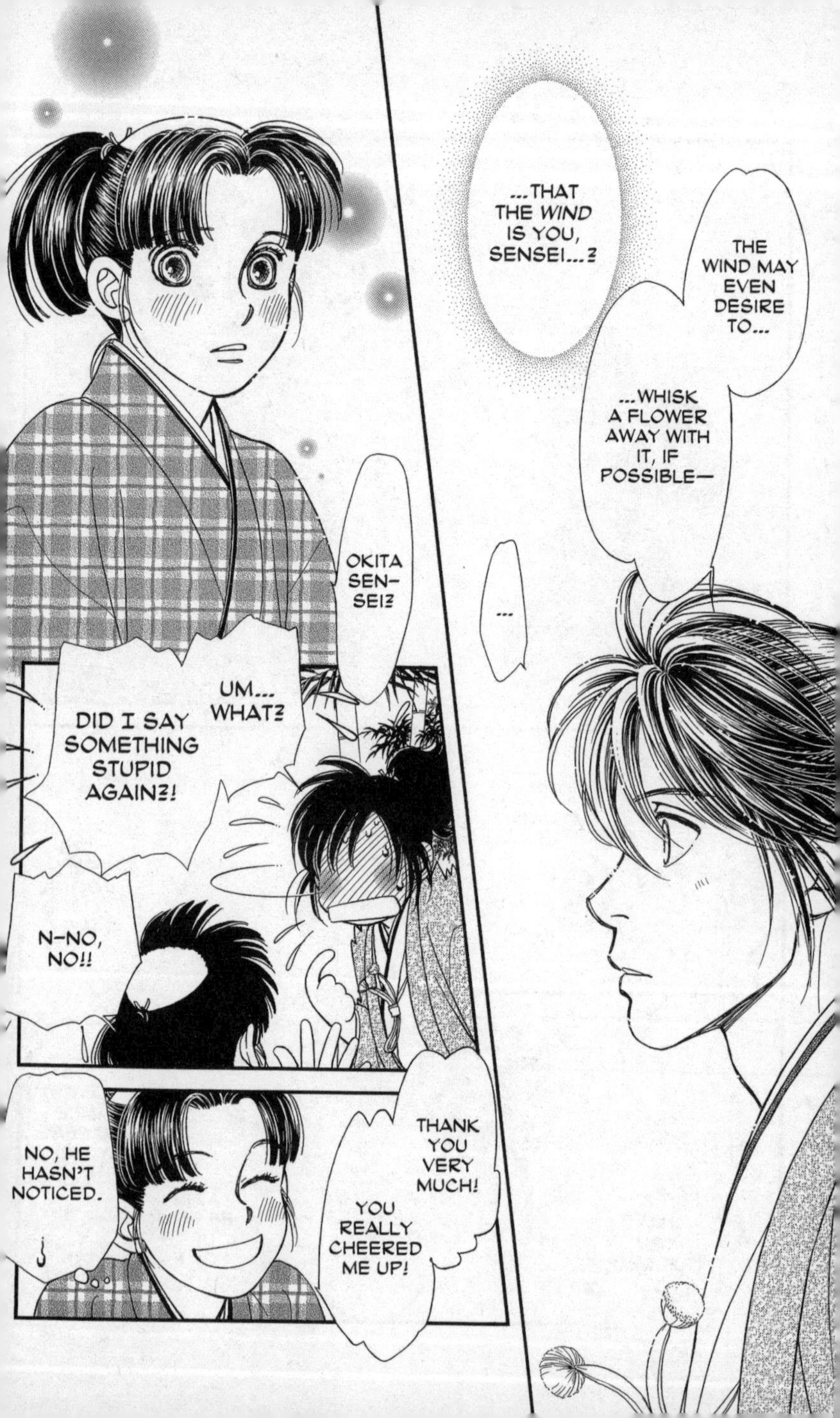

THE WIND MAY EVEN DESIRE TO...
...WHISK A FLOWER AWAY WITH IT, IF POSSIBLE—
...THAT THE *WIND* IS YOU, SENSEI...?
...
OKITA SEN-SEI?
UM... WHAT?
DID I SAY SOMETHING STUPID AGAIN?!
N-NO, NO!!
THANK YOU VERY MUCH!
YOU REALLY CHEERED ME UP!
NO, HE HASN'T NOTICED.

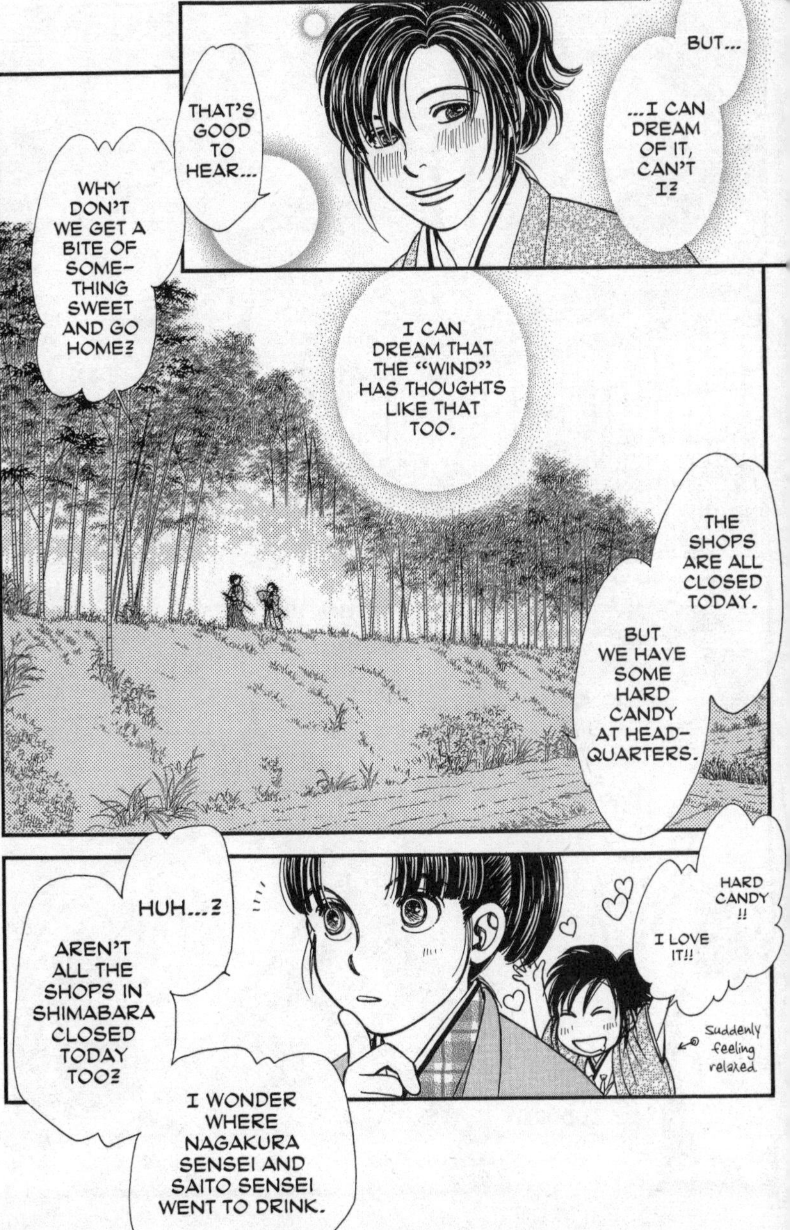

BUT...
...I CAN DREAM OF IT, CAN'T I?
THAT'S GOOD TO HEAR...
I CAN DREAM THAT THE "WIND" HAS THOUGHTS LIKE THAT TOO.
WHY DON'T WE GET A BITE OF SOME-THING SWEET AND GO HOME?
THE SHOPS ARE ALL CLOSED TODAY.
BUT WE HAVE SOME HARD CANDY AT HEAD-QUARTERS.
HARD CANDY !!
I LOVE IT!!
Suddenly feeling relaxed
HUH...?
AREN'T ALL THE SHOPS IN SHIMABARA CLOSED TODAY TOO?
I WONDER WHERE NAGAKURA SENSEI AND SAITO SENSEI WENT TO DRINK.

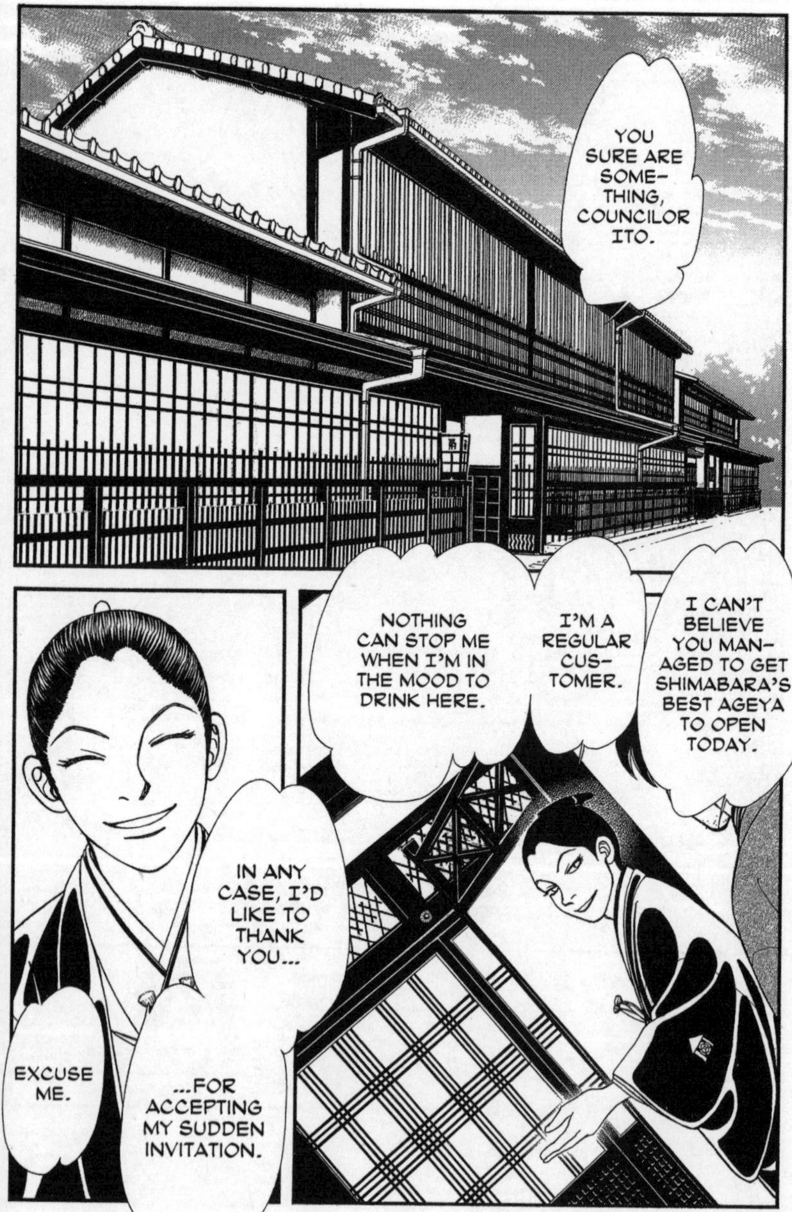
YOU SURE ARE SOME-THING, COUNCILOR ITO.
I CAN'T BELIEVE YOU MAN-AGED TO GET SHIMABARA'S BEST AGEYA TO OPEN TODAY.
I'M A REGULAR CUS-TOMER.
NOTHING CAN STOP ME WHEN I'M IN THE MOOD TO DRINK HERE.
IN ANY CASE, I'D LIKE TO THANK YOU...
...FOR ACCEPTING MY SUDDEN INVITATION.
EXCUSE ME.

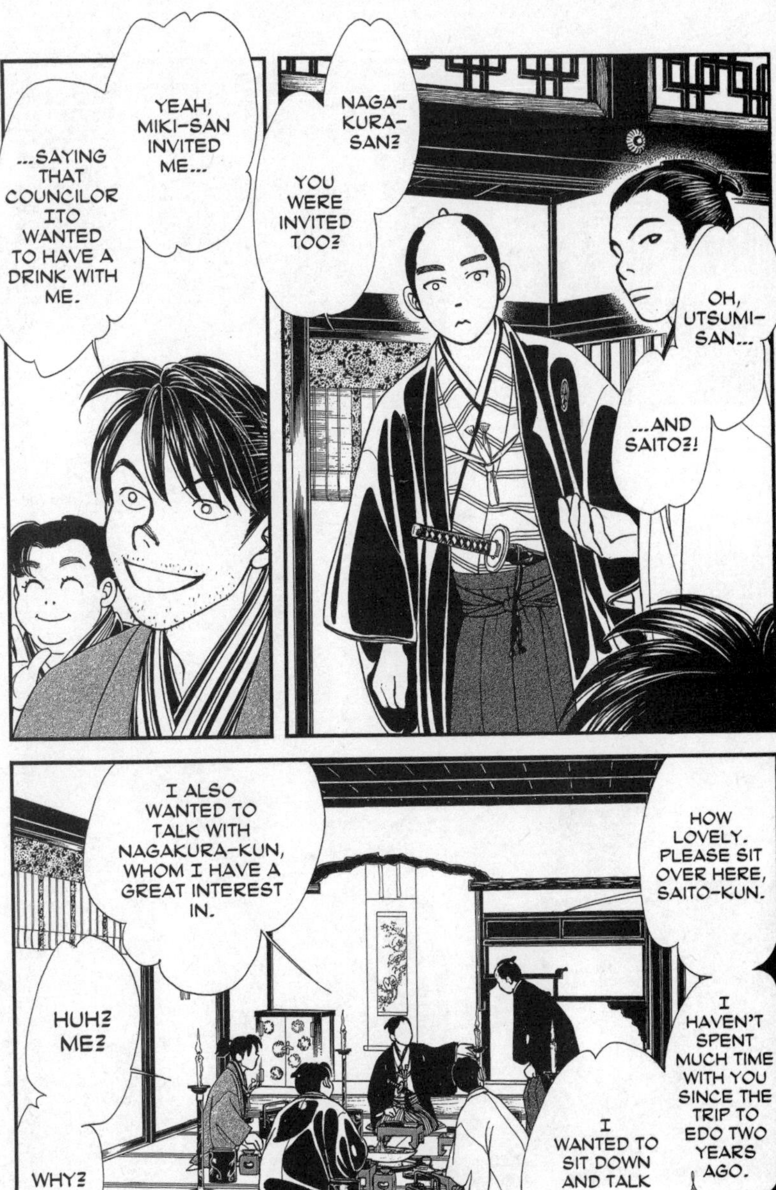
OH, UTSUMI-SAN...
...AND SAITO?!
NAGA-KURA-SAN?
YOU WERE INVITED TOO?
YEAH, MIKI-SAN INVITED ME...
...SAYING THAT COUNCILOR ITO WANTED TO HAVE A DRINK WITH ME.
HOW LOVELY. PLEASE SIT OVER HERE, SAITO-KUN.
I HAVEN'T SPENT MUCH TIME WITH YOU SINCE THE TRIP TO EDO TWO YEARS AGO.
I WANTED TO SIT DOWN AND TALK WITH YOU.
I ALSO WANTED TO TALK WITH NAGAKURA-KUN, WHOM I HAVE A GREAT INTEREST IN.
HUH? ME?
WHY?

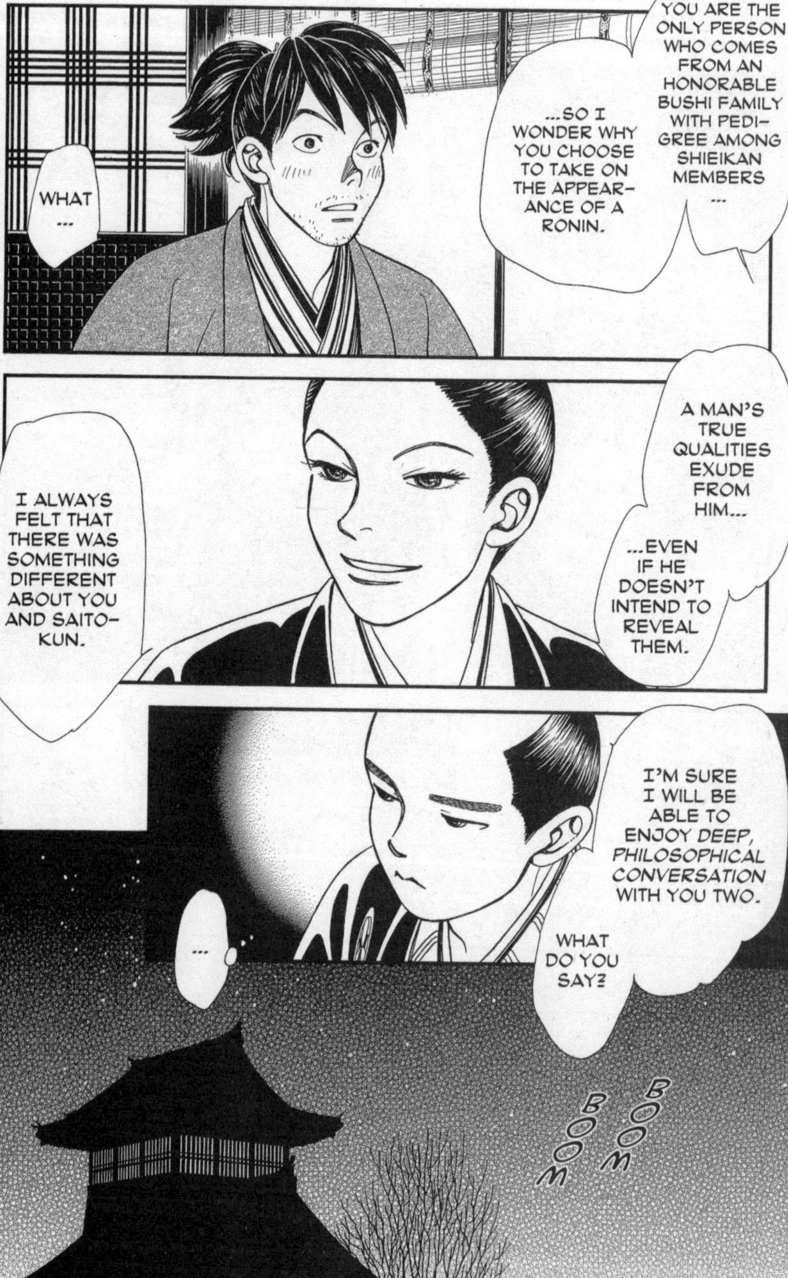

YOU ARE THE ONLY PERSON WHO COMES FROM AN HONORABLE BUSHI FAMILY WITH PEDI- GREE AMONG SHIEIKAN MEMBERS ...
...SO I WONDER WHY YOU CHOOSE TO TAKE ON THE APPEAR- ANCE OF A RONIN.
WHAT ...
A MAN'S TRUE QUALITIES EXUDE FROM HIM...
...EVEN IF HE DOESN'T INTEND TO REVEAL THEM.
I ALWAYS FELT THAT THERE WAS SOMETHING DIFFERENT ABOUT YOU AND SAITO- KUN.
I'M SURE I WILL BE ABLE TO ENJOY *DEEP, PHILOSOPHICAL* CONVERSATION WITH YOU TWO.
WHAT DO YOU SAY?
...
BOOM
BOOM

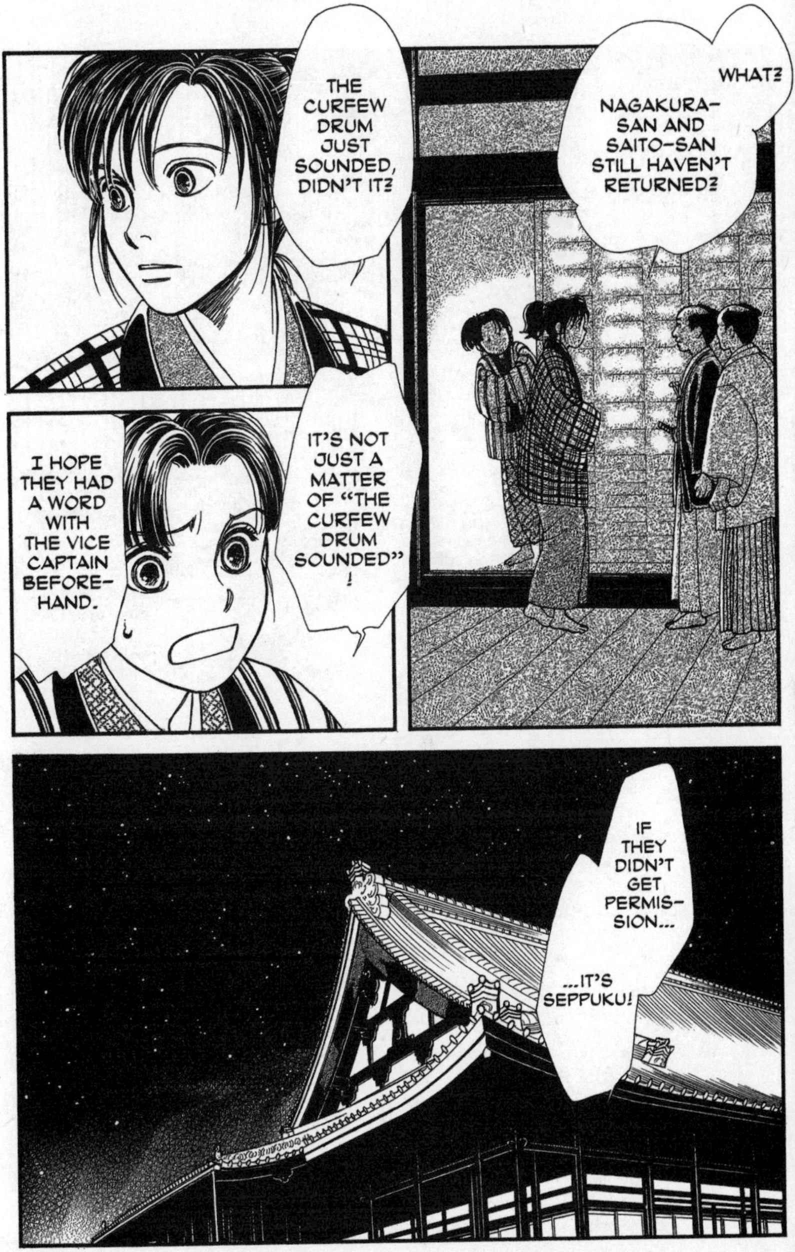
WHAT?
NAGAKURA-SAN AND SAITO-SAN STILL HAVEN'T RETURNED?
THE CURFEW DRUM JUST SOUNDED, DIDN'T IT?
IT'S NOT JUST A MATTER OF "THE CURFEW DRUM SOUNDED"!
I HOPE THEY HAD A WORD WITH THE VICE CAPTAIN BEFOREHAND.
IF THEY DIDN'T GET PERMISSION...
...IT'S SEPPUKU!

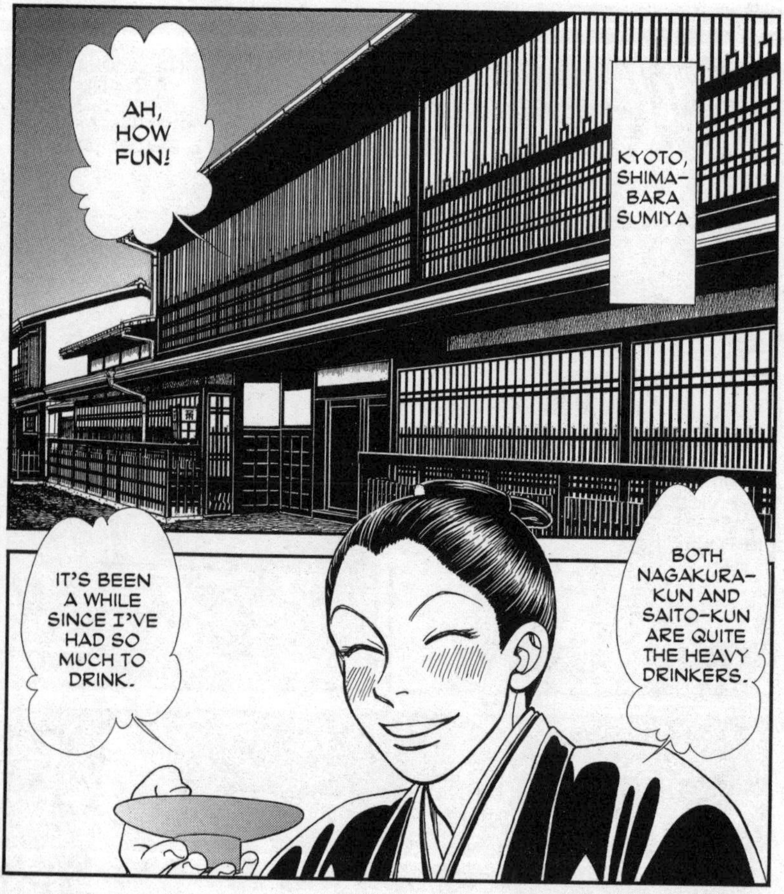
KYOTO, SHIMABARA SUMIYA
AH, HOW FUN!
BOTH NAGAKURA-KUN AND SAITO-KUN ARE QUITE THE HEAVY DRINKERS.
IT'S BEEN A WHILE SINCE I'VE HAD SO MUCH TO DRINK.

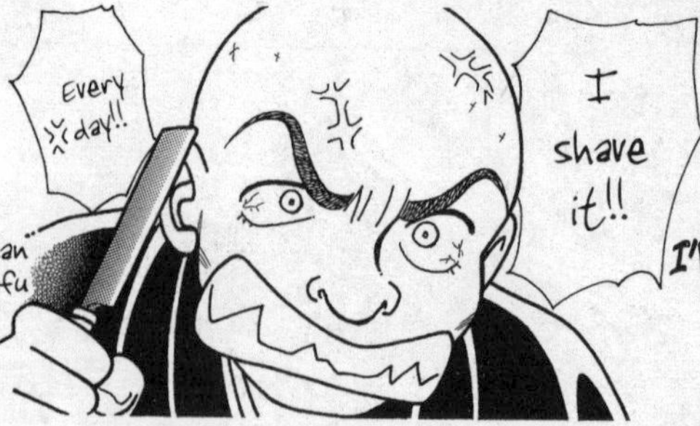
I shave it!!
Every day!!

By TOKO-san from Gifu

KAZE HIKARU SENRYU

**DARN IT
I'VE HAD MY BALD HEAD
AND DROOPY EYES
SINCE BIRTH**

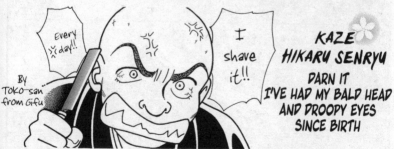

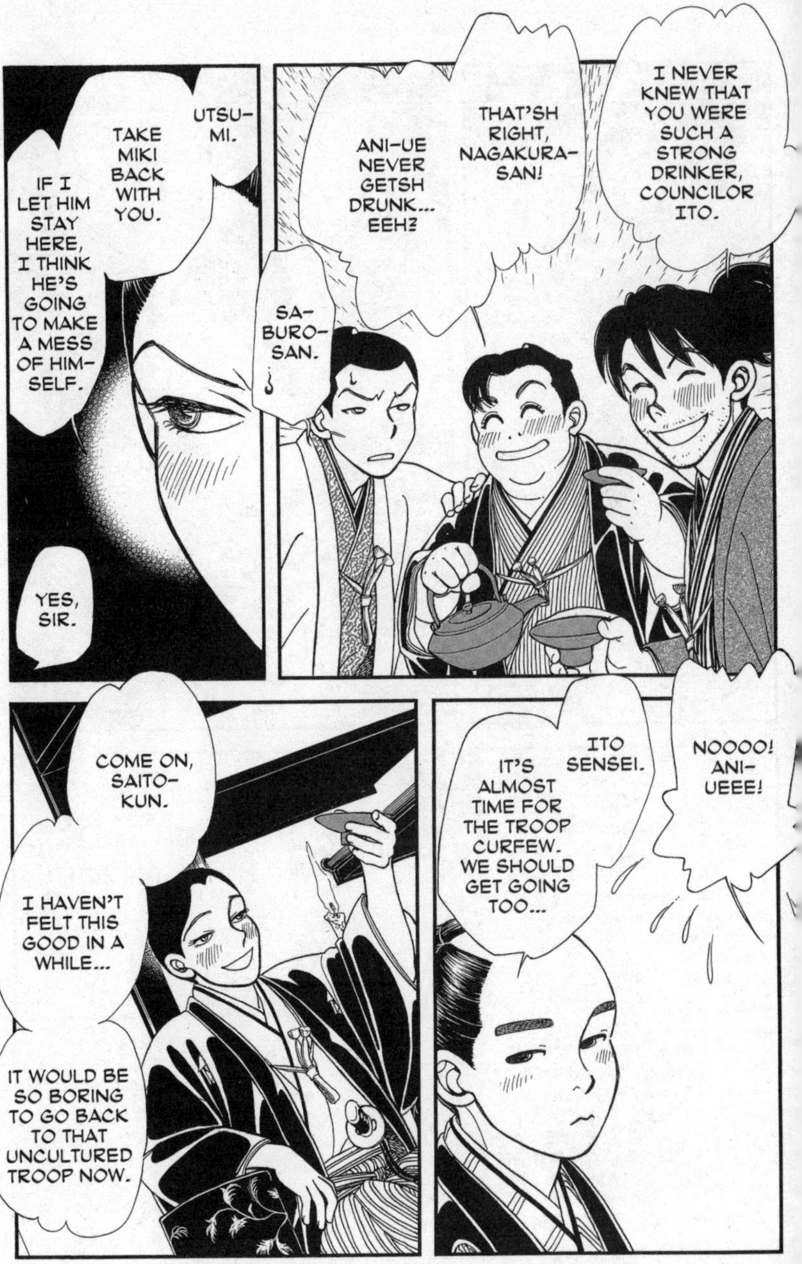
I NEVER KNEW THAT YOU WERE SUCH A STRONG DRINKER, COUNCILOR ITO.
THAT'SH RIGHT, NAGAKURA-SAN!
ANI-UE NEVER GETSH DRUNK... EEH?
SABURO-SAN.
UTSUMI.
TAKE MIKI BACK WITH YOU.
IF I LET HIM STAY HERE, I THINK HE'S GOING TO MAKE A MESS OF HIMSELF.
YES, SIR.
NOOOO! ANI-UEEE!
ITO SENSEI.
IT'S ALMOST TIME FOR THE TROOP CURFEW. WE SHOULD GET GOING TOO...
COME ON, SAITO-KUN.
I HAVEN'T FELT THIS GOOD IN A WHILE...
IT WOULD BE SO BORING TO GO BACK TO THAT UNCULTURED TROOP NOW.

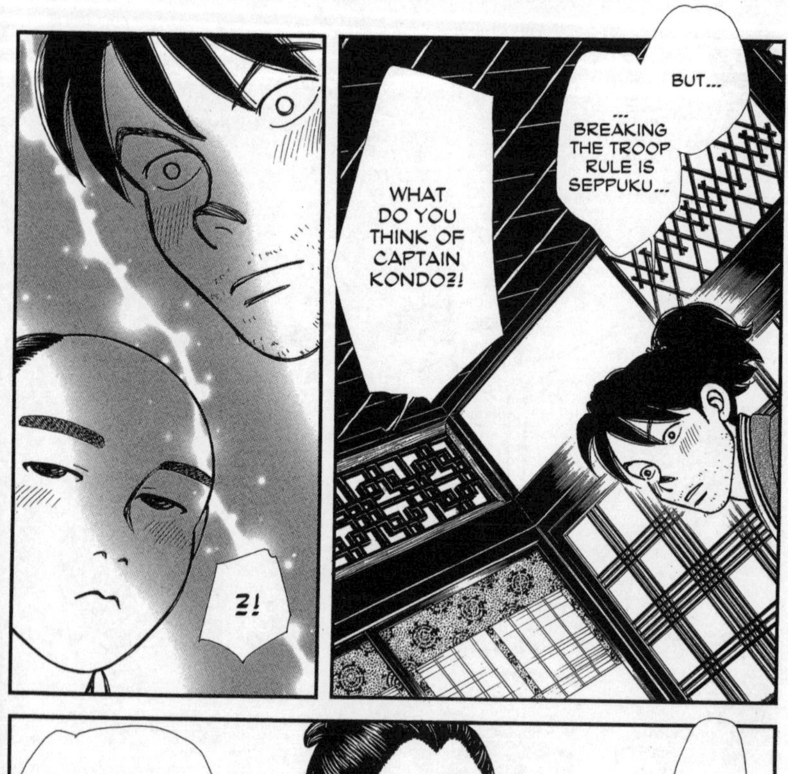
BUT... ...BREAKING THE TROOP RULE IS SEPPUKU...
WHAT DO YOU THINK OF CAPTAIN KONDO?!
?!
FOR EXAM-PLE...
...EVEN IF THE THREE OF US DISOBEYED THE RULES AND STAYED HERE...
...DO YOU THINK THE CAPTAIN IS SUCH A FOOL THAT HE WOULD THOUGHTLESSLY ORDER THE SEPPUKU OF THREE IMPORTANT TROOP MEMBERS?

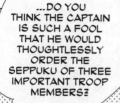

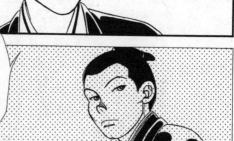

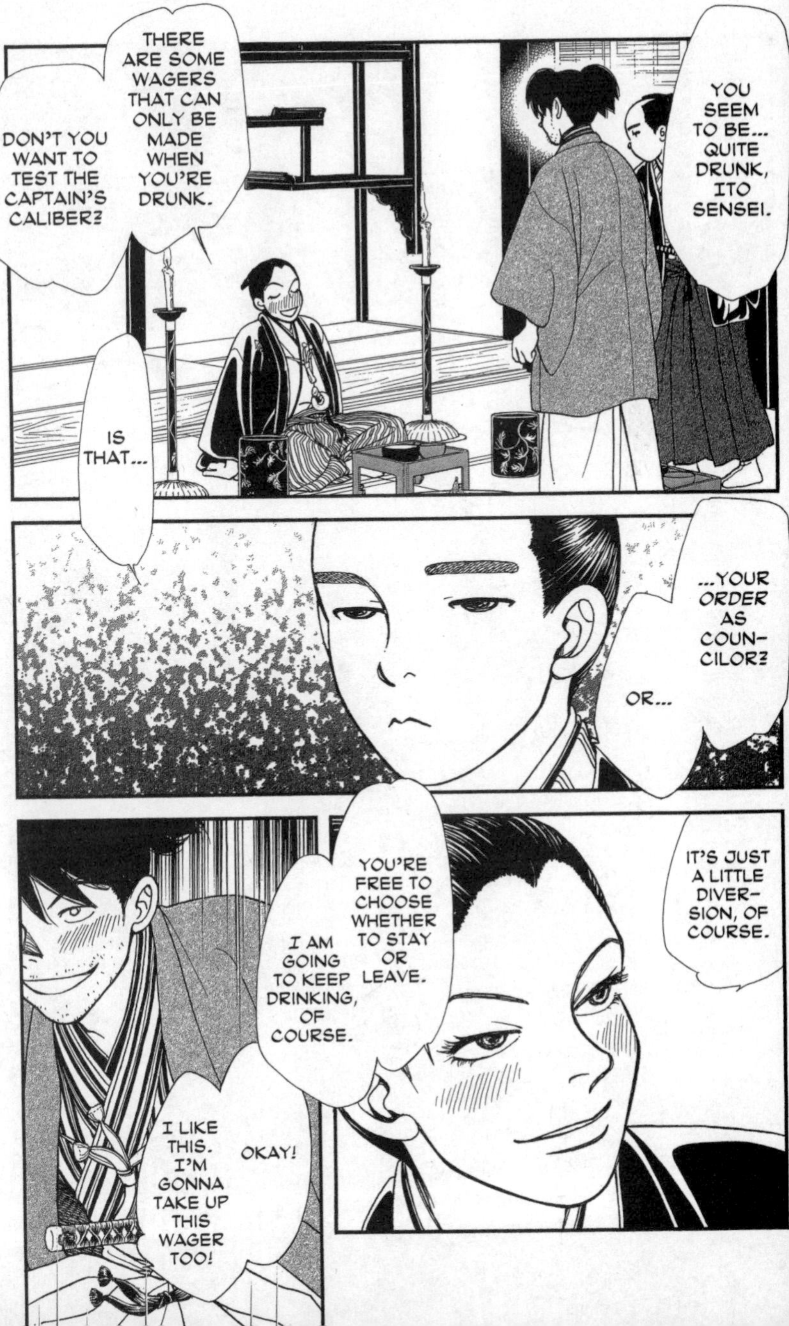
YOU SEEM TO BE... QUITE DRUNK, ITO SENSEI.
THERE ARE SOME WAGERS THAT CAN ONLY BE MADE WHEN YOU'RE DRUNK.
DON'T YOU WANT TO TEST THE CAPTAIN'S CALIBER?
IS THAT...
...YOUR ORDER AS COUNCILOR?
OR...
IT'S JUST A LITTLE DIVERSION, OF COURSE.
YOU'RE FREE TO CHOOSE WHETHER TO STAY OR LEAVE.
I AM GOING TO KEEP DRINKING, OF COURSE.
OKAY!
I LIKE THIS. I'M GONNA TAKE UP THIS WAGER TOO!

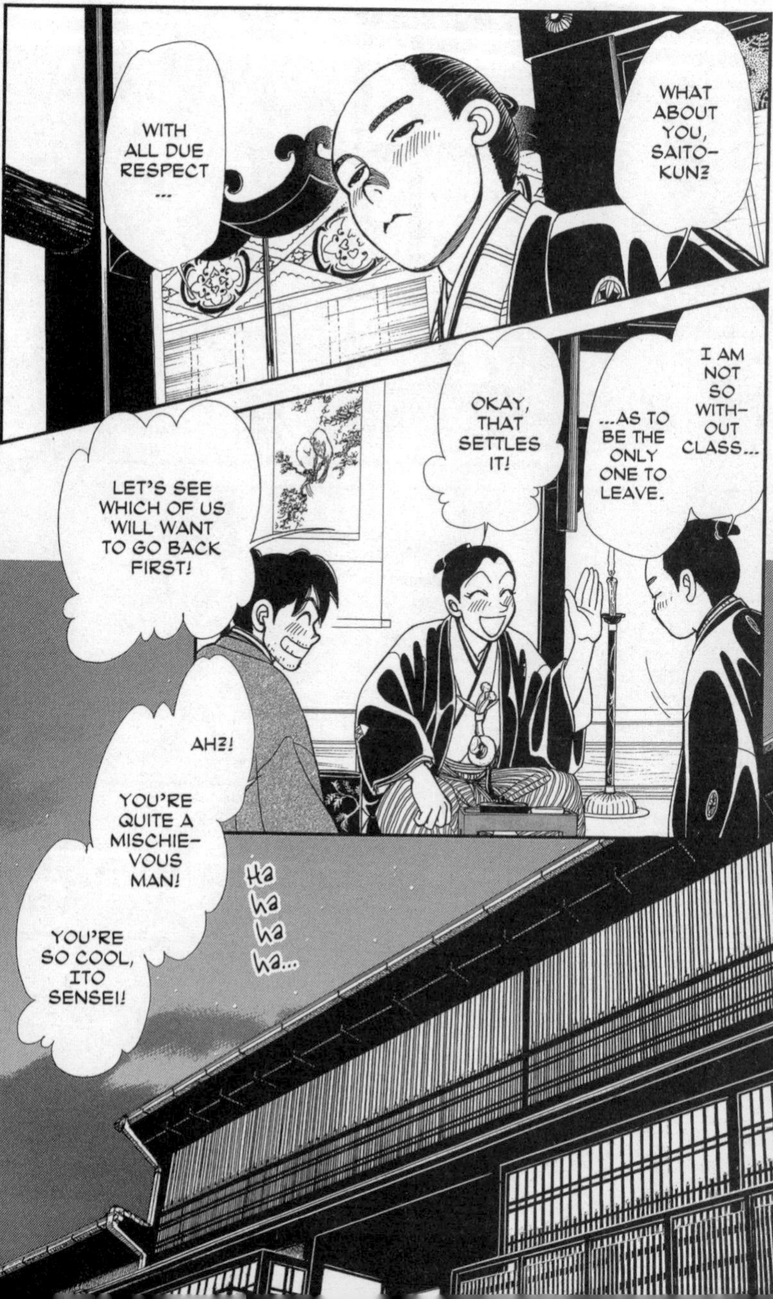
WHAT ABOUT YOU, SAITO-KUN?
WITH ALL DUE RESPECT...
I AM NOT SO WITHOUT CLASS...
...AS TO BE THE ONLY ONE TO LEAVE.
OKAY, THAT SETTLES IT!
LET'S SEE WHICH OF US WILL WANT TO GO BACK FIRST!
AH?!
YOU'RE QUITE A MISCHIEVOUS MAN!
YOU'RE SO COOL, ITO SENSEI!
Ha ha ha ha...

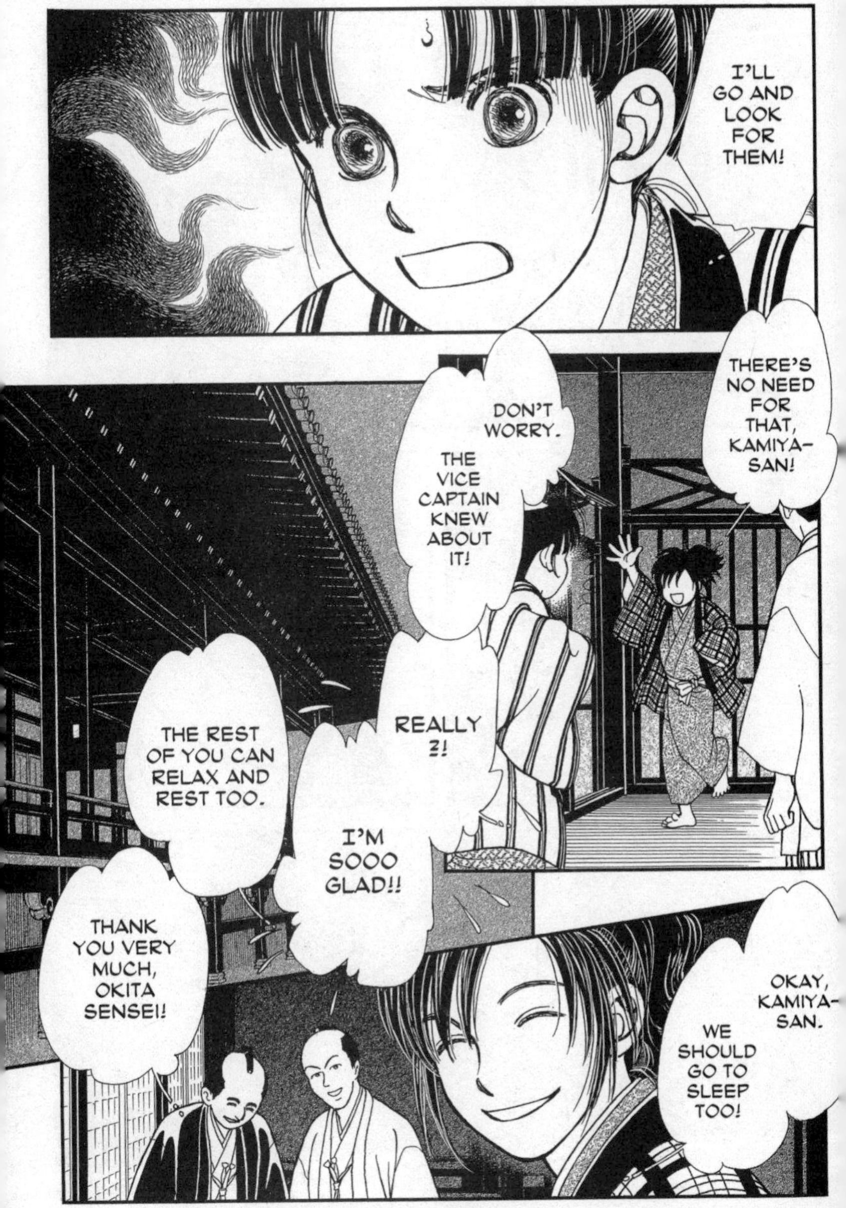
I'LL GO AND LOOK FOR THEM!
THERE'S NO NEED FOR THAT, KAMIYA-SAN!
DON'T WORRY.
THE VICE CAPTAIN KNEW ABOUT IT!
REALLY ?!
THE REST OF YOU CAN RELAX AND REST TOO.
I'M SOOO GLAD!!
THANK YOU VERY MUCH, OKITA SENSEI!
OKAY, KAMIYA-SAN.
WE SHOULD GO TO SLEEP TOO!

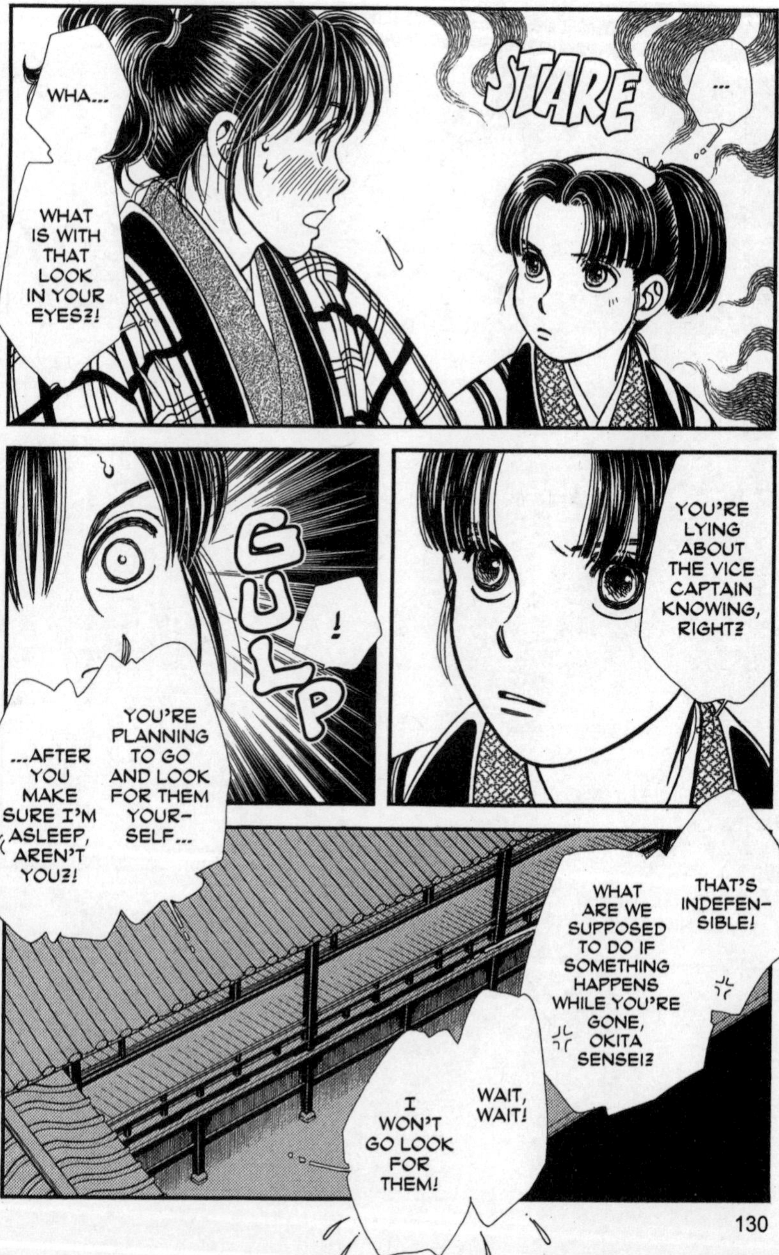
STARE
...
WHA...
WHAT IS WITH THAT LOOK IN YOUR EYES?!
YOU'RE LYING ABOUT THE VICE CAPTAIN KNOWING, RIGHT?
GULP
!
YOU'RE PLANNING TO GO AND LOOK FOR THEM YOURSELF...
...AFTER YOU MAKE SURE I'M ASLEEP, AREN'T YOU?!
THAT'S INDEFENSIBLE!
WHAT ARE WE SUPPOSED TO DO IF SOMETHING HAPPENS WHILE YOU'RE GONE, OKITA SENSEI?
WAIT, WAIT!
I WON'T GO LOOK FOR THEM!

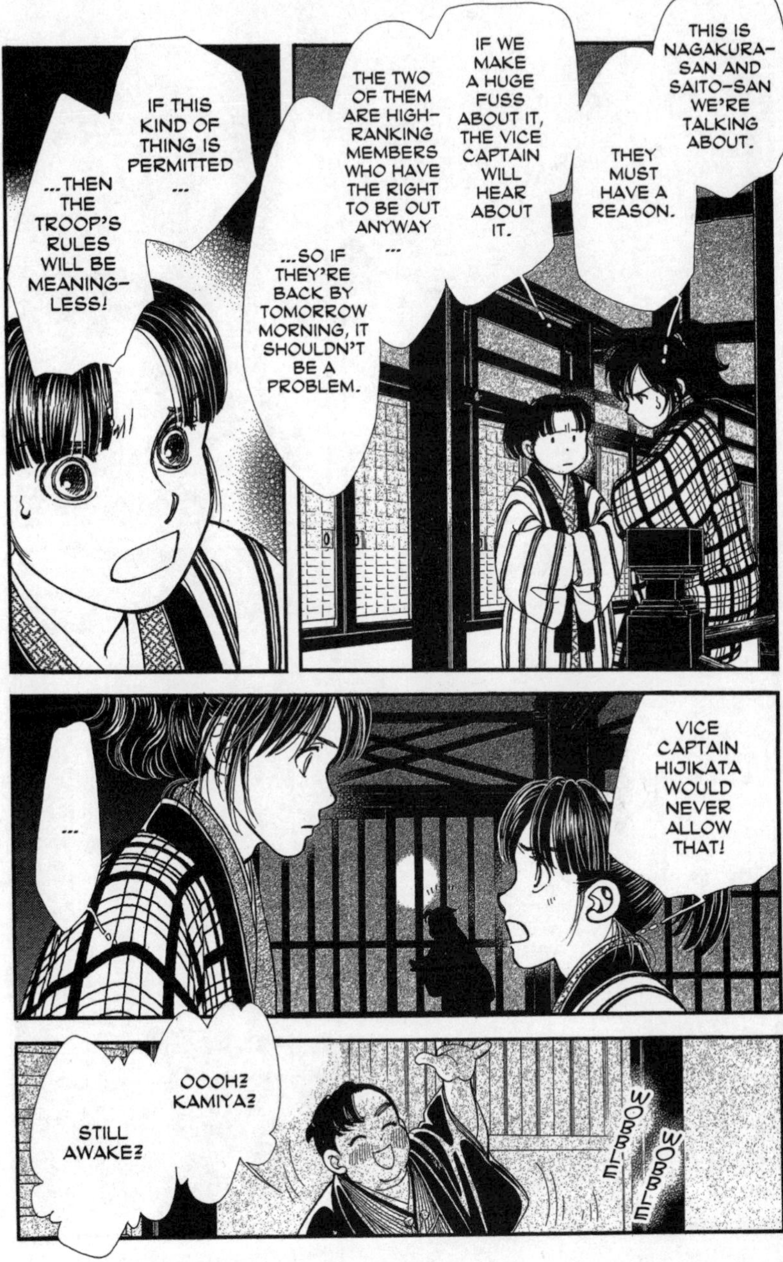
THIS IS NAGAKURA-SAN AND SAITO-SAN WE'RE TALKING ABOUT.
THEY MUST HAVE A REASON.
IF WE MAKE A HUGE FUSS ABOUT IT, THE VICE CAPTAIN WILL HEAR ABOUT IT.
THE TWO OF THEM ARE HIGH-RANKING MEMBERS WHO HAVE THE RIGHT TO BE OUT ANYWAY ...
...SO IF THEY'RE BACK BY TOMORROW MORNING, IT SHOULDN'T BE A PROBLEM.
IF THIS KIND OF THING IS PERMITTED ...
...THEN THE TROOP'S RULES WILL BE MEANINGLESS!
VICE CAPTAIN HIJIKATA WOULD NEVER ALLOW THAT!
...
WOBBLE WOBBLE
OOOH? KAMIYA?
STILL AWAKE?

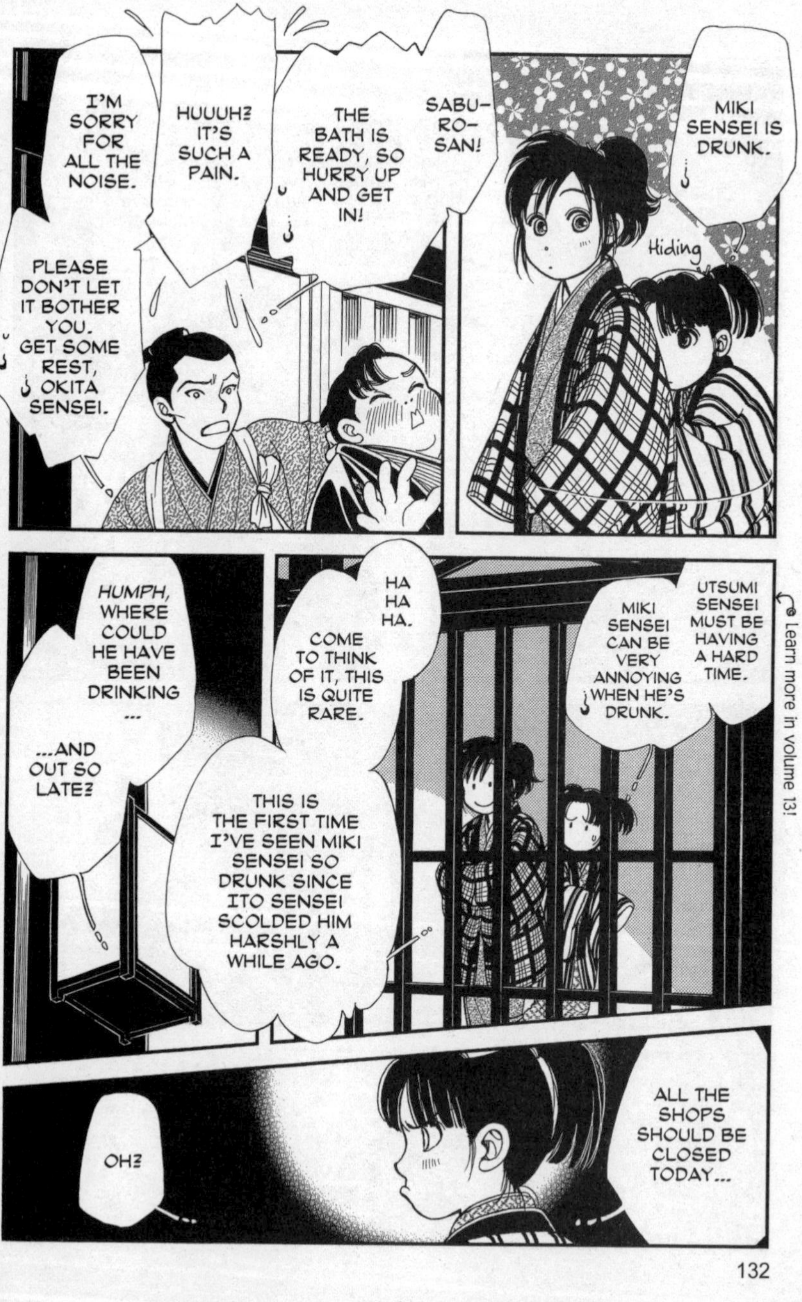
MIKI SENSEI IS DRUNK.
Hiding
SABU-RO-SAN!
THE BATH IS READY, SO HURRY UP AND GET IN!
HUUUH? IT'S SUCH A PAIN.
I'M SORRY FOR ALL THE NOISE.
PLEASE DON'T LET IT BOTHER YOU. GET SOME REST, OKITA SENSEI.
UTSUMI SENSEI MUST BE HAVING A HARD TIME.
Learn more in volume 13!
MIKI SENSEI CAN BE VERY ANNOYING WHEN HE'S DRUNK.
HA HA HA.
COME TO THINK OF IT, THIS IS QUITE RARE.
THIS IS THE FIRST TIME I'VE SEEN MIKI SENSEI SO DRUNK SINCE ITO SENSEI SCOLDED HIM HARSHLY A WHILE AGO.
HUMPH, WHERE COULD HE HAVE BEEN DRINKING...
...AND OUT SO LATE?
ALL THE SHOPS SHOULD BE CLOSED TODAY...
OH?

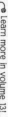

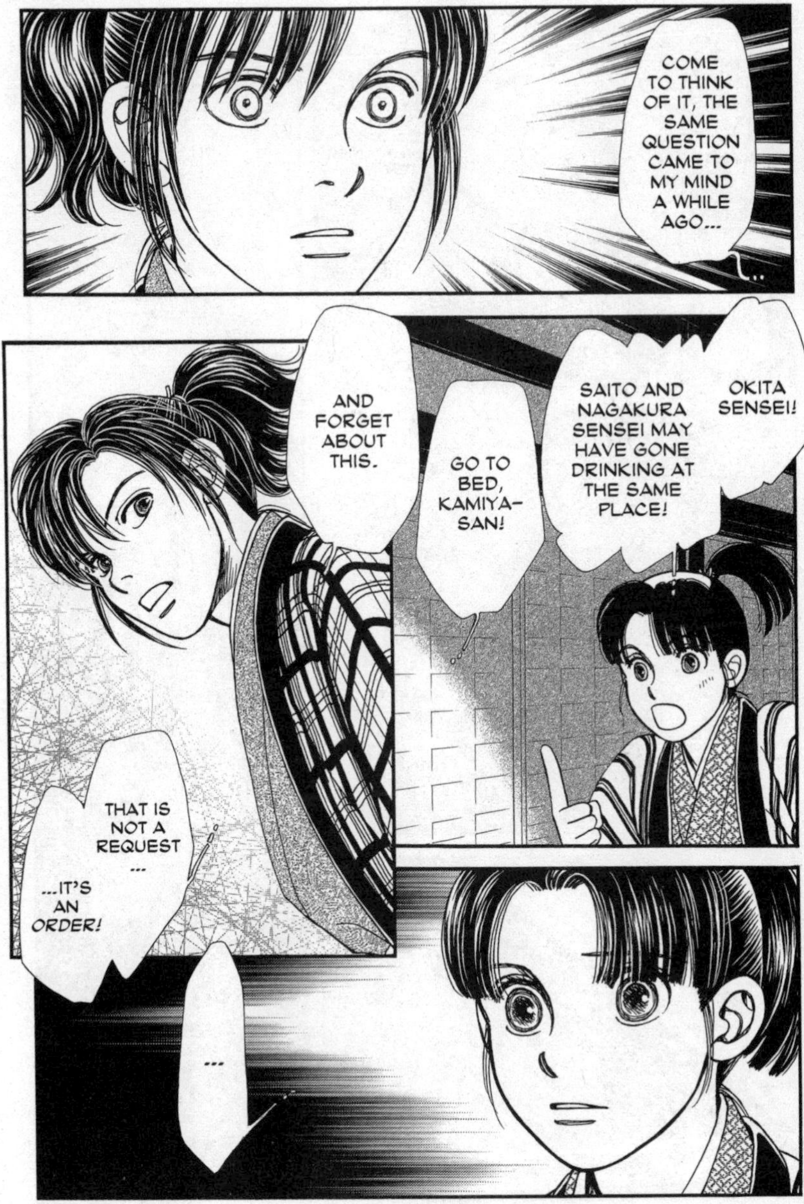
COME TO THINK OF IT, THE SAME QUESTION CAME TO MY MIND A WHILE AGO...
OKITA SENSEI!
SAITO AND NAGAKURA SENSEI MAY HAVE GONE DRINKING AT THE SAME PLACE!
GO TO BED, KAMIYA-SAN!
AND FORGET ABOUT THIS.
THAT IS NOT A REQUEST ...
...IT'S AN *ORDER!*
...

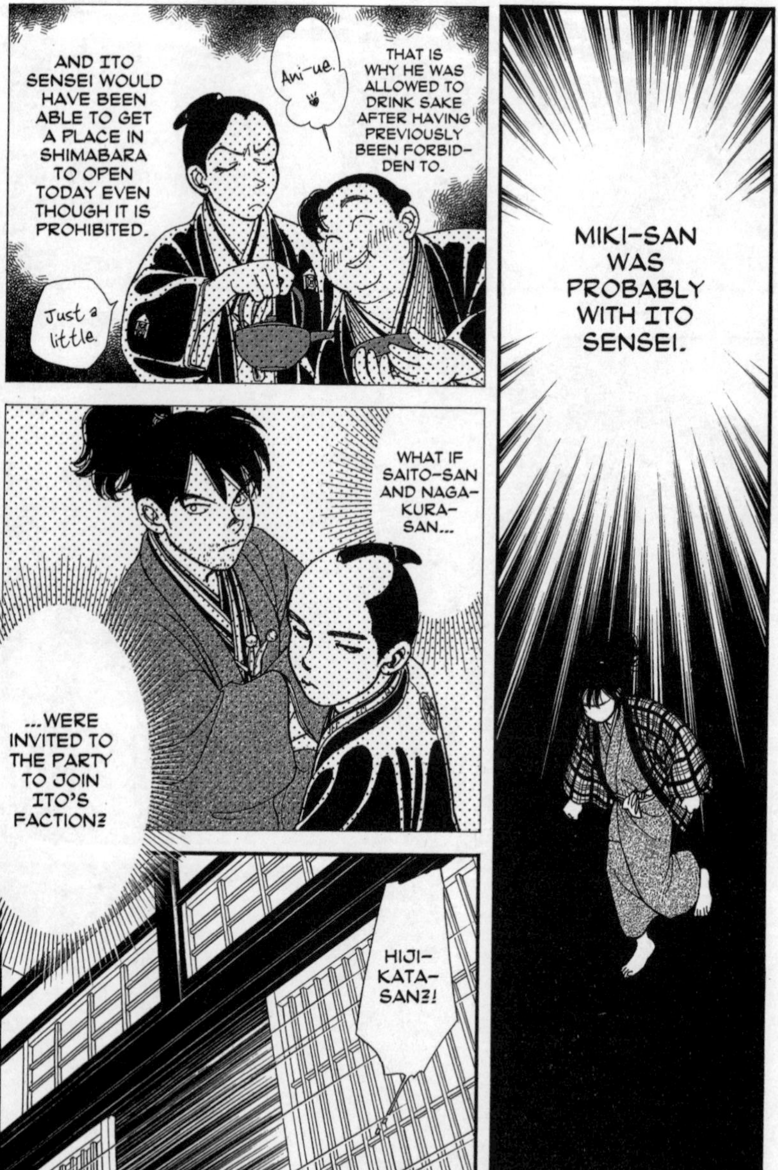
MIKI-SAN WAS PROBABLY WITH ITO SENSEI.
THAT IS WHY HE WAS ALLOWED TO DRINK SAKE AFTER HAVING PREVIOUSLY BEEN FORBID-DEN TO.
Ani-ue.
AND ITO SENSEI WOULD HAVE BEEN ABLE TO GET A PLACE IN SHIMABARA TO OPEN TODAY EVEN THOUGH IT IS PROHIBITED.
Just a little.
WHAT IF SAITO-SAN AND NAGA-KURA-SAN...
...WERE INVITED TO THE PARTY TO JOIN ITO'S FACTION?
HIJI-KATA-SAN?!

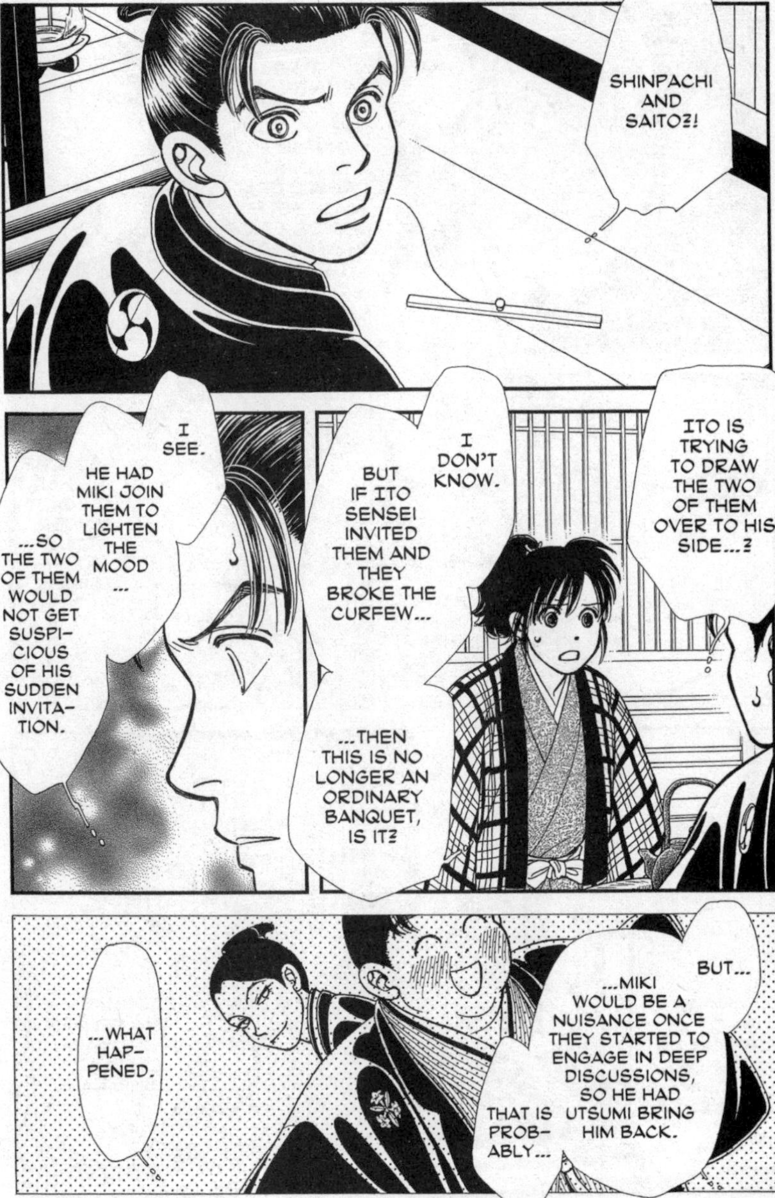

SHINPACHI AND SAITO?!
ITO IS TRYING TO DRAW THE TWO OF THEM OVER TO HIS SIDE...?
I DON'T KNOW.
BUT IF ITO SENSEI INVITED THEM AND THEY BROKE THE CURFEW...
...THEN THIS IS NO LONGER AN ORDINARY BANQUET, IS IT?
I SEE.
HE HAD MIKI JOIN THEM TO LIGHTEN THE MOOD...
...SO THE TWO OF THEM WOULD NOT GET SUSPICIOUS OF HIS SUDDEN INVITATION.
BUT...
...MIKI WOULD BE A NUISANCE ONCE THEY STARTED TO ENGAGE IN DEEP DISCUSSIONS, SO HE HAD UTSUMI BRING HIM BACK.
THAT IS PROBABLY...
...WHAT HAPPENED.

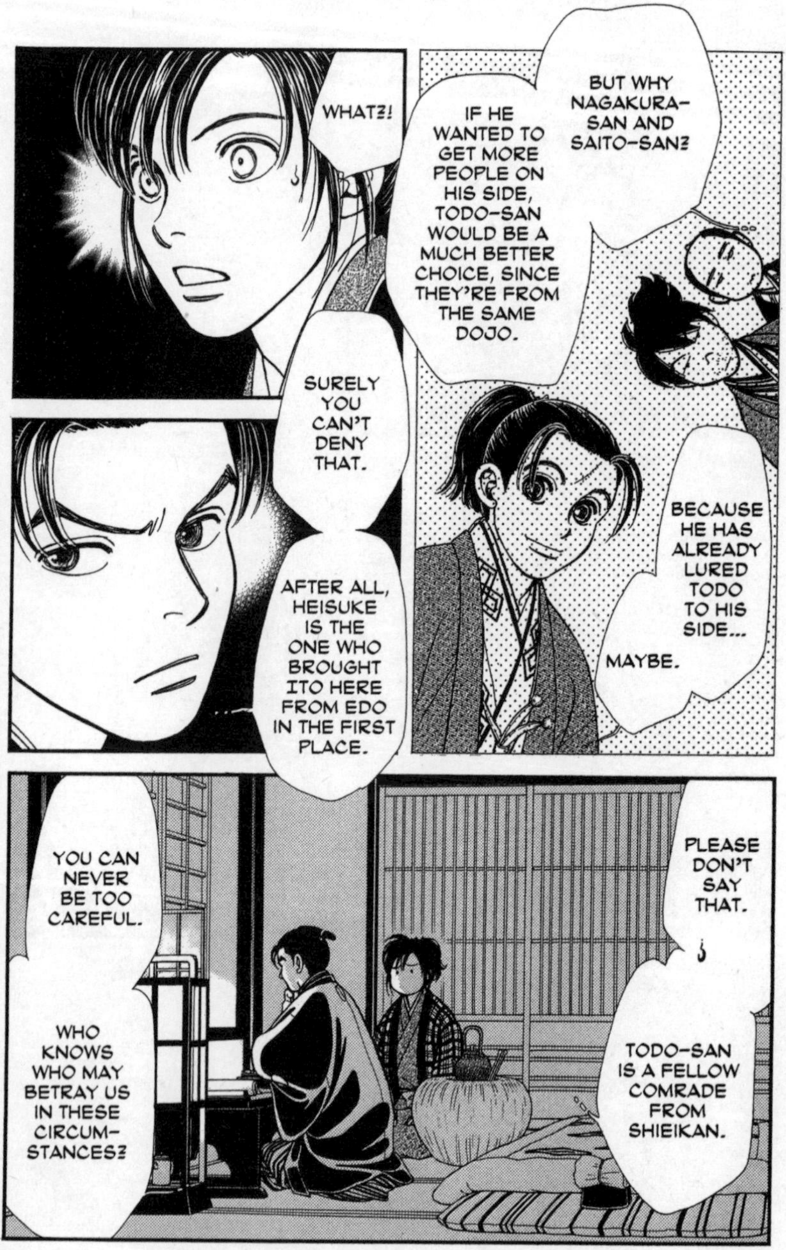
BUT WHY NAGAKURA-SAN AND SAITO-SAN?
IF HE WANTED TO GET MORE PEOPLE ON HIS SIDE, TODO-SAN WOULD BE A MUCH BETTER CHOICE, SINCE THEY'RE FROM THE SAME DOJO.
BECAUSE HE HAS ALREADY LURED TODO TO HIS SIDE...
MAYBE.
WHAT?!
SURELY YOU CAN'T DENY THAT.
AFTER ALL, HEISUKE IS THE ONE WHO BROUGHT ITO HERE FROM EDO IN THE FIRST PLACE.
PLEASE DON'T SAY THAT.
TODO-SAN IS A FELLOW COMRADE FROM SHIEIKAN.
YOU CAN NEVER BE TOO CAREFUL.
WHO KNOWS WHO MAY BETRAY US IN THESE CIRCUMSTANCES?

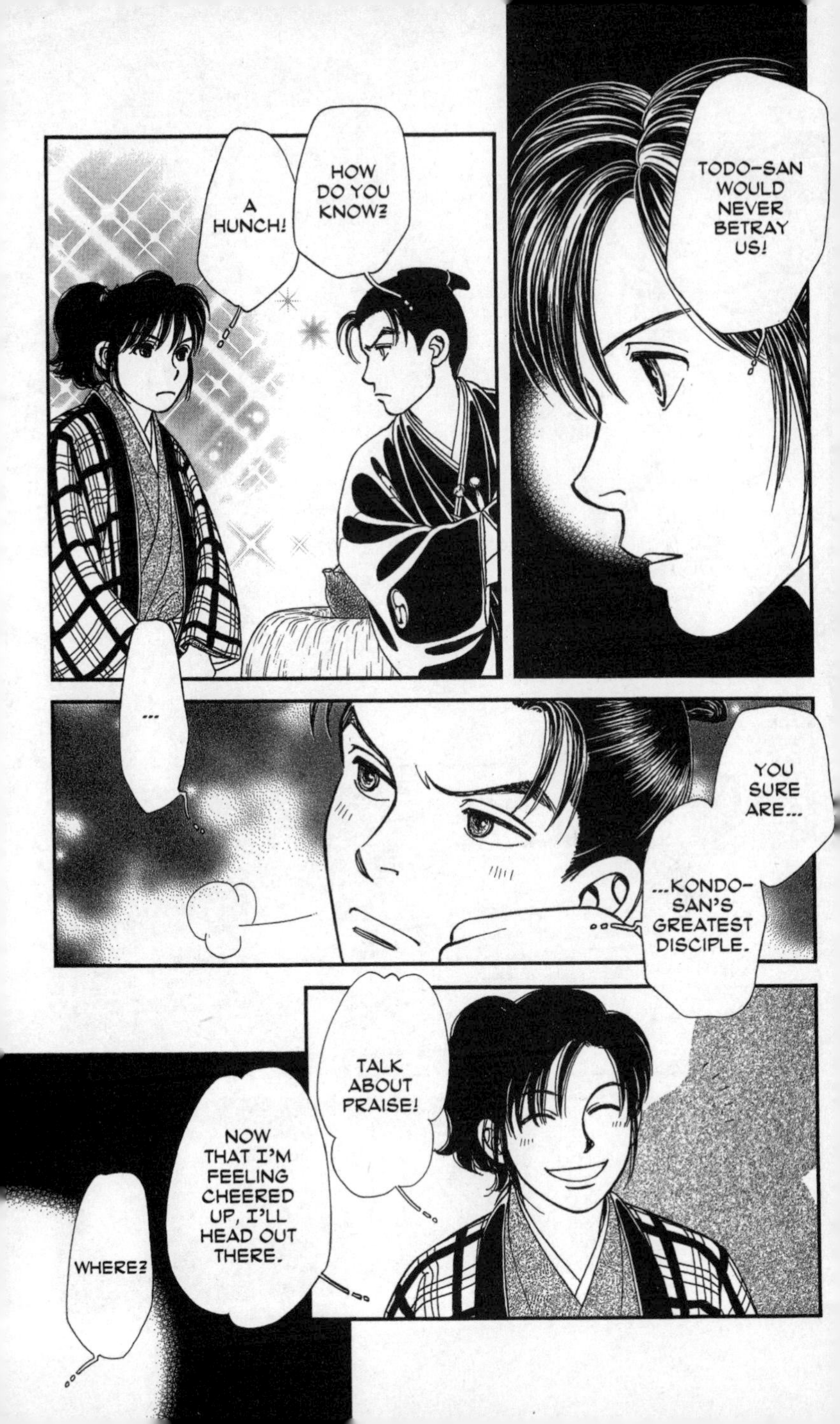
TODO-SAN WOULD NEVER BETRAY US!
HOW DO YOU KNOW?
A HUNCH!
...
YOU SURE ARE...
...KONDO-SAN'S GREATEST DISCIPLE.
TALK ABOUT PRAISE!
NOW THAT I'M FEELING CHEERED UP, I'LL HEAD OUT THERE.
WHERE?

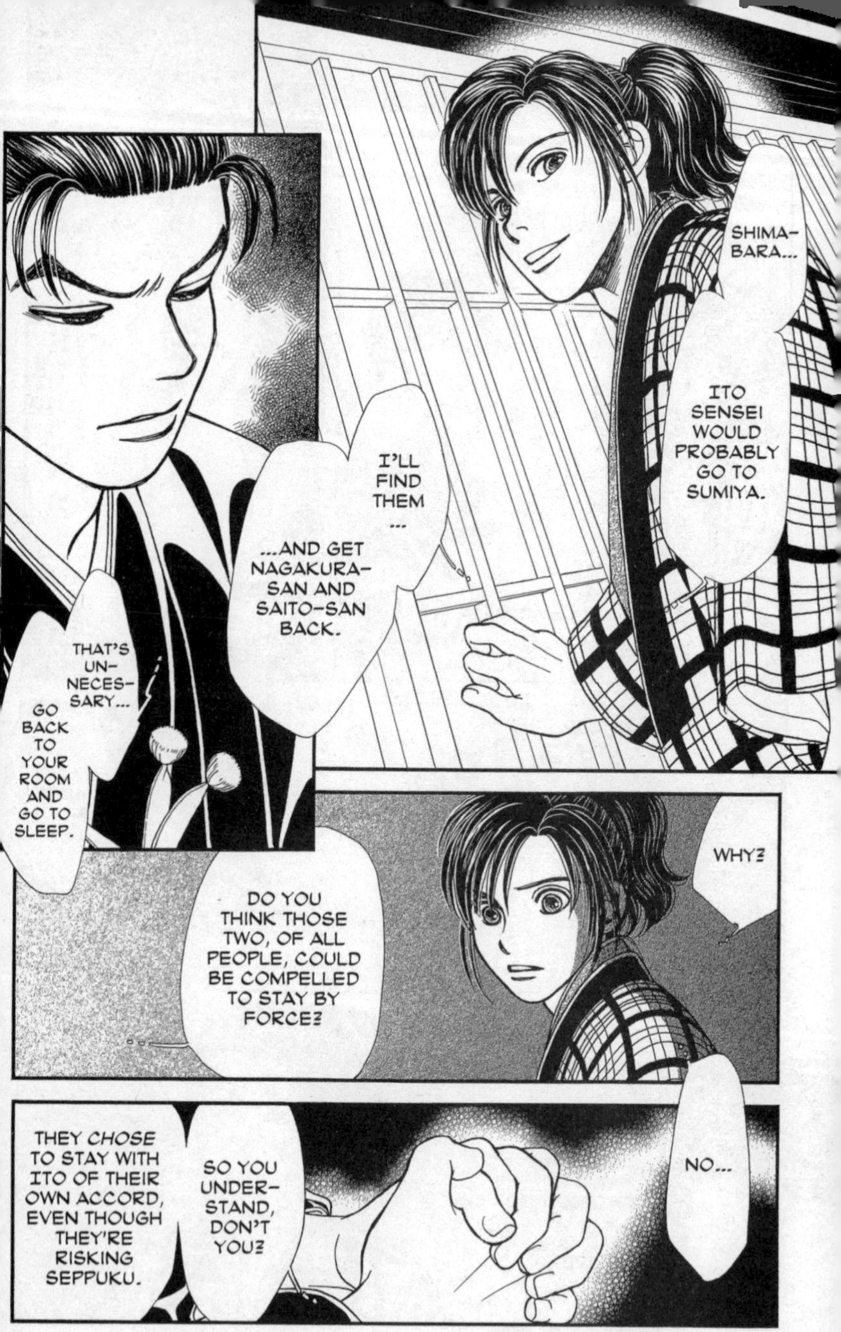
SHIMA-BARA...
ITO SENSEI WOULD PROBABLY GO TO SUMIYA.
I'LL FIND THEM...
...AND GET NAGAKURA-SAN AND SAITO-SAN BACK.
THAT'S UNNECES-SARY...
GO BACK TO YOUR ROOM AND GO TO SLEEP.
WHY?
DO YOU THINK THOSE TWO, OF ALL PEOPLE, COULD BE COMPELLED TO STAY BY FORCE?
NO...
SO YOU UNDER-STAND, DON'T YOU?
THEY *CHOSE* TO STAY WITH ITO OF THEIR OWN ACCORD, EVEN THOUGH THEY'RE RISKING SEPPUKU.

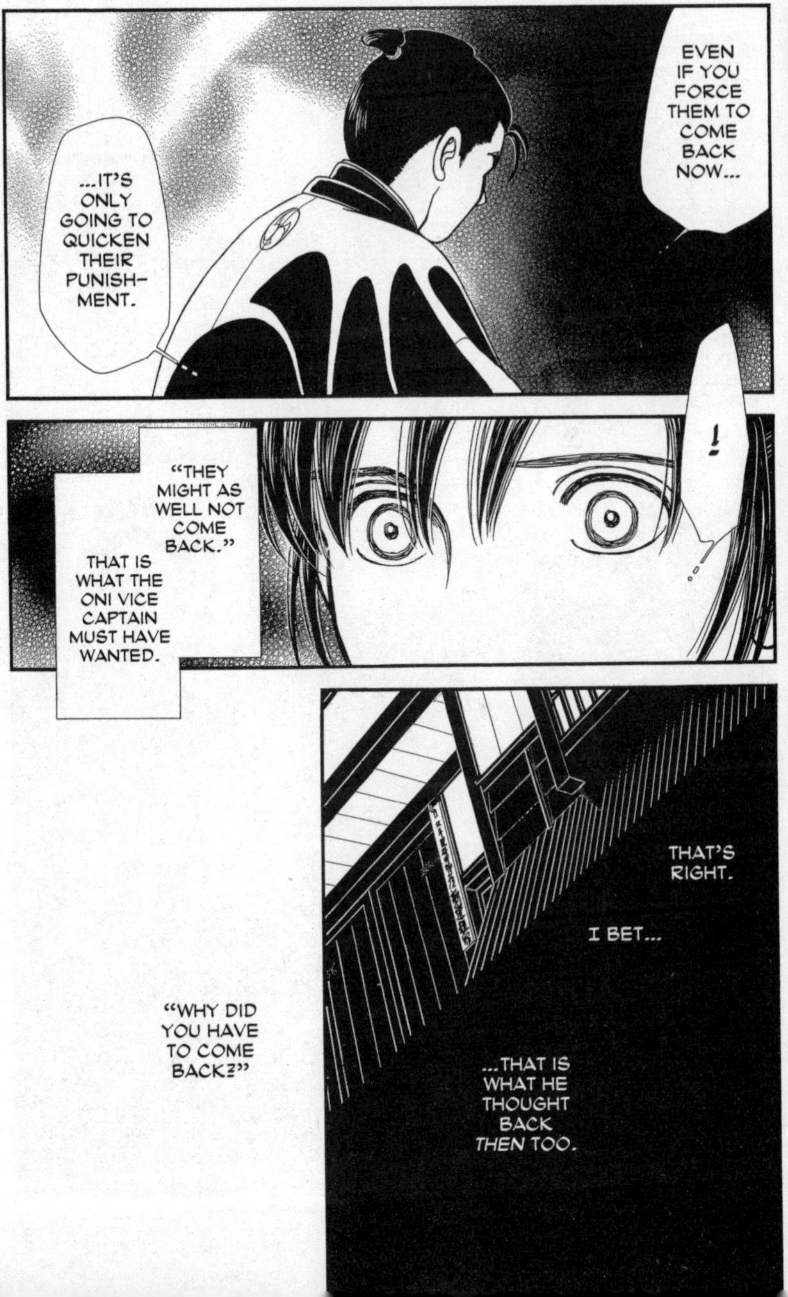
EVEN IF YOU FORCE THEM TO COME BACK NOW...
...IT'S ONLY GOING TO QUICKEN THEIR PUNISHMENT.
!
"THEY MIGHT AS WELL NOT COME BACK."
THAT IS WHAT THE ONI VICE CAPTAIN MUST HAVE WANTED.
THAT'S RIGHT.
I BET...
"WHY DID YOU HAVE TO COME BACK?"
...THAT IS WHAT HE THOUGHT BACK *THEN* TOO.

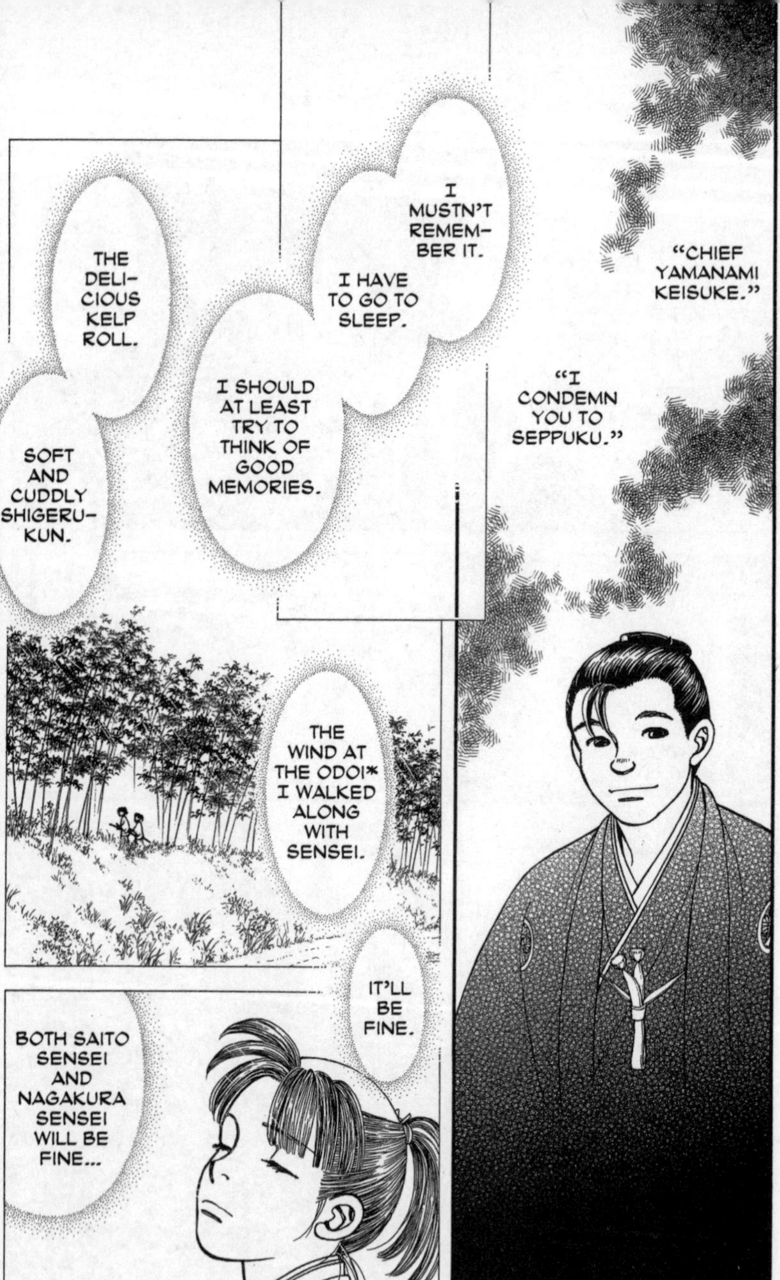
"CHIEF YAMANAMI KEISUKE."
"I CONDEMN YOU TO SEPPUKU."
I MUSTN'T REMEMBER IT.
I HAVE TO GO TO SLEEP.
I SHOULD AT LEAST TRY TO THINK OF GOOD MEMORIES.
THE DELICIOUS KELP ROLL.
SOFT AND CUDDLY SHIGERU-KUN.
THE WIND AT THE ODOI* I WALKED ALONG WITH SENSEI.
IT'LL BE FINE.
BOTH SAITO SENSEI AND NAGAKURA SENSEI WILL BE FINE...

*An earthen wall created by Toyotomi Hideyoshi in the 19th year of Tensho (1591) to protect the city from enemies and flooding by the Kamo River. The 14-mile wall divided inner and outer Kyoto, but by the Bakumatsu period the city had spread eastward and most of the wall along the Kamo River was cleared away.

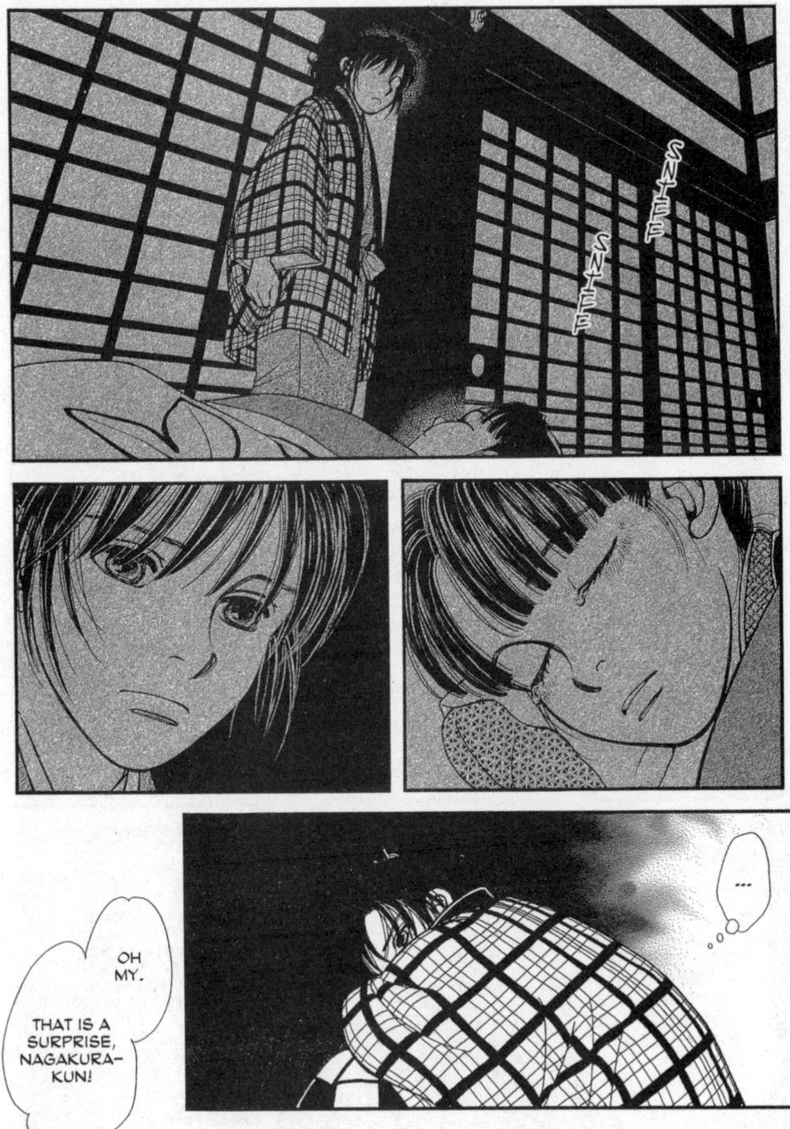
SNIFF
SNIFF
...
OH MY.
THAT IS A SURPRISE, NAGAKURA-KUN!

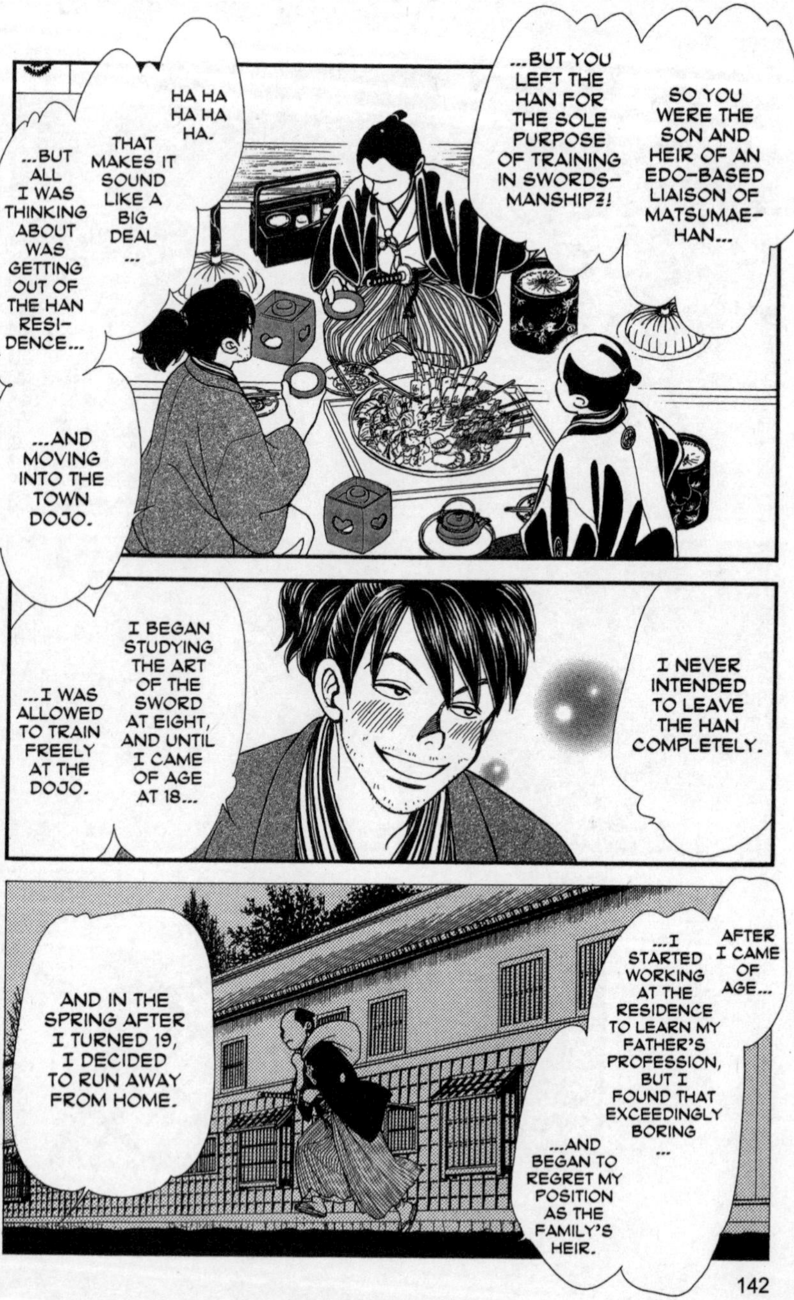
SO YOU WERE THE SON AND HEIR OF AN EDO-BASED LIAISON OF MATSUMAE-HAN...
...BUT YOU LEFT THE HAN FOR THE SOLE PURPOSE OF TRAINING IN SWORDSMANSHIP?!
HA HA HA HA HA.
THAT MAKES IT SOUND LIKE A BIG DEAL...
...BUT ALL I WAS THINKING ABOUT WAS GETTING OUT OF THE HAN RESIDENCE...
...AND MOVING INTO THE TOWN DOJO.
I NEVER INTENDED TO LEAVE THE HAN COMPLETELY.
I BEGAN STUDYING THE ART OF THE SWORD AT EIGHT, AND UNTIL I CAME OF AGE AT 18...
...I WAS ALLOWED TO TRAIN FREELY AT THE DOJO.
AFTER I CAME OF AGE...
...I STARTED WORKING AT THE RESIDENCE TO LEARN MY FATHER'S PROFESSION, BUT I FOUND THAT EXCEEDINGLY BORING...
...AND BEGAN TO REGRET MY POSITION AS THE FAMILY'S HEIR.
AND IN THE SPRING AFTER I TURNED 19, I DECIDED TO RUN AWAY FROM HOME.

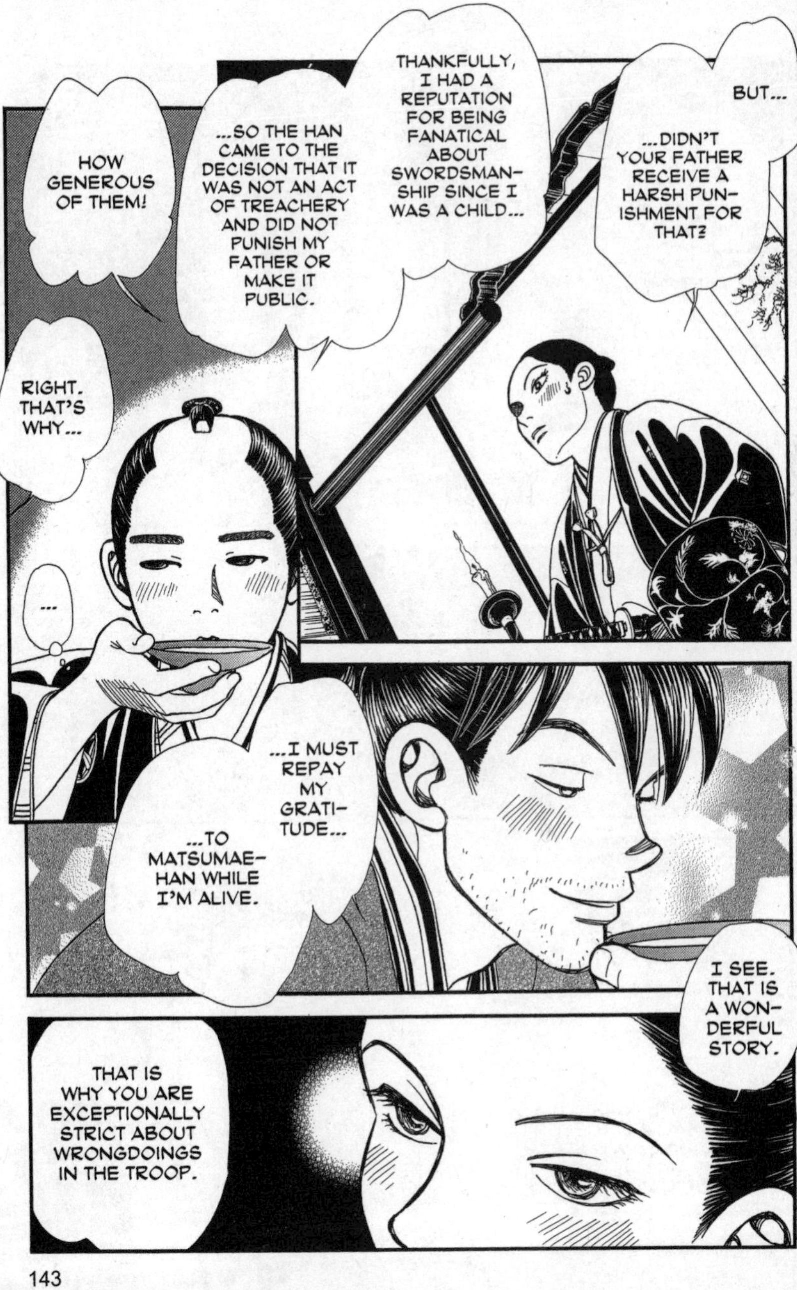
BUT...
...DIDN'T YOUR FATHER RECEIVE A HARSH PUNISHMENT FOR THAT?
THANKFULLY, I HAD A REPUTATION FOR BEING FANATICAL ABOUT SWORDSMANSHIP SINCE I WAS A CHILD...
...SO THE HAN CAME TO THE DECISION THAT IT WAS NOT AN ACT OF TREACHERY AND DID NOT PUNISH MY FATHER OR MAKE IT PUBLIC.
HOW GENEROUS OF THEM!
RIGHT. THAT'S WHY...
...
...I MUST REPAY MY GRATITUDE...
...TO MATSUMAE-HAN WHILE I'M ALIVE.
I SEE. THAT IS A WONDERFUL STORY.
THAT IS WHY YOU ARE EXCEPTIONALLY STRICT ABOUT WRONGDOINGS IN THE TROOP.

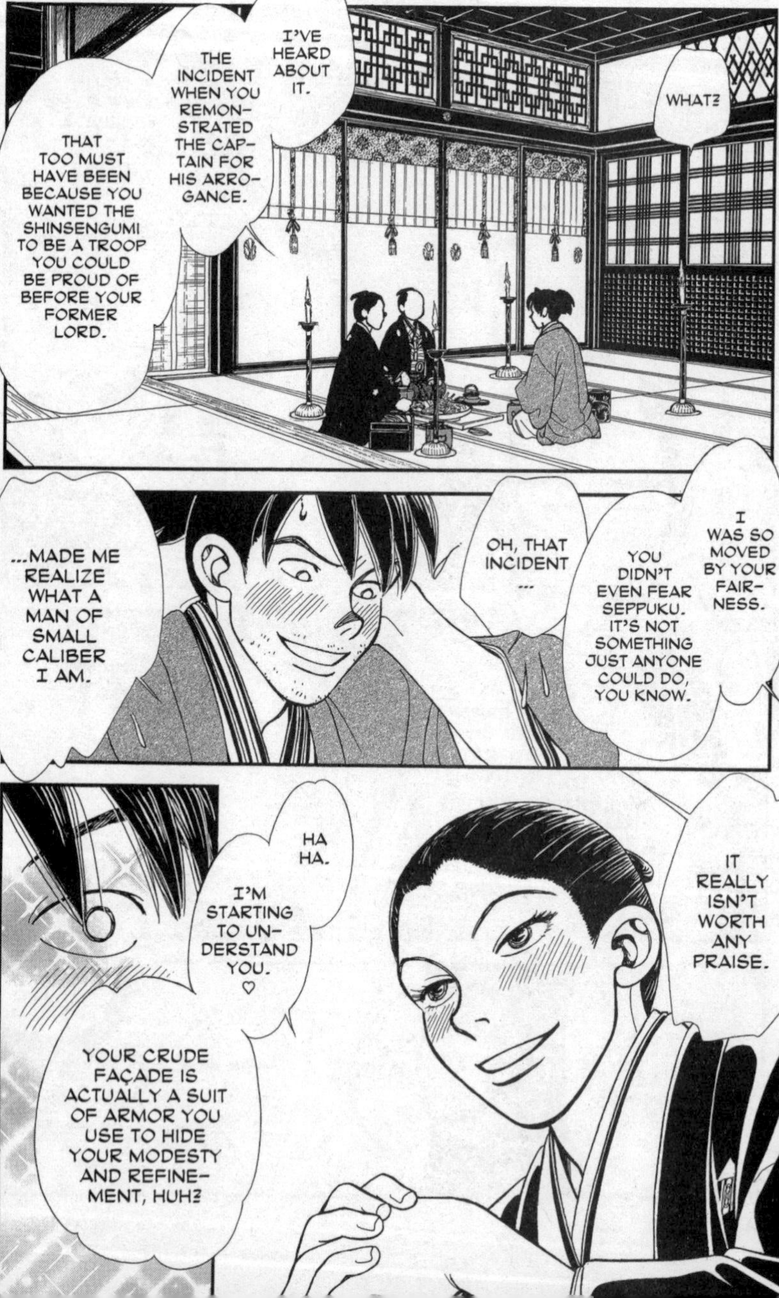
WHAT?
I'VE HEARD ABOUT IT.
THE INCIDENT WHEN YOU REMONSTRATED THE CAPTAIN FOR HIS ARROGANCE.
THAT TOO MUST HAVE BEEN BECAUSE YOU WANTED THE SHINSENGUMI TO BE A TROOP YOU COULD BE PROUD OF BEFORE YOUR FORMER LORD.
I WAS SO MOVED BY YOUR FAIRNESS.
YOU DIDN'T EVEN FEAR SEPPUKU. IT'S NOT SOMETHING JUST ANYONE COULD DO, YOU KNOW.
OH, THAT INCIDENT ...
...MADE ME REALIZE WHAT A MAN OF SMALL CALIBER I AM.
IT REALLY ISN'T WORTH ANY PRAISE.
HA HA.
I'M STARTING TO UNDERSTAND YOU. ♡
YOUR CRUDE FAÇADE IS ACTUALLY A SUIT OF ARMOR YOU USE TO HIDE YOUR MODESTY AND REFINEMENT, HUH?

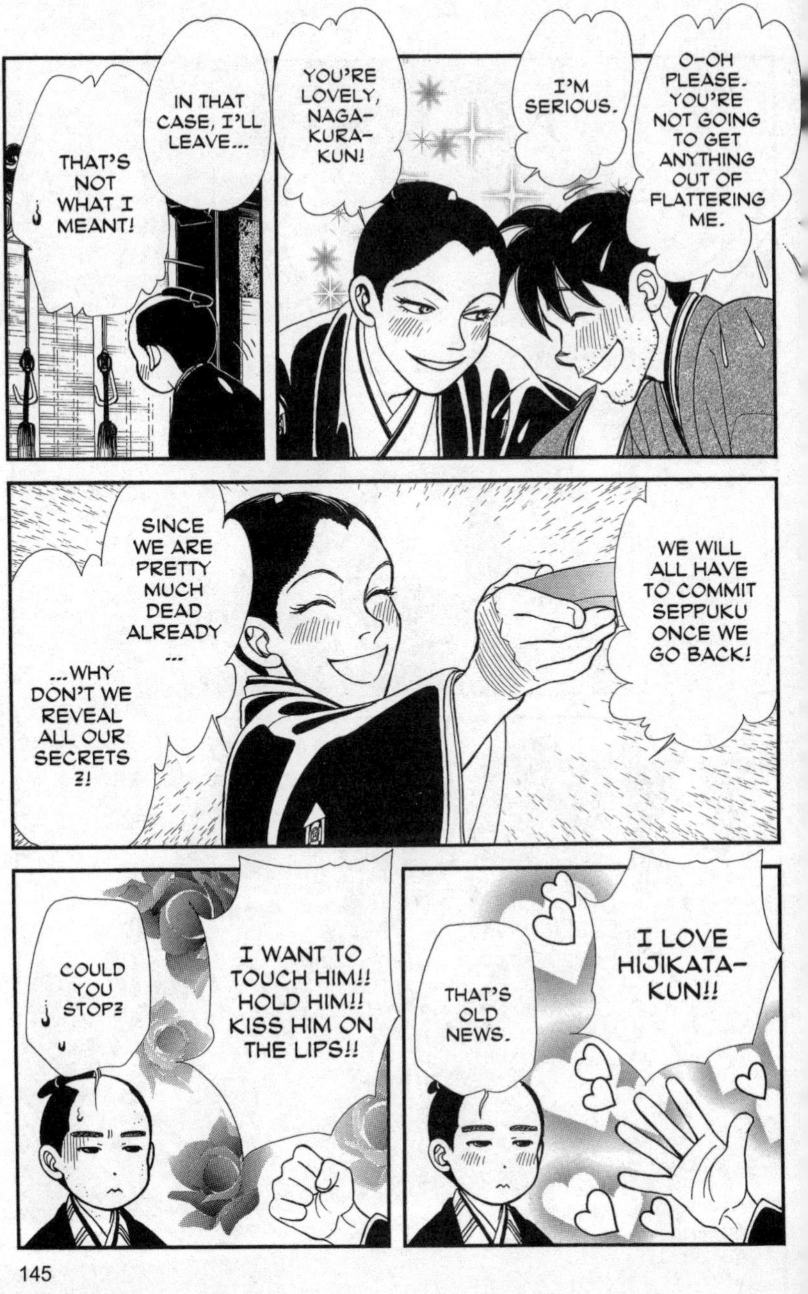
O-OH PLEASE. YOU'RE NOT GOING TO GET ANYTHING OUT OF FLATTERING ME.
I'M SERIOUS.
YOU'RE LOVELY, NAGA-KURA-KUN!
IN THAT CASE, I'LL LEAVE...
THAT'S NOT WHAT I MEANT!
WE WILL ALL HAVE TO COMMIT SEPPUKU ONCE WE GO BACK!
SINCE WE ARE PRETTY MUCH DEAD ALREADY...
...WHY DON'T WE REVEAL ALL OUR SECRETS?!
I LOVE HIJIKATA-KUN!!
THAT'S OLD NEWS.
I WANT TO TOUCH HIM!! HOLD HIM!! KISS HIM ON THE LIPS!!
COULD YOU STOP?

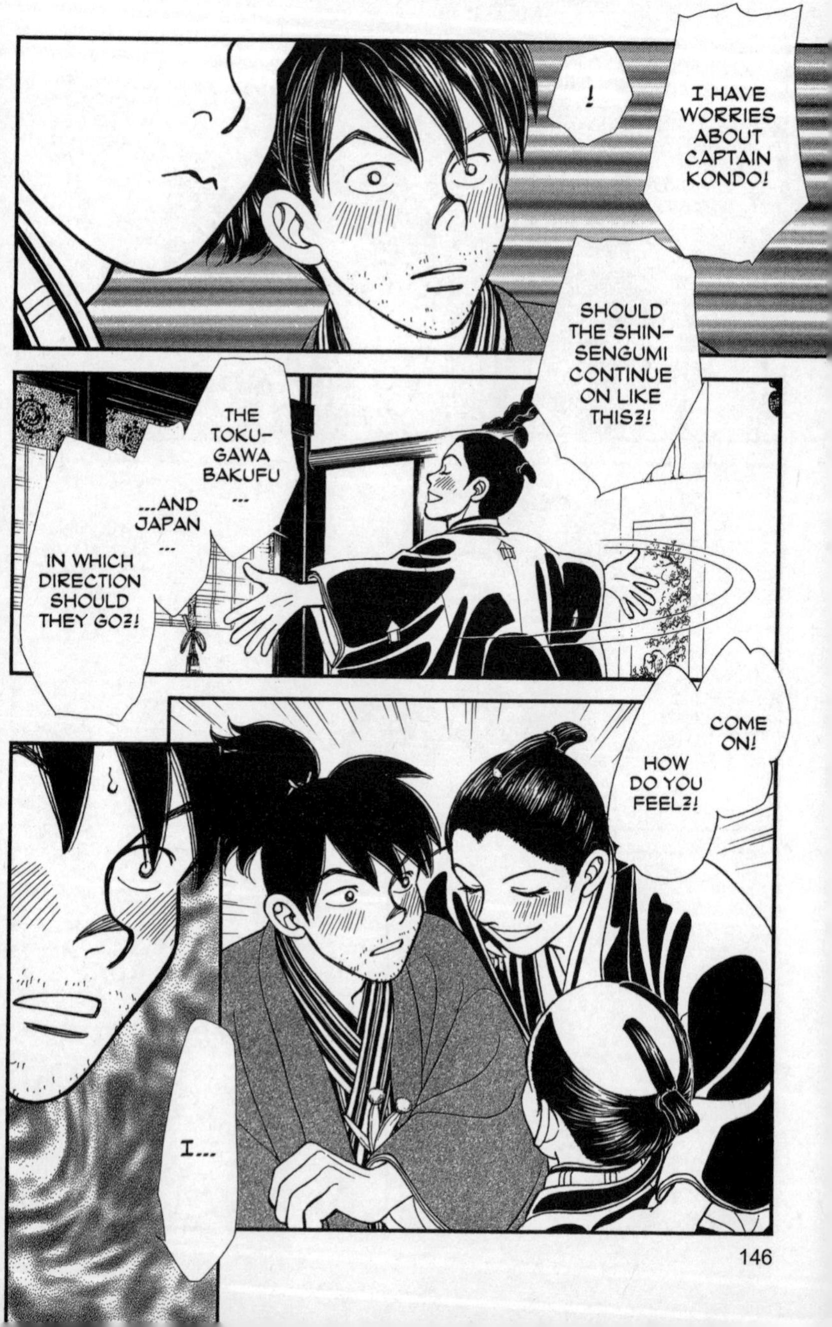
I HAVE WORRIES ABOUT CAPTAIN KONDO!
!
SHOULD THE SHIN-SENGUMI CONTINUE ON LIKE THIS?!
THE TOKU-GAWA BAKUFU ...
...AND JAPAN ...
IN WHICH DIRECTION SHOULD THEY GO?!
COME ON!
HOW DO YOU FEEL?!
I...

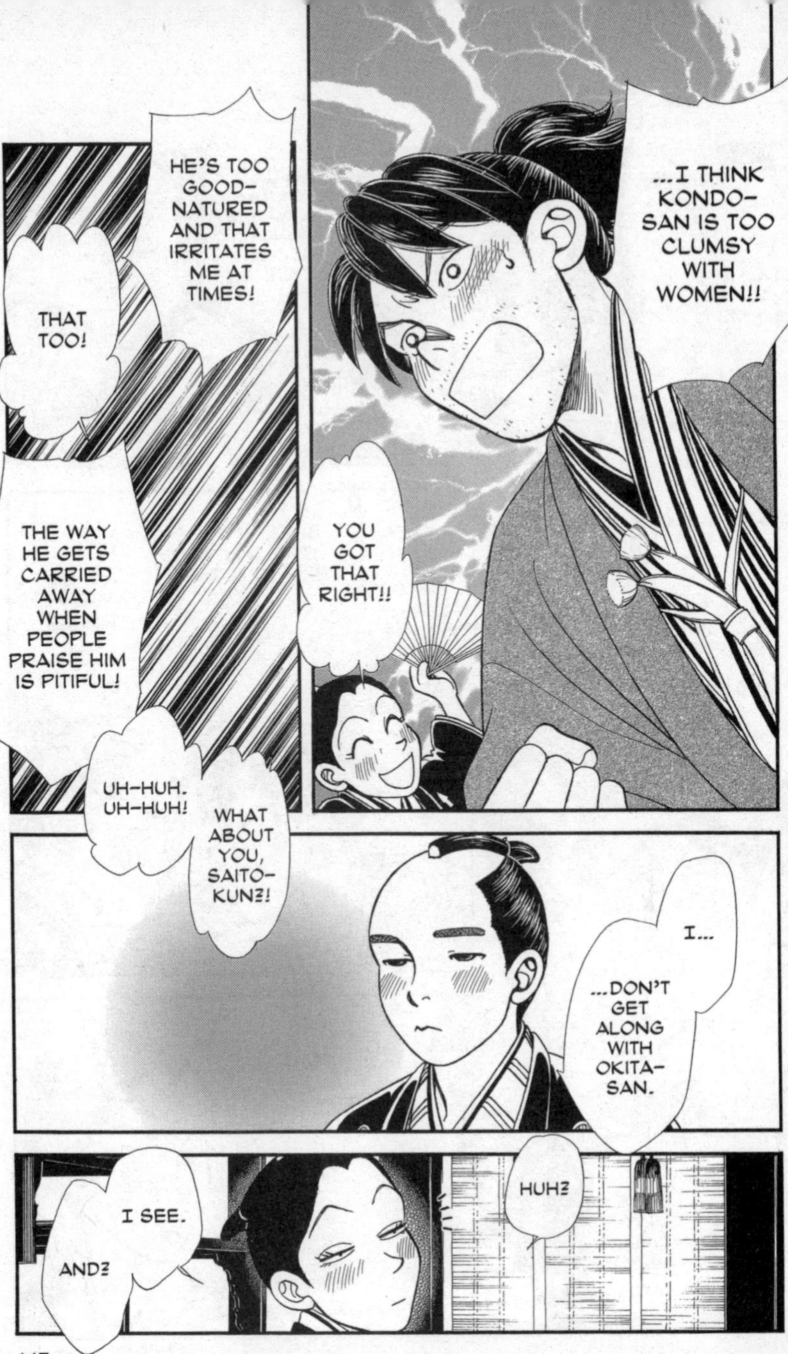
...I THINK KONDO-SAN IS TOO CLUMSY WITH WOMEN!!
YOU GOT THAT RIGHT!!
HE'S TOO GOOD-NATURED AND THAT IRRITATES ME AT TIMES!
THAT TOO!
THE WAY HE GETS CARRIED AWAY WHEN PEOPLE PRAISE HIM IS PITIFUL!
UH-HUH. UH-HUH!
WHAT ABOUT YOU, SAITO-KUN?!
I...
...DON'T GET ALONG WITH OKITA-SAN.
HUH?
I SEE.
AND?

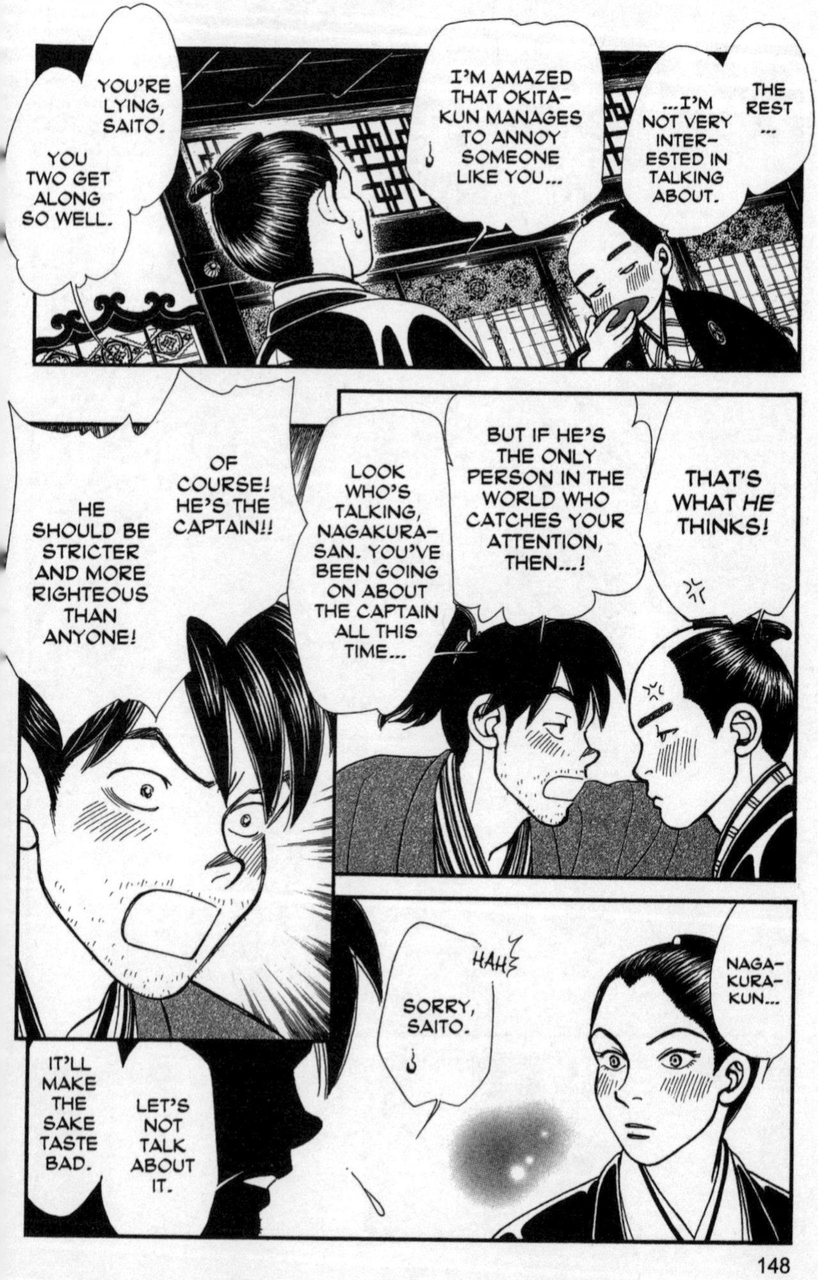
THE REST ...
...I'M NOT VERY INTERESTED IN TALKING ABOUT.
I'M AMAZED THAT OKITA-KUN MANAGES TO ANNOY SOMEONE LIKE YOU...
YOU'RE LYING, SAITO.
YOU TWO GET ALONG SO WELL.
THAT'S WHAT *HE* THINKS!
BUT IF HE'S THE ONLY PERSON IN THE WORLD WHO CATCHES YOUR ATTENTION, THEN...!
LOOK WHO'S TALKING, NAGAKURA-SAN. YOU'VE BEEN GOING ON ABOUT THE CAPTAIN ALL THIS TIME...
OF COURSE! HE'S THE CAPTAIN!!
HE SHOULD BE STRICTER AND MORE RIGHTEOUS THAN ANYONE!
NAGA-KURA-KUN...
HAH
SORRY, SAITO.
LET'S NOT TALK ABOUT IT.
IT'LL MAKE THE SAKE TASTE BAD.

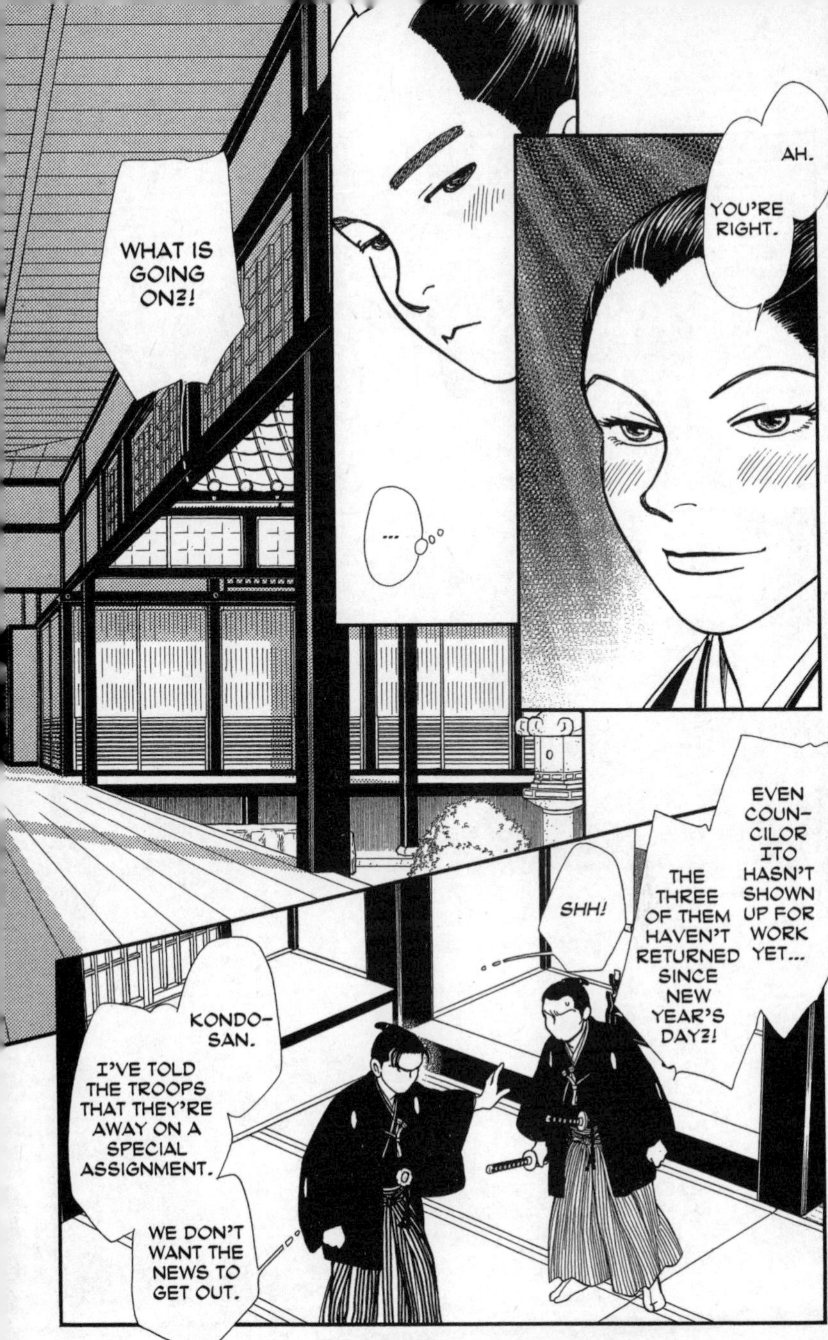
AH.
YOU'RE RIGHT.
...
WHAT IS GOING ON?!
EVEN COUNCILOR ITO HASN'T SHOWN UP FOR WORK YET...
THE THREE OF THEM HAVEN'T RETURNED SINCE NEW YEAR'S DAY?!
SHH!
KONDO-SAN.
I'VE TOLD THE TROOPS THAT THEY'RE AWAY ON A SPECIAL ASSIGNMENT.
WE DON'T WANT THE NEWS TO GET OUT.

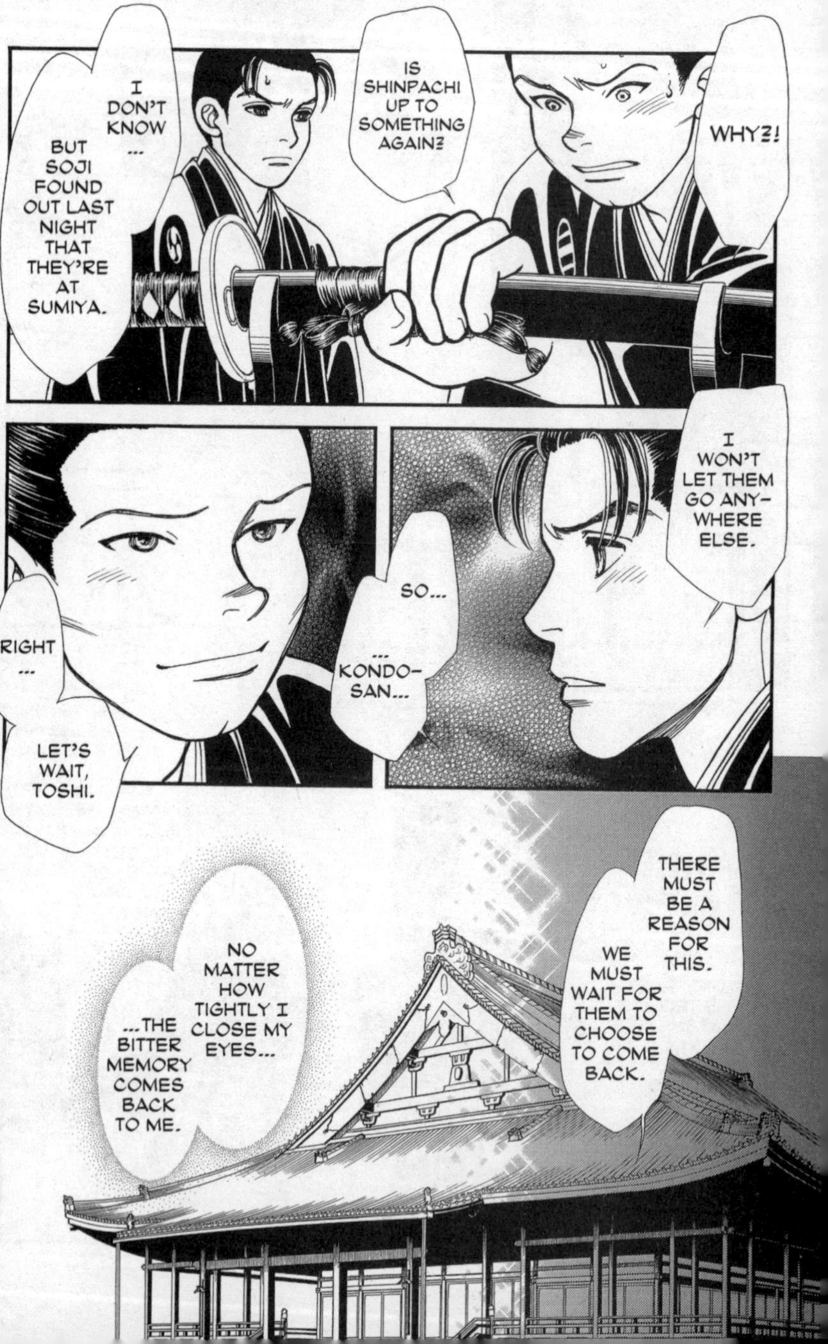
WHY?!
IS SHINPACHI UP TO SOMETHING AGAIN?
I DON'T KNOW...
BUT SOJI FOUND OUT LAST NIGHT THAT THEY'RE AT SUMIYA.
I WON'T LET THEM GO ANYWHERE ELSE.
SO...
...KONDO-SAN...
RIGHT...
LET'S WAIT, TOSHI.
THERE MUST BE A REASON FOR THIS.
WE MUST WAIT FOR THEM TO CHOOSE TO COME BACK.
NO MATTER HOW TIGHTLY I CLOSE MY EYES...
...THE BITTER MEMORY COMES BACK TO ME.

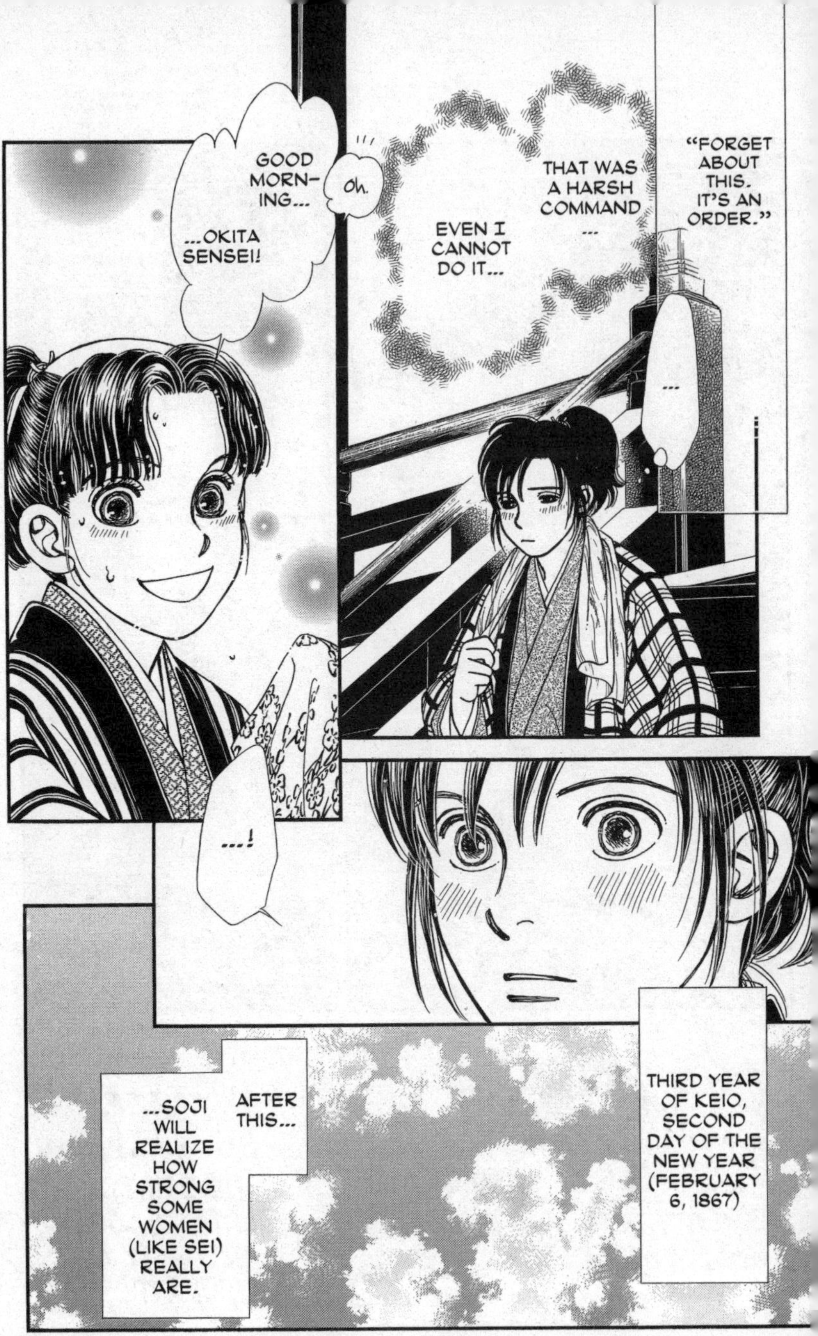
"FORGET ABOUT THIS. IT'S AN ORDER."
THAT WAS A HARSH COMMAND...
EVEN I CANNOT DO IT...
...
Oh.
GOOD MORN-ING... ...OKITA SENSEI!
...!
THIRD YEAR OF KEIO, SECOND DAY OF THE NEW YEAR (FEBRUARY 6, 1867)
AFTER THIS...
...SOJI WILL REALIZE HOW STRONG SOME WOMEN (LIKE SEI) REALLY ARE.

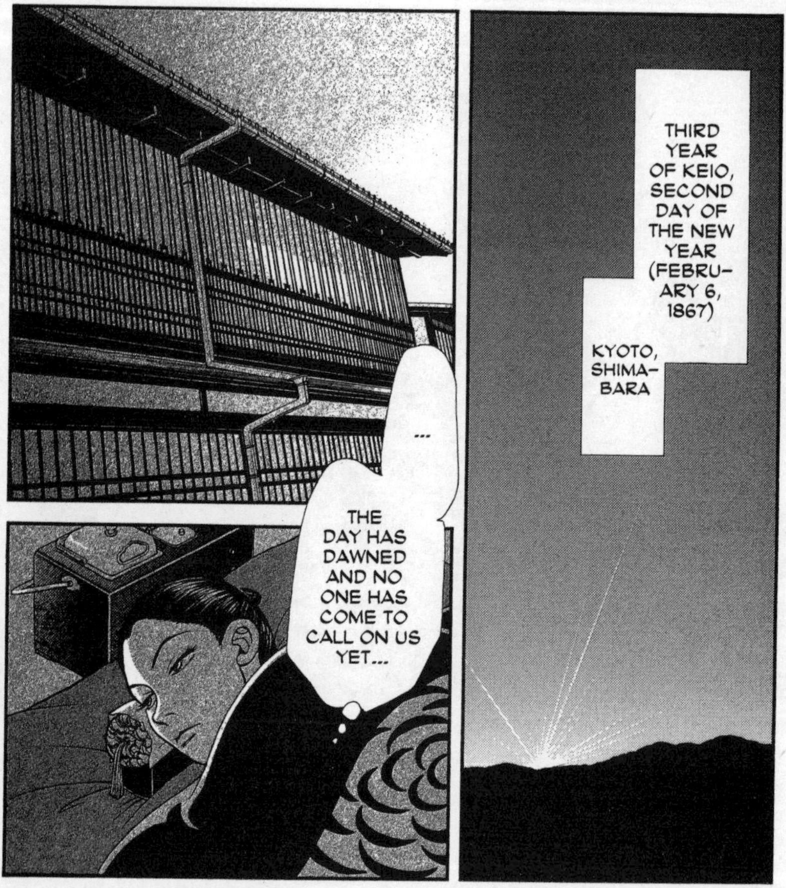
THIRD YEAR OF KEIO, SECOND DAY OF THE NEW YEAR (FEBRUARY 6, 1867)
KYOTO, SHIMABARA
...
THE DAY HAS DAWNED AND NO ONE HAS COME TO CALL ON US YET...

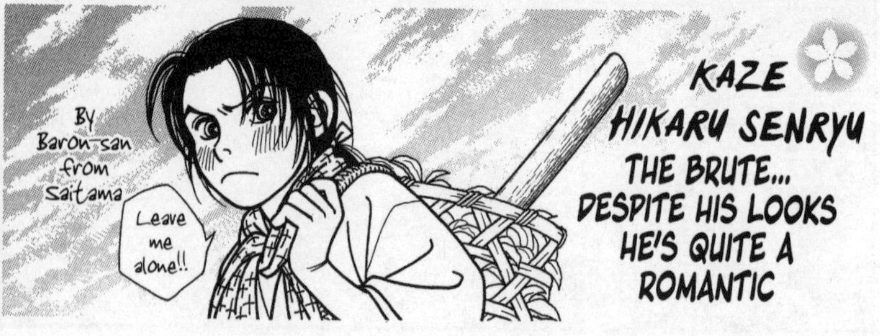
KAZE HIKARU SENRYU
THE BRUTE... DESPITE HIS LOOKS HE'S QUITE A ROMANTIC
Leave me alone!!
By Baron-san from Saitama

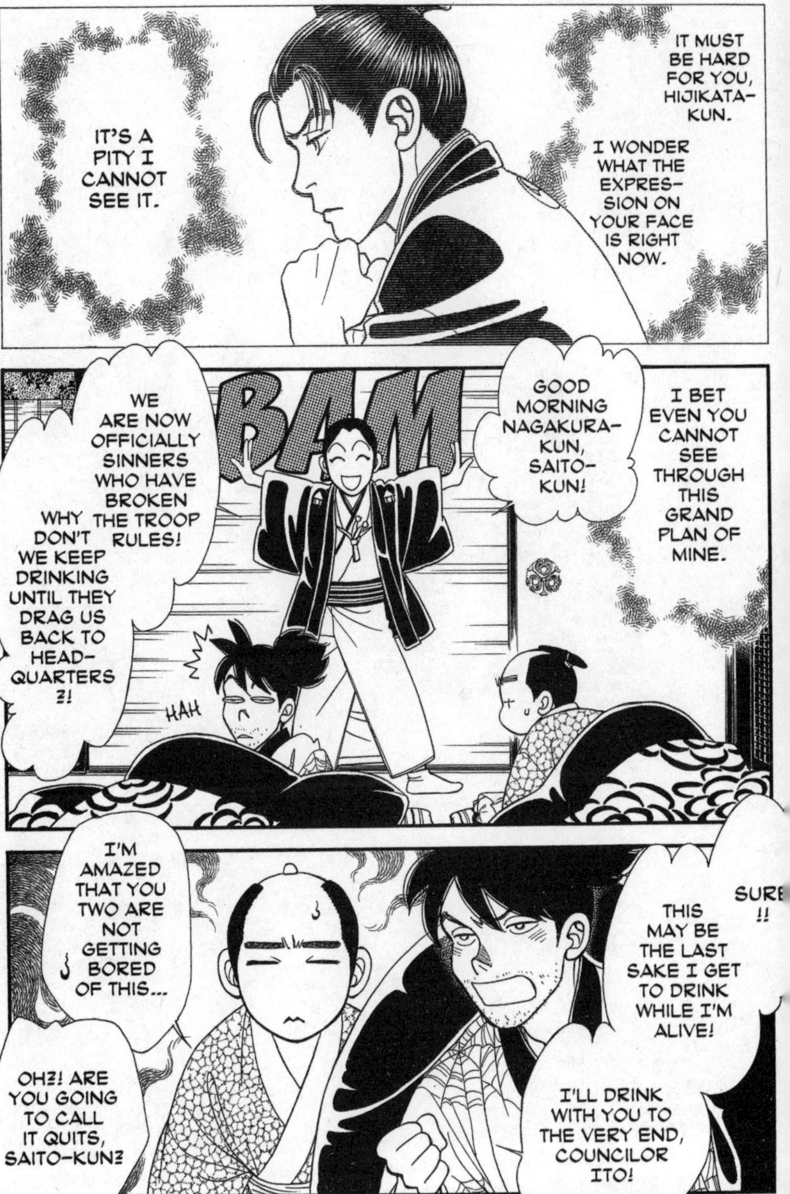
IT MUST BE HARD FOR YOU, HIJIKATA-KUN.
I WONDER WHAT THE EXPRES-SION ON YOUR FACE IS RIGHT NOW.
IT'S A PITY I CANNOT SEE IT.
I BET EVEN YOU CANNOT SEE THROUGH THIS GRAND PLAN OF MINE.
GOOD MORNING NAGAKURA-KUN, SAITO-KUN!
BAM
WE ARE NOW OFFICIALLY SINNERS WHO HAVE BROKEN THE TROOP RULES!
WHY DON'T WE KEEP DRINKING UNTIL THEY DRAG US BACK TO HEAD-QUARTERS?!
HAH
SURE!!
THIS MAY BE THE LAST SAKE I GET TO DRINK WHILE I'M ALIVE!
I'LL DRINK WITH YOU TO THE VERY END, COUNCILOR ITO!
I'M AMAZED THAT YOU TWO ARE NOT GETTING BORED OF THIS...
OH?! ARE YOU GOING TO CALL IT QUITS, SAITO-KUN?

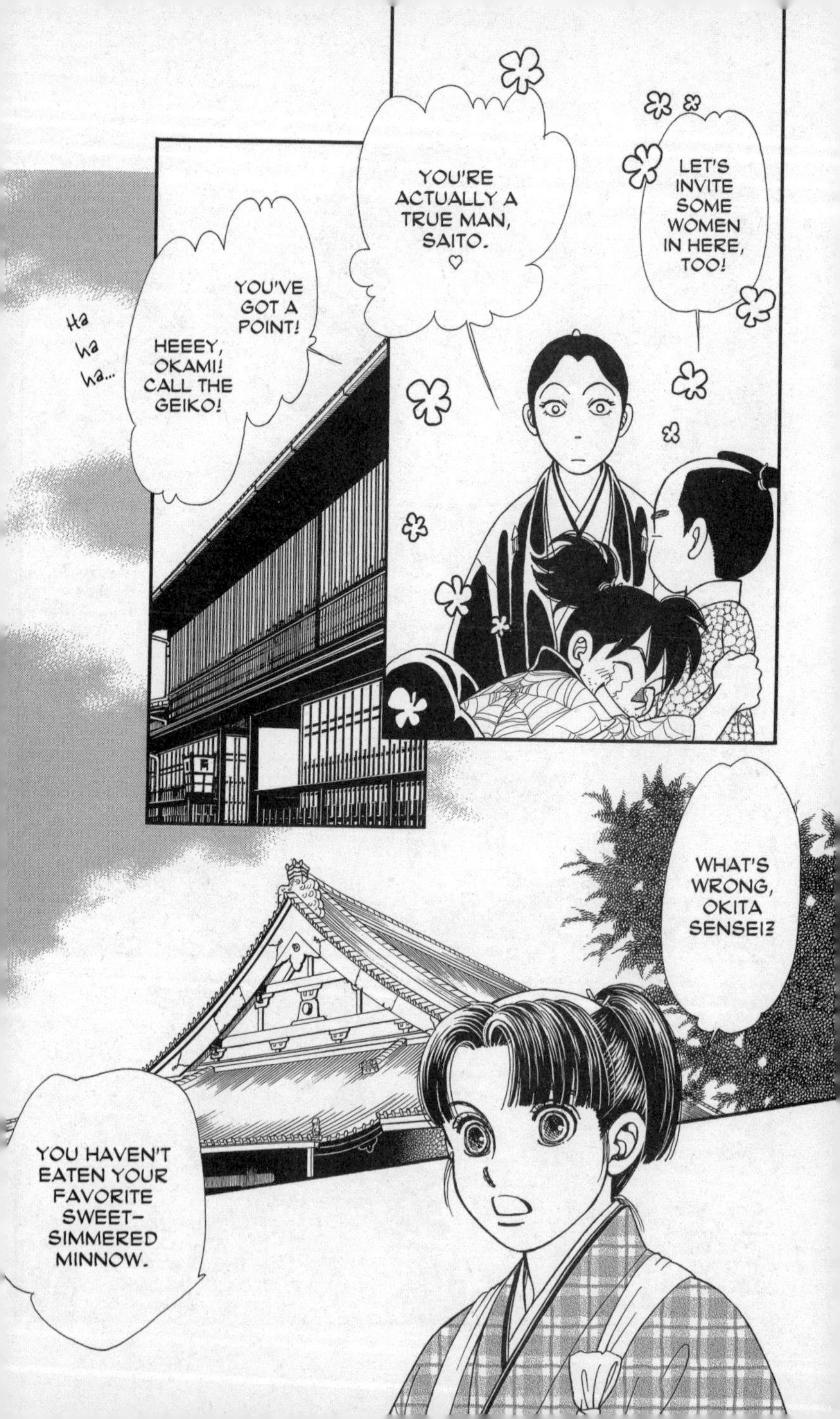
LET'S INVITE SOME WOMEN IN HERE, TOO!
YOU'RE ACTUALLY A TRUE MAN, SAITO. ♡
YOU'VE GOT A POINT!
HEEEY, OKAMI! CALL THE GEIKO!
Ha ha ha...
WHAT'S WRONG, OKITA SENSEI!?
YOU HAVEN'T EATEN YOUR FAVORITE SWEET-SIMMERED MINNOW.

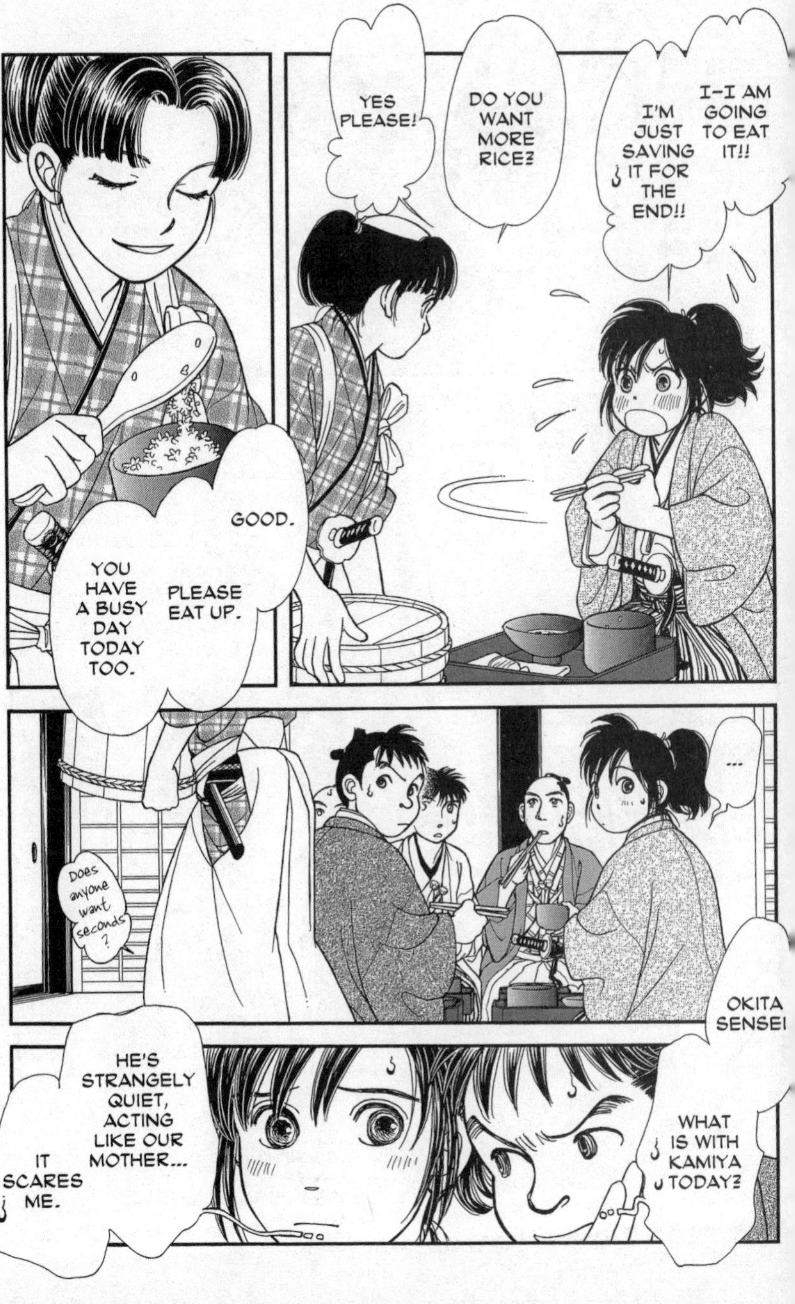
I-I AM GOING TO EAT IT!!
I'M JUST SAVING IT FOR THE END!!
DO YOU WANT MORE RICE?
YES PLEASE!
GOOD.
PLEASE EAT UP.
YOU HAVE A BUSY DAY TODAY TOO.
...
Does anyone want seconds?
OKITA SENSEI
WHAT IS WITH KAMIYA TODAY?
HE'S STRANGELY QUIET, ACTING LIKE OUR MOTHER...
IT SCARES ME.

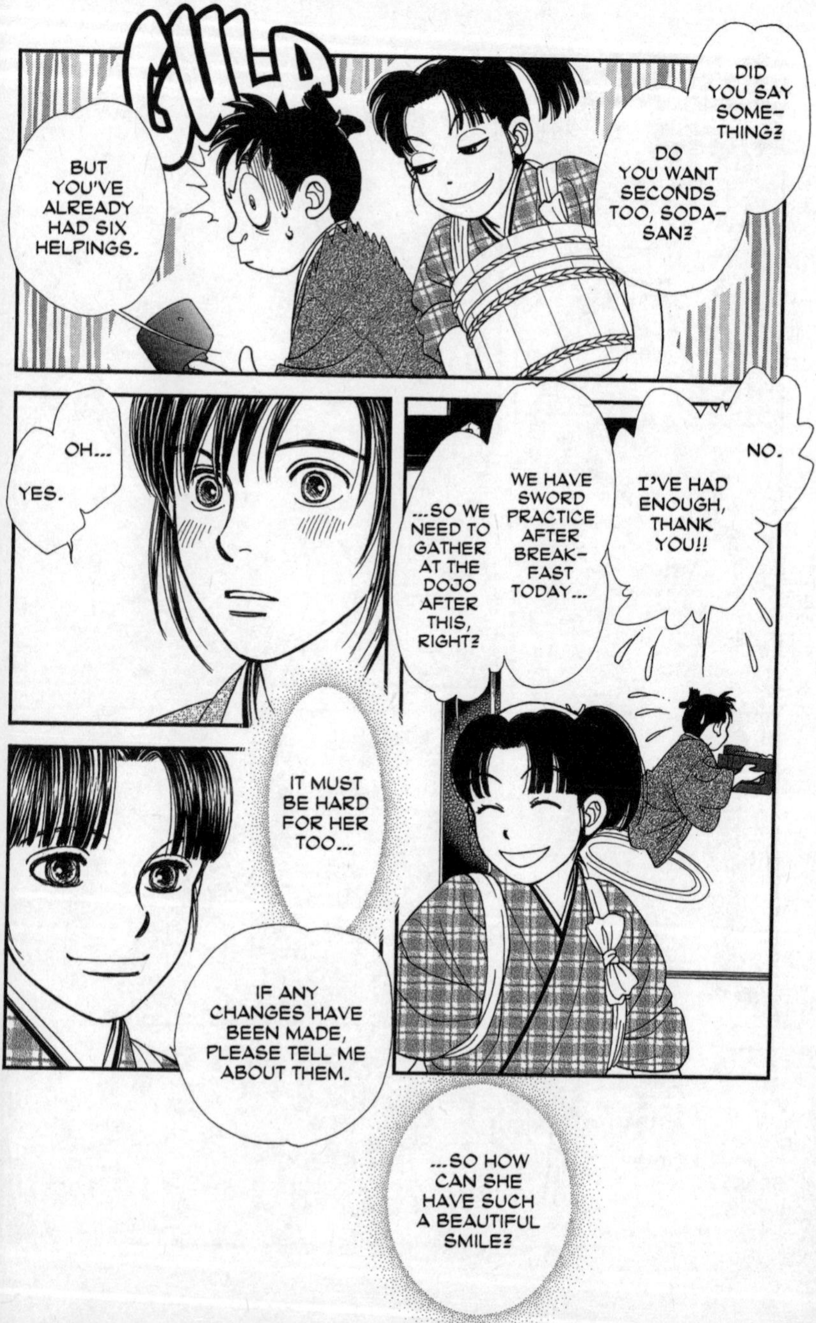
DID YOU SAY SOMETHING?
DO YOU WANT SECONDS TOO, SODA-SAN?
GULP
BUT YOU'VE ALREADY HAD SIX HELPINGS.
NO.
I'VE HAD ENOUGH, THANK YOU!!
WE HAVE SWORD PRACTICE AFTER BREAKFAST TODAY...
...SO WE NEED TO GATHER AT THE DOJO AFTER THIS, RIGHT?
OH...
YES.
IT MUST BE HARD FOR HER TOO...
IF ANY CHANGES HAVE BEEN MADE, PLEASE TELL ME ABOUT THEM.
...SO HOW CAN SHE HAVE SUCH A BEAUTIFUL SMILE?

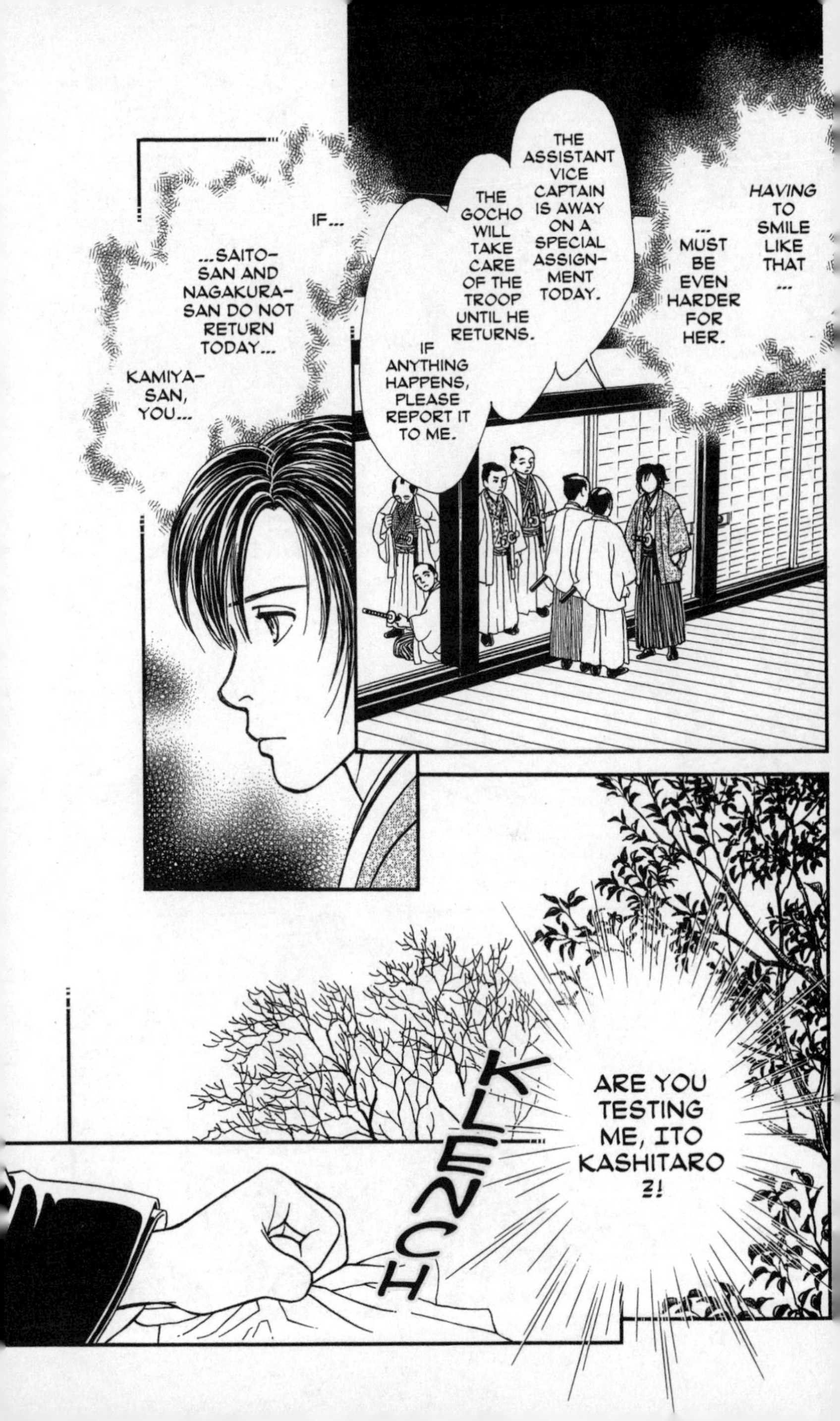
HAVING TO SMILE LIKE THAT...
...MUST BE EVEN HARDER FOR HER.
THE ASSISTANT VICE CAPTAIN IS AWAY ON A SPECIAL ASSIGNMENT TODAY.
THE GOCHO WILL TAKE CARE OF THE TROOP UNTIL HE RETURNS.
IF ANYTHING HAPPENS, PLEASE REPORT IT TO ME.
IF...
...SAITO-SAN AND NAGAKURA-SAN DO NOT RETURN TODAY...
KAMIYA-SAN, YOU...
ARE YOU TESTING ME, ITO KASHITARO?!
KLENCH

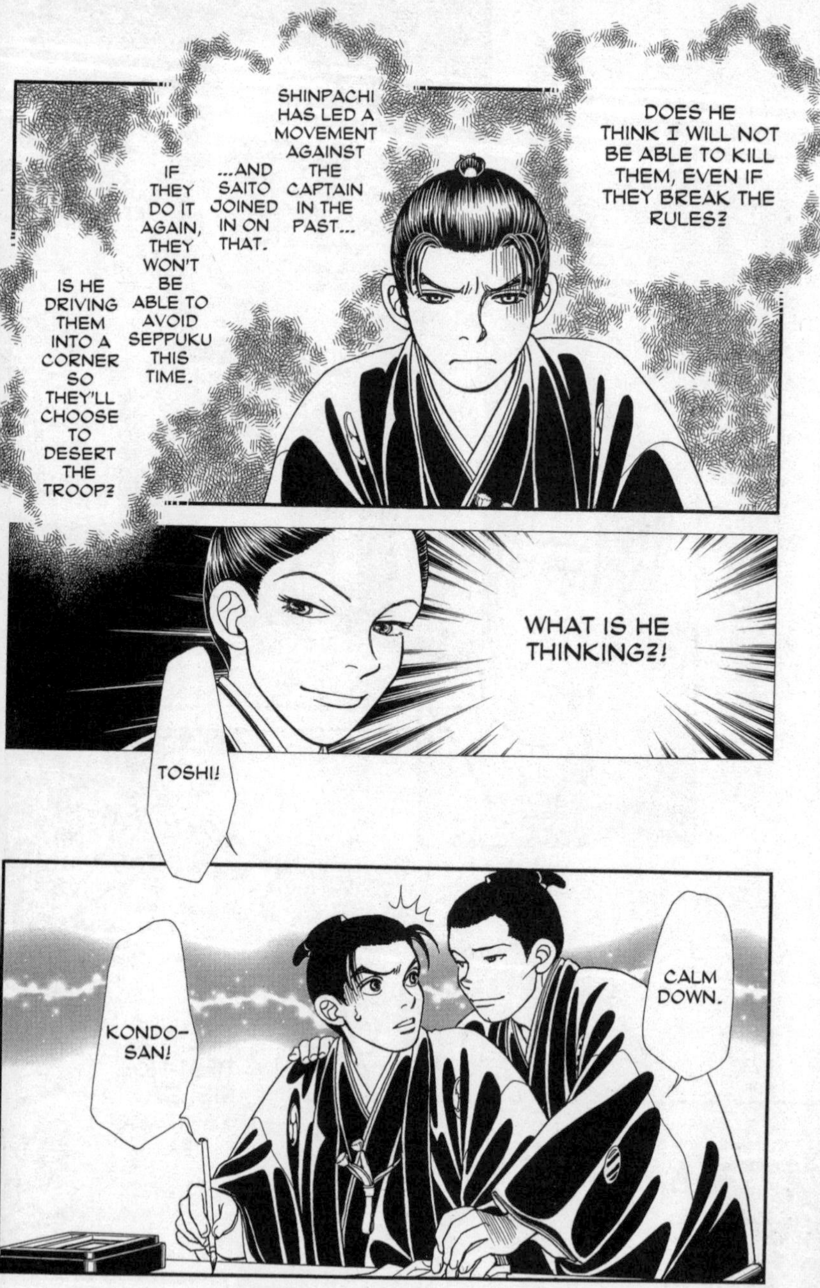
DOES HE THINK I WILL NOT BE ABLE TO KILL THEM, EVEN IF THEY BREAK THE RULES?
SHINPACHI HAS LED A MOVEMENT AGAINST THE CAPTAIN IN THE PAST...
...AND SAITO JOINED IN ON THAT.
IF THEY DO IT AGAIN, THEY WON'T BE ABLE TO AVOID SEPPUKU THIS TIME.
IS HE DRIVING THEM INTO A CORNER SO THEY'LL CHOOSE TO DESERT THE TROOP?
WHAT IS HE THINKING?!
TOSHI!
CALM DOWN.
KONDO-SAN!

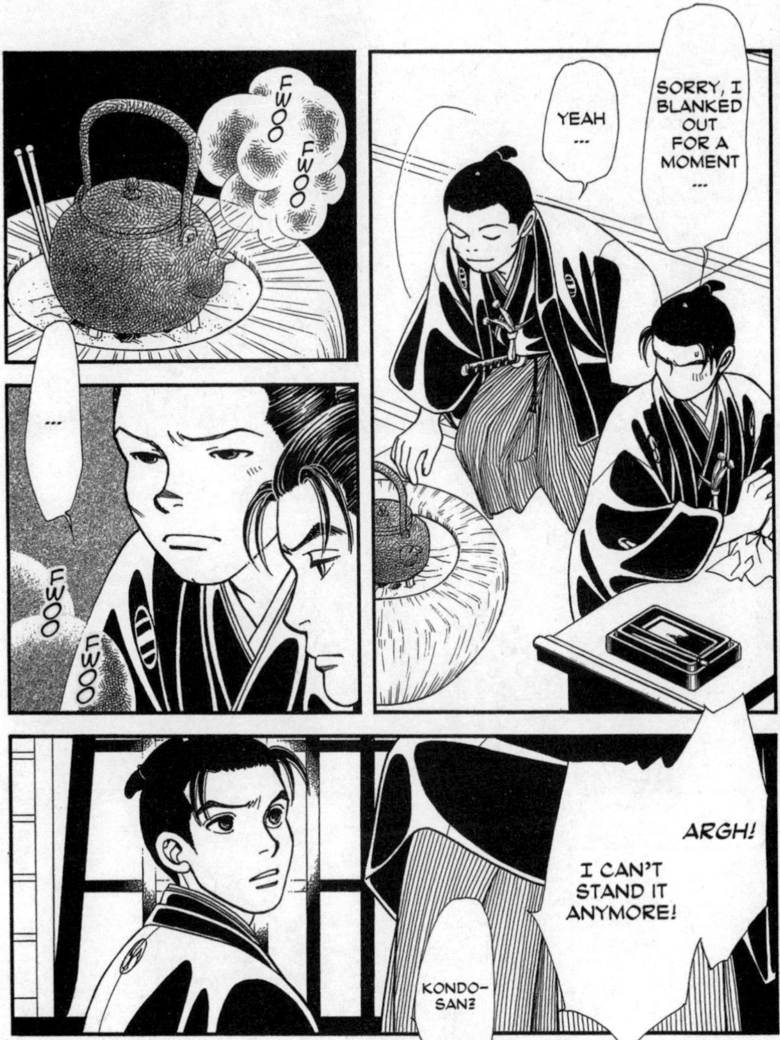
SORRY, I BLANKED OUT FOR A MOMENT ...
YEAH ...
FWOO FWOO
...
FWOO FWOO
ARGH!
I CAN'T STAND IT ANYMORE!
KONDO-SAN?
COME WITH ME, TOSHI!

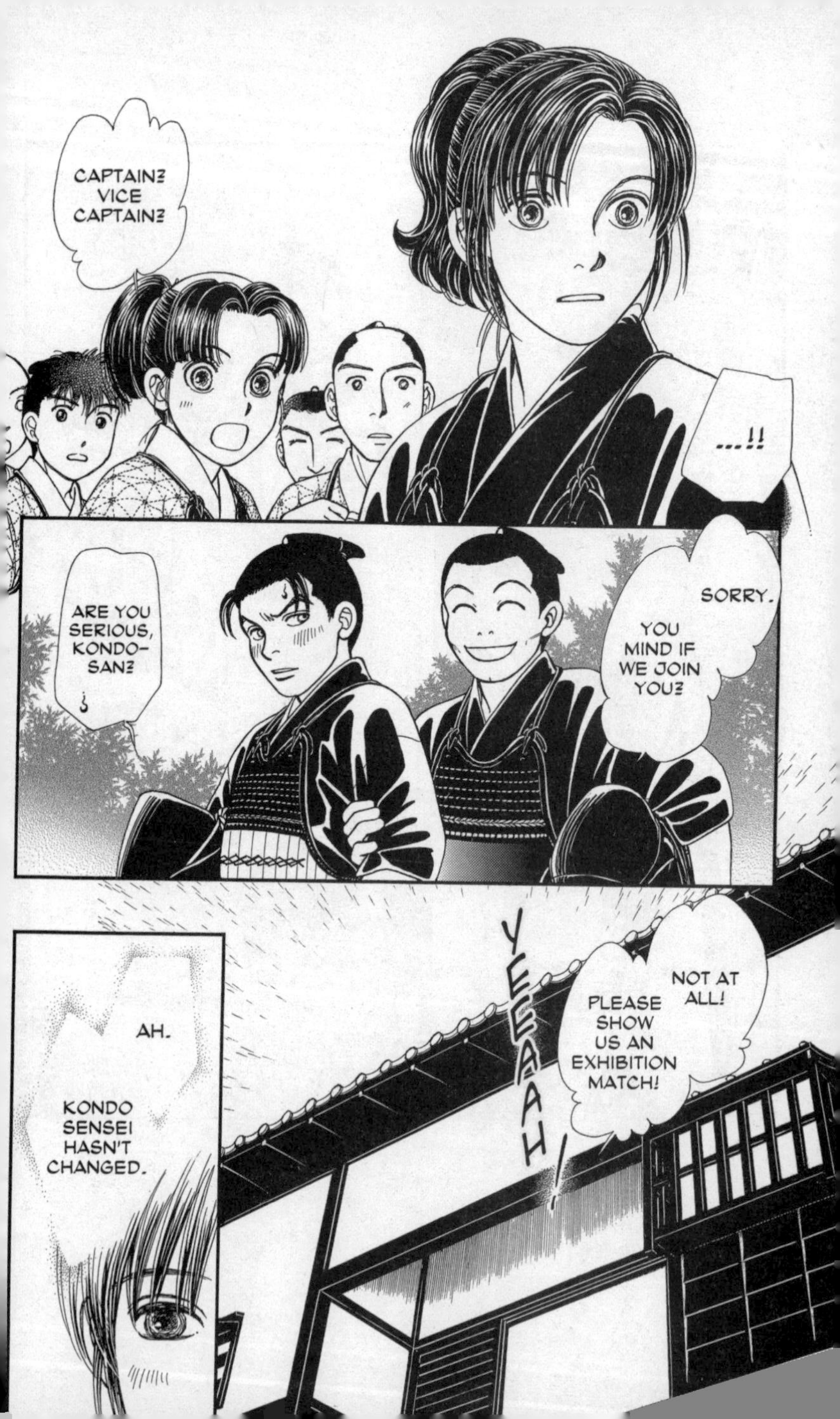
CAPTAIN? VICE CAPTAIN?
...!!
SORRY. YOU MIND IF WE JOIN YOU?
ARE YOU SERIOUS, KONDO-SAN?
NOT AT ALL! PLEASE SHOW US AN EXHIBITION MATCH!
YEEAAH!
AH. KONDO SENSEI HASN'T CHANGED.

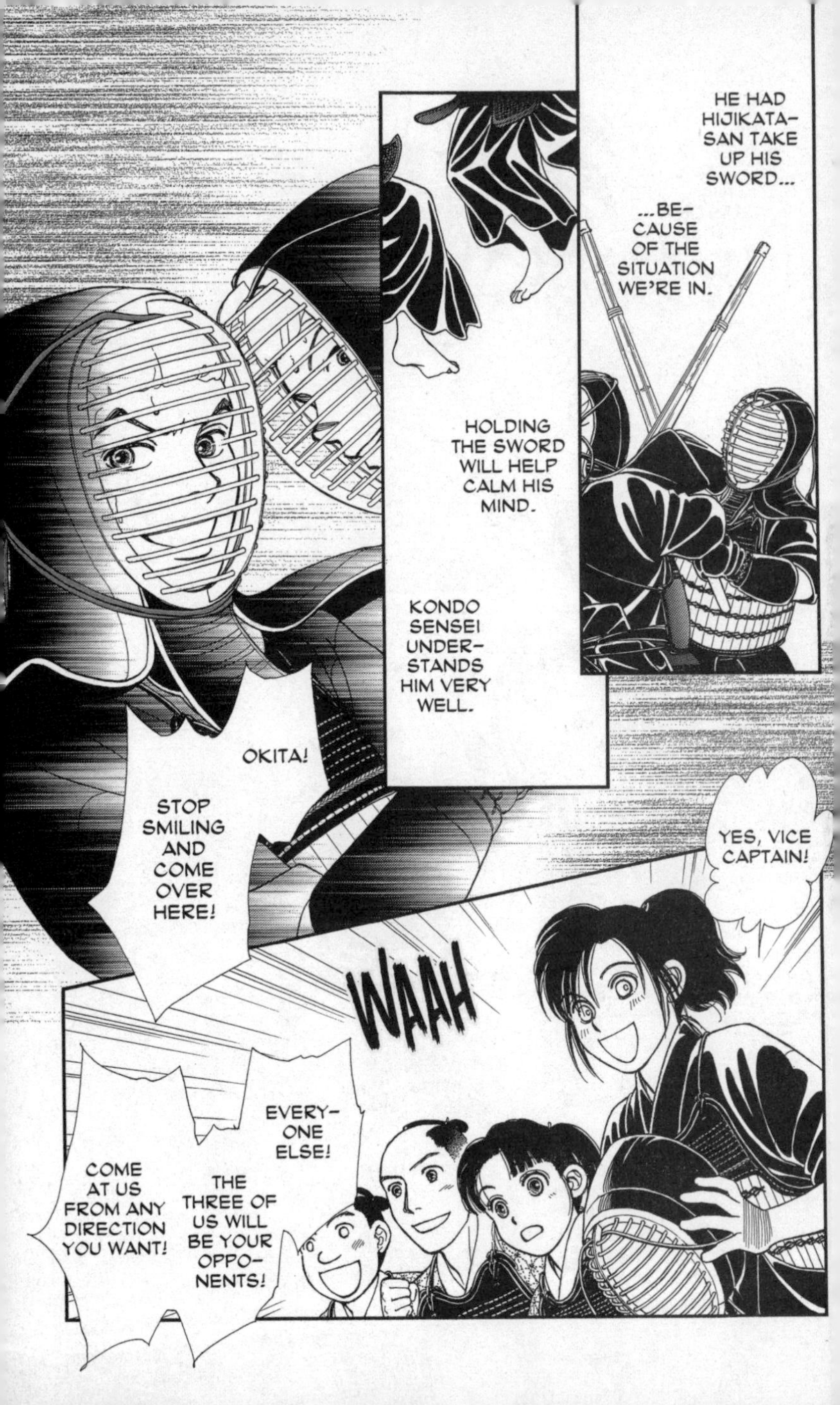
HE HAD HIJIKATA-SAN TAKE UP HIS SWORD...
...BECAUSE OF THE SITUATION WE'RE IN.
HOLDING THE SWORD WILL HELP CALM HIS MIND.
KONDO SENSEI UNDERSTANDS HIM VERY WELL.
OKITA!
STOP SMILING AND COME OVER HERE!
YES, VICE CAPTAIN!
WAAH
EVERYONE ELSE!
THE THREE OF US WILL BE YOUR OPPONENTS!
COME AT US FROM ANY DIRECTION YOU WANT!

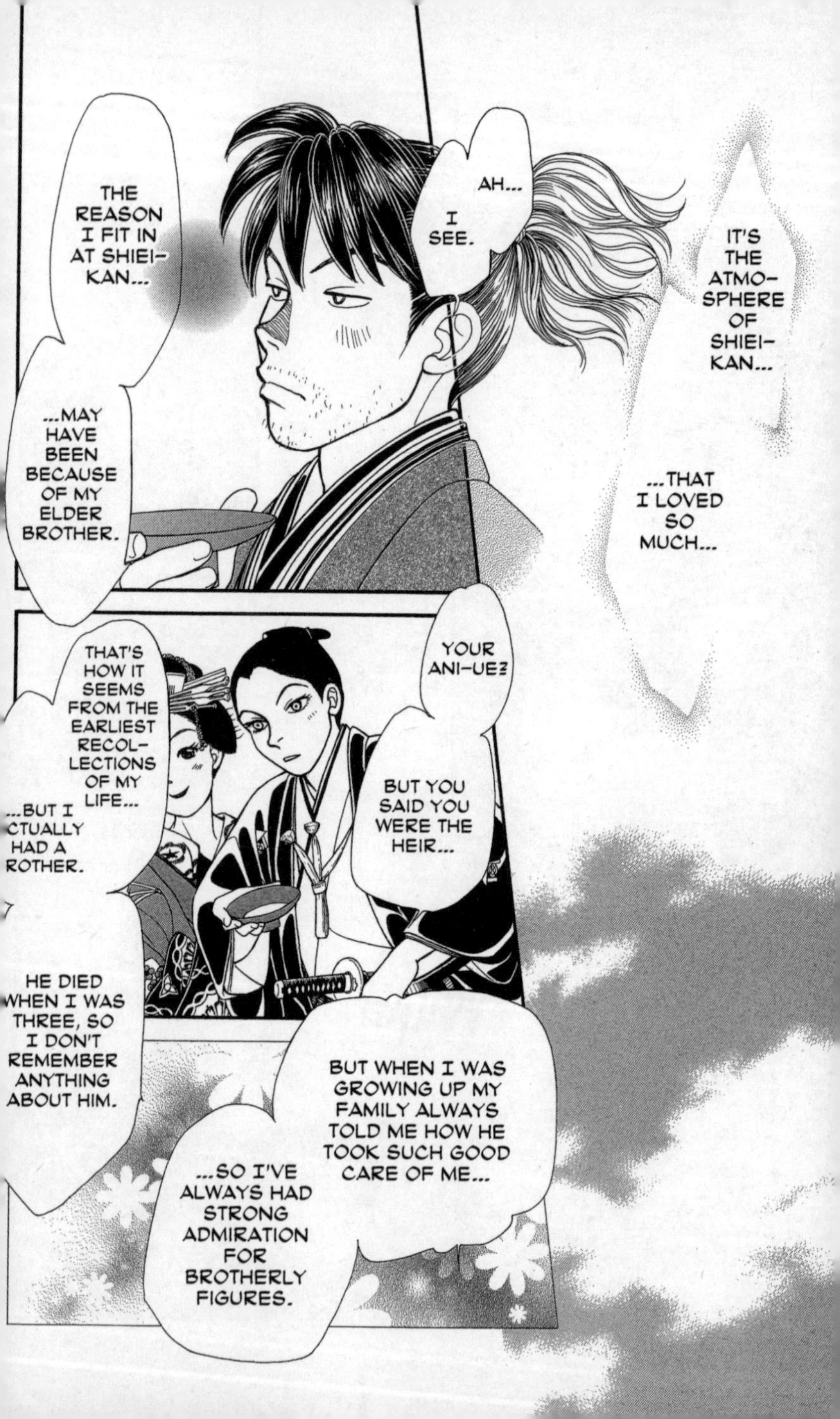
IT'S THE ATMOSPHERE OF SHIEI-KAN...
...THAT I LOVED SO MUCH...
AH... I SEE.
THE REASON I FIT IN AT SHIEI-KAN...
...MAY HAVE BEEN BECAUSE OF MY ELDER BROTHER.
YOUR ANI-UE?
BUT YOU SAID YOU WERE THE HEIR...
THAT'S HOW IT SEEMS FROM THE EARLIEST RECOLLECTIONS OF MY LIFE...
...BUT I CTUALLY HAD A ROTHER.
HE DIED WHEN I WAS THREE, SO I DON'T REMEMBER ANYTHING ABOUT HIM.
BUT WHEN I WAS GROWING UP MY FAMILY ALWAYS TOLD ME HOW HE TOOK SUCH GOOD CARE OF ME...
...SO I'VE ALWAYS HAD STRONG ADMIRATION FOR BROTHERLY FIGURES.

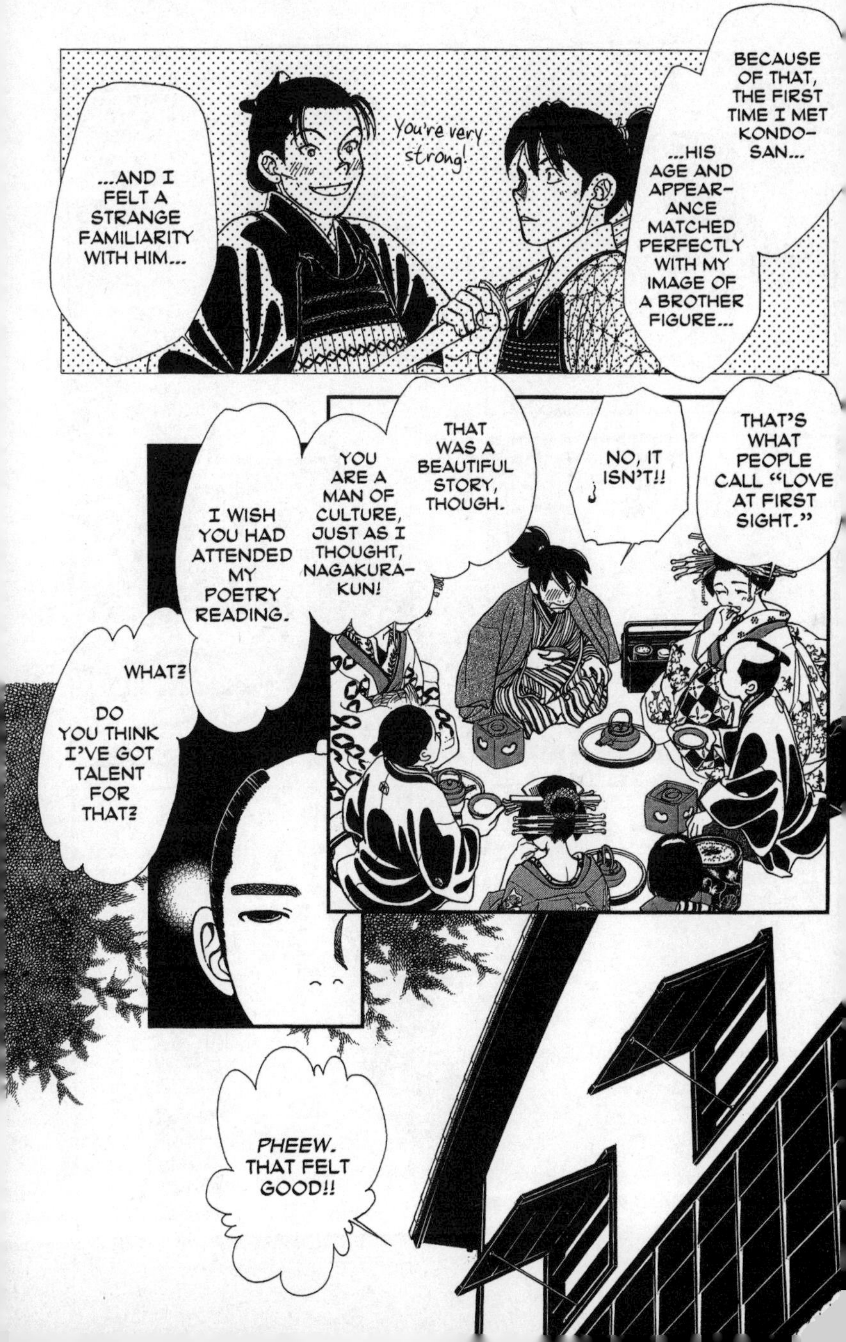
BECAUSE OF THAT, THE FIRST TIME I MET KONDO-SAN...
...HIS AGE AND APPEARANCE MATCHED PERFECTLY WITH MY IMAGE OF A BROTHER FIGURE...
You're very strong!
...AND I FELT A STRANGE FAMILIARITY WITH HIM...
THAT'S WHAT PEOPLE CALL "LOVE AT FIRST SIGHT."
NO, IT ISN'T!!
THAT WAS A BEAUTIFUL STORY, THOUGH.
YOU ARE A MAN OF CULTURE, JUST AS I THOUGHT, NAGAKURA-KUN!
I WISH YOU HAD ATTENDED MY POETRY READING.
WHAT? DO YOU THINK I'VE GOT TALENT FOR THAT?
PHEEW. THAT FELT GOOD!!

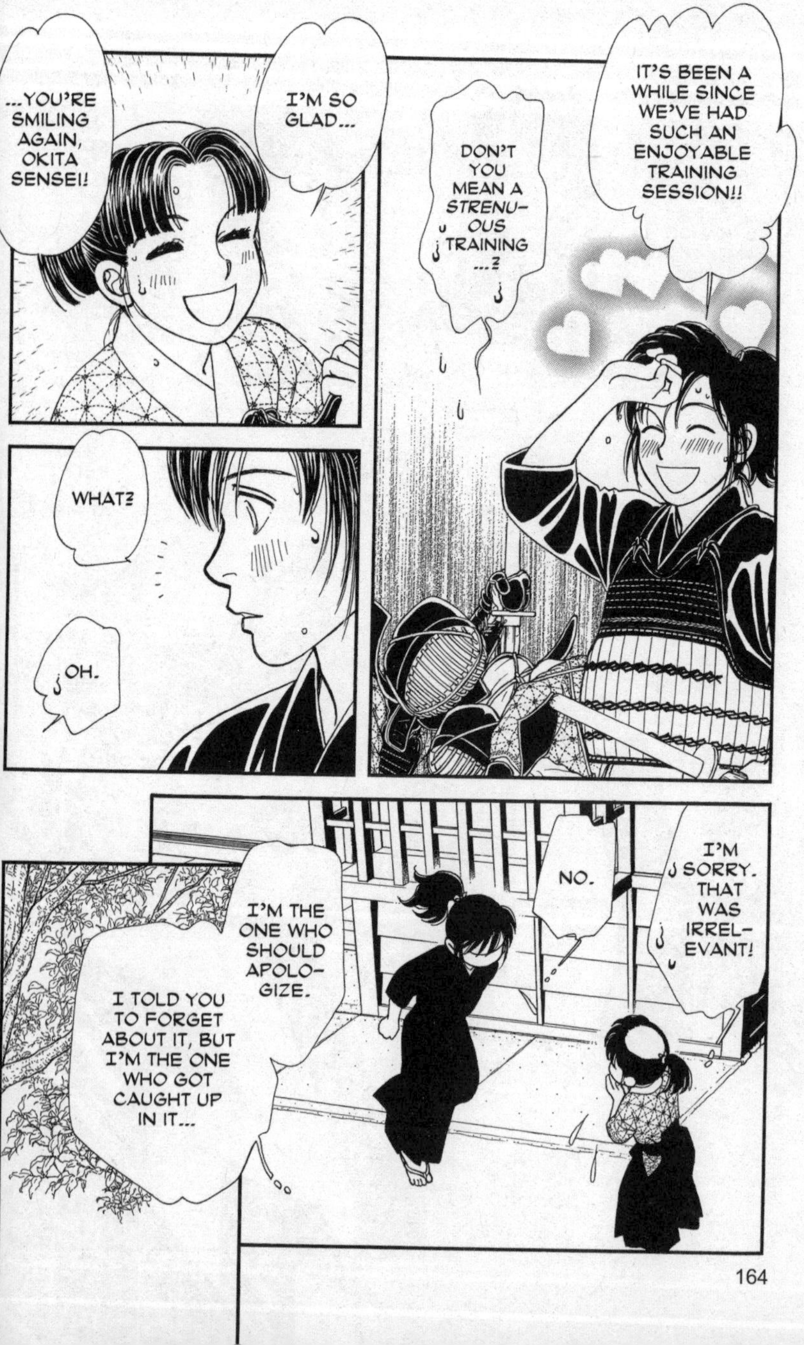
IT'S BEEN A WHILE SINCE WE'VE HAD SUCH AN ENJOYABLE TRAINING SESSION!!
DON'T YOU MEAN A *STRENUOUS* TRAINING ...?
I'M SO GLAD...
...YOU'RE SMILING AGAIN, OKITA SENSEI!
WHAT?
OH.
I'M SORRY. THAT WAS IRRELEVANT!
NO.
I'M THE ONE WHO SHOULD APOLOGIZE.
I TOLD YOU TO FORGET ABOUT IT, BUT I'M THE ONE WHO GOT CAUGHT UP IN IT...

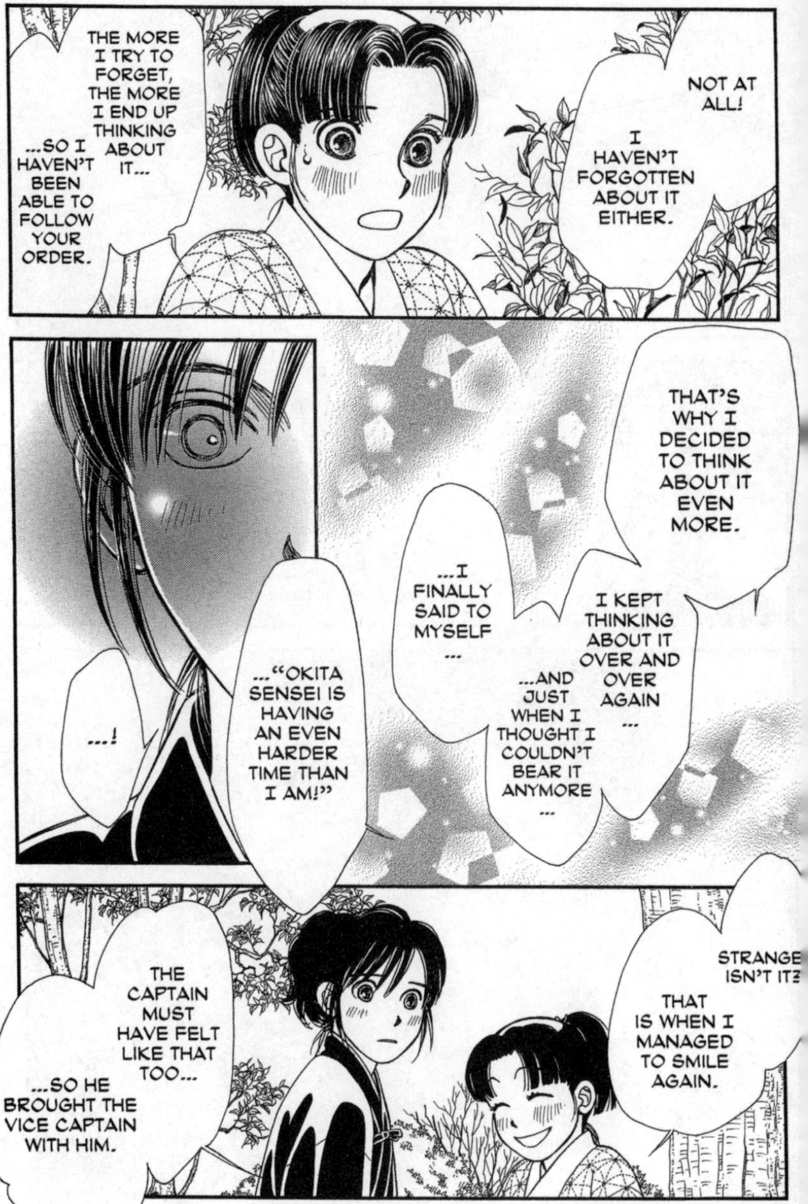
NOT AT ALL!
I HAVEN'T FORGOTTEN ABOUT IT EITHER.
THE MORE I TRY TO FORGET, THE MORE I END UP THINKING ABOUT IT...
...SO I HAVEN'T BEEN ABLE TO FOLLOW YOUR ORDER.
THAT'S WHY I DECIDED TO THINK ABOUT IT EVEN MORE.
I KEPT THINKING ABOUT IT OVER AND OVER AGAIN...
...AND JUST WHEN I THOUGHT I COULDN'T BEAR IT ANYMORE...
...I FINALLY SAID TO MYSELF...
..."OKITA SENSEI IS HAVING AN EVEN HARDER TIME THAN I AM!"
...!
STRANGE ISN'T IT?
THAT IS WHEN I MANAGED TO SMILE AGAIN.
THE CAPTAIN MUST HAVE FELT LIKE THAT TOO...
...SO HE BROUGHT THE VICE CAPTAIN WITH HIM.

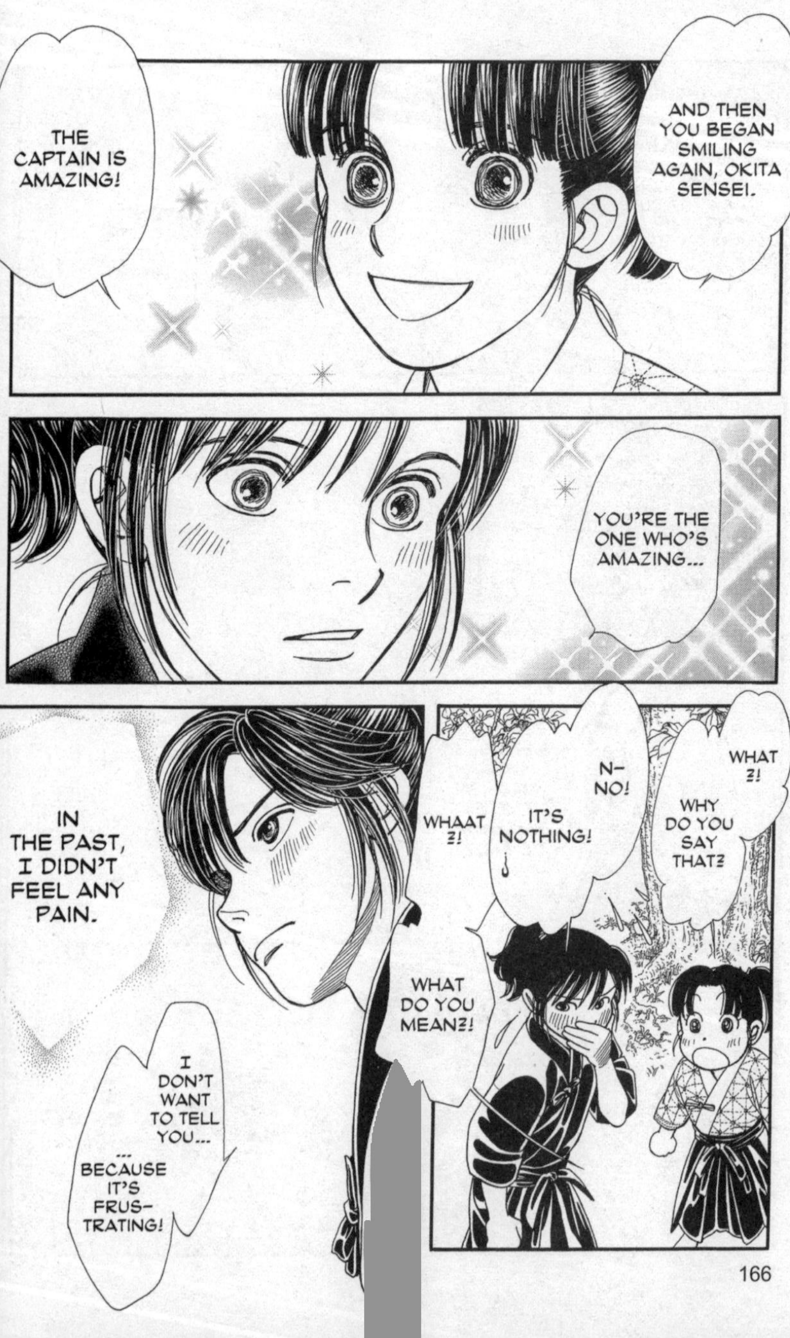
AND THEN YOU BEGAN SMILING AGAIN, OKITA SENSEI.
THE CAPTAIN IS AMAZING!
YOU'RE THE ONE WHO'S AMAZING...
WHAT?! WHY DO YOU SAY THAT?
N-NO! IT'S NOTHING!
WHAAT?!
WHAT DO YOU MEAN?!
IN THE PAST, I DIDN'T FEEL ANY PAIN.
I DON'T WANT TO TELL YOU... ...BECAUSE IT'S FRUS-TRATING!

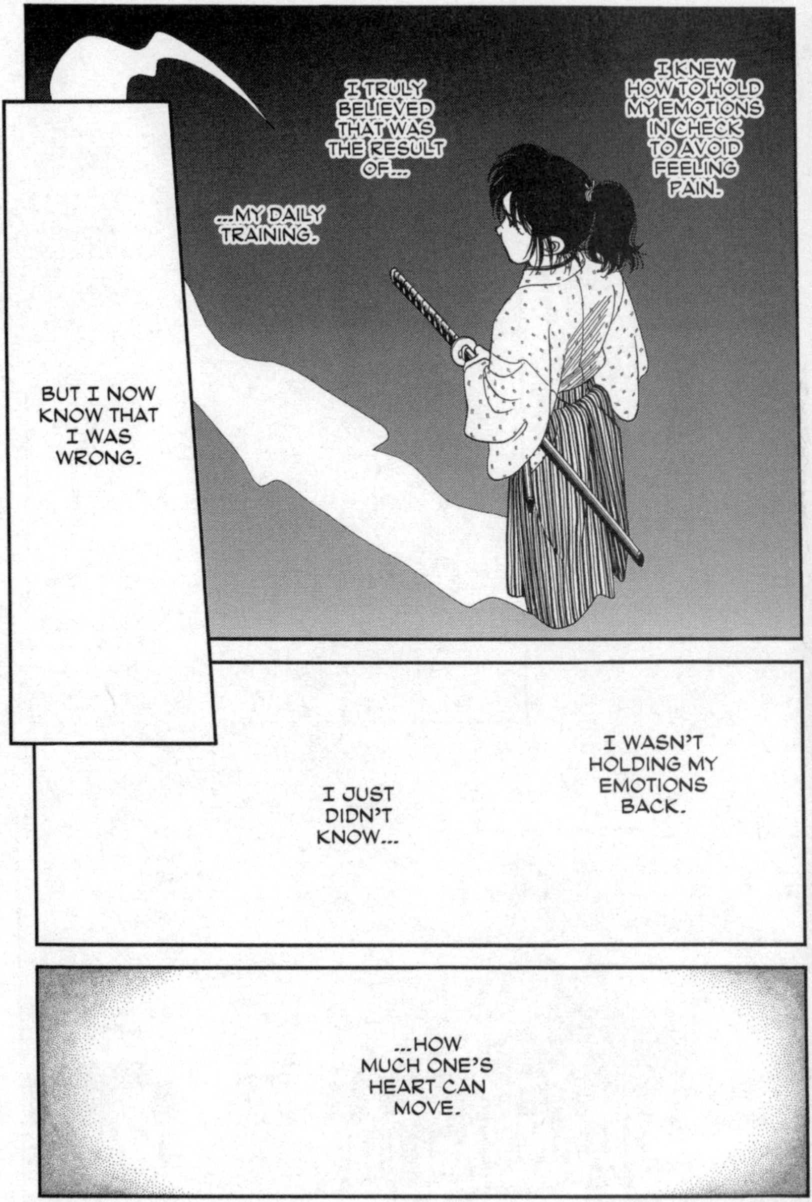
I KNEW HOW TO HOLD MY EMOTIONS IN CHECK TO AVOID FEELING PAIN.
I TRULY BELIEVED THAT WAS THE RESULT OF...
...MY DAILY TRAINING.
BUT I NOW KNOW THAT I WAS WRONG.
I WASN'T HOLDING MY EMOTIONS BACK.
I JUST DIDN'T KNOW...
...HOW MUCH ONE'S HEART CAN MOVE.

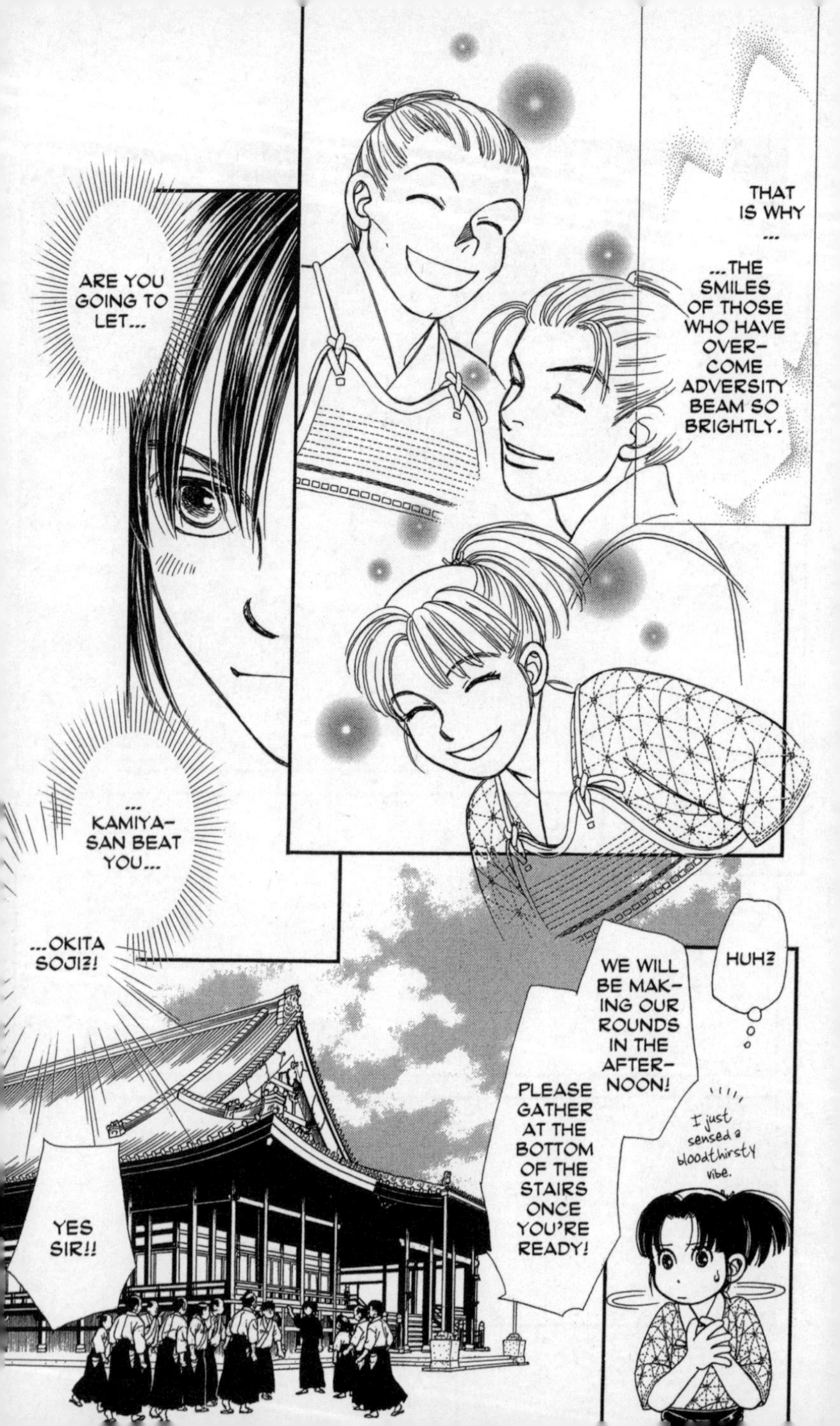
THAT IS WHY ...
...THE SMILES OF THOSE WHO HAVE OVERCOME ADVERSITY BEAM SO BRIGHTLY.
ARE YOU GOING TO LET...
...KAMIYA-SAN BEAT YOU...
...OKITA SOJI?!
HUH?
I just sensed a bloodthirsty vibe.
WE WILL BE MAKING OUR ROUNDS IN THE AFTERNOON!
PLEASE GATHER AT THE BOTTOM OF THE STAIRS ONCE YOU'RE READY!
YES SIR!!

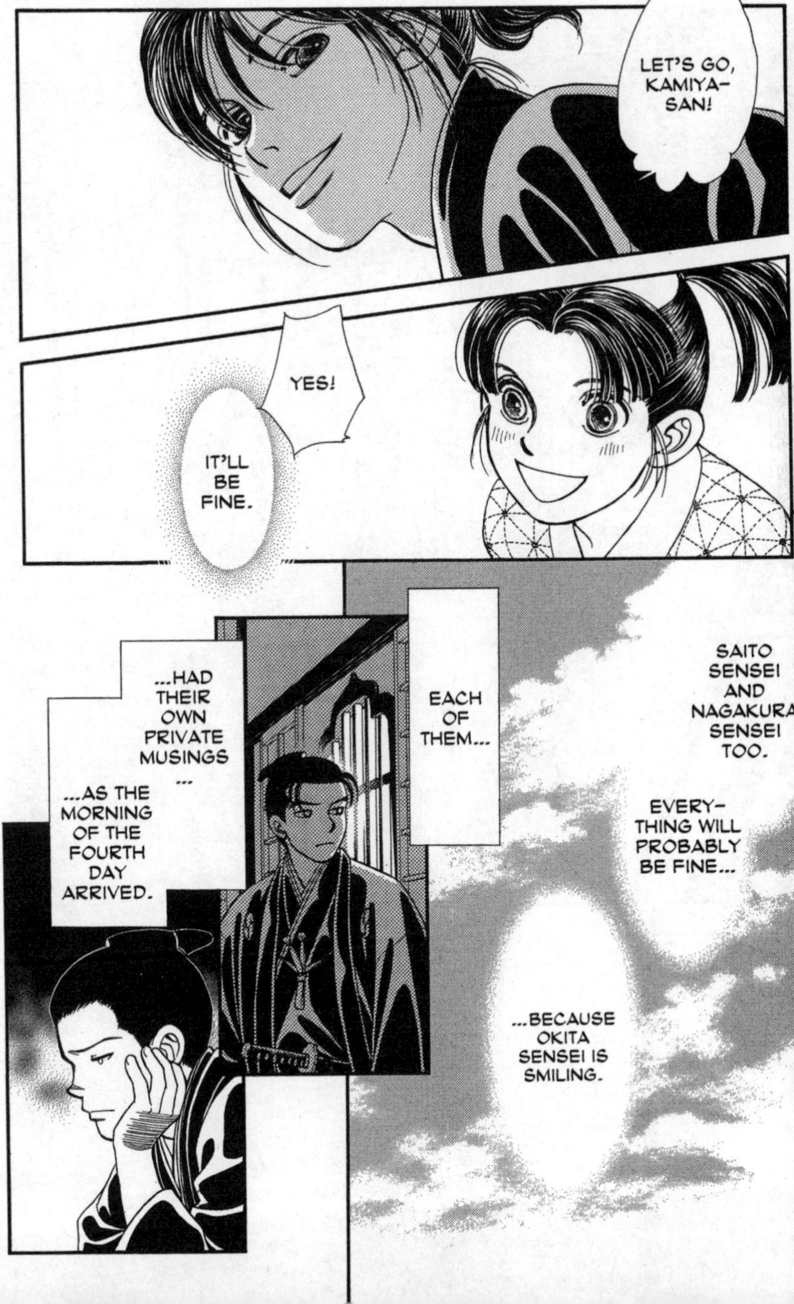
LET'S GO, KAMIYA-SAN!
YES!
IT'LL BE FINE.
SAITO SENSEI AND NAGAKURA SENSEI TOO.
EVERYTHING WILL PROBABLY BE FINE...
...BECAUSE OKITA SENSEI IS SMILING.
EACH OF THEM...
...HAD THEIR OWN PRIVATE MUSINGS...
...AS THE MORNING OF THE FOURTH DAY ARRIVED.

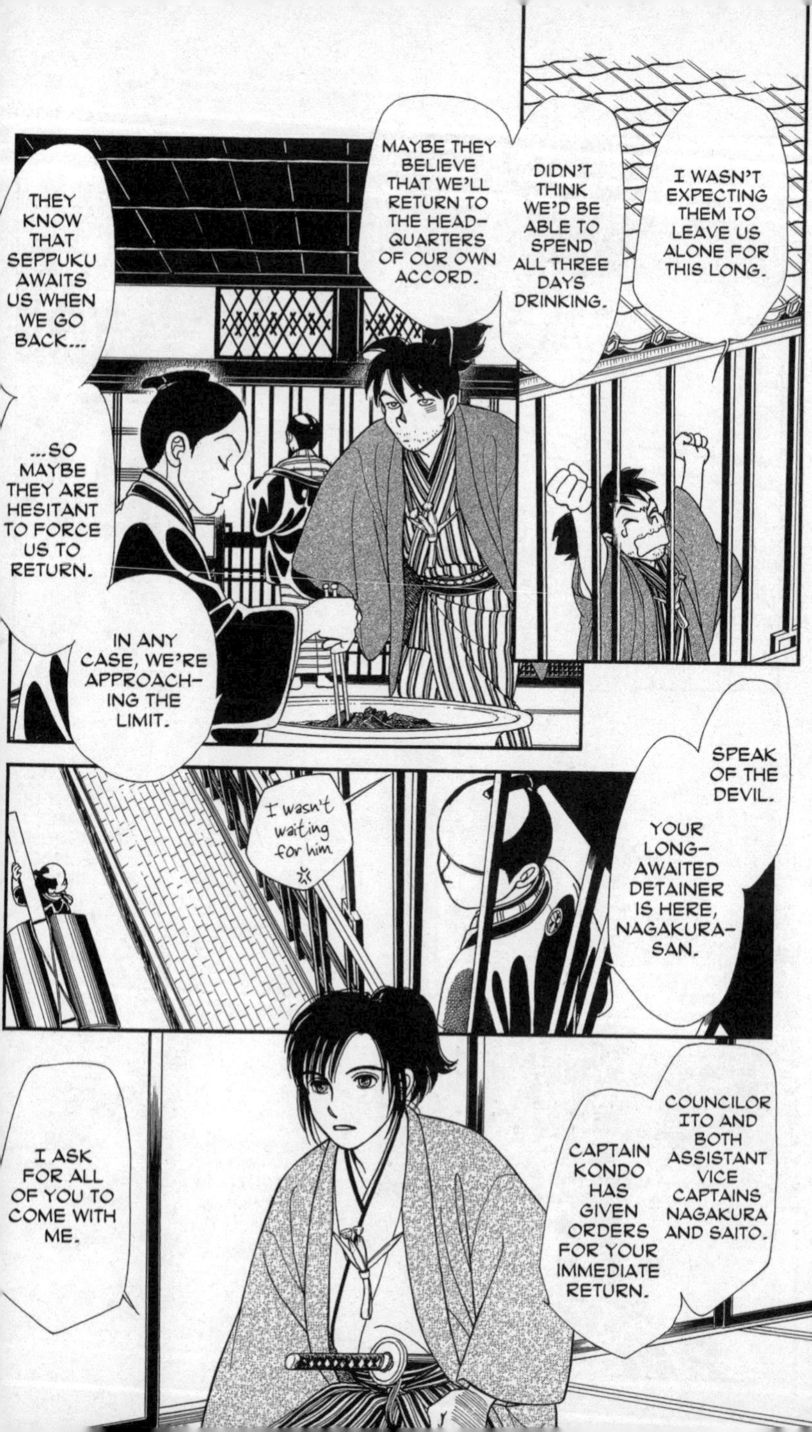
I WASN'T EXPECTING THEM TO LEAVE US ALONE FOR THIS LONG.
DIDN'T THINK WE'D BE ABLE TO SPEND ALL THREE DAYS DRINKING.
MAYBE THEY BELIEVE THAT WE'LL RETURN TO THE HEAD-QUARTERS OF OUR OWN ACCORD.
THEY KNOW THAT SEPPUKU AWAITS US WHEN WE GO BACK...
...SO MAYBE THEY ARE HESITANT TO FORCE US TO RETURN.
IN ANY CASE, WE'RE APPROACH-ING THE LIMIT.
SPEAK OF THE DEVIL.
YOUR LONG-AWAITED DETAINER IS HERE, NAGAKURA-SAN.
I wasn't waiting for him
COUNCILOR ITO AND BOTH ASSISTANT VICE CAPTAINS NAGAKURA AND SAITO.
CAPTAIN KONDO HAS GIVEN ORDERS FOR YOUR IMMEDIATE RETURN.
I ASK FOR ALL OF YOU TO COME WITH ME.

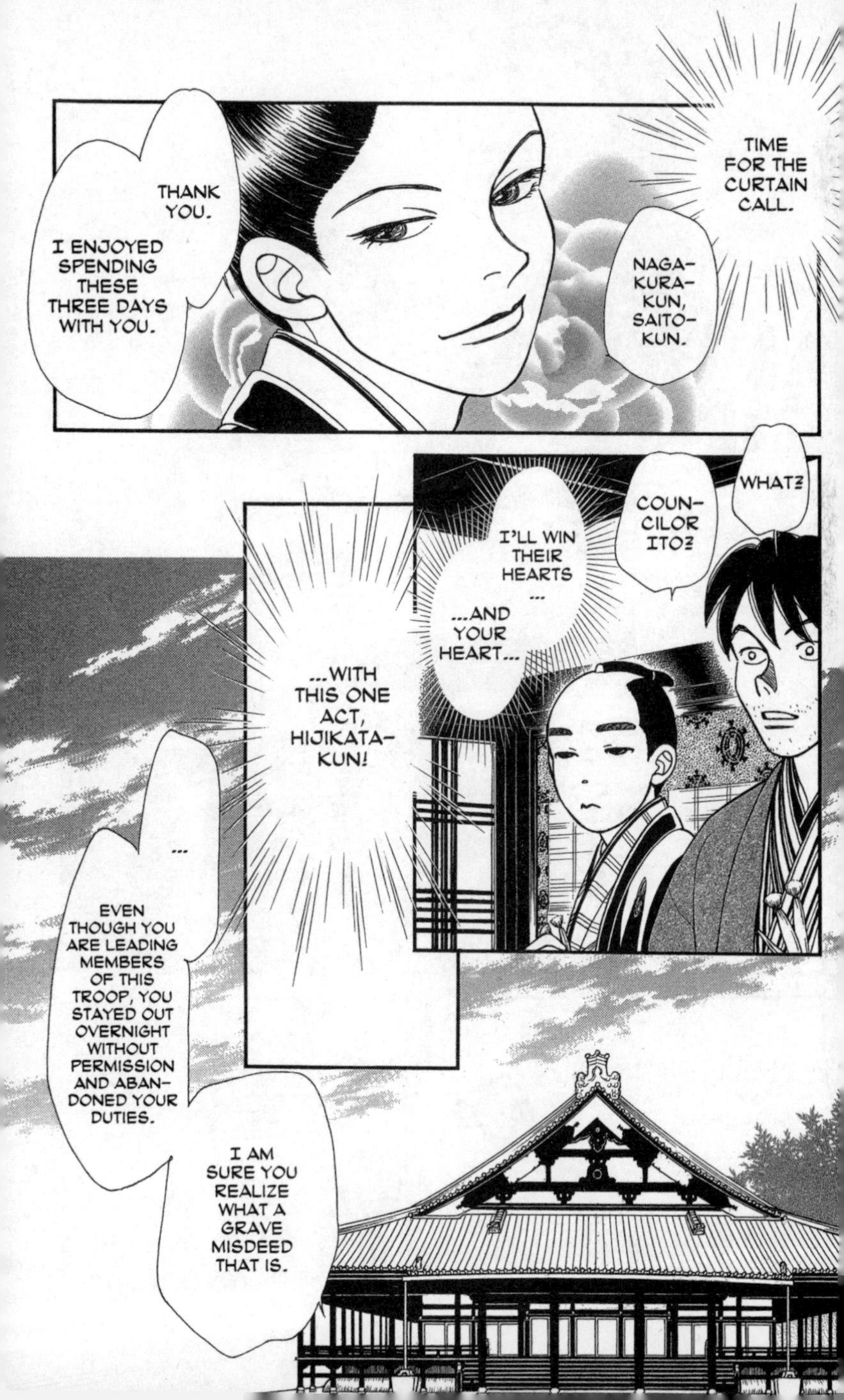
TIME FOR THE CURTAIN CALL.
NAGAKURA-KUN, SAITO-KUN.
THANK YOU.
I ENJOYED SPENDING THESE THREE DAYS WITH YOU.
WHAT?
COUNCILOR ITO?
I'LL WIN THEIR HEARTS ...
...AND YOUR HEART...
...WITH THIS ONE ACT, HIJIKATA-KUN!
...
EVEN THOUGH YOU ARE LEADING MEMBERS OF THIS TROOP, YOU STAYED OUT OVERNIGHT WITHOUT PERMISSION AND ABANDONED YOUR DUTIES.
I AM SURE YOU REALIZE WHAT A GRAVE MISDEED THAT IS.

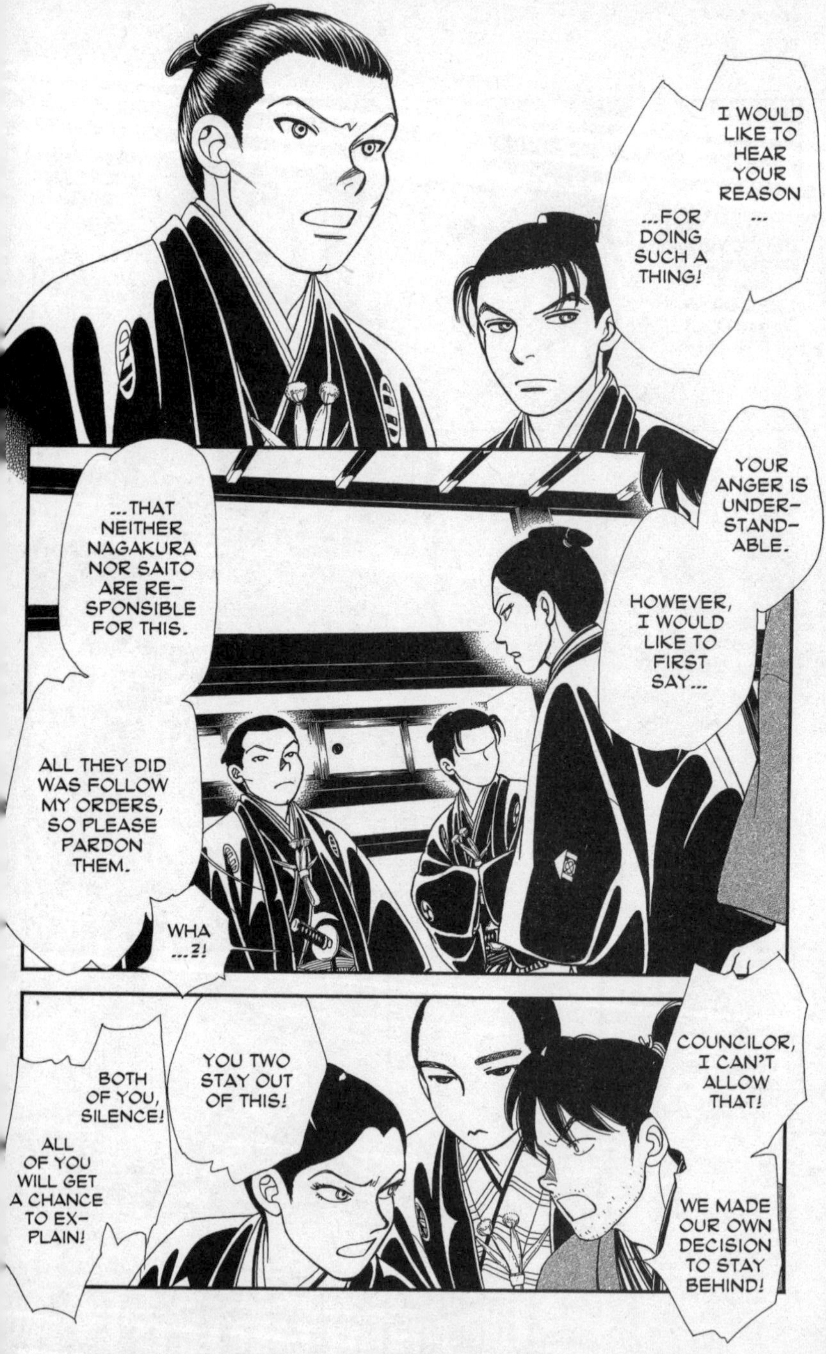
I WOULD LIKE TO HEAR YOUR REASON...
...FOR DOING SUCH A THING!
YOUR ANGER IS UNDERSTANDABLE.
HOWEVER, I WOULD LIKE TO FIRST SAY...
...THAT NEITHER NAGAKURA NOR SAITO ARE RESPONSIBLE FOR THIS.
ALL THEY DID WAS FOLLOW MY ORDERS, SO PLEASE PARDON THEM.
WHA...?!
COUNCILOR, I CAN'T ALLOW THAT!
WE MADE OUR OWN DECISION TO STAY BEHIND!
YOU TWO STAY OUT OF THIS!
BOTH OF YOU, SILENCE!
ALL OF YOU WILL GET A CHANCE TO EXPLAIN!

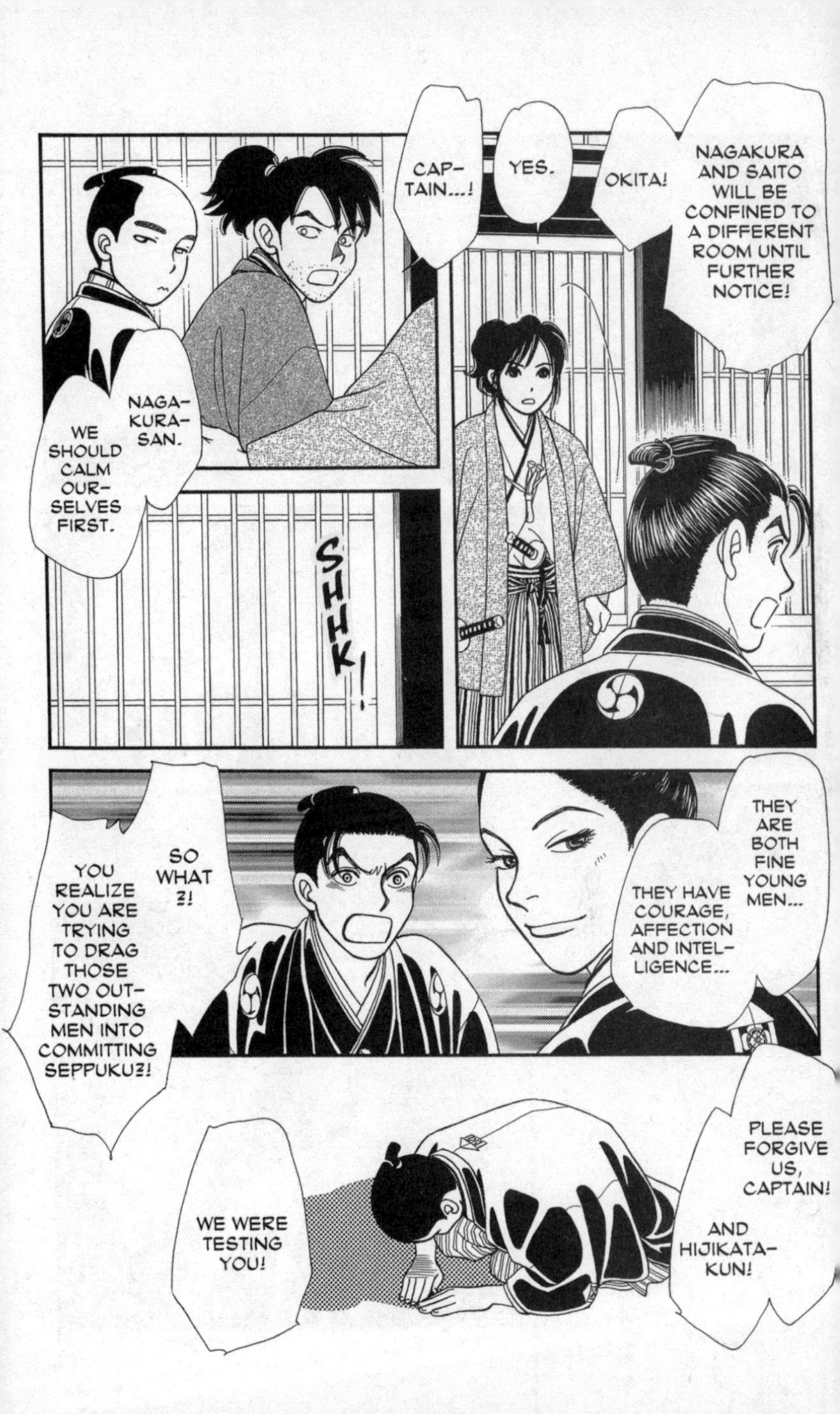
NAGAKURA AND SAITO WILL BE CONFINED TO A DIFFERENT ROOM UNTIL FURTHER NOTICE!
OKITA!
YES.
CAPTAIN...!
NAGAKURA-SAN.
WE SHOULD CALM OURSELVES FIRST.
SHHK!
THEY ARE BOTH FINE YOUNG MEN...
THEY HAVE COURAGE, AFFECTION AND INTELLIGENCE...
SO WHAT?!
YOU REALIZE YOU ARE TRYING TO DRAG THOSE TWO OUTSTANDING MEN INTO COMMITTING SEPPUKU?!
PLEASE FORGIVE US, CAPTAIN!
AND HIJIKATA-KUN!
WE WERE TESTING YOU!

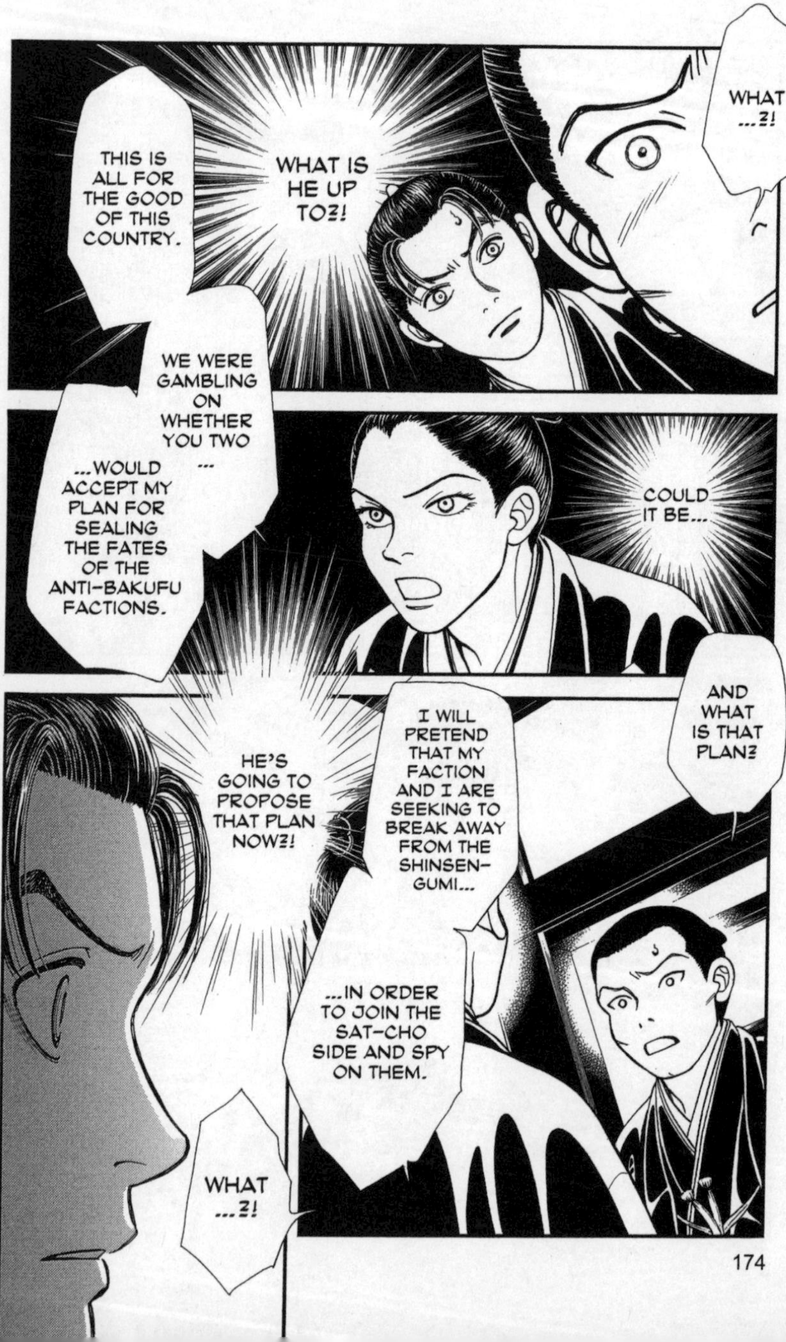
WHAT ...?!
WHAT IS HE UP TO?!
THIS IS ALL FOR THE GOOD OF THIS COUNTRY.
WE WERE GAMBLING ON WHETHER YOU TWO ...
...WOULD ACCEPT MY PLAN FOR SEALING THE FATES OF THE ANTI-BAKUFU FACTIONS.
COULD IT BE...
AND WHAT IS THAT PLAN?
I WILL PRETEND THAT MY FACTION AND I ARE SEEKING TO BREAK AWAY FROM THE SHINSEN-GUMI...
HE'S GOING TO PROPOSE THAT PLAN NOW?!
...IN ORDER TO JOIN THE SAT-CHO SIDE AND SPY ON THEM.
WHAT ...?!

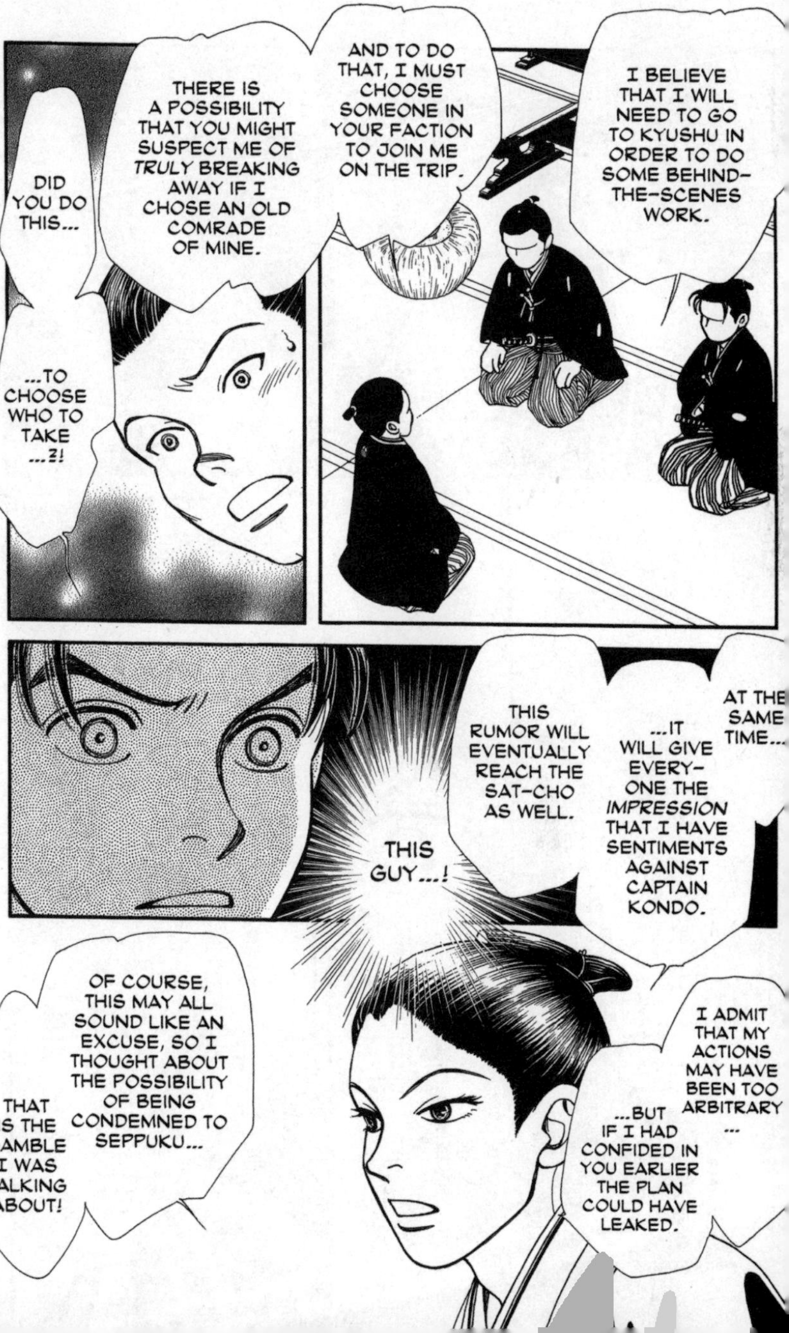
I BELIEVE THAT I WILL NEED TO GO TO KYUSHU IN ORDER TO DO SOME BEHIND-THE-SCENES WORK.
AND TO DO THAT, I MUST CHOOSE SOMEONE IN YOUR FACTION TO JOIN ME ON THE TRIP.
THERE IS A POSSIBILITY THAT YOU MIGHT SUSPECT ME OF *TRULY* BREAKING AWAY IF I CHOSE AN OLD COMRADE OF MINE.
DID YOU DO THIS...
...TO CHOOSE WHO TO TAKE ...?!
AT THE SAME TIME...
...IT WILL GIVE EVERYONE THE *IMPRESSION* THAT I HAVE SENTIMENTS AGAINST CAPTAIN KONDO.
THIS RUMOR WILL EVENTUALLY REACH THE SAT-CHO AS WELL.
THIS GUY...!
I ADMIT THAT MY ACTIONS MAY HAVE BEEN TOO ARBITRARY...
...BUT IF I HAD CONFIDED IN YOU EARLIER THE PLAN COULD HAVE LEAKED.
OF COURSE, THIS MAY ALL SOUND LIKE AN EXCUSE, SO I THOUGHT ABOUT THE POSSIBILITY OF BEING CONDEMNED TO SEPPUKU...
THAT IS THE GAMBLE I WAS TALKING ABOUT!

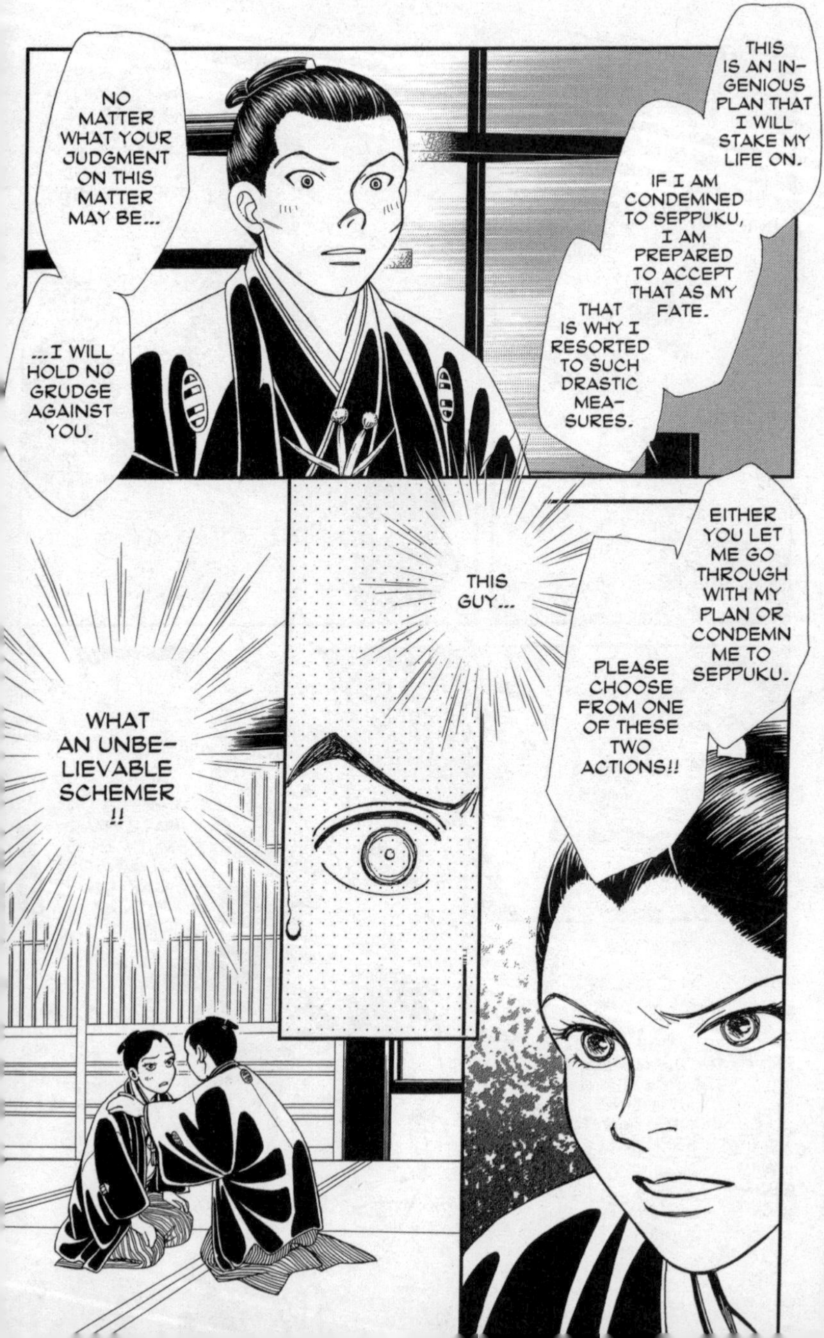
THIS IS AN INGENIOUS PLAN THAT I WILL STAKE MY LIFE ON.
IF I AM CONDEMNED TO SEPPUKU, I AM PREPARED TO ACCEPT THAT AS MY FATE.
THAT IS WHY I RESORTED TO SUCH DRASTIC MEASURES.
NO MATTER WHAT YOUR JUDGMENT ON THIS MATTER MAY BE...
...I WILL HOLD NO GRUDGE AGAINST YOU.
EITHER YOU LET ME GO THROUGH WITH MY PLAN OR CONDEMN ME TO SEPPUKU.
PLEASE CHOOSE FROM ONE OF THESE TWO ACTIONS!!
THIS GUY...
WHAT AN UNBELIEVABLE SCHEMER!!

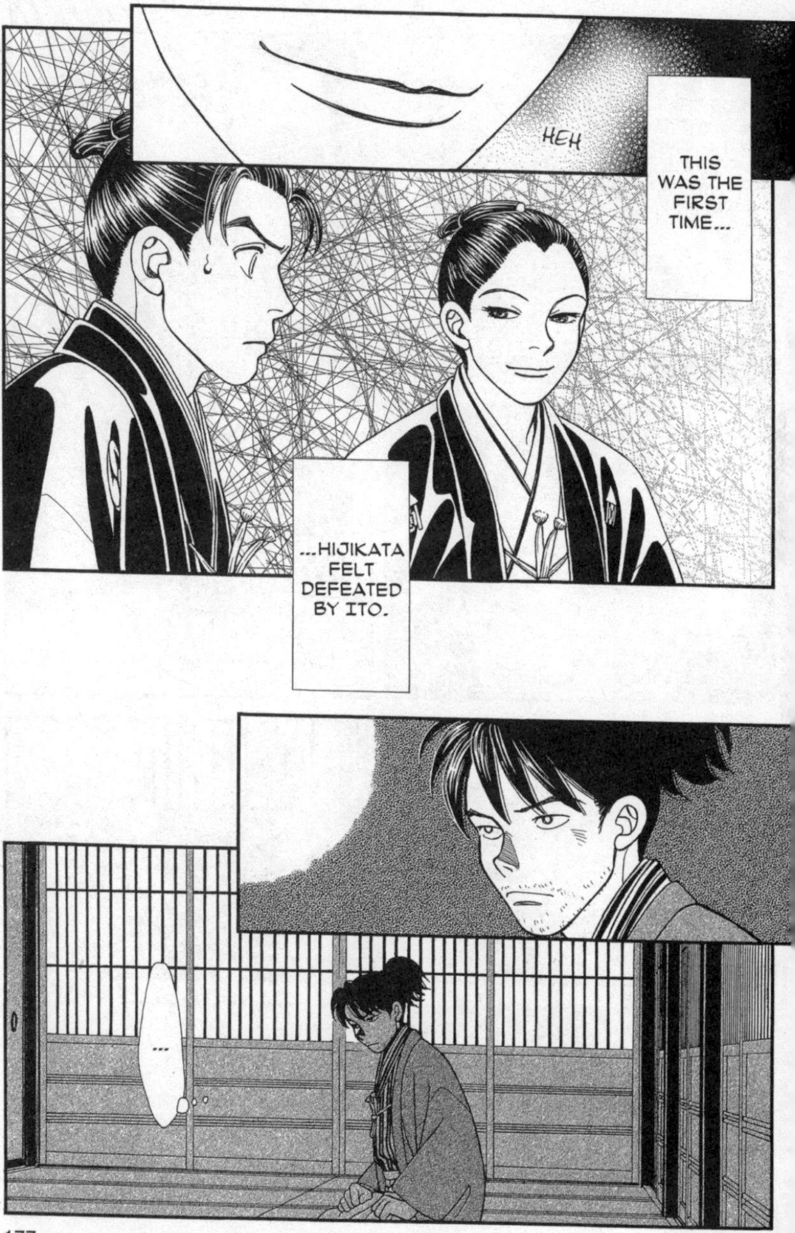
HEH
THIS WAS THE FIRST TIME...
...HIJIKATA FELT DEFEATED BY ITO.
...

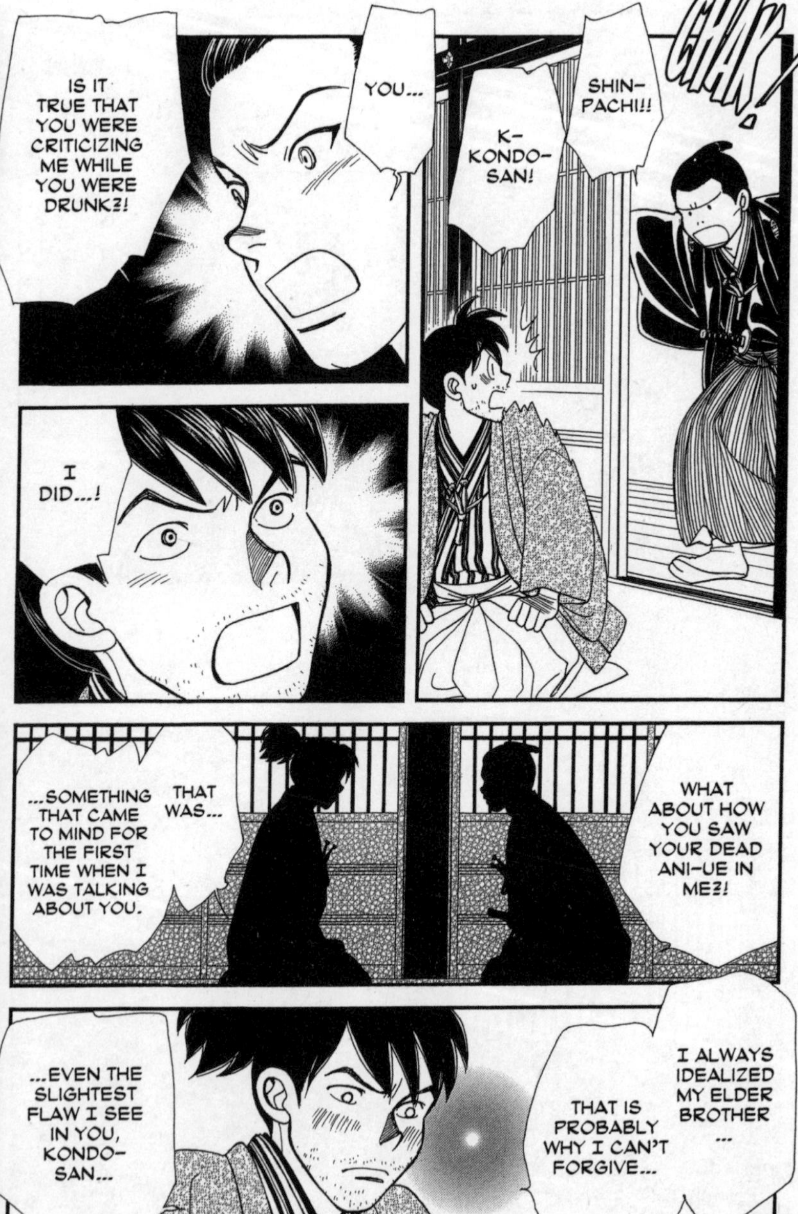
CHAK!
SHIN-PACHI!!
K-KONDO-SAN!
YOU...
IS IT TRUE THAT YOU WERE CRITICIZING ME WHILE YOU WERE DRUNK?!
I DID...!
WHAT ABOUT HOW YOU SAW YOUR DEAD ANI-UE IN ME?!
THAT WAS...
...SOMETHING THAT CAME TO MIND FOR THE FIRST TIME WHEN I WAS TALKING ABOUT YOU.
I ALWAYS IDEALIZED MY ELDER BROTHER...
THAT IS PROBABLY WHY I CAN'T FORGIVE...
...EVEN THE SLIGHTEST FLAW I SEE IN YOU, KONDO-SAN...

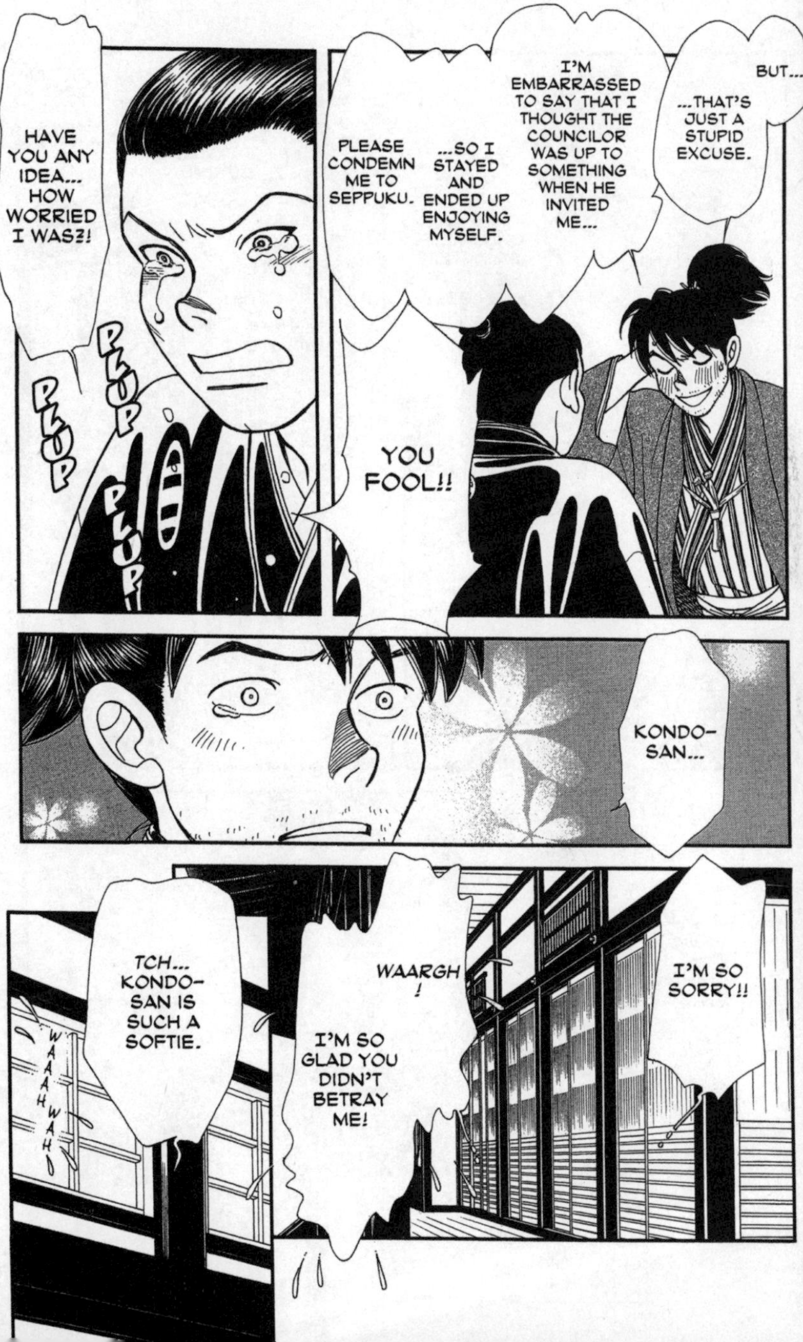
BUT...
...THAT'S JUST A STUPID EXCUSE.
I'M EMBARRASSED TO SAY THAT I THOUGHT THE COUNCILOR WAS UP TO SOMETHING WHEN HE INVITED ME...
...SO I STAYED AND ENDED UP ENJOYING MYSELF.
PLEASE CONDEMN ME TO SEPPUKU.
YOU FOOL!!
HAVE YOU ANY IDEA... HOW WORRIED I WAS?!
PLUP
PLUP
PLUP
PLUP
KONDO-SAN...
I'M SO SORRY!!
WAARGH!
I'M SO GLAD YOU DIDN'T BETRAY ME!
TCH... KONDO-SAN IS SUCH A SOFTIE.
WAAAH
WAH

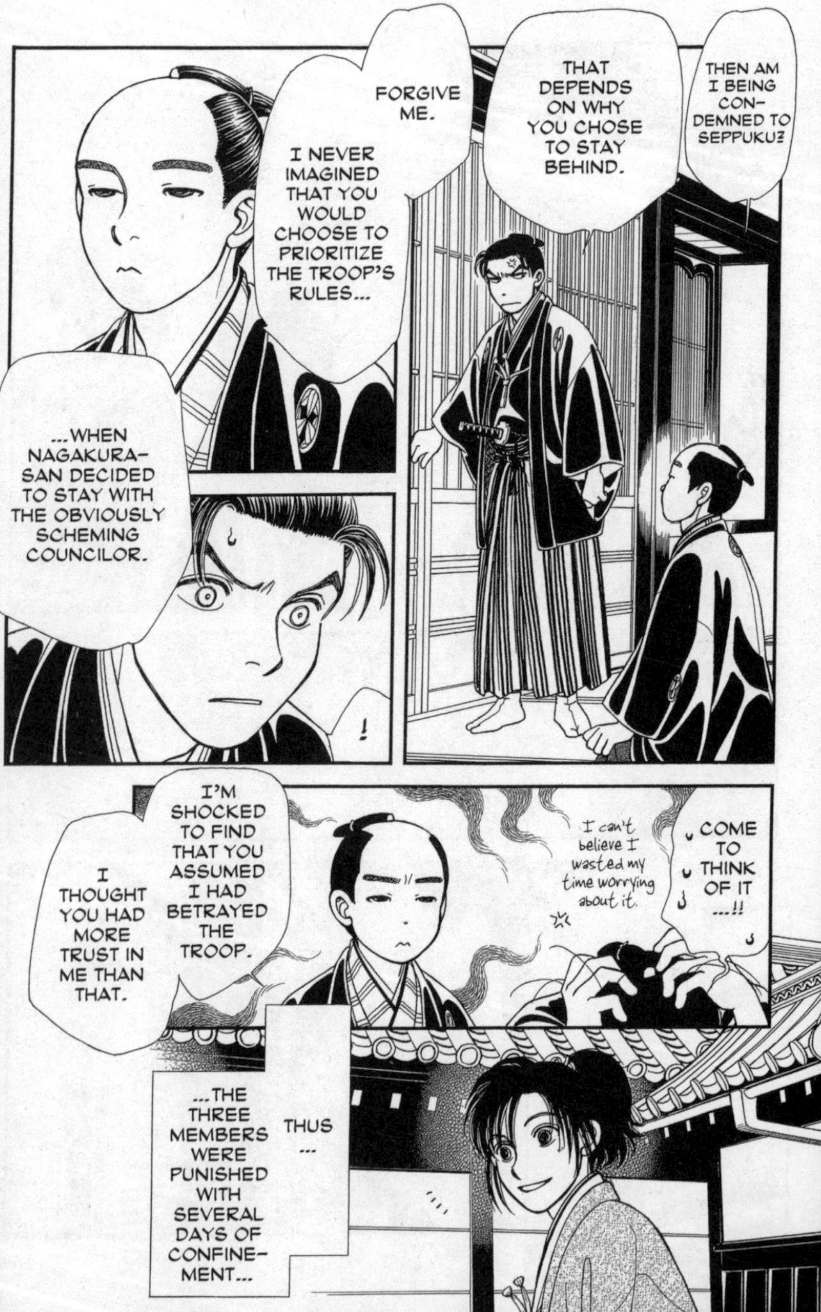
THEN AM I BEING CON-DEMNED TO SEPPUKU?
THAT DEPENDS ON WHY YOU CHOSE TO STAY BEHIND.
FORGIVE ME.
I NEVER IMAGINED THAT YOU WOULD CHOOSE TO PRIORITIZE THE TROOP'S RULES...
...WHEN NAGAKURA-SAN DECIDED TO STAY WITH THE OBVIOUSLY SCHEMING COUNCILOR.
!
COME TO THINK OF IT...!!
I can't believe I wasted my time worrying about it.
I'M SHOCKED TO FIND THAT YOU ASSUMED I HAD BETRAYED THE TROOP.
I THOUGHT YOU HAD MORE TRUST IN ME THAN THAT.
THUS...
...THE THREE MEMBERS WERE PUNISHED WITH SEVERAL DAYS OF CONFINE-MENT...

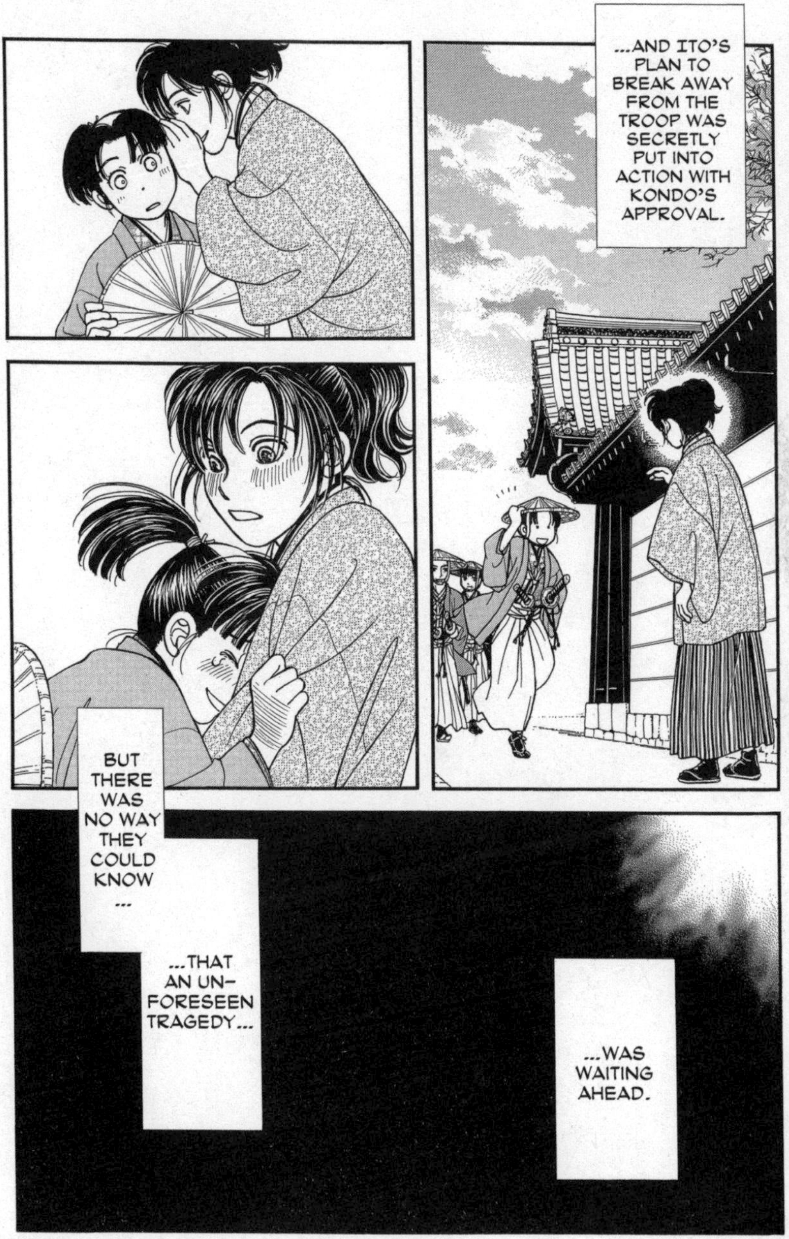
...AND ITO'S PLAN TO BREAK AWAY FROM THE TROOP WAS SECRETLY PUT INTO ACTION WITH KONDO'S APPROVAL.
BUT THERE WAS NO WAY THEY COULD KNOW...
...THAT AN UN-FORESEEN TRAGEDY...
...WAS WAITING AHEAD.

TO BE CONTINUED!

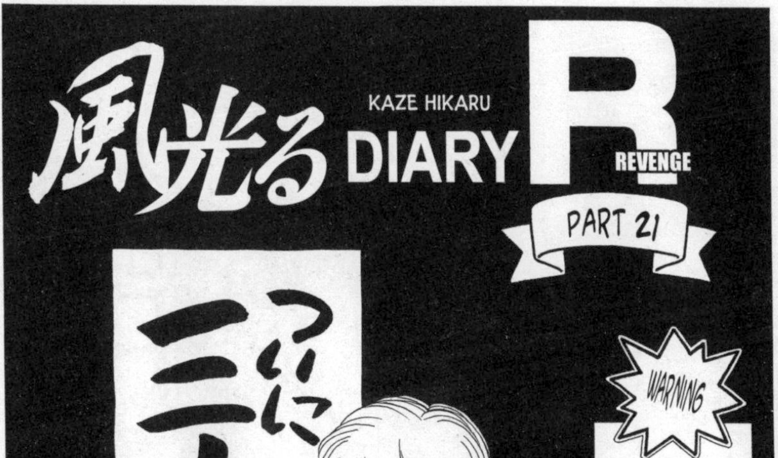
風光る
KAZE HIKARU
DIARY
R
REVENGE
PART 21
WARNING
PLEASE PROCEED ONLY AFTER READING THE MAIN CONTENTS OF KAZE HIKARU.
ついに三十路。

*Finally entering the thirties.

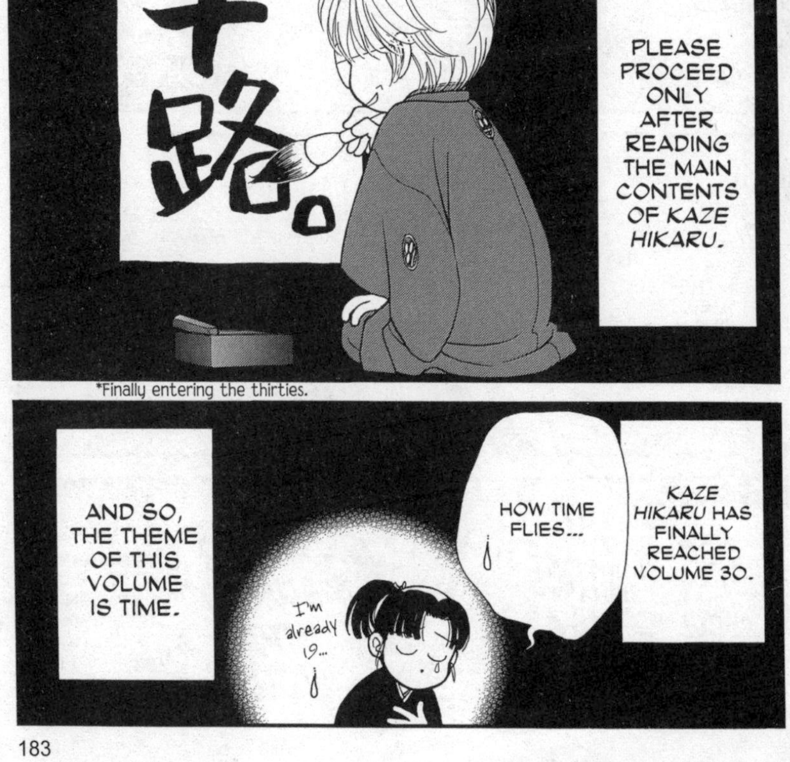
KAZE HIKARU HAS FINALLY REACHED VOLUME 30.
HOW TIME FLIES...
I'm already 19...
AND SO, THE THEME OF THIS VOLUME IS TIME.

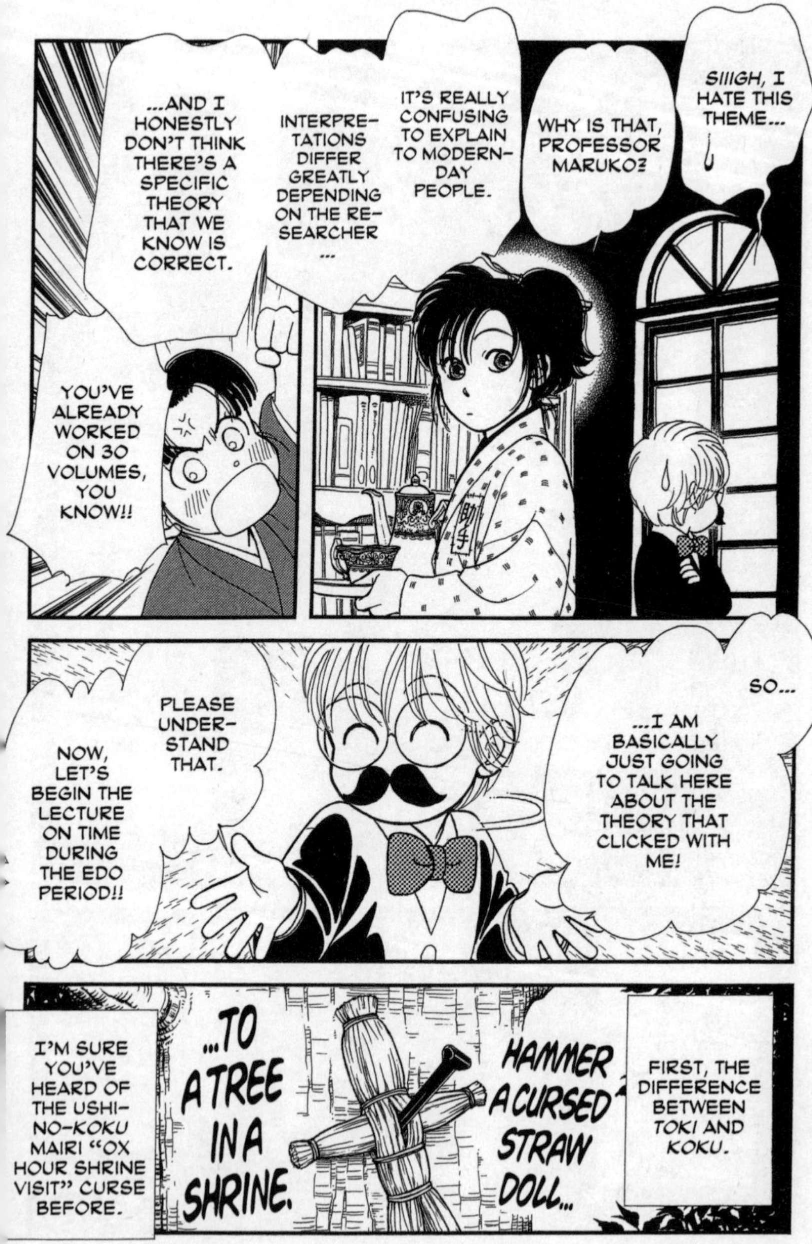
SIIIGH, I HATE THIS THEME...
WHY IS THAT, PROFESSOR MARUKO?
IT'S REALLY CONFUSING TO EXPLAIN TO MODERN-DAY PEOPLE.
INTERPRETATIONS DIFFER GREATLY DEPENDING ON THE RESEARCHER...
助手
...AND I HONESTLY DON'T THINK THERE'S A SPECIFIC THEORY THAT WE KNOW IS CORRECT.
YOU'VE ALREADY WORKED ON 30 VOLUMES, YOU KNOW!!
SO...
...I AM BASICALLY JUST GOING TO TALK HERE ABOUT THE THEORY THAT CLICKED WITH ME!
PLEASE UNDERSTAND THAT.
NOW, LET'S BEGIN THE LECTURE ON TIME DURING THE EDO PERIOD!!
FIRST, THE DIFFERENCE BETWEEN *TOKI* AND *KOKU*.
HAMMER A CURSED STRAW DOLL...
...TO A TREE IN A SHRINE.
I'M SURE YOU'VE HEARD OF THE USHI-NO-KOKU MAIRI "OX HOUR SHRINE VISIT" CURSE BEFORE.

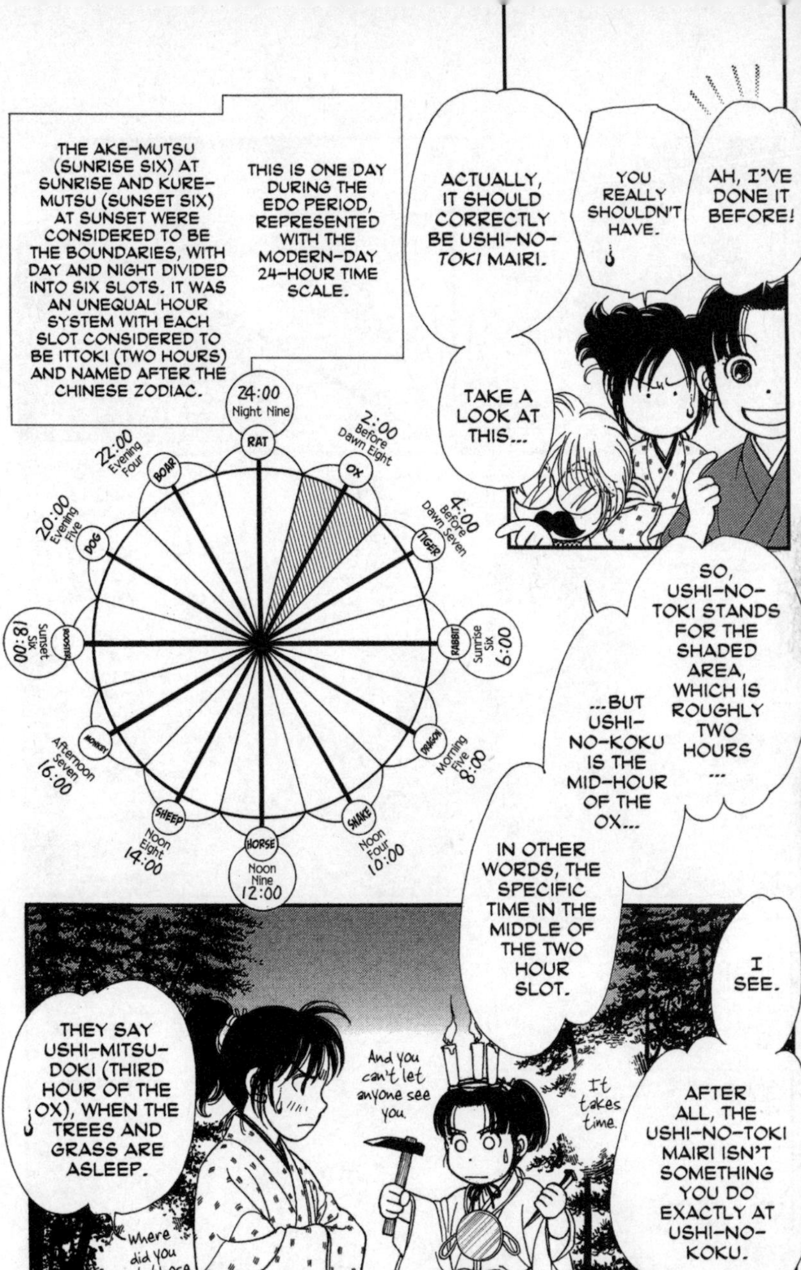
AH, I'VE DONE IT BEFORE!
YOU REALLY SHOULDN'T HAVE.
ACTUALLY, IT SHOULD CORRECTLY BE USHI-NO-*TOKI* MAIRI.
TAKE A LOOK AT THIS...
THIS IS ONE DAY DURING THE EDO PERIOD, REPRESENTED WITH THE MODERN-DAY 24-HOUR TIME SCALE.
THE AKE-MUTSU (SUNRISE SIX) AT SUNRISE AND KURE-MUTSU (SUNSET SIX) AT SUNSET WERE CONSIDERED TO BE THE BOUNDARIES, WITH DAY AND NIGHT DIVIDED INTO SIX SLOTS. IT WAS AN UNEQUAL HOUR SYSTEM WITH EACH SLOT CONSIDERED TO BE ITTOKI (TWO HOURS) AND NAMED AFTER THE CHINESE ZODIAC.
24:00 Night Nine
RAT
2:00 Before Dawn Eight
OX
4:00 Before Dawn Seven
TIGER
6:00 Sunrise Six
RABBIT
8:00 Morning Five
DRAGON
10:00 Noon Four
SNAKE
12:00 Noon Nine
HORSE
14:00 Noon Eight
SHEEP
16:00 Afternoon Seven
MONKEY
18:00 Sunset Six
ROOSTER
20:00 Evening Five
DOG
22:00 Evening Four
BOAR
SO, USHI-NO-TOKI STANDS FOR THE SHADED AREA, WHICH IS ROUGHLY TWO HOURS...
...BUT USHI-NO-KOKU IS THE MID-HOUR OF THE OX...
IN OTHER WORDS, THE SPECIFIC TIME IN THE MIDDLE OF THE TWO HOUR SLOT.
I SEE.
AFTER ALL, THE USHI-NO-TOKI MAIRI ISN'T SOMETHING YOU DO EXACTLY AT USHI-NO-KOKU.
It takes time.
And you can't let anyone see you.
THEY SAY USHI-MITSU-DOKI (THIRD HOUR OF THE OX), WHEN THE TREES AND GRASS ARE ASLEEP.
Where did you get those props?

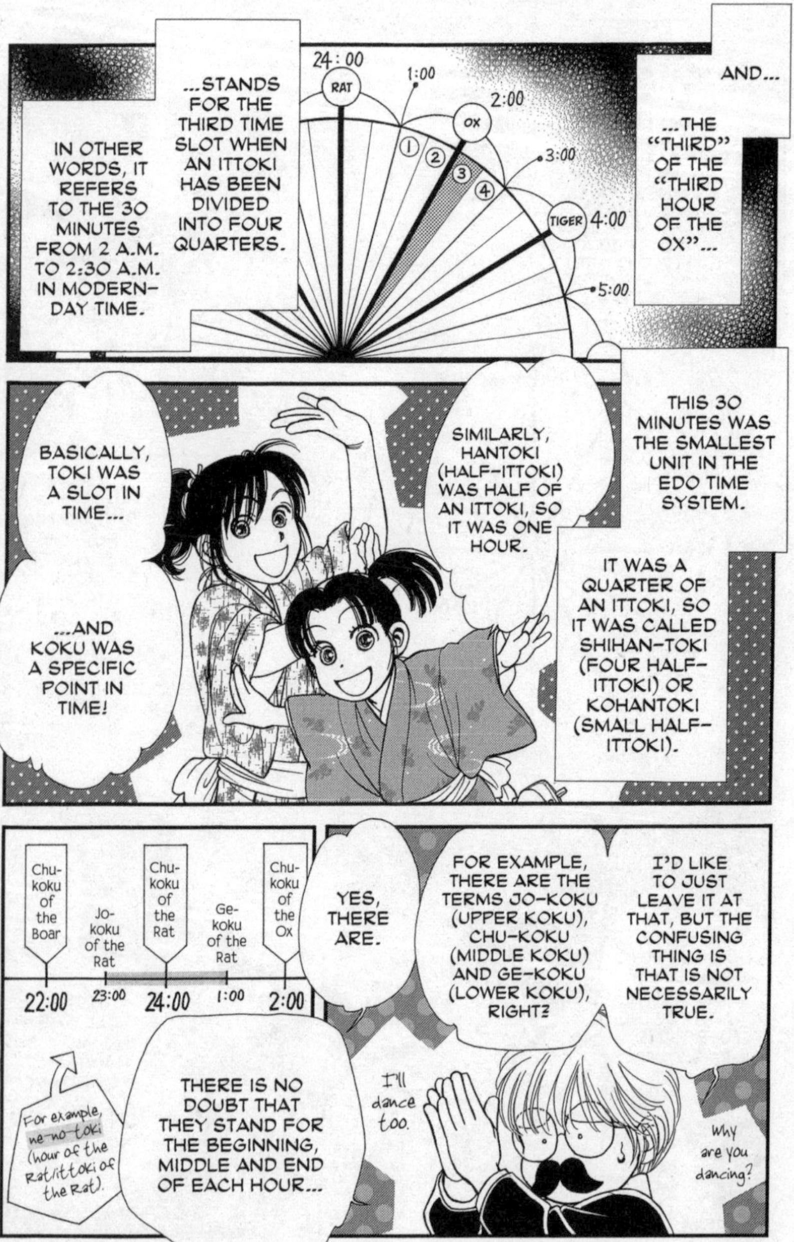
AND...
...THE "THIRD" OF THE "THIRD HOUR OF THE OX"...
24:00
RAT
1:00
2:00
OX
1
2
3
4
3:00
TIGER
4:00
5:00
...STANDS FOR THE THIRD TIME SLOT WHEN AN ITTOKI HAS BEEN DIVIDED INTO FOUR QUARTERS.
IN OTHER WORDS, IT REFERS TO THE 30 MINUTES FROM 2 A.M. TO 2:30 A.M. IN MODERN-DAY TIME.
THIS 30 MINUTES WAS THE SMALLEST UNIT IN THE EDO TIME SYSTEM.
IT WAS A QUARTER OF AN ITTOKI, SO IT WAS CALLED SHIHAN-TOKI (FOUR HALF-ITTOKI) OR KOHANTOKI (SMALL HALF-ITTOKI).
SIMILARLY, HANTOKI (HALF-ITTOKI) WAS HALF OF AN ITTOKI, SO IT WAS ONE HOUR.
BASICALLY, TOKI WAS A SLOT IN TIME...
...AND KOKU WAS A SPECIFIC POINT IN TIME!
I'D LIKE TO JUST LEAVE IT AT THAT, BUT THE CONFUSING THING IS THAT IS NOT NECESSARILY TRUE.
FOR EXAMPLE, THERE ARE THE TERMS JO-KOKU (UPPER KOKU), CHU-KOKU (MIDDLE KOKU) AND GE-KOKU (LOWER KOKU), RIGHT?
YES, THERE ARE.
Why are you dancing?
I'll dance too.
THERE IS NO DOUBT THAT THEY STAND FOR THE BEGINNING, MIDDLE AND END OF EACH HOUR...
Chu-koku of the Boar
Jo-koku of the Rat
Chu-koku of the Rat
Ge-koku of the Rat
Chu-koku of the Ox
22:00
23:00
24:00
1:00
2:00
For example, ne-no-toki (hour of the Rat/ittoki of the Rat).

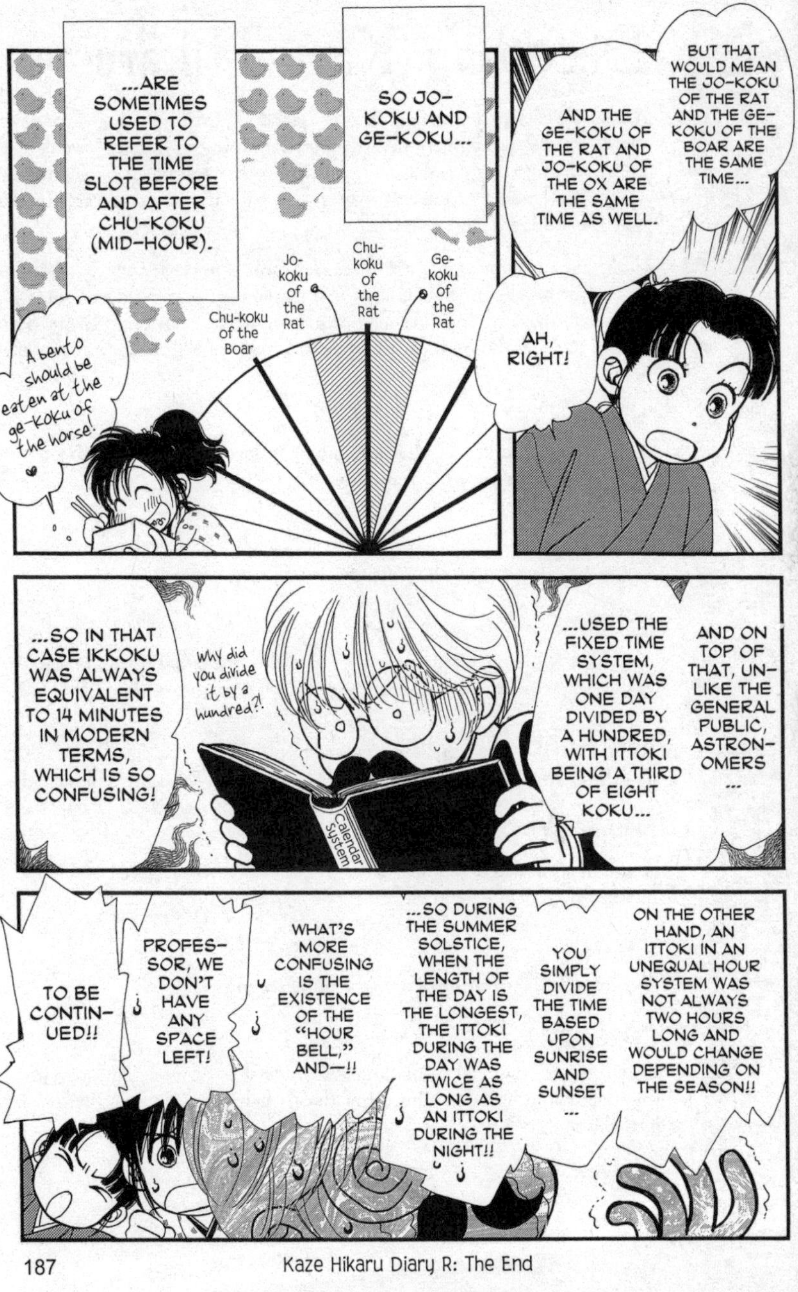
BUT THAT WOULD MEAN THE JO-KOKU OF THE RAT AND THE GE-KOKU OF THE BOAR ARE THE SAME TIME...
AND THE GE-KOKU OF THE RAT AND JO-KOKU OF THE OX ARE THE SAME TIME AS WELL.
AH, RIGHT!
SO JO-KOKU AND GE-KOKU...
...ARE SOMETIMES USED TO REFER TO THE TIME SLOT BEFORE AND AFTER CHU-KOKU (MID-HOUR).
Ge-koku of the Rat
Chu-koku of the Rat
Jo-koku of the Rat
Chu-koku of the Boar
A bento should be eaten at the ge-koku of the horse!
AND ON TOP OF THAT, UNLIKE THE GENERAL PUBLIC, ASTRONOMERS...
...USED THE FIXED TIME SYSTEM, WHICH WAS ONE DAY DIVIDED BY A HUNDRED, WITH ITTOKI BEING A THIRD OF EIGHT KOKU...
Why did you divide it by a hundred?!
...SO IN THAT CASE IKKOKU WAS ALWAYS EQUIVALENT TO 14 MINUTES IN MODERN TERMS, WHICH IS SO CONFUSING!
Calendar System
ON THE OTHER HAND, AN ITTOKI IN AN UNEQUAL HOUR SYSTEM WAS NOT ALWAYS TWO HOURS LONG AND WOULD CHANGE DEPENDING ON THE SEASON!!
YOU SIMPLY DIVIDE THE TIME BASED UPON SUNRISE AND SUNSET...
...SO DURING THE SUMMER SOLSTICE, WHEN THE LENGTH OF THE DAY IS THE LONGEST, THE ITTOKI DURING THE DAY WAS TWICE AS LONG AS AN ITTOKI DURING THE NIGHT!!
WHAT'S MORE CONFUSING IS THE EXISTENCE OF THE "HOUR BELL," AND—!!
PROFESSOR, WE DON'T HAVE ANY SPACE LEFT!
TO BE CONTINUED!!

Decoding Kaze Hikaru

Kaze Hikaru is a historical drama based in 19th century Japan and thus contains some fairly mystifying terminology. In this glossary we'll break down archaic phrases, terms and other linguistic curiosities for you so that you can move through life with the smug assurance that you are indeed a know-it-all.

First and foremost, because *Kaze Hikaru* is a period story, we kept all character names in their traditional Japanese form—that is, family name followed by first name. For example, the character Okita Soji's family name is Okita and his personal name is Soji.

AGEYA:
A high-class tea house/pleasure house where patrons could host parties or socialize with geiko and Tayu.

ANI-UE:
Formal term for an older brother.

BAKUFU:
Literally, "tent government." This was the Shogunate; the feudal, military government that dominated Japan for more than 200 years.

BAKUMATSU:
The final years of the Bakufu, ending with the Tokugawa shogunate.

BUSHI:
A samurai or warrior (part of the compound word *bushido*, which means "way of the warrior").

-CHAN:
A diminutive suffix that conveys endearment.

CHIKYO:
This form of imperial punishment forbids the receiver from leaving their bedroom for anything other than washing and using the bathroom.

DAIMYO:
A landholding feudal lord.

-DAYU:
An honorific suffix used following the names of high-ranking courtesans.

-DONO:
An honorific suffix that implies "Lord" or "Master."

EDO:
The former name of Tokyo.

GEIKO:
The term used in Kyoto for "geisha."

GION:
Kyoto's entertainment district.

GOCHO:
The rank below assistant vice captain in the Shinsengumi hierarchy.

GOSANKE:
Literally, "three families." Three land-owning families, each ruling over their own Han, who are dependents of the shogun and take the Tokugawa name. Ieyasu, the first Tokugawa shogun, created the Gosanke to provide an heir in case the shogun did not have a son. Gosanke family heads rank directly below the shogun.

HAN OR -HAN:
A feudal domain of Japan during the Edo period.

IKEDAYA INCIDENT:
A Shinsengumi raid on an inn in Kyoto where anti-Shogunate rebels had gathered. Seven rebels were killed and scores were arrested.

KOSHO:
A Shinsengumi captain's personal assistant.

-KO:
An honorific suffix added to the names of lords and those of high status.

-KUN:
An honorific suffix that indicates a difference in rank and title. The use of -kun is also a way of indicating familiarity and friendliness between students or compatriots.

OBI:
Belt worn with a kimono.

OKAMI:
The landlady or manager of an entertainment house.

ONI:
Literally, "ogre."

RONIN:
Masterless samurai.

-SAMA:
An honorific suffix used for one of higher rank; a more respectful version of *-san*.

-SAN:
An honorific suffix that carries the meaning of "Mr." or "Ms."

SENRYU:
A humorous, haiku-like poem.

SENSEI:
A teacher, master, or instructor.

SEPPUKU:
A ritualistic suicide that was considered a privilege of the nobility or the samurai elite.

SHIEIKAN DOJO:
The martial arts school that taught Ten'nen Rishin-ryu.

SHIMABARA:
Formerly the red-light district in Kyoto.

SHUDO:
A romantic relationship between a younger samurai and his older mentor.

SONJO-HA:
Those loyal to the emperor and dedicated to the expulsion of foreigners from the country.

SUMIYA:
A well-known ageya in Shimabara.

TAYU:
A term of address for the highest-ranking courtesans (*yujo*).

TOKUGAWA BAFUKU:
The last feudal military government of Japan's premodern period, it was directed by hereditary leaders–shoguns–of the Tokugawa clan.

TOSA:
The leaders of Tosa-han were in favor of reforming the Bakufu.

TEN'NEN RISHIN-RYU:
The martial art practiced by members of the Shinsengumi.

UKINOSUKE-SAN:
When Sei and Soji previously interacted with the current Shogun, Yoshinobu, he was operating under the alias "Ukinosuke."

YUJO:
A prostitute.

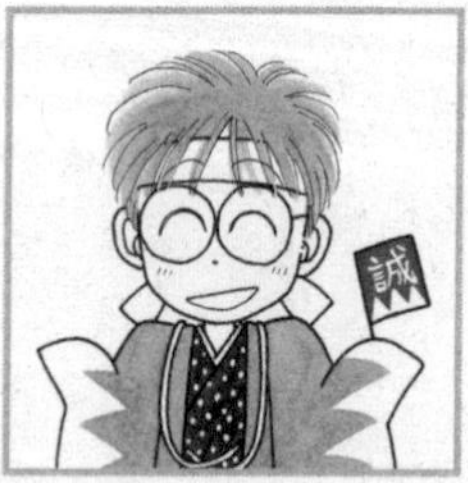

I wasn't sure whether I should write about this, but I think I should. On March 11, 2011, when the Great East Japan Earthquake struck, I was working on the final draft of this volume.* I had never experienced such a strong and long-lasting earthquake before. It was quite surprising to me that I felt rather calm. I thought, "So this is how I'm going to die," as I hid under my desk with the final draft in my hands. The next thought that came to mind was, "This is a war." I was thankful from the bottom of my heart that it turned out not to be the kind of war that involves people killing people, and then I thought, "I will start my own battle to rebuild Japan from this moment on." It was the first time I felt such an intense inner passion, one that perhaps resembled the feelings experienced by these guys from the Bakumatsu era.

Volume 30's seasonal theme is summer. On the cover Soji and Sei are wishing upon a rainbow, and I believe their wish will reach us here in the future. Let's do our best, Japan!

*This volume was published in Japan in June 2011, two months after the Great East Japan Earthquake.

Taeko Watanabe debuted as a manga artist in 1979 with her story *Waka-chan no Netsuai Jidai* (Love Struck Days of Waka). *Kaze Hikaru* is her longest-running series, but she has created a number of other popular series. Watanabe is a two-time winner of the prestigious Shogakukan Manga Award in the girls' category—her manga *Hajime-chan ga Ichiban!* (Hajime-chan Is Number One!) claimed the award in 1991, and *Kaze Hikaru* took it in 2003.

Watanabe read hundreds of historical sources to create *Kaze Hikaru.* She is from Tokyo.

KAZE HIKARU
VOL. 30
Shojo Beat Edition

STORY AND ART BY
TAEKO WATANABE

KAZE HIKARU Vol. 30
by Taeko WATANABE
© 1997 Taeko WATANABE
All rights reserved.
Original Japanese edition published by SHOGAKUKAN.
English translation rights in the United States of America and Canada arranged with SHOGAKUKAN.

Translation & English Adaptation/Tetsuichiro Miyaki
Touch-up Art & Lettering/Rina Mapa
Design/J. Shikuma
Editor/Megan Bates

Printed in the U.S.A.

Published by VIZ Media, LLC
P.O. Box 77010
San Francisco, CA 94107

10 9 8 7 6 5 4 3 2 1
First printing, August 2022

VIZ MEDIA
viz.com

shojobeat.com

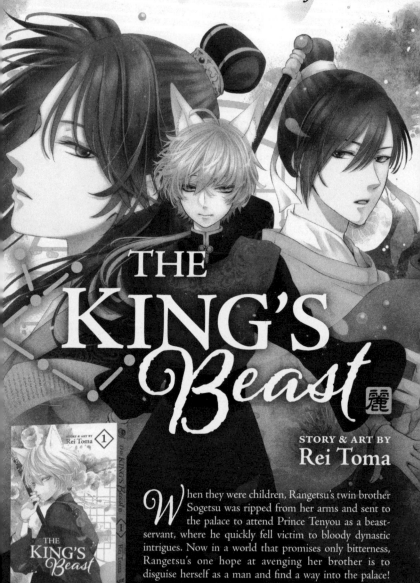

A smoldering tale of romance and revenge set in the world of the *New York Times* best seller *Dawn of the Arcana!*

THE KING'S *Beast*

STORY & ART BY
Rei Toma

When they were children, Rangetsu's twin brother Sogetsu was ripped from her arms and sent to the palace to attend Prince Tenyou as a beast-servant, where he quickly fell victim to bloody dynastic intrigues. Now in a world that promises only bitterness, Rangetsu's one hope at avenging her brother is to disguise herself as a man and find a way into the palace!

Revolutionary Girl
UTENA

COMPLETE DELUXE BOX SET

Story and Art by
CHIHO SAITO

Original Concept by
BE-PAPAS

Utena strives to be strong and noble like the childhood prince she yearns to meet again. But when she finds herself seduced into the twisted duels of Ohtori Academy, can she become the prince she's been waiting for?

VIZ

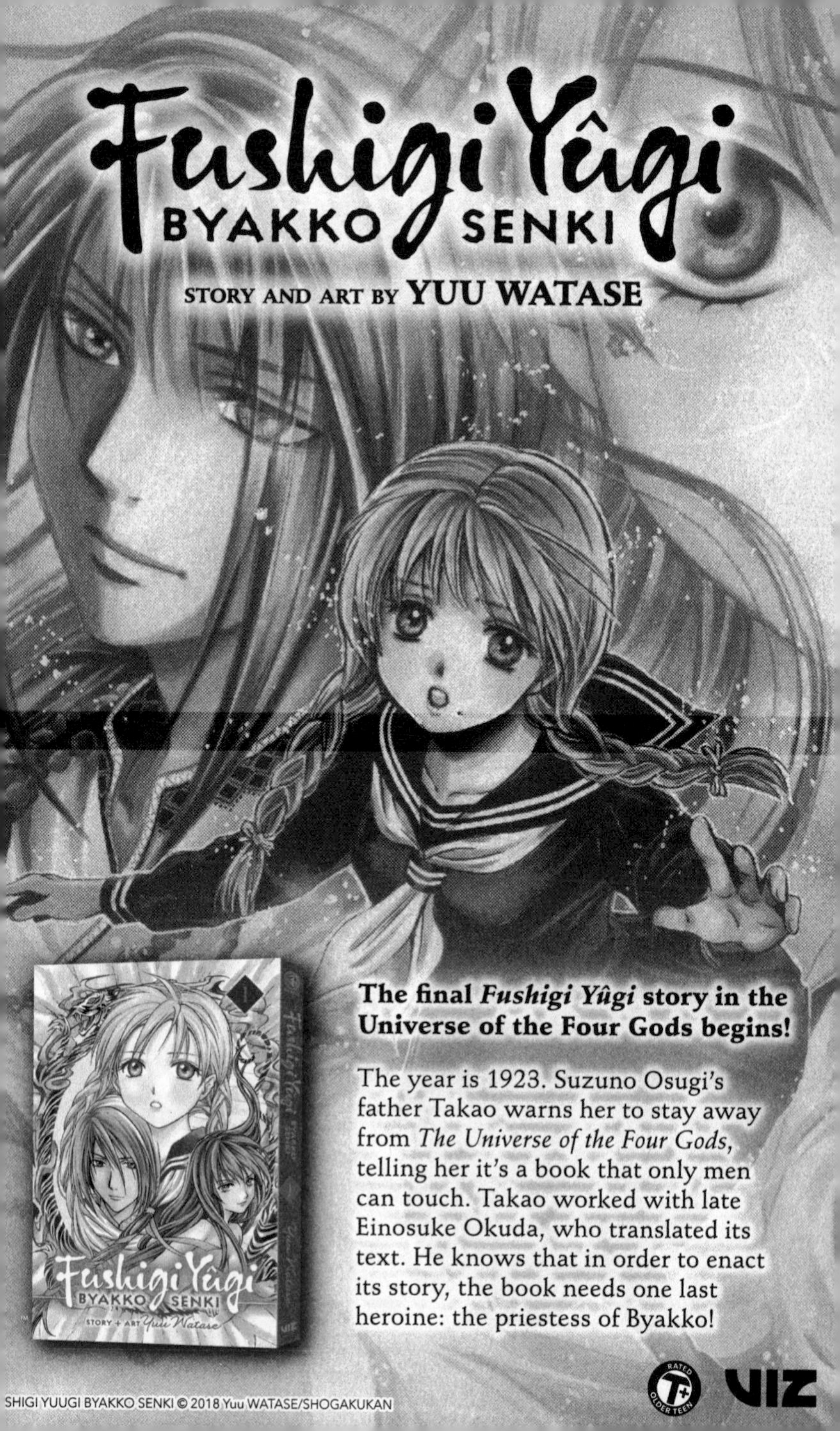
Fushigi Yûgi
BYAKKO SENKI
STORY AND ART BY YUU WATASE
1
Fushigi Yûgi
BYAKKO SENKI
STORY + ART Yuu Watase
The final Fushigi Yûgi story in the Universe of the Four Gods begins!
The year is 1923. Suzuno Osugi's father Takao warns her to stay away from The Universe of the Four Gods, telling her it's a book that only men can touch. Takao worked with late Einosuke Okuda, who translated its text. He knows that in order to enact its story, the book needs one last heroine: the priestess of Byakko!
RATED T+ OLDER TEEN
VIZ
SHIGI YUUGI BYAKKO SENKI © 2018 Yuu WATASE/SHOGAKUKAN

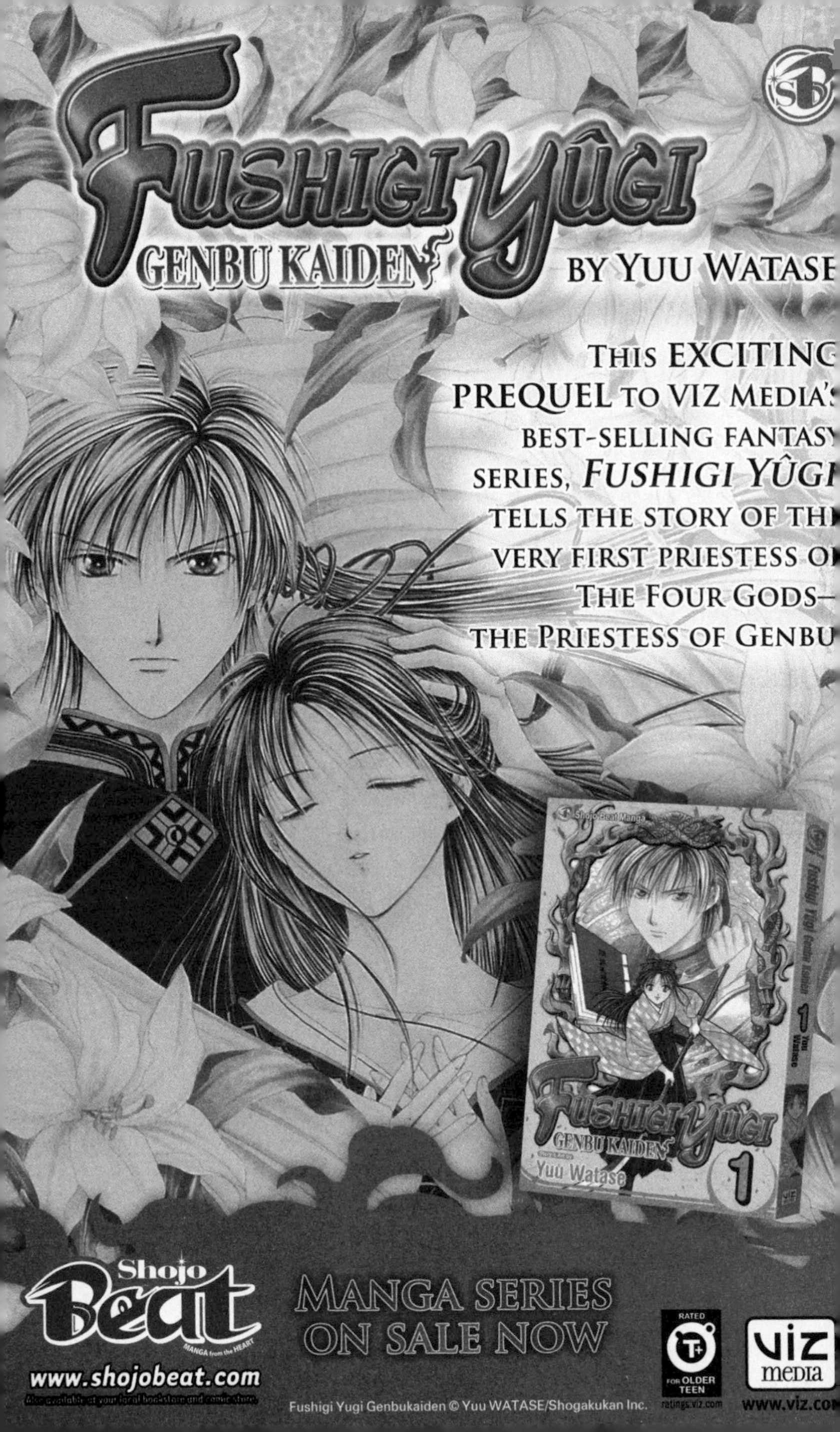

FUSHIGI YÛGI
GENBU KAIDEN
BY YUU WATASE
THIS EXCITING
PREQUEL TO VIZ MEDIA'S
BEST-SELLING FANTASY
SERIES, FUSHIGI YÛGI
TELLS THE STORY OF THE
VERY FIRST PRIESTESS OF
THE FOUR GODS—
THE PRIESTESS OF GENBU
Shojo Beat Manga
Fushigi Yûgi Genbu Kaiden
1
Yuu Watase
FUSHIGI YÛGI
GENBU KAIDEN
Yuu Watase
1
Shojo Beat
MANGA from the HEART
www.shojobeat.com
Also available at your local bookstore and comic store.
MANGA SERIES
ON SALE NOW
RATED
T+
FOR OLDER TEEN
ratings.viz.com
viz media
www.viz.com
Fushigi Yugi Genbukaiden © Yuu WATASE/Shogakukan Inc.

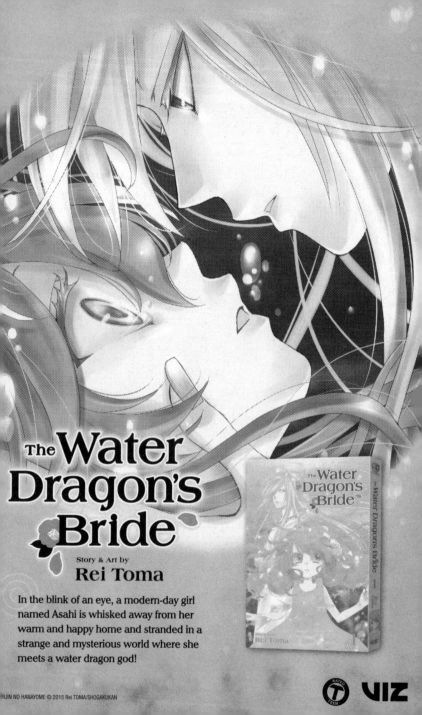

The Water Dragon's Bride

Story & Art by
Rei Toma

In the blink of an eye, a modern-day girl named Asahi is whisked away from her warm and happy home and stranded in a strange and mysterious world where she meets a water dragon god!

RATED TEEN

VIZ

Queen's Quality

**Story & Art by
Kyousuke Motomi**

Fumi Nishioka lives with Kyutaro Horikita
and his family of "Sweepers," people who
specialize in cleaning the minds of those
overcome by negative energy and harmful
spirits. Fumi has always displayed mysterious
abilities, but will those powers be used for
evil when she begins to truly awaken
as a Queen?

SURPRISE!

You may be reading the wrong way!

It's true: In keeping with the original Japanese comic format, this book reads from right to left—so action, sound effects, and word balloons are completely reversed. This preserves the orientation of the original artwork—plus, it's fun! Check out the diagram shown here to get the hang of things, and then turn to the other side of the book to get started!

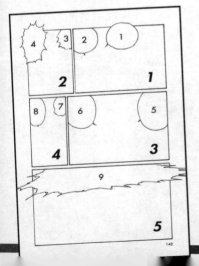